Human Diversity in Education

An Integrative Approach

Human Diversity in Education

An Integrative Approach

THIRD EDITION

Kenneth Cushner

Averil McClelland

Philip Safford

Kent State University

Boston   Burr Ridge, IL   Dubuque, IA   Madison, WI   New York   San Francisco   St. Louis
Bangkok   Bogotá   Caracas   Lisbon   London   Madrid
Mexico City   Milan   New Delhi   Seoul   Singapore   Sydney   Taipei   Toronto

McGraw-Hill Higher Education

A Division of The **McGraw-Hill** *Companies*

HUMAN DIVERSITY IN EDUCATION: AN INTEGRATIVE APPROACH,
THIRD EDITION

This book is printed on acid-free paper.

4 5 6 7 8 9 0 QWF/QWF 7 6 5 4 3 2 1

ISBN 0–07–228724–1

Editorial director: *Jane E. Vaicunas*
Sponsoring editor: *Beth Kaufman*
Developmental editor: *Cara Harvey*
Marketing manager: *Daniel M. Loch*
Project manager: *Joyce M. Berendes*
Senior production supervisor: *Mary E. Haas*
Coordinator of freelance design: *Rick Noel*
Photo research coordinator: *John C. Leland*
Supplement coordinator: *Tammy Juran*
Compositor: *Electronic Publishing Services, TN*
Typeface: *10/12 Times Roman*
Printer: *Quebecor Printing Book Group/Fairfield, PA*

Cover design: *Ellen Pettengell*
Interior design: *Kathy Theis*
Cover image: *S.I.S. Stock Illustrations Source art by Jose Ortega*
Photo research: *Connie Mueller*

The credits section for this book begins on page 358 and is considered an extension of the copyright page.

Library of Congress Cataloging-in-Publication Data

Cushner, Kenneth.
    Human diversity in education : an integrative approach / Kenneth Cushner, Averil McClelland, Philip Safford. — 3rd ed.
      p.   cm.
    Includes bibliographical references and indexes.
    ISBN 0–07–228724–1
    1. Multicultural education—United States. 2. Individual differences in children—United States. 3. Sex differences in education—United States. I. McClelland, Averil. II. Safford, Philip L. III. Title.
LC1099.3.C87   2000
370.117'0973—dc21
                                        99–27510
                                          CIP

www.mhhe.com

About the Authors

KENNETH CUSHNER is Associate Dean for Student Life and Intercultural Affairs, and Professor of Education in the College and Graduate School of Education at Kent State University. He received his doctorate at the University of Hawaii while on scholarship with the Institute of Culture and Communication at the East-West Center. Dr. Cushner is a frequent contributor to the professional development of educators and other professionals through workshops, writing, consulting, and travel programs. Among his publications, he is co-author *of Intercultural Interactions: A Practical Guide,* second edition, (Sage Publications, 1996); co-editor of *Improving Intercultural Interactions: Modules for Cross-Cultural Training Programs,* volume 2, (Sage Publications, 1997); editor *of International Perspectives on Intercultural Education,* (Lawrence Erlbaum Associates, 1998); and author of the multicultural education workbook, *Human Diversity in Action: Developing Multicultural Competencies for the Classroom,* (McGraw-Hill, 1999). He has taught in schools or developed educational programs for teachers and youths on all seven continents, and is current director of COST – The Consortium for Overseas Student Teaching. In his spare time, Dr. Cushner enjoys photography, travel, and playing guitar and percussion.

AVERIL MCCLELLAND is currently an Associate Professor of Cultural Foundations of Education at Kent State University. She received her Ph.D. from Kent State University. Dr. McClelland has had extensive experience in curriculum design and program evaluation, as well as considerable experience with addressing issues of gender and education, and cultural diversity in education. She is a consultant to the international journal, *Gender and Education*, and she received the Distinguished Teaching award from Kent State University in 1996. Her special interests are the history and sociology of education, multicultural education, and the reconstruction of teacher education.

PHILIP SAFFORD is Emeritus Professor and former chair of Special Education at Kent State University. His Ph.D. was earned through the combined program in education and psychology of the University of Michigan, with specialization in special education and developmental psychology. Previously he had been a teacher of emotionally disturbed children and also a coordinator and director of special education in residential treatment programs. Dr. Safford has authored four books, all concerning special education for infants, toddlers, and preschool age children with disabilities, as well as numerous journal articles. He has directed or co-directed a number of training, research, and demonstration projects supported by federal and state grants in special education.

Contents

PREFACE   **xvii**

Part One
FOUNDATIONS FOR MULTICULTURAL TEACHING

1. Education in a Changing Society   3

   THE REALITY OF SOCIAL CHANGE   6

   Demographics in Transition   *7*
   Institutions in Transition   *7*
     Economics and Politics   /   Marriage and Family Life   /   Organized
     Religion

   SCHOOLS AS A REFLECTION OF SOCIAL CHANGE   10

   Demographics   *10*
   Language   *10*
   Ability   *10*
   Gender   *11*
   Students and Teachers: A Clash of Cultures?   *11*
   Rethinking Schools and Teaching   *12*

   SCHOOLS IN TRANSITION   13

   Characteristics of Second Wave Schools: Classrooms for the
   Industrial Age   *13*
     Standardization   /   Synchronization   /   Specialization   /
     Centralization   /   Large Scale

   Characteristics of Third Wave Schools: Classrooms for the
   Information Age   *15*
     Individualization and Choice   /   Collaboration   /   Diversity   /
     Decentralization   /   Small Scale

   Where We Are Today   *17*
   The Difficulty of Change   *17*

GOALS OF THIS BOOK   19

Goal 1: Recognize Social and Cultural Changes   *20*
Goal 2: Understand Culture and the Culture-Learning
Process   *21*
Goal 3: Improve Intergroup and Intragroup Interactions   *21*
Goal 4: Transmit Cross-Cultural Understanding and
Skills to Students   *21*

THE ROLE OF STORIES, CASES, AND ACTIVE EXERCISES IN THIS BOOK   22

Stories   *22*
Cases   *22*
Active Exercises   *23*
Accessing the World Wide Web: Resources for Diversity   *23*

REFERENCES   24

2. Multicultural Education: Historical and Theoretical Perspectives   27

HISTORICAL PERSPECTIVES ON PLURALISM   30

We Have Been Different from the Beginning   *30*
Industrialization, Immigration, and Religious Pluralism   *31*
The Civil War: Freedmen's Schools and the Issue of Race   *32*
The Civil Rights Movement and the Schools   *33*

HISTORICAL PERSPECTIVES ON MULTICULTURAL EDUCATION   34

Anglo-Conformity and Assimilationist Ideology   *34*
Multiculturalism and the Pluralist Ideology   *36*
Legislative and Judicial Landmarks   *37*
Public Responses to Multicultural and Bilingual Education
Reforms   *38*
Judicial and Legislative Mandates Regarding Equity   *40*
Reaction to Multicultural Education in the 1980s and 1990s   *42*

CONTEMPORARY APPROACHES TO
MULTICULTURAL EDUCATION PROGRAMS   43

The Sleeter and Grant Categories   *43*
    Teaching the Culturally Different   /   Human Relations   /   Single-
    Group Studies   /   Inclusive Multicultural Education   /   Education
    That Is Multicultural and Social Reconstructionist

The Mitchell Typology   *46*
    Models of Cultural Understanding   /   Models of Cultural Competence
    /   Models of Cultural Emancipation and Social Reconstruction

THE OUTCOMES OF MULTICULTURAL EDUCATION   48

Student Outcomes   *48*
Program Outcomes   *48*

Active Exercises   49
Accessing the World Wide Web: Resources for Diversity   50

REFERENCES   50

3. Culture and the Culture-Learning Process   55

EXPLORING THE CONCEPT OF CULTURE   59

THREE VIEWS OF CULTURE   59

Anthropology   59
  Humans Construct Culture   /   Culture Is Shared   /   Culture Is Both
  Objective and Subjective   /   Culture Is Nurtured

Sociology   63
  Subculture   /   Microculture   /   Minority Group   /   Ethnic Group   /
  People of Color

Cross-Cultural Psychology   65
  Culture-Specific vs. Culture-General Frameworks   /   Themes from
  Cross-Cultural Psychology

THE CULTURE-LEARNING PROCESS   68

What Is Learned: The Sources of Cultural Knowledge   69
  Race   /   Sex/Gender   /   Health   /   Ability/Disability   /
  Social Class   /   Ethnicity/Nationality   /   Religion/Spirituality   /
  Geographic Location   /   Age   /   Sexuality   /   Language   /
  Social Status

How Culture Is Learned: The Socializing Agents   75
When Culture Is Learned   77
  Primary Socialization: Cultural Similarities   /   Secondary Socialization

SOME RESULTS OF SOCIALIZATION   80

Ethnocentrism   80
Perception   81
Categorization   81
Stereotypes   82
Some Limits on Socialization   83

UNDERSTANDING CULTURAL DIFFERENCES   84

*Variations in Cultural Environments: Returning to
Grover's Corners*   84
*Variations in Cultural Attributes, Socializing Agents, and
Cultural Learners*   86
Active Exercises   88
Accessing the World Wide Web: Resources for Diversity   88

REFERENCES   89

4. Classrooms and Schools as Cultural Crossroads   93

SCHOOLS AND CLASSROOMS: WHERE CULTURES INTERSECT   94

Student Culture   94
Teacher Culture   94
School Culture   95
Teachers as Cultural Mediators   96
Reshaping of Cultural Identity   96

A MODEL OF CROSS-CULTURAL INTERACTION   99

Stage One: Understanding Emotional Responses in Intercultural
Interaction   101
   Anxiety / Ambiguity / Disconfirmed Expectations /
   Belonging/Rejection / Confronting Personal Prejudice

Stage Two: Understanding the Cultural Basis of
Unfamiliar Behavior   103
   Communication and Language / Values / Rituals / Situational
   Behavior / Roles / Social Status / Time and Space Orientation
   / Relationship to the Group

Stage Three: Making Adjustments and Reshaping
Cultural Identity   106
   Categorization / Differentiation / Attribution / Ingroups and
   Outgroups / Learning Style

APPLICATION OF THE CULTURE-GENERAL MODEL   109

Commonalities Among Groups   110
Differences Within a Group   110
Critical Incidents at Alden High   111
Active Exercises   116
Accessing the World Wide Web: Resources for Diversity   117

REFERENCES   117

Part Two
MULTICULTURAL TEACHING IN ACTION

5. Developing Learning Communities:
   Language and Learning Style   121

CHARACTERISTICS OF A LEARNING COMMUNITY   130
Pedagogies: Old and New   132
Roles: Old and New   133
Place of Content Knowledge: Old and New   133
Assessment: Old and New   134

PERSPECTIVES ON LANGUAGE ACQUISITION   134

Language and the Family   *134*
Institutional Aspects of Language   *135*

PERSPECTIVES ON LANGUAGE VARIATION   136

Verbal Communication   *136*
   Accents / Dialects / Bidialectalism / Sign Language

Nonverbal Communication   *139*
   Proxemics

Kinesics   *139*
   Paralanguage

CULTURE, LANGUAGE, AND LEARNING STYLE   140

Components of Learning Style   *141*
Origins of Learning Style   *142*
The Relation of Language and Learning Style to Culture   *142*
Communication Style   *144*
   Formal vs. Informal Communication / Emotional vs. Subdued
   Communication / Direct vs. Indirect Communication / Objective
   vs. Subjective Communication / Responses to Guilt and Accusations

Bilingual Education   *145*
   Types of Bilingual Programs / An Explanation of Bilingual
   Functioning / Why Bilingual Education Is Important / Outcomes
   of Bilingual Education Efforts / Ethical Issues in Bilingual Education

SOME REFLECTIVE QUESTIONS   151

Active Exercises   *152*
Accessing the World Wide Web: Resources for Diversity   *154*

REFERENCES   155

6. Creating Developmentally Appropriate Classrooms:
   The Importance of Age and Developmental Status   161

RATIONALE FOR DEVELOPMENTALLY APPROPRIATE EDUCATIONAL
PRACTICES   167

Economic Aims for Schooling   *168*
Early Childhood Education and Developmentally
Appropriate Practice   *169*
Constructivist Thought in Developmentally Appropriate
Practice   *169*

CHARACTERISTICS OF A DEVELOPMENTALLY APPROPRIATE CLASSROOM   171

Pedagogies: Old and New   *171*
Roles: Old and New   *173*

Place of Content Knowledge: Old and New   175
Assessment: Old and New   175

PERSPECTIVES ON AGE AND DEVELOPMENT   176

Sensitive Periods and Developmental Crises   176
Individual Differences and Developmental Domains   177
The Importance of Developmental Knowledge   178
Active Exercises   180
Accessing the World Wide Web: Resources for Diversity   180

REFERENCES   181

7. Creating Inclusive Classrooms: The Health Dimension
    and Ability/Disability Continuum   185

    RATIONALE FOR INCLUSIVE CLASSROOMS   190

    CHARACTERISTICS OF AN INCLUSIVE CLASSROOM   193

    Pegagogies: Old and New   194
    Roles: Old and New   194
    Place of Content Knowledge: Old and New   196
    Assessment: Old and New   196

    PERSPECTIVES ON HEALTH AND THE ABILITY/DISABILITY CONTINUUM   198

    The Health Dimension   198
    The Ability/Disability Continuum   200
    What Is "Exceptionality?"   201
    Historical Perspectives on Special Education   201
    The Importance of Collaboration   204
    What Does "Flexibility" Involve?   205
    Ethical Issues   206
    Active Exercises   209
    Accessing the World Wide Web: Resources for Diversity   209

    REFERENCES   210

8. Developing a Collaborative Classroom: Gender and
    Sexual Orientation   213

    RATIONALE FOR COLLABORATIVE TEACHING AND LEARNING   219

    CHARACTERISTICS OF A COLLABORATIVE CLASSROOM   220

    Pedagogies: Old and New   221
    Roles: Old and New   223
    Place of Content Knowledge: Old and New   225
    Assessment: Old and New   225

    PERSPECTIVES ON GENDER AND SEXUAL ORIENTATION   226

    Sex Role Socialization   226

Sex Role Socialization in the Middle Class   227
Masculine and Feminine Behavior   228

PERSPECTIVES ON SCHOOLS AS SOCIALIZING AGENTS   229

Sex Role Stereotypes in School   230
Recent Studies   232

PERSPECTIVES ON GENDER AND SCHOOL CULTURE   233

Productive and Reproductive Processes   233
*Gender and European American Values in Traditional
School Culture*   233
Gender and School Rules   235
Homophobia and School Culture   235
Ethical Issues   238

SOME REFLECTIVE QUESTIONS   238

Active Exercises   239
Accessing the World Wide Web: Resources for Diversity   239

REFERENCES   240

9. The Classroom as a Global Community: Race,
   Ethnicity/Nationality, and Region   243

RATIONALE FOR THE CLASSROOM AS A GLOBAL COMMUNITY   253

Education for a Global Perspective   254
Hoopes's Model of Intercultural Education   254

CHARACTERISTICS OF A GLOBAL CLASSROOM   256

Pedagogies: Old and New   256
Roles: Old and New   257
Place of Content Knowledge: Old and New   258
Assessment: Old and New   258
Case Analysis   259

PERSPECTIVES ON A GLOBALLY ORIENTED CURRICULUM   259

Curriculum Transformation: The Case of Prejudice   259
  The Functions of Prejudice / Extreme Cases of Prejudice: Hate
  Groups / The Components of Prejudice / White Privilege /
  Prejudice Formation / Prejudice Reduction

Curriculum Transformation: The International Perspective   268
  Perspective Consciousness / State of the Planet Awareness /
  Cross-Cultural Awareness / Knowledge of Global Dynamics or
  World Systems / Awareness of Human Choice / Teaching the
  Global Perspective

Ethical Issues   275

SOME REFLECTIVE QUESTIONS 276

Active Exercises 277
Some Critical Incidents 277
   A Delayed Response / Nurturing a Gang?

Accessing the World Wide Web: Resources for Diversity 278

REFERENCES 279

10. Religious Pluralism in Secular Classrooms 283

RATIONALE FOR ATTENDING TO RELIGION IN PUBLIC SCHOOLS 286

Definitions of Religion 287
Religious Pluralism in the United States 288

CHARACTERISTICS OF A CLASSROOM THAT ATTENDS TO RELIGIOUS
PLURALISM 290

Pedagogies: Old and New 290
Roles: Old and New 291
Place of Content Knowledge: Old and New 292
Assessment: Old and New 293
Analysis of the Case Study 294

PERSPECTIVES ON RELIGION AND SCHOOLING IN THE UNITED STATES 294

Private Freedoms: Religion and Compulsory Attendance 295
*Private Freedoms: The Practice of Religious Beliefs in
Classrooms* 297
Public Freedoms: Public Funding for Religious Schools 298
Public Freedoms: The Provision of Religious Instruction 300

PERSPECTIVES ON RELIGIOUS IDENTITY 301

Religion as a Form of Personal Identity 301
The Influence of the "Religious Right" 302
Ethical Issues 304

SOME REFLECTIVE QUESTIONS 305

Active Exercises 306
Accessing the World Wide Web: Resources for Diversity 306

REFERENCES 306

11. Assessing Progress: The Importance of Social Class and
Social Status 309

RATIONALE FOR A BROADENED DEFINITION OF ASSESSMENT 316

The Case Against Standardized Testing 317
The Case for Alternative Forms of Assessment 318

CHARACTERISTICS OF A CLASSROOM USING BOTH TRADITIONAL AND
ALTERNATIVE ASSESSMENTS   319

Pedagogies: Old and New   320
Roles: Old and New   320
Place of Content Knowledge: Old and New   320
Assessment: Old and New   321
The Importance of Criteria   322
The Issue of Grading   322
  Sorting / Motivation / Feedback

Case Analysis   325

PERSPECTIVES ON SOCIAL CLASS AND SOCIAL STATUS   328

Definitions of Social Class   328
Social Class and Minority Group Membership   329
The Working Poor   330
Social Class and Childrearing Practices   330
Social Status   332
The Importance of Teacher Expectations   332

PERSPECTIVES ON ALTERNATIVE ASSESSMENT   333

Demand Versus Support   333
Ethical Issues   335

SOME REFLECTIVE QUESTIONS   336

Accessing the World Wide Web: Resources for Diversity   337

REFERENCES   338

12. Classrooms of Today and Tomorrow   341

CREATION OF AN INCLUSIVE ENVIRONMENT   342

Sociocultural Inclusion   343
Curriculum Inclusion and Expansion   345
Modification of Pedagogy   346
Modification of Assessment Strategies   347

COMMUNITY AND THE SCHOOL   347

THE PROCESS OF CHANGE: FROM SELF TO OTHER   353

IN CONCLUSION   355

REFERENCES   356

PHOTO CREDITS   358

AUTHOR INDEX   359

SUBJECT INDEX   362

Preface

The opportunities and challenges which people face at the beginning of a new millennium continue to reflect the face of diversity. Here in the United States, as well as in many countries around the world, educators struggle with the question of how to provide an education that is responsive to the needs of different communities while maintaining a sense of unity. In response, the fields of multicultural, intercultural, and international/global education continue to grow and develop.

This third edition of *Human Diversity in Education: An Integrative Approach* continues to address the preparation of teachers for the wide diversity of students they are certain to meet in their classrooms, schools, and communities. At the same time, if they are fully understood and embraced by teachers, the concepts presented in this book provide a foundation that will assist young people to take a proactive role in an increasingly interdependent, global and multicultural society.

Given the extremely positive feedback received from users of the second edition, we have maintained much of the familiar format. Regular users, however, will notice some changes. The book continues to provide a broad treatment of the various forms of human diversity found in today's schools; including nationality, ethnicity, race, religion, gender, class, language, sexual orientation, and handicapping condition. This book maintains its unique approach; that is, its research-based cross-cultural psychological emphasis, based on the assumption that it is at the level of the individual teacher where the change that must occur with regard to diversity in schools begins. That is, little in terms of institutional or systemic change will occur until each individual fully understands the role of culture in determining his or her thoughts and actions, and acquires the means to begin to alter its powerful influence. Culture learning, thus, is central to this book. The use of case studies and critical incidents has been expanded. Instead of being embedded within chapters, most begin with a case study, thus setting the context for what is to follow. An increased number of critical incidents related to the case studies are also included. Each chapter identifies a number of related websites which students can access for up-to-date references related to the topic of each chapter.

An accompanying workbook has also been developed, and reference to relevant activities is made at the end of each chapter. This workbook, *Human Diversity in Action: Developing Multicultural Competencies for the Classroom,* (by Kenneth Cushner, McGraw-Hill,1999) provides a wide-range of activities designed to actively engage students in the concepts presented in the text. Finally, a teacher's-guide provides direction for instructors as well as classroom activities and suggested test questions.

The general format of this edition remains similar to the previous one. Part One provides historical background to current efforts in multicultural education. Chapters 1 and 2 examine the broad social, cultural, and economic changes which confront society today. Chapter 3 explores how cultural differences develop in groups and individuals. Chapter 4 examines how individuals with different cultural identities go through similar adjustment processes as they confront cross-cultural situations. Part Two then examines what teachers can do to make their classrooms and schools more responsive to diversity and more effective learning communities; that is, into classrooms that are collaborative, inclusive, developmentally appropriate, globally oriented, and religiously pluralistic. Each of the chapters in Part Two centers around a case study that illustrates how teachers can adapt their curriculum and instruction to fit the many differences that their students bring into the classroom: language and learning style (Chapter 5); developmental and ability levels (Chapter 6 and 7); gender and sexual orientation (Chapter 8); race, ethnicity, and region (Chapter 9); religion (Chapter 10); and social class and social status (Chapter 11).

Kenneth Cushner
Averil McClelland
Philip Safford

Foundations for Multicultural Teaching

Education in a Changing Society

CHAPTER OUTLINE

THE REALITY OF SOCIAL CHANGE
- Demographics in Transition
- Institutions in Transition

SCHOOLS AS A REFLECTION OF
SOCIAL CHANGE
- Demographics
- Language
- Ability
- Gender
- Students and Teachers: A Clash of Cultures?
- Rethinking Schools and Teaching

SCHOOLS IN TRANSITION
- Characteristics of Second Wave Schools: Classrooms for the Industrial Age
- Characteristics of Third Wave Schools: Classrooms for the Information Age
- Where We Are Today

The Difficulty of Change

GOALS OF THIS BOOK
- Goal 1: Recognize Social and Cultural Changes
- Goal 2: Understand Culture and the Culture-Learning Process
- Goal 3: Improve Intergroup and Intragroup Interaction
- Goal 4: Transmit Cross-Cultural Understanding and Skills to Students

THE ROLE OF STORIES, CASES, AND ACTIVE EXERCISES IN THIS BOOK
- Stories
- Cases

ACTIVE EXERCISES

ACCESSING THE WORLD WIDE WEB: RESOURCES FOR DIVERSITY

REFERENCES

Despite the formidable difficulties, I remain optimistic, perhaps because there is to me a contradiction in being simultaneously pessimistic and an educator. Whatever our individual experiences with a place called school, to think seriously about education conjures up intriguing possibilities both for schooling and a way of life as yet scarcely tried.

John Goodlad

Jim McDowell's Sixth Grade: A Case Study

It was late on a June afternoon in the year 2000 when Jim McDowell was packing up the usual assortment of books, games, bulletin board materials, and stuff that he had accumulated during the year to enhance his sixth graders' educational experiences. It was a task he had done many times

*before, but this time was quite different. This was the last time he would put
all these things away: he was retiring after thirty years in the classroom.*

*As he cleaned out closets and drawers, took down favorite pictures
and posters, and packed up assorted plants, he thought about all the
changes that had occurred since he began teaching in the district in 1970.
He had been in a different school then, a K–6 school that served the neighborhood in which it was located, a neighborhood that was comfortably if
not ostentatiously middle-class. There had been eighteen teachers on the
staff, including a music teacher, an art teacher, one principal, and no
Chapter I reading or math teachers. All but he and the principal were
women, and most of them had taught at this school for at least fifteen years
(except for the times several had been on leave to have children). This
hadn't changed much over the years. Although a few men had taught in
the building, most stayed only a short time before moving to another site,
taking a position in administration, or leaving the field of education altogether. There were still only two male teachers in his current building, and
the principal was a woman.*

*That first year had been, as it often is for new, young teachers, some-
thing of a blur, but it was a pleasant one. Nearly all of his students had
lived in the neighborhood all their lives; indeed, many of them were the
children of parents who had also attended that elementary school. Almost
all of his students' mothers were at home during the day, and a number of
them made themselves available to help with class field trips and parties
for Halloween, Christmas, and Valentine's Day. Only two of his students
did not live with both parents, and fall and spring open houses were
crowded with mothers and fathers eager to see their children's work posted
on every available wall and to listen to him talk about their progress. All
his students were white; indeed, the only African American children in the
building were two students in the primary Educable Mentally Retarded
class, which housed all the youngest EMR students in the district. The
materials he had to work with consisted primarily of paper, pencils, paint,
books, and chalk.*

*He had been at his present school for nine years. In the early 1980s, the
district had been forced to close two of its six elementary schools due to
declining enrollment, and this school, one of two intermediate schools in the
district, served half of the district's children in grades 4, 5, and 6. In many
ways, it was an exciting school to teach in because of the challenges faced
by its student body and staff. The staff consisted of eighteen regular classroom teachers, two Chapter I reading teachers, one Chapter I math teacher,
a part-time music teacher, a part-time art teacher, a teacher who taught a
Developmentally Handicapped class, a teacher who taught a Severe Behavior Disorders class, a full-time social worker, a drug-education professional
who was in the building three days a week, a two-day-a-week school nurse,
and a principal and an assistant principal.*

*His class this year had twenty-five students. Half of them lived in fam-
ilies headed by a single parent (one of them a father); one-third of the class
were reading below grade level; and one-third were eligible for free
lunches. Far from being an all-white class, 35 percent of his students were*

African American and 40 percent were white, with the remaining students from East Indian, Vietnamese, Puerto Rican, and Central American backgrounds. Half his students were Catholic, three belonged to the local Jehovah's Witness church, two were Muslim, one was Buddhist, and four were Jewish—far below the number that were in each classroom when he began teaching in the district. One child, who had suffered injuries in an automobile accident that had left him unable to walk, was in a wheelchair. Two students were still waiting to be tested to determine their eligibility for the Severe Behavior Disorders class. All of them loved using the computer that had been installed in his room five years earlier.

Looking back now, the times seemed quite different. When he first started teaching in 1970, things were somewhat more turbulent, yet hopeful. Jim entered the teaching force, initially, as a means of avoiding the Vietnam War. Teaching, at the time, was one of the few ways in which young people could obtain draft-exempt status. He felt lucky to have been a natural teacher, as many had said to him over the years—he had a genuine liking of young people, and both they and most parents trusted him. Young people were central to the social upheaval of the 1960s and 1970s. The 1960s saw the peak of the Civil Rights Movement. In 1969, just before Jim's last year in college, Neal Armstrong walked on the moon for the first time, the Hippy movement was in full swing, and Woodstock had brought together half a million people, who made a statement about music and peace. And, just a few months later, in May 1970, just when he was graduating from college, four students were killed on the campus of Kent State University in Ohio and two at Jackson State in Alabama for protesting against a war in which they did not believe. Kids, then, were growing up in a time of social uncertainty, but optimism.

In a way, Jim regretted leaving the job he had had for so many years. Science had always been one of his great interests, and he had spent several summers in classes offered by the regional NASA installation, where he got many ideas and resources for his classes. One year he was even able to borrow some moon rocks, which created all kinds of excitement throughout the school and community. He still enjoyed the kids, and he knew he would feel a tug to return to the school next September. The decision to retire had been difficult, but the state was doing a buy-out designed to remove the highest-paid teachers from the classroom; financially, it was beneficial for him to retire now. And everything had changed so much that he could not be quite sure about the future of his students. Children today had so many more seemingly intractable problems than had the children when he began teaching; so many more were poor; so many more had difficulty concentrating on schoolwork; so many more had family difficulties. Babies born to mothers addicted to crack cocaine and children born with fetal alcohol syndrome were entering schools with greater frequency. More and more children were being diagnosed with ADHD—attention deficit/hyperactivity disorder. High school and college graduates were less certain of obtaining good positions as companies were downsizing and many people were being laid off from their jobs, yet corporations were posting record profits. It didn't seem to make much sense. Financial aid to *support applications for college were getting more difficult to obtain, and violence seemed to be on the increase in schools and communities. Perhaps, he thought, it really was best to leave now.*

The children who had entered Jim McDowell's sixth grade classroom in the fall of 2000 will be graduating from high school in the year 2007. His classroom and the diversity of the students in it are not atypical. Indeed, his classroom in many ways represents the wave of the future in public education in the United States, not only in urban districts but in suburban and rural ones as well. The school district in which Jim teaches is a suburban one in a region of the country just beginning to emerge from the industrial depression of the rust belt, with its aging steel mills, auto factories, and rubber plants. It is composed of two suburban communities with a total population of about sixty-five thousand people. There are two private universities nearby, as well as a major urban state university just eight miles away. As a whole, the district is reasonably well mixed in terms of race and social class. However, the two communities differ in several respects. One is largely white, was more recently built, has a considerable upper-middle-class population, and is more completely residential than the other. The other major community, the older of the two, is generally middle- and lower-middle-class, has a few small shopping districts, and has a large group of families that has been there for many generations. This community has a rather large African American population, which over the years has replaced an aging and more mobile Jewish community; however, some of the orthodox Jewish communities remain so they can be close to the synagogues to which they must walk on their Sabbath. This community also has a number of Italian American families who have lived in the area for generations, as well as more recent immigrants reflecting Asian, Middle Eastern, and Latino backgrounds. Many families in the district are Catholic, although a large number of these families send their children to public school. Nevertheless, the district also has two Catholic elementary schools and one Catholic high school, as well as several Protestant Christian schools. The district is split politically on most issues, some reflecting liberal ideology and others remaining rather conservative in their orientation.

Several years ago, rather than waiting for the state to mandate a state-designed desegregation plan, the local school board developed its own reorganization plan, transforming its neighborhood school structure to one in which all students of the same age went to four primary schools (grades K–3), three intermediate schools (grades 4–6), one middle school (grades 7–8), and one high school (grades 9–12). By virtue of the age criterion, all schools became demographically mixed. It is important to note, however, that these demographic characteristics are relatively new. Thirty years ago, within the memory of most teachers in the district, both communities were relatively homogeneous, the population was almost entirely white and middle-class, and divorce and family poverty were statistical exceptions. What has happened in the intervening years?

THE REALITY OF SOCIAL CHANGE

As we begin the twenty-first century, we are witnessing two fundamental social changes that have widespread importance for the future of our country: (1) a rapid shift in the demographic makeup of our population and (2) an equally profound shift in the nature of our basic institutions. A brief discussion of each follows.

Demographics in Transition

Three factors are of primary importance in the shifting demographics of our population. First, immigration from non-European countries currently rivals the great immigrations from Europe that were experienced at the turn of the twentieth century. In the early part of the twentieth century, the majority of immigrants arrived from Europe, and, except for language, it was relatively easy for them to fit into the cultural landscape of the country (after all, many looked similar to the majority of those around them). Today's immigrants come from such diverse regions as the Middle East, Central and Latin America, Southeast Asia and the Pacific, and Eastern Europe and Russia. Most look somewhat different from the mainstream, which immediately sets them apart from others. Indeed, many communities are becoming increasingly international.

Second, birthrates are considerably higher among nonwhite populations than they are among whites. About the time that most current teacher education students were born (the early to mid 1980s), approximately one in four schoolchildren was a child of color (traditionally referred to as a minority student). By the year 2020, it is likely that the figure will increase to one child in two, and many of these children will be poor. In 1994 in the twenty-five largest school districts in the United States, children of color comprised about 72 percent of the total school enrollment.[1] By 2056, the average U.S. resident, as defined by Census statistics, will trace his or her descent to Africa, Asia, the Hispanic world, the Pacific Islands, Arabia—almost anywhere but white Europe.[2] Compounding this demographic phenomenon is the academic underachievement of many minority students. For example, The President's Initiative on Race reports the following percentages of the population age 25 to 29 who have finished high school: whites, 93 percent; blacks, 87 percent; Hispanics, 62 percent. The lower rate among Hispanics reflects lower average levels of education among immigrants, 38 percent of whom were foreign-born in 1997.[3]

Third, the total population of children in relation to adults in the United States is changing as the public grows older. The Commission on Work, Family, and Citizenship of the William T. Grant Foundation notes that the number of American youth has shrunk dramatically. Between 1980 and 1996, the youth population between the ages of 15 and 25 fell 21 percent, from 43 to 34 million. Young people as a percentage of the nation's population also declined from 18.8 to 13 percent.[4] Only recently are these figures beginning to turn around. There is increasing concern that there will not be enough workers to support the aging baby boom population, which will be a tremendous drain on the nation's social security system in future decades.

Institutions in Transition

We are also witnessing profound changes in the nature of our basic institutions. Alvin Toffler asserts that these changes are so fundamental as to constitute a shift in the very nature of our civilization, away from what he calls Second Wave institutions—characterized by reliance on standardization, synchronization, specialization, centralization, and valuing bigness—toward Third Wave institutions, characterized by individualization, choice, diversity, and valuing smallness.[5] He writes:

> . . . many of today's changes are not independent of one another. Nor are they random. For example, the crack-up of the nuclear family, the global energy crisis, the spread of cults and cable television, the rise of flextime and the new fringe-benefit

packages, the emergence of separatist movements from Quebec to Corsica, may all seem like isolated events. Yet precisely the reverse is true. These and many other seemingly unrelated events or trends are interconnected. They are, in fact, parts of a much larger phenomenon: the death of industrialism and the rise of a new civilization.[6]

Economics and Politics

While it is relatively easy, particularly at the beginning of a new millennium, to fall prey to exaggerated notions of the future, Toffler's views are more than a little intriguing. Clearly, all of our institutions are showing signs of transition, and the direction seems to be toward increased choice, increased diversity, and increased interdependency. Our economy, for example, is now firmly global in scale, in large measure because of advances in computer technology and high-speed travel. Indeed, the much revered American corporation can hardly be said to exist any longer; the acquisition of raw material for manufacturing and the distribution of goods by such giants as Chrysler, General Motors, and General Electric are done worldwide. Robert Reich, secretary of labor in the first Clinton administration, writes:

> Consider some examples: Precision ice hockey equipment is designed in Sweden, financed in Canada, and assembled in Cleveland and Denmark for distribution in North America and Europe, respectively, out of alloys whose molecular structure was researched and patented in Delaware and fabricated in Japan. An advertising campaign is conceived in Britain; film footage for it is shot in Canada, dubbed in Britain, and edited in New York. A sports car is financed in Japan, designed in Italy, and assembled in Indiana, Mexico, and France, using advanced electronic components invented in New Jersey and fabricated in Japan. A microprocessor is designed in California and financed in America and West Germany, containing dynamic random-access memories fabricated in South Korea. A jet airplane is designed in the state of Washington and in Japan, and assembled in Seattle, with tail engines from Britain, special tail sections from China and Italy, and engines from Britain. A space satellite designed in California, manufactured in France, and financed by Australians is launched from a rocket made in the Soviet Union. Which of these is an American product? Which a foreign? How does one decide? Does it matter?[7]

Such economic realities have their counterparts in the political sphere as well. As we increasingly interact with people from other nations in matters of trade, we also increasingly interact with them politically, and political events occurring in other countries have a much more profound effect on our own political agenda than they used to. For example, the North American Free Trade Agreement (NAFTA) and the GATT (General Agreement on Tariffs and Trade) Treaty are political responses to the facts of international trade. Similarly, the end of the Cold War as the defining feature of international politics and the recurring ethnic and religious wars around the world are expressions of new realities with which the United States must contend.

Marriage and Family Life

In the family, too, we are witnessing profound changes in structure and organization. Recent research on the changing demographics of our families graphically portrays the changing nature of family life. For instance, in 1942, 60 percent of families could be described as nuclear families consisting of two parents and their children. Furthermore, if one believes the images often portrayed in basal readers until relatively recently, this nuclear family includes a dog and a cat all living happily together in a white house surrounded by a neat picket fence. In these families, the father's role is to leave home every day to earn the money to support the family, and the mother's role is to stay at home and raise the children. Today, less than 10 percent of American families match that picture.

It is estimated today that approximately two-thirds of all marriages in the United States will be disrupted through divorce or separation. More than ten different family configurations are represented in today's classrooms—a significant one being the single-parent family, often a mother and child or children living in poverty. Increasingly, this single parent is a teenage mother. Another increasing family configuration is one in which two adults of the same sex, committed to one another over time, are raising children who may be biologically related to one of the adults or who may have been adopted by them.

Consider some of these facts: every thirty-two seconds a baby is born into poverty, every minute a baby is born to a teen mother, every two minutes a baby is born at low birth-weight, every three minutes a baby is born to a mother who received late or no prenatal care, every fifteen minutes a baby dies, and a teenager is twice as likely to give birth out of wedlock in the United States than in any other country in the world.[8]

Another increasing family issue is poverty, and it is not limited to the children of children, or even to children of single parents. In the United States, the number of children living in poverty has risen 43 percent since 1970, and more than 12 million American youngsters live below the poverty level. A quarter of all students are from lower socioeconomic backgrounds, 20 percent live in single-parent homes, 14 percent are at risk of dropping out, 14 percent are children of teenage mothers, 40 percent will live with divorced parents before the age of 18, and 25 to 33 percent will be latchkey children with no one to greet them when they come home from school. Most disturbing is the fact that every nine seconds a child drops out of school, every ten seconds a child is reported abused or neglected, every two hours a child is killed by firearms, every four hours a child commits suicide, and every five hours a child dies from abuse or neglect.[9] Thus, a random sample of 100 children in the United States would reveal 12 born out of wedlock, 40 born to parents who will divorce, 15 born to parents who will separate in the next five years, 2 born to parents who will die in the next five years, and 41 who will reach age 16 "normally." Clearly, the family pattern that was once considered normal, that provided the image of the right and proper kind of family, and that guided the policies of our institutions is now a minority pattern.

Organized Religion

In times of transition like this, organized religion can serve as a stabilizing influence. Here, too, however, the institutionalized churches of all faiths are undergoing change. Once largely a nation steeped in the Judeo-Christian heritage, the United States is now home to a growing number of faiths that are unfamiliar to many people. Buddhism, Islam, and other religions of the East and Middle East are growing, as new immigrants bring their religious ideas with them, with Islam being the fastest-growing religion in America. Similarly, a wide variety of relatively small but active congregations built around scientific, philosophical, and psychological ideas appear to proliferate the so-called New Age religious sects. At the same time, conservative branches of mainline Protestant, Catholic, Jewish, and Muslim religions serve as havens for those for whom social change seems too rapid and too chaotic, and fundamentalist denominations (usually Protestant) are the fastest-growing religious organizations in the nation. Indeed, the tension between so-called liberal and conservative elements in the organized church may become one of the most profound social conflicts of contemporary life.

SCHOOLS AS A REFLECTION OF SOCIAL CHANGE

Demographics

All the institutional changes discussed thus far are inevitably reflected in the institution of schooling—its purposes, policies, and practices. For example, the demographic statistics cited in the previous sections in terms of the total population of the United States are first seen in our schools. It is projected that, by the year 2020, children of color will comprise upwards of one-half of the children in classrooms, up from approximately one-third at the beginning of the twenty-first century. Startling changes are already occurring in a number of places in the country. For example, more than a decade ago, students from so-called minority groups comprised more than 50 percent of the school populations in California, Arizona, New Mexico, Texas, and Colorado.[10] In these states, minority children may find themselves in the uncomfortable position of being the majority in a world whose rules are set by a more powerful minority, not unlike the former situation in South Africa.

Language

Along with ethnic and racial diversity often comes linguistic diversity. Increasing numbers of children are entering school from minority-language backgrounds and have little or no competence in the English language. While Spanish is the predominant language of many children in the United States (the United States is currently the fifth largest Spanish-speaking country in the world), an increasing number of students are entering the schools speaking Arabic, Chinese, Hmong, Khmer, Lao, Thai, and Vietnamese.[11] Since a person's language provides the symbols used to understand the world, children whose symbol systems differ from those of the dominant group are likely to see the world from a different perspective, to look for meaning in different ways, and to attribute different meanings to common objects and processes.

Ability

Life in classrooms is different in other ways as well. Before the enactment of The Education of All Handicapped Children Act of 1975 (Public Law 94-142), more than 1 million children with disabilities were excluded from public school, because the community (or state) had not yet taken any responsibility for their welfare or education. In addition, many who were in school were given inappropriate labels and were segregated from their peers. With amendments enacted in 1990, the law was renamed The Individuals with Disabilities Education Act and a significant change was made in that the law now affects students through the age of 21, not only children. As a result of PL 94-142 and its successors, however, students with a variety of disabilities now spend increasing amounts of time in traditional classrooms, while still receiving the services they need. The trend is toward more inclusion, which enables students with disabilities to be educated side-by-side with their nondisabled peers. While this benefits students with special needs, the benefits are not one-sided. Children do learn from each other, and students with disabilities also have *abilities* to share.

Gender

Finally, there is new awareness in many classrooms of a difference among children that is so fundamental that it has been overlooked as a matter of inquiry throughout most of our history. That difference is gender. Because we have included both girls and boys, at least in elementary education, since the very beginning of the common school, and because our political and educational ideals assume that school is gender neutral, the effect of gender on children's education has not been analyzed until quite recently. In the past thirty years, however, considerable research on differences in the social and educational lives of boys and girls in school has been done. Shakeshaft writes:

> Two messages emerge repeatedly from the research on gender and schooling. First, what is good for males is not necessarily good for females. Second, if a choice must be made, the education establishment will base policy and instruction on that which is good for males.[12]

For the most part, girls have not been considered educationally different from boys, yet the experiences of girls in school are in many ways quite different from the experiences of boys. It is also the case that the educational outcomes of girls differ from those of boys. In short, girls who sit in the same classroom with boys, read the same materials as boys, do the same homework as boys, and take the same examinations as boys often are not treated in the same ways as boys and, consequently, may not achieve the same educational outcomes as boys.

Students and Teachers: A Clash of Cultures?

There exists a considerable discrepancy between the makeup of the student population in most schools and that of the teaching force. Most of our nation's teachers come from a rather homogeneous group; approximately 88 to 90 percent are European American and middle-class. Female teachers outnumber male teachers by three to one, with nearly two-thirds of Pre K–6 teachers being women (male teachers in grades 7–12 do outnumber female teachers two to one). This contrasts sharply with the student diversity that currently exists in schools and that is projected to increase in the years ahead. A considerable number of children of color are therefore missing important role models who represent their background within the school setting. Majority students, as well, miss having role models who represent cultures other than their own. Equally critical is the fact that teachers (like many other people) tend to be culture-bound and have little knowledge or experience with people from other cultures. This, of course, limits their ability to interact effectively with students who are different from themselves. Today, fewer than 10 percent of teacher education students in the United States claim fluency in a language other than English, fully three-fifths are completely monolingual, most live within 100 miles of their birthplace, and most wish to teach in communities similar to those in which they grew up.[13] Sixty-nine percent of white teacher education students report spending all or most of their free time with people of their own racial or ethnic background.[14] More disturbing, a substantial number of teacher education students do not believe that low-income and minority learners are capable of learning high-level concepts in the subjects they are preparing to teach.[15] Finally, the traditional identification of teaching as women's work means that even multiculturally sophisticated teachers are sometimes powerless to make their school's culture more accommodating to female and minority students, because it is often males who are in key decision-making roles.

Rethinking Schools and Teaching

In terms of traditional definitions of social order, it appears that most of our social institutions, including schools, are not working very well in the beginning of this new millennium. Numerous governmental and private reports have said so; college teachers say so; classroom teachers say so; politicians say so; and your neighbors say so. In this context, the principle values of democracy—equality, liberty, and community—appear to be in jeopardy. What does equality mean when many culturally different people are competing for scarce jobs? What does liberty mean when language barriers prevent common understanding? What does community mean when allegiance to one's group prevents commonality with people in other groups?

Some have argued that the changes we are experiencing require a shift from the ideals of a Jeffersonian political democracy (in which democratic principles are defined by individualism) to the ideals of a cultural democracy, in which democratic principles are defined by cultural pluralism.[16] Such a shift involves a radical change in our beliefs about how we are to get along with one another, what kinds of information and skills we need to develop, and how we are to interpret our national ideals and goals. Among other things, this cultural view of democracy requires a fundamental rethinking of our national goals and the way in which we structure or organize schools in relation to those goals. The school, after all, is the institution charged not only with teaching necessary information and skills but also with ensuring that young people develop long-cherished democratic attitudes and values. While schooling alone cannot completely alter the larger society in which it exists,[17] schooling can influence as well as reflect its parent society. Since teachers can either engender or stifle new ideas and new ways of doing things with their students, they are in a position to influence both the direction and the pace of change in our society.

Fortunately, there are teachers who have begun to exercise this power in positive ways. They work in classrooms in all regions of the country, sometimes alone and sometimes with colleagues who are turned on to new possibilities. They work with students of all backgrounds: white and nonwhite, wealthy and poor, boys and girls, rural and urban. They work with students of various religions and of no particular religion, with students who have vastly different abilities, and with students who have different sexual orientations. They work in wealthy districts, which spend a great deal of money on each student, and in poor districts, which have little in the way of resources. And, most important, their classrooms reflect their belief that all children can succeed.

SCHOOLS IN TRANSITION

Twenty-first-century schools and classrooms, in which teachers must learn to see change as an opportunity rather than a problem and to see difference as a resource rather than a deficit, are fundamentally different from the traditional schools and classrooms that characterized nineteenth- and twentieth-century America. Underlying these differences between past and future schools are fundamental differences in the larger society in which the schools are found. During the nineteenth and twentieth centuries, most schools were designed to reflect the emerging industrial (factory) mode of organization. Toffler refers to this as "Second Wave Civilization" to distinguish it from its predecessor, the agrarian, or "First Wave Civilization." As mentioned earlier, central to this Second Wave Civilization are the ideas of *standardization, synchronization, specialization, centralization, and a value placed on bigness*. Conversely, the organizational model that seems to be emerging as we enter the Information Age of the twenty-first century, which Toffler refers to as the "Third Wave Civilization," differs sharply from its predecessor. Central to Third Wave Civilization, including its schools, are the ideas of *individualization and choice* rather than standardization, *decentralization* rather than centralization, *diversity* rather than specialization, and *smallness* rather than bigness. In the next two sections, we will take a closer look at how the current progression from Second to Third Wave Civilizations is likely to influence the nature of twenty-first-century schooling and teaching. We will then examine where today's schools are in relation to this transition and the primary obstacles that must be dealt with as the change proceeds. Finally, we will discuss the goals of this book in terms of preparing teachers for this change process.

Characteristics of Second Wave Schools: Classrooms for the Industrial Age

In Second Wave schools, administrators are viewed as "bosses," teachers as "workers," and students as "raw material." The "work" of teachers is to lecture, ask questions, and give directions that will "produce" students who meet the vocational and citizenship needs of the society. Students, as befitting "raw material," are largely passive.

Standardization

Standardization is important in such schools. Teachers and other school personnel are hired based on well-defined standards of certification. Standards of dress and behavior for both school personnel and students are enforced through well-publicized, standardized rules. Curriculum is based largely on standardized textbooks and on a districtwide standardized course of study that each teacher is expected to follow. Standards of performance for students and teachers are well defined, and grades reflect a student's ability to learn standardized lessons as demonstrated through standardized paper-and-pencil tests. Competition for grades is encouraged, and work is normally done individually. "Keep your eyes on your own paper" and "Don't talk to your neighbors" are common statements made by teachers to reinforce ideals of individualism and competition. It is expected, and therefore accepted, that some students, being poorer "raw material," will fail.

Children are initially grouped by age in standard grade levels without regard to individual development. Children who do not fit a particular grade level are "put down" a grade level, "kept back" for a year, advanced a grade, or placed in remedial or special classes. In the past, the last option was likely to continue throughout the course of a child's schooling. Print is the instructional medium of choice, while the use of art, music, drama, video, computers, and other alternative media is considered an extra, if it is considered at all.

Synchronization

In Second Wave schools, the synchronization of time is a major part of the school structure. The school year lasts a certain number of days. There is a time to come to school and a time to leave. Classes last for a certain number of minutes. Indeed, in some states, time allotments per subject per week are mandated by the state department of education. Special events, such as field trips and assemblies, are carefully scheduled so as to offer the least interference with the standard school day.

Specialization

Specialization is also a central element of Second Wave schools. In elementary school, specialized subject areas are taught separately throughout the day. Above the elementary grades, knowledge is divided into disciplines and offered in specialized courses by different teachers separated from one another by physical distance, time, and often a hierarchy of value. Home economics, vocational education, music, and art, for example, are not valued as highly as mathematics, English, and science. Roles in Second Wave schools are also specialized. Administrators do certain kinds of things; teachers do other kinds of things. Teachers in secondary schools teach only certain subjects, while special teachers teach only special students. Other professional and nonprofessional staff (nurses, counselors, custodians) do still other kinds of things.

Centralization

Similarly, Second Wave schools are highly centralized. Most rules and customs are decided by centralized district staff, who usually work out of what is accurately called the "central office." Curriculum decisions, budgets, purchasing, and school policies regarding attendance, discipline, acceptable teaching practices, and annual scheduling are effected from a centralized point. For students receiving special education, such responsibilities are administered separately, as a centralized system-within-a-system.

Large Scale

An inclination toward bigness is also characteristic of Second Wave schools, particularly at the secondary level. It's an old American belief that "bigger is better," and that applies to almost all aspects of schools—except class size, where the norm is about twenty-five students per class. An elementary principal once said, sadly, "Every time my school population declines to its most educable level—about 300 students—the district talks about consolidating us with another school." Educators know from experience that, the larger a school is, the more impersonal it becomes, the less chance there is for the school to become a community and more students will "fall through the cracks." Nevertheless, for financial reasons, the consolidation of small schools is a major trend in the United States. Finally, most people seem attracted to the idea of bigness—a big football team, a big band, a big choir, a big building.

Reich describes the school that expresses a desire to fit students for an industrial, mass-production society:

> Children [move] from grade to grade through a preplanned sequence of standard subjects, as if on factory conveyor belts. At each stage, certain facts [are] poured into their heads. Children with the greatest capacity to absorb the facts, and with the most submissive demeanor, [are] placed on a rapid track through the sequence; those with the least capacity for fact retention and self-discipline, on the slowest. Most children [end] up on a conveyor belt of medium speed. Standardized tests [are] routinely administered at certain checkpoints in order to measure how many of the facts [have] stuck in the small heads, and product defects [are] taken off the line and returned for retooling. As in the mass-production system, discipline and order [are] emphasized above all else.[18]

Characteristics of Third Wave Schools: Classrooms for the Information Age

The model for Third Wave schools and classrooms is not the factory; it is the learning community. In learning communities, teachers, students, support staff, parents, administrators, and others who are involved in the school from time to time are viewed as members of a single community, whose common purpose, for everyone, is learning. Learning is defined not only as the acquisition of factual knowledge but also as the development of critical thinking skills and the ability to apply knowledge in varied situations (problem solving). Emphasis is placed not only on the acquisition of information and skills but also on the *understanding* of their theoretical and research base. In such an atmosphere, *why* is often a more important question than *what*. It also means that the *process* of learning—how material is structured and is presented in order to help students learn—is considered an important issue.

Individualization and Choice

Individualization and choice will increasingly characterize Third Wave classrooms. Teachers and students often decide together, within a broad curricular framework, what to study and how to study it, what materials are required, what rules are needed, and how much time is given to various activities. Such collaboration enables teachers to share their knowledge and skills. Students and teachers are viewed as resources, each with unique contributions to the learning community.

Collaboration

As befits a "community," tasks are often accomplished by people working together, using what they already know and figuring out what they need to know and how to get it. Since the primary goal of the community is learning, not sorting out those who have learned from those who have not, everyone's knowledge is put to use in the service of that goal. It is expected, and accepted, that everyone will learn and contribute to the learning of others. Cooperation is emphasized, and competition is reduced to an occasional activity. Mistakes are accepted and considered instructive, so the logical next step after failure is to try again. Some of these schools and classrooms have abandoned letter grades in favor of narrative progress reports or portfolio assessment. Where grades are given, they are sometimes given to groups rather than to individuals and, in any case, are used more as a measure of progress than as a measure of the person.

In learning communities, it is understood that children learn at different rates. Standardized grade levels are sometimes abandoned in favor of mixed age or ability groupings. Where grade levels are maintained, mixed age and ability groupings are often used for part of the day, so that older or more advanced students can help those who are younger or less advanced. One way to accomplish this is to block part of the day, so that all students are simultaneously working on math or another subject in different parts of the school. Another way is to organize learning in an individual classroom around small-group projects, which allows students to collaborate in solving some problems. In this case, the acquisition of knowledge becomes a means for accomplishing the project. Still another community strategy is to study a particular object from an interdisciplinary point of view, applying knowledge from science, art, music, history, language arts, mathematics, and so forth to further understanding. For example, a unit on food production might integrate content from the sciences (plant growth), social studies (geography, economics, anthropology), language arts (writing from the perspective of a farmer), health (preservation of food), music (production of advertising jingles), and art (marketing and advertising). In most learning communities, all three patterns are present, sometimes sequentially and sometimes simultaneously.

Diversity

It is also understood in learning communities that everyone (students, teachers, support staff) has his or her own unique characteristics. Individuals learn, teach, and interact in any number of ways, depending on their innate characteristics and their cultural conditioning. Such social diversity is viewed as normal rather than deviant and as enriching rather than dividing the community. Consequently, in such schools and classrooms, social and physical differences are explicitly acknowledged and appreciated. This attitude has some important educational consequences. First, a continuing effort is made to help all children understand and appreciate the characteristics of those who differ from themselves. Second, the tools of such understanding and appreciation—the skills of questioning, negotiating, and conflict resolution—are explicitly taught as a part of the ongoing routines of the day. And, perhaps most important, teaching is seen as a process of adapting to different styles and needs.

Because learning communities are likely to "mix up" traditional divisions of age, time, and disciplines, both adults and children in the school are likely to find themselves working outside of their normal age groups and knowledge specialties. Thus, everyone in the school, both adults and students, may serve as resources to one another. Students may find themselves working with many different adults and a wide variety of other students.

Decentralization

Because people in learning community schools and classrooms think of themselves as decision makers, the organization of these schools and classrooms is largely decentralized. That is, the goals and objectives of learning are dictated less by external or centralized personnel and directed more by the participants themselves. This is also true in terms of budgeting, attendance and dress policies, the hiring of staff, and so forth. In many schools, this process is called *site-based management*—that is, the community's decision making is done on-site by those who will carry out these decisions.

Small Scale

Finally, learning communities tend to be small enough to enable everyone to know everyone else reasonably well and to engage in the kind of face-to-face interaction that characterizes most communities. This issue of scale can be addressed in a variety of ways. In some schools, enrollment is deliberately kept low. In larger schools that have been formed for cost-saving purposes, students and teachers are often divided in "schools-within-schools." For example, three or four teachers in an elementary school may teach 75 to 100 children, or five or six subject-area teachers may teach 150 high school students. This arrangement permits the greater flexibility and creativity that comes with smaller-scale organization. The ultimate goal in all cases is to enable both children and adults to feel a sense of belonging to the community and a sense of responsibility for its welfare.

Where We Are Today

As we begin the transition to the twenty-first century and the Information Age, schools are also in transition. Few schools today can be described as being entirely Second Wave or Third Wave in their organization and governance. Rather, most schools are somewhere between the two models. Furthermore, the Third Wave school is not entirely new. Some of its elements, such as cross-age grouping and the learning community atmosphere, have historical roots that go back to the one-room schoolhouse of the nineteenth century. What seems to separate the school as a learning community from the school as a factory are the characteristics associated with each model. And those characteristics, in turn, depend largely on the beliefs, attitudes, and values of the people who comprise the entity we call "school."

The Difficulty of Change

Change is difficult, particularly when it deals with the fundamental beliefs, attitudes, and values around which we organize our lives. Attempts at such change often result in hostility or in an effort to preserve, at any cost, our familiar ways of doing things and thinking about the world around us. The universal nature of such resistance to change is illustrated in the following parable.

This parable speaks to us on both a literal and a metaphorical level. On the metaphorical level, it carries many messages: it applauds diversity and recognizes that a society cannot function to its fullest when it ignores the ideas, contributions, efforts, and concerns of any of its people. It illustrates some of the consequences of

A Parable

Once upon a time there was a group of people who lived in the mountains in an isolated region. One day a stranger passed through their area and dropped some wheat grains in their field. The wheat grew. After a number of years, people noticed the new plant and decided to collect its seeds and chew them. Someone noticed that when a cart had accidentally ridden over some of the seeds, a harder outer covering separated from the seed and what was inside was sweeter. Someone else noticed that when it rained, the grains that had been run over expanded a little, and the hot sun cooked them. So, people started making wheat cereal and cracked wheat and other wheat dishes. Wheat became the staple of their diet.

Years passed. Because these people did not know anything about crop rotation, fertilizers, and cross-pollination, the wheat crop eventually began to fail.

About this time, another stranger happened by. He was carrying two sacks of barley. He saw the people starving and planted some of his grain. The barley grew well. He presented it to the people and showed them how to make bread and soup and many other dishes from barley. But they called him a heretic.

"You are trying to undermine our way of life and force us into accepting you as our king." They saw his trick. "You can't fool us. You are trying to weaken us and make us accept your ways. Our wheat will not let us starve. Your barley is evil."

He stayed in the area, but the people avoided him. Years passed. The wheat crop failed again and again. The children suffered from malnutrition. One day the stranger came to the market and said, "Wheat is a grain. My barley has a similar quality. It is also a grain. Why don't we just call the barley grain?"

Now since they were suffering so much, the people took the grain, except for a few who staunchly refused. They loudly proclaimed that they were the only remaining followers of the True Way, the Religion of Wheat. A few new people joined the Wheat Religion from time to time, but most began to eat barley. They called themselves The Grainers.

For generations, the Wheat Religion people brought up their children to remember the true food called wheat. A few of them hoarded some wheat grains to keep it safe and sacred. Others sent their children off in search of wheat, because they felt that if one person could happen by with barley, wheat might be known somewhere else too.

And so it went for decades, until the barley crop began to fail. The last few Wheat Religion people planted their wheat again. It grew beautifully, and because it grew so well, they grew bold and began to proclaim that their wheat was the only true food. Most people resisted and called them heretics. A few people said, "Why don't you just admit that wheat is a grain?"

The wheat growers agreed, thinking that they could get many more wheat followers if they called it grain. But by this time, some of the children of the Wheat Religion people began to return from their adventures with new seed, not just wheat, but rye and buckwheat and millet. Now people began to enjoy the taste of many different grains. They took turns planting them and trading the seed with each other. In this way, everyone came to have enough sustenance and lived happily ever after.[19]

---

unreasonable prejudice but also recognizes the powerful emotions that underlie a prejudiced attitude. It indicates the power of naming something in a way that is familiar and comfortable to those who are uncomfortable about accepting something new. Perhaps most important, the parable recognizes the tendency people have to resist change. People are creatures of habit who find it difficult to change, whether at the individual level, the institutional level, or the societal level. People often work from one set of assumptions, one pattern of behavior. Because of the way in which they are socialized, these habits of thought and behavior are so much a part of them that they find it very difficult to think that things can be done in any other way. Some habits people develop are positive and constructive; others are negative and limiting. The story shows us that sometimes even a society's strengths can become weaknesses, yet new circumstances and opportunities arise in each generation that demand that new perspectives, attitudes, and solutions be sought.[20] Such circumstances are evident today in the changing face of the American classroom, and much of the responsibility for change must lie with teachers and teacher educators.

GOALS OF THIS BOOK

This book is about change. It is about teaching all children in a society that is growing more diverse each year. It is about changes in classrooms and in the act of teaching within those classrooms. It is about changes in schools and in the larger society in which these schools are embedded. All these environments (classrooms, schools, and society) are connected, so that changes in any one of them produce disequilibrium and change in the others. Their connectedness and the mutual influence that each exerts on the others is visually depicted in Figure 1.1.

As a teacher in the twenty-first century, your career will be spent in ever changing schools, whose mission will be to help American society make an orderly transition from a Second Wave (industrially-oriented) Civilization to a Third Wave (information-oriented) Civilization that is more inclusive of all its members. Your ability to feel comfortable and operate effectively within such a changing environment will require unique cultural understandings and interpersonal skills, which go beyond traditional pedagogy. These skills, perspectives, and attitudes, which you as a teacher must adopt in order to coalesce diverse students into an effective learning

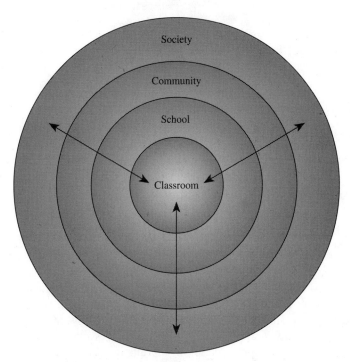

FIGURE 1.1. Interconnected environments.

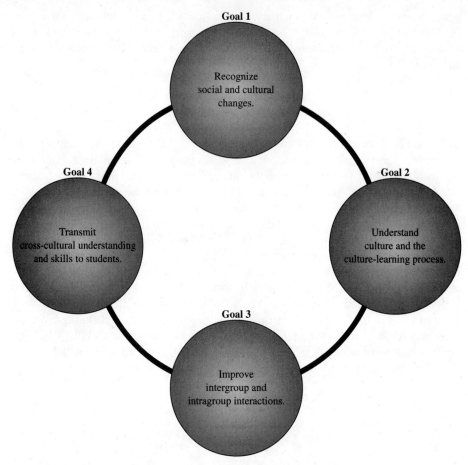

FIGURE 1.2. Goals of this book.

community, must also be transmitted to the students in your charge, who will live their lives in the same kind of highly interconnected and interdependent world.

Figure 1.2 illustrates four basic goals of this book, which can be viewed as steps in understanding multicultural education and your role as an educator in an inclusive system. A word about each follows.

Goal 1: Recognize Social and Cultural Changes

The first step in providing an education that is truly multicultural is to improve student understanding of the concept of pluralism in American society. Pluralism in this context must consider such sources of cultural identity as nationality, ethnicity, race, gender, socioeconomic status, religion, sexual orientation, geographic region, health, and ability/disability and must look particularly at how each of these has had an impact on the individual as well as the group. This means understanding the social changes that are taking place in our pluralistic society and are providing the underlying rationale for multicultural education. Chapters 1 and 2 provide this rationale. They examine various social and cultural changes that have been taking place in our pluralistic society and that have led to the emergence of various types of multicultural education programs.

Goal 2: Understand Culture and the Culture-Learning Process

After establishing the need for an education that is multicultural, it is necessary to understand just what is meant by that term. What does the term *culture* refer to and how do people acquire different cultural identities? With what knowledge do children already come to school? Too often schools do not legitimize the experiences children bring with them to school, instead labeling them as failures because their backgrounds, including their language and culture, are not seen as adequate or legitimate. We must thus expand the knowledge base of culture and the various groups found in the United States, as well as abroad. At a content level, this considers curriculum inclusion and expansion. At a process level, this considers pedagogical and communication processes. Chapter 3 examines these issues and, in the process, provides models of the sources of cultural learning and of the culture-learning process. An important recognition here is that differences *within* groups are often as important as differences *between* groups. Individuals belong simultaneously to many different groups, and their behavior can be understood only in terms of their *simultaneous* affiliation with these groups. These models illustrate how culture filters down to the individual learner, who actively engages with it, accepting and absorbing certain elements and rejecting and modifying others.

Goal 3: Improve Intergroup and Intragroup Interactions

Having examined how individuals acquire their particular cultural identity, the next step is to show how culturally different people interact with one another and how these interactions can be improved. We must work to improve intergroup and intragroup interactions. This demands attention to such issues as cross-cultural understanding and interaction, attribution and assessment across groups, and conflict management. Teachers, in particular, must broaden their instructional repertoire, so that it reflects an understanding of the various groups they will teach. To help you understand the interaction between culturally different individuals (whether from different groups or from the same group), Chapter 4 develops a "culture-general" model of behavior. This simple, three-stage model analyzes the nature of cross-cultural interaction and shows how key concepts of the model can be applied to various types of school situations. The culmination of this model is showing how its repeated application causes teachers and students to broaden their cultural horizons and, thereby, to modify their own cultural identity.

Goal 4: Transmit Cross-Cultural Understanding and Skills to Students

The final goal of this book is to help teachers transmit to students the same understandings and skills that are contained in (1) the subsequent model for explaining cultural differences (see Chapter 3) and (2) the subsequent model for improving cross-cultural interaction in order to prepare multicultural citizen-actors who are able and willing to participate in an interdependent world (see Chapter 4). That is, a major goal of this book is to strive to empower action-oriented, reflective decision makers who are able and willing to be socially and politically active in the school, community, nation, and world. We are thus not only concerned with developing the knowledge and skill of practicing teachers but are equally concerned with transferring this knowledge to the pupils in their charge. Thus, individuals become proactive teachers and reflective practitioners who can ultimately prepare reflective citizen-actors (their students) for an interdependent world. The content of these models is universal. That is, it applies to all multicultural situations, not just to those confronted by teachers in classrooms and schools. Teaching these understandings and skills to students can be accomplished both through teacher modeling and through explicit instruction, and they are illustrated in the remaining chapters of this book.

THE ROLE OF STORIES, CASES, AND ACTIVE EXERCISES IN THIS BOOK

Stories

There are a great many stories in this book. Some are about real people and events, while others, like the story of the wheat people, are folktales and parables. We use these for their power to speak about complex human experiences—in this case, about how people experience the fact of human diversity. Stories help us see the universals within the experience. Everyone, no matter what his or her unique cultural and biological characteristics, goes through similar stages of experience when confronted with change. Stories, like no other literary device, help us cut through the morass of individual and cultural differences that separates us and allow us to focus on the universals of the experience as we come to grips with those changes.

Cases

Because it is difficult to imagine situations with which one has had little experience, the series of case studies and critical incidents in this book describes multicultural teaching situations you might encounter. These are either actual or synthesized real-life situations as they have been described by a number of researchers and practitioners. Think of them as scenes in a play about schools with a multicultural student population. Most cases were generated from multiple sources, each of which is noted in the list of references.

Since the cases cover a variety of communities and classrooms with diverse kinds of people in them, multiple issues are embedded in most of the cases. Although each case is designed to illustrate one or more issues related to the topic at hand, our hope is that the portraits of people, places, ideas, and activities will be rich enough that they can also be used to discuss topics in other chapters. Some characters will be more memorable than others; some situations will reveal issues found in other parts of the book or, perhaps, not found in the book at all. Taken together, these cases attempt to illustrate a number of complex classroom realities that defy simple right and wrong solutions. Rather, they present small dramas in which a number of interpretations are possible and a number of ideas can be used to develop plans of action and fallback positions.

Active Exercises

So much of culture learning is dependent on actual interactions and the development of an experience base. It is thus suggested that you use these activities to "make real" the concepts introduced in the book. The following exercises from *Human Diversity in Action: Developing Multicultural Competencies for the Classroom*[21] complement this chapter well:

Activity 1:   Mental Maps of Culture: An Icebreaker, p. 2

Activity 6:   Proverbs as a Window into One's Culture, p. 33

Accessing the World Wide Web: Resources for Diversity

The following web sites can provide you with up-to-date information and current data regarding the content of this chapter.

For demographic and statistical information on the nation and the world, the following web sites are useful:

http://www.sccoe.k12.ca.us/demo4.html

http://www.sccoe.k12.ca.us/demo5.html

For more information about Alvin Toffler and his ideas, the following web sites contain a variety of perspectives:

http://www.skypoint.net/members/mfinley/toffler.html   "Alvin Toffler and the Third Wave" provides an explanation of Toffler's ideas about the future, especially his "wave" theory of social change.

http://www.microtimes.com/toffler.html   "Perspectives for a Changing World: A Return Visit with Alvin Toffler," by Mary Eisenhart.

http://www.zdnet.com/zdtv/thesite/0497w4/iview/iview534_042397.html Another interview with Alvin Toffler, by Sam Whitmore, covers Toffler's ideas on the future of computers, war, work, crime, and science.

http://www.extropy.com/~sasha/thinkers.html   A web site called "Great Thinkers and Visionaries," which includes links to a wide variety of people (including Alvin Toffler) whose ideas seem to be shaping the world around us.

For more information on schools in transition, there are a variety of web sites dealing with school reform proposals. Among the most helpful might be the following:

http://www.naesp.org The National Association of Elementary School Principals.

http://www.nassp.org The National Association of Secondary School Principals.

http://www.ncrel.org The North Central Clearinghouse on Education Laboratory, which has numerous articles available on line regarding specific school reform issues and activities.

References

1. National Center for Educational Statistics, 1997.
2. William A. Henry III, "Beyond the Melting Pot," *Time,* 9 April 1990, p. 28.
3. The President's Initiative on Race, prepared by the Council of Economic Advisors, cited in the Akron (Ohio) *Beacon Journal,* 18 September 1998, p. A5.
4. Commission on Work, Family, and Citizenship, "American Youth: A Statistical Snapshot," cited in Marian Wright Edelman, "Children at Risk," in *Caring for America's Children,* ed. Frank J. Macchiarola and Alan Gartner (New York: The Academy of Political Science, 1989), p. 21.
5. Alvin Toffler, *The Third Wave* (New York: William Morrow and Company, 1980).
6. Ibid., p. 18.
7. Robert Reich, *The Work of Nations* (New York: Vintage Books, 1992), p. 112.
8. *America's Children Yearbook* (Washington, DC: Children's Defense Fund, 1996).
9. Statistics on these kinds of categories vary depending on the methods (and, often, the purposes) of those compiling them. These statistics can be found in the following publications: Center for Education Statistics, Digest of Education Statistics (Washington, DC: U.S. Government Printing Office, 1987); "Here They Come, Ready or Not," *Education Week* (14 May 1986); Hodgkinson, H. *All One System: Demographics of Education—Kindergarten Through Graduate School* (Washington, D.C.: Institute of Educational Leadership, 1985); M. M. Kennedy, R. K. Jung, and M. E. Orland, *Poverty, Achievement, and the Distribution of Compensatory Education Services* (Washington, DC: U.S. Government Printing Office, 1986); and *America's Children Yearbook*, op cit.
10. *From Minority to Majority Education and the Future of the Southwest* (Boulder, CO: Western Interstate Compact of Higher Education, 1988).
11. R. Oxford-Carpenter, L. Pol, M. Gendell, and S. Peng, *Demographic Projections of Non-English-Background and Limited-English-Proficient Persons in the United States to the Year 2000 by State, Age, and Language Group* (Washington, DC: National Clearinghouse for Bilingual Education, Inter-America Research Associates, 1984).
12. Carol Shakeshaft, "A Gender at Risk," *Phi Delta Kappan* 67, 7 (March 1986): 500.
13. N. L. Zimpher, "The RATE Project: A Profile of Teacher Education Students," *Journal of Teacher Education* 40, 6 (November-December 1989): 27–30.
14. Ibid.
15. Ibid.
16. Averil E. McClelland and Normand R. Bernier, "A Rejoinder to Steve Tozer's 'Toward a New Consensus Among Social Foundations Educators,'" *Educational Foundations* 7, 4 (fall 1993): 61.
17. George Counts, *Dare the Schools Build a New Social Order?* (Carbondale, IL: Southern Illinois University Press, 1978 [1932]).
18. Reich, op. cit., pp. 59–60.

19. Told by J. E. Rash at the Mediterranean Youth Environment Conference, Cartagena, Spain, August 1985.
20. Ibid.
21. Kenneth Cushner, *Human Diversity in Action: Developing Multicultural Competencies for the Classroom* (New York: McGraw-Hill, 1999).

Multicultural Education: Historical and Theoretical Perspectives

CHAPTER OUTLINE

HISTORICAL PERSPECTIVES ON PLURALISM
  We Have Been Different from the
    Beginning
  Industrialization, Immigration, and
    Religious Pluralism
  The Civil War: Freedmen's Schools
    and the Issue of Race
  The Civil Rights Movement and
    the Schools
HISTORICAL PERSPECTIVES ON
  MULTICULTURAL EDUCATION
  Anglo-Conformity and
    Assimilationist Ideology
  Multiculturalism and the Pluralist
    Ideology
  Legislative and Judicial Landmarks
  Public Responses to Multicultural
    and Bilingual Education
    Reforms

  Judicial and Legislative Mandates
    Regarding Equity
  Reaction to Multicultural
    Education in the 1980s and
    1990s
CONTEMPORARY APPROACHES TO
  MULTICULTURAL EDUCATION
  PROGRAMS
  The Sleeter and Grant Categories
  The Mitchell Typology
THE OUTCOMES OF MULTICULTURAL
  EDUCATION
  Student Outcomes
  Program Outcomes
ACTIVE EXERCISES
ACCESSING THE WORLD WIDE WEB:
  RESOURCES FOR DIVERSITY
REFERENCES

*Scholars describe the United States as one of history's first universal or world nations—
its people are a microcosm of humanity with biological, cultural, and social ties to
all other parts of the earth.*

National Council for the Social Studies,
"The Columbus Quincentenary Position Statement"

When Noah Webster observed that "our national character is not yet formed . . . ,"[1] he identified a central dilemma that still faces the United States, as well as many other multiethnic nations. This land of immigrants is, indeed, an odd land in which many feel themselves to be strangers in their own country.

In the United States, one major instrument for creating unity out of diversity has been the public school system, which, for most of our history, has been used as a tool for socializing us into a common culture. This helps explain why the public schools have always been a battleground where various groups have sought to control the school curriculum and, through it, to shape our common culture. The way schools address American pluralism has been publicly debated from the beginning of our republic and continues with renewed vigor today in light of our position as a leading player in the global community.

Educational literature over the past 170 years reflects profound disagreement about how to educate the young while forging a nation-state from a multiethnic population. Should differences of language and culture be recognized and taken into account, or should we work as hard and as fast as we can to assimilate newcomers to "the American way of life"? Indeed, as our nation becomes increasingly diverse and increasingly part of an interdependent global community, there is currently some debate on whether or not there really is any longer something called "the American way of life." What *is* certain is that advocates on all sides have never been fully satisfied with the role played by the school and the way it carries out its socializing mission.

Central High School, Little Rock, Arkansas, 1957: A Case Study

On 4 September 1957, nine black teenagers attempting to enter Central High School in Little Rock, Arkansas, for the first time were turned away by the National Guard, which was called out by Governor Orval Faubus "to preserve the peace and avert violence." While this event was not the final chapter in the story of the integration of Central High School, it was not the first chapter, either. It was, however, one that—shown widely on national television—riveted the nation. If any episode in the history of the Civil Rights Movement in public education can be said to remain in the public mind, it is this one.

Contrary to what many people believe, the state of Arkansas and the city of Little Rock had made some strides in desegregating its public facilities prior to the integration of Central High School. As early as 1949, the School of Law at the University of Arkansas was integrated, and in 1951 the Little Rock Public Library board approved the integration of its facilities. In 1956, the city's public buses were quietly desegregated with little fuss. However, as in many other places in the United States, integrating schools was a more difficult—and emotional—matter.

In May of 1954, five days after the Supreme Court decision in Brown v. Board of Education of Topeka, Kansas, the Little Rock School Board issued a policy statement, offering to comply with the Brown decision "when the Court outlines the method to be followed and the time to be allowed." Two days later, the board voted unanimously to adopt the superintendent's plan of gradual integration, beginning in September 1957, at the high school level and adding the lower grades over the next six years. But, for those who yearned for faster action, this plan was insufficient.

In January 1956, twenty-seven students attempted to register in all-white Little Rock schools and were turned down. One month later, the National

Association for the Advancement of Colored People (NAACP) filed suit on behalf of thirty-three black children denied admittance to four white schools, and, in August of that year, a federal judge dismissed the suit, ruling that the Little Rock School Board had acted in good faith in proposing its plan. The students would have to wait.

As the fall of 1957 approached, those opposed to integration began to organize. Specifically, a member of the Mother's League of Central High School attempted to block integration by asking for an injunction, which was granted in a local court on 27 August and then nullified in a federal court three days later. Central High School would be integrated in September.

But it was not that simple. On 23 September, surrounded by an angry crowd of about one thousand people, the nine students again tried to enter the school—this time through a side door. When the crowd discovered that the students were inside, it became unruly and police feared that they could not maintain control. The black students were taken out of the school, again through a side door. The next day, the mayor of Little Rock asked President Eisenhower for federal troops to maintain order; the president sent one thousand members of the 101st Airborne Division to Little Rock and federalized the Arkansas National Guard. On 25 September, escorted by federal troops, the nine black students were escorted back into Central High School.

During the 1957-1958 school year, the "Little Rock Nine" (as the students came to be called) tried to maintain their composure and their studies in an atmosphere of student unrest and adult confrontations—in court and outside of it. In December, one of the nine students, at the end of her patience with taunting by white students, dumped a bowl of chili on her tormentors in the cafeteria; she was suspended for six days and, after further altercations, ultimately for the rest of the year. She transferred to a high school in New York City.

In February 1958, the Little Rock School Board filed a request to delay integration until the concept "all deliberate speed" was defined. In June, a federal judge granted the delay, writing that, although black students had a constitutional right to attend white schools, the "time has not come for them to enjoy that right." The NAACP appealed that decision, and in August it was reversed by a federal Court of Appeals.

Over the summer of 1958, the school board asked for a stay of the Appeals Court ruling to enable them to appeal to the Supreme Court; the Supreme Court called a special session to discuss the Little Rock case; Governor Faubus asked the Arkansas legislature for a law enabling him to close public schools to avoid integration and to lease the closed schools to private school corporations; the Supreme Court ruled that Little Rock must continue with its integration plan; the school board announced the opening of the city's high schools on 15 September; Governor Faubus ordered Little Rock's three high schools closed. At the end of September, voters overwhelmingly opposed integration by a vote of 129,470 to 7,561. Public high schools in Little Rock were closed for the year.

In November 1958, five of the six members of the Little Rock School Board resigned in frustration, having been ordered to proceed with integration of the high schools, even though it had no high schools to integrate. In December, a new school board was elected, evenly divided between *"pro" and "con" factions. In May of 1959, segregationist members of the school board attempted to fire forty-four teachers and administrators suspected of integrationist sympathies. Three moderates on the board walked out, refusing to participate. In June 1959, a federal court declared the state's school-closing law unconstitutional, and the new school board announced it would reopen the schools in the fall of 1959.*

Fifteen years later, in the fall of 1972, all grades in Little Rock public schools were finally integrated. Forty years later, in the fall of 1997, President Clinton—who was an 11-year-old student in a nearby town when the first attempt to integrate Central High School occurred—held the door to the high school open for the returning members of the Class of 1957, including most of the "Little Rock Nine." One of those students, Ernest Green (who was the first of the nine to graduate from the high school) spoke for all of them—and, perhaps, for all those involved in this drama—when he said, "We were a part not just of civil rights history, but of American history. . . . It's something to see your name in your kid's history book."[2]

If, as argued in Chapter 1, fundamental changes must be undertaken in the way we "do school" for an increasingly diversified population, then it will be helpful for us to examine the history of education, not only of specific incidents in the struggle for equal educational opportunity, but also of the debate surrounding multicultural education. What follows is a somewhat abbreviated account of how educators have reached their current place with respect to this debate and what the major issues are today.

HISTORICAL PERSPECTIVES ON PLURALISM

We Have Been Different from the Beginning

One might argue that intolerance toward differences in the Americas began with the introduction of European culture in the 1490s. There is considerable evidence that the Native American populations, which existed in the Americas before European settlement, exhibited far greater tolerance toward diversity of thought and lifestyle than did the arriving Europeans. The Taino people, for instance, greeted Columbus with food, shelter, and open festivity when the Spaniards first arrived on their small Caribbean island in 1492. At first intrigued with the Taino, Columbus wrote that "their manner is both decorous and praiseworthy."[3] The Taino's hospitality, however, was soon met with severe cruelty by the Spaniards. Within twenty years of Columbus's landing, the Taino people became extinct. In fact, the Spaniards' tendency toward intolerance of both religious and cultural diversity may have prevented them from becoming the dominant culture in North America. So much energy was spent repressing and fighting the native populations that the northern spread of Spanish culture was halted in the southwest.

The emergence of the English as the dominant force in the new lands may be partially attributed to their somewhat greater tolerance, born, perhaps, of their own need for religious freedom. However, even though the English government allowed, even encouraged, immigrants from a variety of ethnic backgrounds to settle in America, it was the white, English-born Protestants who, by the time the United States became a nation in 1776, had emerged as the dominant group. This group, too, was fearful of "different" kinds of immigrants. In 1698, for example, South Carolina passed an act exempting Irish and Roman Catholics from new bounties.[4] In 1729, Pennsylvania placed a duty on all servants of Scotch-Irish descent. One official at the time wrote, "The common fear is that if they continue to come, they will make themselves proprietors of the province."[5] Ironically, the very people who originally had come to the new world to escape religious persecution were among those who actively engaged in the persecution of others for their beliefs, values, and lifestyles.

Industrialization, Immigration, and Religious Pluralism

In the early years of the nineteenth century, an influx of European immigrants followed the Industrial Revolution across the Atlantic. At the same time, the United States was developing the idea of the "common school," heralded in part as a way to give all children, no matter what their cultural, religious, or economic background, a common experience that would help them understand one another and that would provide the common basis for citizenship in a democracy. Despite a growing network of public elementary schools, the increasing diversity within the United States began to be viewed as a "problem" for public schooling. The first battles within these pluralistic common schools were not waged around the issue of race or ethnicity, as is common today, but around the issue of religion.

Many new immigrants in this period were Catholic and, to native-born Protestants, represented a threat to the stability of the republic—as well as competition for newly created industrial jobs. Many suspected that newly arrived Catholics owed a greater allegiance to the pope than to the U.S. government, an issue that was not finally settled until the election of John F. Kennedy to the presidency in 1960. Second-, third-, and fourth-generation Protestants also opposed the emergence of Catholic schools, believing that they were intended to instill undemocratic values in Catholic children. Catholic parents, on the other hand, felt that a Catholic education was necessary to preserve their children's religious faith and was an important vehicle for maintaining Catholic communities.

Opposition to Catholic schooling often became violent, both in word and deed. Political cartoonists had a field day with caricatures of the pope as an ogre attempting to "swallow" the United States. More serious, however, were physical attacks on Catholic schools, exemplified by the burning of the Ursuline convent in Charleston, Massachusetts, by a Protestant mob in 1834.[6]

In the 1830s, the common school movement, which was supposedly nonsectarian but was largely Protestant-driven, came into dramatic conflict with those who wished to educate their children in religious-based schools. If the emphasis in Catholic schools was toward a religious faith, the emphasis in the common school was toward a secular government that would maintain the new forms of democracy being developed in the United States. The democracy that was taking shape was rapidly becoming a kind of civic religion, and the development of loyalty to that idea was one of the foundations of public schooling. Thus, Catholics had some justification for the belief that the common school might socialize their children away from their religious faith. As the number of Catholic immigrants increased, and the network of Catholic schools grew, Catholic parents began to insist that public funds raised through taxation to support public schools also be used to fund private Catholic institutions. That debate continues to this day.

Catholics were not the only group that was feared and persecuted. In 1835, The Indian Removal Act saw the last vestige of Native American culture in the eastern United States swept westward across the Mississippi River in the tragic roundup known today as the Trail of Tears. In the case of Jews, the last barrier to their voting rights was not abolished in New Hampshire until 1877. And in 1882 the Immigration Department passed an act that prohibited the entry of Chinese into the country.

The Civil War: Freedmen's Schools and the Issue of Race

Issues of race in *public* education became important only after the Civil War. In the pre–Civil War South, it was against the law to educate black slave children, so no racial problem existed in southern schools. In the North, blacks who had bought or had been given their freedom achieved some education in the common schools, in African American church communities, and through abolitionist efforts. After the Civil War, the education of black children was still not perceived to be a "national problem" by most whites because, where African Americans were educated at all, they were educated in separate schools.

Southern states, notably resistant to providing public education for blacks, were not above taxing them for white schools. In some places—Florida, Texas, and Kentucky, for example—black schools were built only after black citizens paid a second tax to build their own schools.[7]

In 1865, Congress established the Freedmen's Bureau to help freed slaves with the transition to citizenship. In 1866, the law was amended to assist in the provision of black schools. Many of the teachers in these schools were northern white women, often daughters of abolitionist families. Indeed, the story of the women, both black and white, who taught in the "Freedmen's Schools" is among the proudest in the history of teaching. By 1870, nearly 7,000 white and black "schoolmarms" were teaching 250,000 black students and learning to cross the barriers of race and class that have characterized American history. The legacy of these teachers is enormous. Not only did they educate the children who later became the teachers in segregated schools, but they also educated a generation of free black leaders, too seldom talked about today.[8]

Violence characterized the development of black schools after the Civil War, as it had the development of Catholic schools earlier. The burning of buildings and harassment of black teachers and students were commonplace. However, passage of the Fourteenth Amendment to the Constitution in 1868 made responsibility for civil rights a federal rather than a state function; as a result, African Americans began to gain more access to public education. Fully aware that education was a way out of poverty, black parents saw that their children got to school, one way or another. When they were needed on the farm, they would alternate between school and work, as one Alabama boy described:

> I took turns with my brother at the plow and in school; one day I plowed and he went to school, the next day he plowed and I went to school; what was learned on his school day he taught me at night and I did the same for him.[9]

Black children remained in segregated schools that were funded at minimal rates and often open for only part of the year. Indeed, despite efforts through the courts to equalize the rights of blacks in all spheres of public life, in 1896, in the *Plessy v. Ferguson* decision, the Supreme Court held that segregation was not prohibited by the

Constitution. *Plessy v. Ferguson,* which upheld the doctrine that "separate but equal" facilities for blacks and whites were constitutionally permissible, justified the separate (usually inferior) education of African American children in both the North and South until 1954.

Very few African American children with disabilities received any schooling at all in the nineteenth century, but the tiny number who did, mainly those with visual impairments, experienced double segregation. Among the thirty public and private residential schools for blind pupils established in the United States between 1832 and 1875 was the first school for "the colored blind," in North Carolina.[10] By 1931, there were five such separate schools for black children and youth. Ten other black schools maintained separate (inferior) departments for blind students, most of which used second-hand materials, such as badly worn braille books that were virtually impossible to read. Moreover, ". . . segregation not only kept black children in separate schools staffed by black teachers, but prevented those teachers from attending courses given at white southern colleges."[11] Their lower salaries made attendance at northern colleges prohibitive.

The Civil Rights Movement and the Schools

Six decades after *Plessy*, diversity in American society and in its schools again became the subject of major social turmoil. During the 1960s and 1970s, fueled by the general social ferment of the Civil Rights Movement and the war in Vietnam, educational reform legislation was enacted in the following areas: desegregation, multicultural and bilingual education, the mainstreaming of students with special needs into regular classrooms, and gender-sensitive education. These programs recognized the pluralistic nature of this society in a positive rather than a negative sense. Each one attempted to help an educationally disadvantaged group to receive a better education within a pluralistic framework.

It is important to realize that these educational mandates were not achieved in isolation but as part of the larger human and civil rights struggles of the 1960s and 1970s. During this period, Congress passed a number of antidiscriminatory statutes: the Voting Rights Act (1963), dealing with voter registration; the Equal Pay Act (1963), which required that men and women occupying the same position be paid equally; the Civil Rights Act (1964), dealing with housing and job discrimination as well as with education; the Bilingual Education Act of 1968 (Title VII of the Elementary and Secondary Education Act), which established programs for children whose first language was not English; Title IX of the Education Amendments (1972), prohibiting sex discrimination against students and employees of educational institutions; and the Education of All Handicapped Children Act (1975), requiring schools to assume the responsibility for educating all children in the least restrictive environment possible. It was, in the words of one partisan observer, a period of "intensity of concern and commitment to do something about the problems in America stemming from the continued growth of its pluralistic character."[12]

In education, the chief concerns were for access and equity: access to public education for excluded groups and a guarantee that such education would be equitable—that is, that it would be commensurate with the best that public education could offer. All these efforts rested on the belief that previously excluded groups had an inherent *right* to educational equity. Why was it important to emphasize the *rights* of racial and ethnic minorities, women, and persons with disabilities? Why was it important to enact legislation that protected their rights? Quite simply, it was important because these rights had not been recognized in the past, and large numbers of people had experienced discrimination and unequal opportunity in a society that rests on the principle that *all* citizens are equal under the law. The Civil Rights Movement was a reaffirmation of the beliefs that form the very basis of American society and an insistence that we live up to our ideals in education, as well as in other aspects of social life.

The debate about the precise way that public schooling should serve the interests of a diverse population did not end with the passage of these laws, however. Political and educational reformers (often the same people) repeatedly confronted political and ideological impediments as they sought to implement the new civil rights laws. The first set of policy initiatives to be considered concerned children of racial, ethnic, and linguistic minorities who, it was asserted, were being discriminated against in public schools. One evidence of such discrimination was their disproportionately large representation in classes for students labeled "mildly retarded" or "behavior disordered." To understand the difficulties encountered by these "multicultural education" reformers, we turn once again to history.

HISTORICAL PERSPECTIVES ON MULTICULTURAL EDUCATION

During the earlier years of massive immigration, from about 1870 to 1920, the "problem" of diversity in the schools was largely perceived as a problem of how to assimilate children of other nationalities. In short, it was thought to be the school's task to make immigrant children as much like white, middle-class, Anglo-Saxon Protestants as possible in as short a time as possible.

Interestingly, a key strategy used by public schools to accomplish this goal involved establishing the field of speech therapy (formally termed speech/language pathology). Immigrant children placed in New York's "vestibule" or "steamer classes" were instructed in the proper use of English by speech teachers, who very soon, at parents' requests, were also assigned to work with children who had medically impaired articulation or fluency.

Anglo-Conformity and Assimilationist Ideology

Described as *Anglo-conformity* or the *assimilationist model,* the rationale for this strategy was typified by the following words of Ellwood Cubberly, a prominent educator around the turn of the twentieth century:

> Everywhere these people settle in groups or settlements to set up their national manners, customs, and observances. Our task is to break up these groups or settlements, to assimilate and amalgamate these people as part of our American race and to implant in their children so far as can be done, the Anglo-Saxon conception of righteousness, law and order, and our popular government and to awaken in them a reverence for our democratic institutions and for those things in our national life which we as a people hold to be of abiding worth.[13]

The assimilationist strategy was applied to each new ethnic group as immigrants poured through Ellis Island and other ports of entry. Jews, Poles, Slavs, Asians, and Latin Americans all became the "raw material" from which the "new American" would be made. Between 1860 and 1920, 37 million immigrants became naturalized citizens. Their sheer numbers changed the ethnic makeup of America. By 1916, for example, only 28 percent of San Francisco's population claimed English as its first language.

Despite the high number of immigrants, however, the *dominant* American culture retained its English, Protestant identity. The nation's public schools, staffed largely by white, middle-class, Protestant women, did little or nothing to encourage the expression of ethnicity or to address the special needs of an increasingly diverse student population. Indeed, in the eyes of the nativist population, the schools were supposed to prevent such expression. The idea of a melting pot was used to describe the process of helping immigrants shed their native languages, learn English, and assimilate into the dominant American culture.

The term *melting pot* actually came from the name of a play written in 1909 by Israel Zangwill. The goal of creating one homogeneous culture from the many that arrived on the shores of the United States is captured in the following speech from that play:

> America is God's Crucible, the great Melting Pot where all the races of Europe are melting and reforming! Here you stand, good folk, think I, when I see them at Ellis Island, here you stand in your fifty groups with your fifty languages and histories, and your fifty hatreds and rivalries, but you won't be long like that, brothers, for these are the fires of God. A fig for your feuds and vendettas! Germans and Frenchmen, Irishmen and Englishmen, Jews and Russians—into the Crucible with you all! God is making the American. . . . The real American has not yet arrived. He is only in the Crucible. I tell you—he will be the fusion of all races, the coming superman.[14]

James Banks suggests that assimilationists believe that one's identification with an ethnic group should be temporary, as it presents an obstacle to one's long-term interests and needs.[15] Assimilationists believe that, for a society to advance, individuals must give up their ethnic identities, languages, and ideologies in favor of the norms and values of the larger, national society. From an assimilationist perspective, the goal of the school should be to socialize individuals into the society at large so all can function in an "appropriate" manner—that is, in a manner that supports the goals of the nation as expressed through its leaders. Ethnic group identification, if it is to be developed, should be confined to small community organizations. In short, the goal for assimilationists is to make it possible for everyone to be "melted" into a homogeneous whole.

The assimilationist view, sometimes called a *monocultural* perspective, shares an *image* or a *model* of American culture. In this view, there is a core "American" culture composed of common knowledge, habits, values, and attitudes. For people who think of American culture this way, these common characteristics might include the following. "Real" Americans are mostly white, middle-class adults (or are trying to be); they are heterosexual, are married, and go to church (mostly Protestant but sometimes Catholic). They live in single-family houses (which they own, or are trying to); they work hard, eat well, and stand on "their own two feet"; they expect their children to behave themselves; they wash themselves a good deal and generally try to smell "good"; they are patriotic and honor the flag; they are often charitable and, in return, expect only that those receiving their charity will try to "shape up." They are not very interested in "highfalutin" ideas found in books written by overly educated people; instead, they believe in "good, old-fashioned common sense." Of course, this is a composite picture. Not all monoculturalists fit neatly into this view of "real" Americans, but most share many of these characteristics, and divergence from some of them (for example, from heterosexuality) almost automatically disqualifies a person, even if that is the only way in which he or she differs. For people who see American culture in this narrow way, those who do not share these characteristics are clearly not "real" Americans, whether they happen to have been born here or not. Moreover, their difference makes them dangerous to the maintenance of America as it is "supposed" to be. It is, therefore, a primary role of schooling to make the children of the culturally different into "American" children—that is, to teach these children the ways of thinking, behaving, and valuing that will help them fit harmoniously into the monoculturalists' culture. Children of monoculturalists, of course, do not need such help, because they already match the model.

While exceptional individuals, those who have disabilities and those who are intellectually or otherwise gifted, may be considered "real" Americans, they also have been viewed in some sense as "others." Beginning in the 1870s, large urban school districts formed separate classes for "unrulies" and for "backward" or "dull" pupils. In actuality, most such classes were repositories for children, who for some reason "didn't fit" the regular program. From these beginnings, special education emerged as a separate, smaller system within the public school.

Multiculturalism and the Pluralist Ideology

Those who believe strongly in the idea of the melting pot have been both bemused and angered by the fact that the contents of the pot never melted. Eventually, in opposition to the assimilationist ideology, came the call for cultural pluralism by a small group of philosophers and writers who argued that a political democracy must also be a cultural democracy.[16] To these pluralists, immigrant groups were entitled to maintain their ethnic cultures and institutions within the greater society. The analogy they used was that of a salad bowl; in order to have a rich, nutritious salad (society), it was necessary to include a variety of cultures. In short, American society would be strengthened, not weakened, by the presence of various cultures.

Pluralists view one's social group as critical to the socialization process in modern society. The group provides the individual with identity, a sense of belonging or psychological support, particularly when faced with discrimination by the larger society. It is through one's group, usually the ethnic group, that one develops a primary language, values, and interpersonal relationships, as well as a particular lifestyle. Pluralists believe the identity group (racial/ethnic, religious, and so forth) to be so important that the schools should actively promote their interests and recognize their importance in the life of the individual. Because pluralists assume a "difference" rather than a "deficit" orientation, they stress the importance of a curriculum addressing different learning styles and patterns of interaction and fully recognizing students' cultural histories. The assumption is that, the more congruent the school experience is with the child's other experiences, the better the child's chance of success.

One set of programs responsive to cultural and other forms of diversity fell under the umbrella term *multicultural education*. Growing out of the Civil Rights Movement of the 1960s, these programs tried to address the needs of racial, ethnic, and linguistic minorities. Specifically, Spanish-speaking Americans in the Southwest, Puerto Ricans on the East Coast, Asian Americans on the West Coast, Native Americans on reservations and in urban settlements, and African Americans throughout the United States began to seek their fair share of what America had to offer and to demand that the nation live up to the ideals it professed. The powerful buildup of unrest and frustration born of the discrepancy between American ideals and American practices sought an outlet. From the *Brown v. Board of Education of Topeka* decision in 1954 through the Civil Rights Act of 1964 and through the Vietnam War, those groups marched out of the ghettos and into the courts.

Legislative and Judicial Landmarks

The start of these events is usually marked by the 1954 Supreme Court decision in *Brown v. Board of Education of Topeka.* This landmark decision stated that segregated schools were inherently unequal and that state laws which allowed separate schools for black and white students were unconstitutional. In 1967, the U.S. Commission on Civil Rights was established primarily to investigate complaints alleging the denial of people's right to vote by reason of race, color, religion, sex, or national origin.

About the same time (1966), the National Education Association issued a study supporting the teaching of Spanish to Mexican Americans in Tucson, and the American Association of Colleges of Teacher Education produced a policy statement on pluralism entitled "No One Model American." These and other investigative, judicial, and legislative moves were directed toward ending educational discrimination and the comfortable middle-class perceptions about cultural assimilation that supported discrimination. Together, these reports and judicial proceedings began to dim the embers under the American melting pot.

In the twelve-year period from 1963 to 1975, private and governmental studies and hearings and a series of lawsuits regarding rights to native language instruction, the placement of children with disabilities, and desegregation produced many mandates for the schooling of minority students. Concurrently, new educational strategies and curricula, especially in bilingual and bicultural education, appeared in districts across the nation.

The Civil Rights Act of 1964 made it illegal for public schools that received federal or state funds to assign students to schools based on their color, race, religion, or country of origin. The Bilingual Education Act was passed in 1968 as Title VII of the Elementary and Secondary Education Act. President Lyndon Johnson clarified the intent of this law in the following words:

> This bill authorizes a new effort to prevent dropouts; new programs for handicapped children; new planning help for rural schools. It also contains a special provision establishing bilingual education programs for children whose first language is not English. Thousands of children of Latin descent, young Indians, and others will get a better start—a better chance—in school. . . .[17]

In 1970, the Office of Civil Rights Guidelines tried to make special training for non-English-speaking students a requirement for public schools that received federal aid. The office stated:

> Where inability to speak and understand the English language excludes national origin-minority group children from effective participation in the education program offered by a school district, the district must take affirmative steps to rectify the language deficiency in order to open its instructional program to these students.[18]

Also during the 1960s and early 1970s, members of the women's movement began to pressure Congress to enact legislation that would guarantee equitable educational experience for girls and women. The result was Title IX of the Education Amendments of 1972. Intending to prohibit discrimination in elementary and secondary schools on the basis of sex, the preamble to this statute reads, in part:

> No person in the United States shall, on the basis of sex, be excluded from participation in, be denied the benefits of, or be subjected to discrimination under any education program or activity receiving federal financial assistance.[19]

It was not until 1975, however, that the rules and regulations enforcing Title IX were published and sent to state departments of education and to school districts. In the interim, there was heated controversy (and ten thousand written comments from citizens).[20]

Similarly, the Education of All Handicapped Children Act of 1975 (PL 94-142) became the basis for the educational rights of children and youth with disabilities. Like other educational equity efforts, PL 94-142 was not enacted in a vacuum but was the culmination of a long-lived movement. In 1948, for example, prior to the *Brown* decision, Congress prohibited discrimination against people with disabilities by the U.S. Civil Service Commission. In 1968, the Architectural Barriers Act prohibited the use of government funds to construct facilities that were inaccessible to the handicapped. With the enactment of amendments to the Vocational Rehabilitation Act of 1973 (PL 93-112), amended by PL 93-516, even more far-reaching policies were established. The most familiar part of this legislation, Section 504, specifically prohibits any form of discrimination against persons with disabilities by any agency receiving government funds. Enactment of the Americans with Disabilities Act of 1991 extended that prohibition to the private sector.

Public Responses to Multicultural and Bilingual Education Reforms

Passage of civil rights laws, however, did not guarantee equality of educational opportunity to all American children. Frequently, court assistance was needed to ensure compliance with congressional mandates. A significant case in the development of multicultural and bilingual education was *Lau v. Nichols,* decided by a 1974 Supreme Court ruling. This decision declared that a San Francisco school district violated a non-English-speaking Chinese student's right to equal educational opportunity when it failed to provide needed English language instruction and other special programs. An important consequence of the *Lau* decision was the declaration that school districts across the country must provide students an education in languages that meet their needs.

While *Lau v. Nichols,* filed on behalf of 1,800 Chinese-American pupils, did not involve special education directly, the ruling underscored the responsibility of schools to address language differences in making decisions about placing students, as well as in teaching them. Two previous judicial decisions in class action suits brought by parents had directly addressed the issue of the overrepresentation of minority children in special education. In 1970, in *Diana v. State Board of Education,* parents charged that the number of Hispanic students placed in special classes for children with mental retardation in California was approximately twice what would be expected, based on the proportion of Hispanic children enrolled in that state. In *Larry P. v. Riles,* a similar overrepresentation of black children was found in the San Francisco Unified School District. In both cases, the disproportions were attributed to the invalid use of IQ tests as the basis for placement decisions; *Diana* revealed that Spanish-speaking children were administered tests in English, while African American pupils in *Larry P. v. Riles* were found to score within the normal range when retested.

In terms of schooling mandates, educators and the public have responded (and still respond) to multicultural efforts in various ways. In direct conflict are those who advocated special programs, such as bilingual and multicultural education, and those who opposed them. Opponents of special programs fall into two categories. First, there are those who believe the American educational system in its "traditional" form has always provided for the upward mobility of culturally diverse peoples who were "willing to work." Other opponents believe that the nation-state would be destroyed if the schools did not continue offering a monocultural and monolinguistic education. In the latter group, some moralize that pluralistic approaches to education, especially bilingualism, can "handicap a child—perhaps permanently—by offering him a crutch that won't hold up in the work-a-day world in which he must live in later life."[21] Others worry that "ethnics" will now be mandated for available (and scarcer) teaching positions. Still others warn that ethnic (and racial) identity movements weaken the cultural "glue" that holds the nation together, thereby aggravating tensions rather than diminishing differences among groups.

A third group, composed primarily of educators and speaking in a somewhat softer voice, asserts that pluralism in education should not be viewed as a remedial effort or a form of reparation but, rather, as the long overdue affirmation of a social reality. Pluralism, in their view, is not an ethnic or a racial property but a national characteristic, long ignored in education. Rudolph Schmerl at the University of Michigan, for example, observed:

> Intercontinental origin is still much more apparent in our electoral process than in our educational system. Our politics cultivate the immigrant and ethnic ethos as a matter of simple realism. Our educational system seems to be capable, so far, of no more than cursory, half-embarrassed hints about the diversity of our origins and experience, memories, and loyalties, fears, hopes, bitterness, and pride.[22]

Similarly, the American Association of Colleges for Teacher Education policy statement on pluralism states:

> Multicultural education affirms that schools should be oriented toward the cultural enrichment of all children and youth through programs rooted to the preservation and extension of cultural diversity as a fact of life in American society. . . . To endorse cultural pluralism is to understand and appreciate the differences that exist among the nation's citizens. . . . Cultural pluralism is more than a temporary accommodation to placate racial and ethnic minorities.[23]

This view, however, has not dominated the educational scene. While nearly forty years of advocacy has produced a legacy of judicial and legislative mandates aimed at educational equity, the realization of that legacy in practice is still a long way off. More than a decade ago, James Boyer of Kansas State University, speaking at a conference on exploring issues in teacher education, described the status of multicultural education:

Concepts of multi-culturalism have had difficulty gaining both academic respectability within teacher education and within the context of instructional delivery in public elementary and secondary schools. Not only has the topic been mis-used, misunderstood, and under-studied, it has been rejected as a critical entity because it forces us to re-examine so many of our practices, policies, and research endeavors.[24]

Judicial and Legislative Mandates Regarding Equity

Multicultural education as an approach to schooling developed over time as the debate over pluralism and civil rights developed in the nation's legislatures and courts. In the forty years from 1952 to 1992, the following court decisions and pieces of legislation provided the foundation on which multicultural education grew.

Most court decisions and laws having to do with schooling are based on provisions of the First and Fourteenth Amendments to the Constitution of the United States:

> *First Amendment:* Congress shall make no law respecting the establishment of religion or prohibiting the free exercise thereof; or abridge the freedom of speech or of the press; or the right of people peaceably to assemble and to petition the government for redress of grievances.

> *Fourteenth Amendment:* No state shall make or enforce any law which shall abrogate the privileges or immunities of citizens of the United States; nor shall any state deprive any person of life, liberty, or property without due process of law; nor deny any person within its jurisdiction the equal protection of the laws.

Issues of Race

1954   In *Brown v. Board of Education of Topeka,* the U.S. Supreme Court rescinded the Court's view in *Plessy v. Ferguson* (1896), which supported the "separate but equal" doctrine. The Court declared that "separate but equal has no place in public education" and that "separate facilities are inherently unequal."

1964   Title VI of the Civil Rights Act (PL 88-352) prohibits discrimination on the basis of race, color, or national origin against students of any school receiving federal financial assistance.

1964   Title VII of the Civil Rights Act (PL 88-352) prohibits discrimination on the basis of race, color, or national origin against employees of any school receiving federal financial assistance.

1965   The Voting Rights Act prohibits discrimination on the basis of race, color, or national origin against U.S. citizens' right to vote.

1972   In *Larry P. v. Riles,* a California State Court found that some African American children placed in special education classes has been inappropriately placed. The case changed the assessment and placement practices in California and had an impact throughout the nation.

Issues of Religion

1952   In *Zorach v. Clausen,* the U.S. Supreme Court ruled that religious instruction during school hours does not violate the First Amendment of the Constitution as long as it takes place off school grounds and is conducted by teachers or religious figures independent of and not paid by the school.

1963   In *Abington School District v. Schempp,* the U.S. Supreme Court ruled that public schools cannot start the day with required prayer or Bible reading.

1968   In *Epperson v. State of Arkansas,* the Supreme Court found that the statute criminalizing the teaching of evolutionary theory was unconstitutional on the grounds that the statute breached the constitutional criteria against establishing religion by the state.

1971   In *Lemon v. Kurtzman,* the Supreme Court outlined what has become known as the "Three-Pronged Test" for deciding whether or not any statute violates the establishment clause of the First Amendment regarding religion.

1972 In *Wisconsin v. Yoder,* (sometimes called "the Amish exception"), the Supreme Court upheld the right of Amish families to withdraw their children from public schools after the eighth grade on religious grounds.

1980 In *Palmer v. Board of Education,* the U.S. Supreme Court ruled that a teacher's right to religious beliefs must be respected, but those beliefs cannot be required of students. Thus, teachers much follow district curricula, even though portions of such curricula may include matters to which they have religious objections.

1990 In *Board of Education of Westside Community Schools v. Mergens,* the Supreme Court upheld the right of students to form religious clubs in schools.

Issues of Language

1967 In the Elementary and Secondary Education Act, the U.S.Congress provided federal funds for schools that wished to implement bilingual education programs designed for language minority students.

1968 With the Bilingual Education Act, the U.S. Congress established that language and cultural heritage are basic means by which a child learns and provided funding for bilingual programs. This law was reauthorized in 1974, 1978, 1984, 1988, and 1990.

1968 In *Diana v. State Board of Education,* a suit brought on behalf of Mexican American, Spanish-speaking children who had been placed in special education classes based on IQ tests in English, the U.S. Supreme Court ruled that testing for eligibility for special education services must be done in the dominant language of the student.

1972 In *Guadalupe Organization, Inc. v. Tempe Elementary School District No. 3,* a suit brought in an Arizona State Court on behalf of Yaquii Indian and Mexican American children disproportionately placed in special education classes based on IQ tests given in English, an out-of-court settlement involved the reevaluation of these students and testing in their primary language.

1974 The Equal Educational Opportunities Act reaffirmed that the failure of any educational agency to take action to overcome language barriers that impeded equal participation by students is a denial of equal educational opportunity.

1974 In *Lau v. Nichols,* a suit brought on behalf of Chinese-speaking children in California who had been disproportionately placed in special education classes, the U.S. Supreme Court ruled that affirmative steps must be taken by a school district to rectify language deficiency.

1977 In *Keyes v. School District No. 1,* the Tenth U.S. Circuit Court established bilingual education as compatible with desegregation.

1979 In *Martin Luther King, Jr. Elementary School Children v. Ann Arbor School District Board of Education,* filed on behalf of black English-speaking children in Ann Arbor by parents demanding that their children be taught standard English, a U.S. District Court in Michigan found for the parents and mandated linguistic instruction for teachers in Black English as a legitimate dialect.

1988 The Bilingual Education Act of 1988 reauthorized bilingual education but added a "three-year enrollment rule," implying that three years of bilingual education was sufficient for most students with limited English proficiency.

Issues of Gender

1963 With the Vocational Education Act (as amended by the Education Amendment of 1976), the U.S. Congress required states to make efforts to overcome sex discrimination and stereotyping in vocational education.

1972 In Title IX of the Education Amendments (PL 92-318), the U.S. Congress prohibited discrimination on the basis of sex against students and employees of any school receiving federal financial assistance.

1978 With the Pregnancy Discrimination Act (PL 95-555), the U.S. Congress prohibited discrimination on the basis of pregnancy, childbirth, or related medical conditions as unlawful under Title VII of the Civil Rights Act.

Issues of Disability

1973 With the Rehabilitation Act of 1973, the U.S. Congress expanded opportunities available to persons with disabilities. Section 502 requires accessibility in all buildings built after 1968 and financed with federal funds. Section 503 requires affirmative action and nondiscrimination clauses in all contracts valued at more than $2,500. Section 504 provides equal educational opportunity (including accessibility) for "otherwise qualified handicapped individuals" in all educational programs.

1976   In the Education of All Handicapped Children Act, the U.S. Congress established that all school districts are responsible for education "in the least restrictive environment for all children, regardless of handicapping condition."

1990   With the Individuals with Disabilities Education Act (IDEA—PL 101-476), the U.S. Congress introduced the phrase "individuals with disabilities" as language more appropriate and realistic than "handicapped persons" and extended its provisions to serve individuals until age 21.

1992   With the Americans with Disabilities Act (ADA), the U.S. Congress extended to the private sector provisions to ensure the rights of access and freedom from discrimination for persons with disabilities that had previously applied only to agencies and settings receiving federal funds.

Reaction to Multicultural Education in the 1980s and 1990s

The 1980s saw a retrenchment from the ideals of educational equity and a resurgence of old assimilationist arguments in new costumes. In particular, these arguments were masked by a call for "excellence" in the face of "mediocrity." Those calling for excellence generally advocate curricula based on the old European-, white-, male-oriented classics. Frequently, these calls for the traditional model of education have explicitly deplored the attention given to diversity. President Ronald Reagan, for example,

> claimed that one reason that the schools were failing was the attention that had been focused on female, minority, and handicapped students. He asserted that, if the federal government and educators had not been so preoccupied with the needs of these special groups of students, education in the U.S. might not have succumbed to the "rising tide of mediocrity." What the President failed to note is that, if these three groups of students are eliminated, only about 15 percent of the school population remains.[25]

During this period, programs in multicultural education, global or international education, gender-equitable education, and education for exceptional individuals continued to develop, although in a political climate that was far from congenial. Unfortunately, children from diverse backgrounds are still, more often than not, forced into a single, more manageable class group by teachers who are stressed from the demands of a difficult job. Unfortunately, the model for the students in these classes is one in which they are usually treated as if they are Anglo, middle-class, and experientially enriched.

Proponents of multicultural education in the past decade have continued to pursue the goal of equal educational opportunity, as well as to argue that a truly equitable education will also be truly excellent. Scholars in multicultural education have looked both within the field and outside it for ideas and concepts that will broaden the field, taking interest especially in the areas of gender research and inclusionary practices in special education. The past decade has also witnessed the publication of the first handbook of research in multicultural education, as well as the first systematic dictionary of multicultural terms and concepts.[26] With these publications, the field of multicultural education has made a strong claim to being not just an advocacy but a disciplined field of study.

It is safe to say, however, that current media and other attention to perceived deficits in schooling in general have sometimes come into conflict with the development of multicultural practice. Thus, the efforts of those who believe strongly in the affirmation of multicultural principles as principles of good teaching for all students must continue with as much energy and dedication as before.

CONTEMPORARY APPROACHES TO
MULTICULTURAL EDUCATION PROGRAMS

43

CHAPTER 2
Multicultural
Education: Historical
and Theoretical
Perspectives

The Sleeter and Grant Categories

In their analysis of multicultural education in the United States, Sleeter and Grant identify five distinct categories of efforts, described under the label *multicultural education,* that are commonly found in schools.[27] While there is some overlap among them, they represent the various approaches that have been used by educational pluralists in attempting to advance the cause of a positive approach to cultural diversity.

Teaching the Culturally Different

The main purposes of these approaches are to counter a perceived cultural deficiency orientation while assisting individuals in developing and maintaining their own cultural identity. Such efforts attempt to help individuals develop competence in the culture of the dominant group while developing a positive self-identity. The focus of such efforts tend to be on the aspects of the culture and language of specific target groups that a teacher can build on, rather than issues of social and power relationships. Few of these efforts extend beyond attention to culture (in the traditional sense), race, and ethnicity and, therefore, exclude attention to gender, exceptionality, and social class.

Such approaches are evident in situations where the majority group is rather homogeneous and of a different background than the teacher. Also characteristic of such approaches is an emphasis on the transmission of mainstream curriculum content. An example of such efforts includes the extensive KEEP (Kamehameha Early Education Program) project in Hawaii, which aims to modify the school context so that it is more congruent with the culture of the child. Teacher training efforts that teach "all there is to know about teaching the _____ child" reflect such an orientation. Such efforts can transmit a considerable amount of culture-specific information; however, they may mask an assimilationist ideology.

Human Relations

This category views multicultural education as a means by which students of different backgrounds learn to communicate more effectively with others while learning to feel good about themselves. Such efforts provide practical ideas for teachers to improve their communication with others while helping students understand their culturally different peers.

While it is essential that individuals in a pluralistic nation learn to communicate more effectively with one another, such emphasis is only part of the solution. An education that effectively addresses diversity goes well beyond such a limited scope to include attention to such factors as curriculum expansion and inclusion, as well as empowerment.

Single-Group Studies

This category addresses instruction that focuses on the experiences and cultures of one specific group. In response to the early demands of those seeking inclusion in the curriculum, specific courses that reflect the heritage, contributions, and perspectives of these "forgotten" groups have been developed in many schools and universities across the nation. Such courses as African American History, Chicano Literature, and Native American Culture, typically monoethnic courses, have been developed and taught, for the most part, by members of that particular group. Those who take such courses are typically members of the target ethnic group. The primary goals of these courses are twofold: (1) to develop a content dimension as exclusion from mainstream material typically resulted in a lack of information readily available about certain groups and (2) to help individuals develop a more positive perception and self-image.

While such efforts are needed, they may have the tendency to perpetuate a rather ethnocentric orientation, albeit from a different group's perspective. Addressing diversity effectively today demands that *multiple* perspectives be considered. The efforts of all who have contributed to the single-group studies can assist those working to expand the curriculum content for today's students.

Inclusive Multicultural Education

It soon became apparent that the adoption of single-group courses in and of themselves was not sufficient to enable many minority students to achieve in school at levels comparable to those of most of their majority counterparts, or to advance along such a hierarchy. These early efforts seemed to be more akin to educational practices for minorities, rather than practices for an inclusive multicultural education.

A slow shift in direction began to occur that offered a new approach, a new way of looking at the question of what is appropriate multicultural education. Attention began to be paid to broader issues of school reform, which focused on the total school environment. As more and more ethnic groups began to make similar demands, the pressure on schools and universities to develop and deliver courses that reflected the experiences of many groups increased. As similarities in people's experiences and perspectives became evident, schools, colleges, and universities began to offer courses that attempted to link the experiences of ethnic groups from a variety of perspectives while developing a conceptual core. Such course offerings as Ethnic Minority Music, Minority Literature, and The History of Minorities in America became popular.

These courses help raise the consciousness of a number of people concerning the perspectives and contributions of various groups to a variety of disciplines and causes. Underlying all these approaches is a focus on such issues as the strength and value of diversity in a pluralistic nation, human rights as a basic tenet for all, the acceptability of alternative life choices, social justice and equal opportunity, and the equitable distribution of power among members of all ethnic groups.

Still others are interested in educational reform that would consider the educational problems beyond those of ethnic minority groups. Such efforts attempt to address the needs of women, religious groups, individuals with handicaps, and people from particular regions of the country, such as white Appalachia. Teachers who incorporate such a multicultural approach into their teaching would use the material, concepts, and perspectives of many individuals from diverse groups. English literature, for instance, would not be limited to a study of the literature of the so-called dead white men but would include pieces written by women and individuals from a variety of ethnic and cultural groups. In addition, the pieces selected for study would be ones identified as relevant by members of that particular group.

Education That Is Multicultural and Social Reconstructionist

Even the approaches identified in the previous sections did not seem to have a sufficient impact on the experiences of many, at least to the degree that people were empowered to make a difference in their lives. A significant mismatch between the curriculum of the school and the daily experiences and cultural backgrounds of many people of color is assumed to exist that is nearly impossible for many to transcend. Essentially, the schools succeed at placing certain individuals at an advantage while effectively suppressing many others.

Sleeter and Grant speak of providing education that is multicultural and social reconstructionist.[28] This approach goes beyond multicultural education in its attempt to help students critically analyze their circumstances and the social stratification that keeps them from full participation in the society at large. The phrase "education that is multicultural" means that the entire education program should be designed to address the needs of diverse groups regardless of race, ethnicity, culture, religion, exceptionality, or gender. This approach also strives to provide students with the skills necessary to become socially active in creating the necessary changes. Such an effort is designed to enable individuals to shape their own destinies, hence the term *social reconstructionist.*

Sleeter and Grant cite four practices[29] unique to education that is multicultural and social reconstructionist:

1. Schools and classrooms that adopt such an approach are organized in such a way that democracy is put into action. That is, students are not told in a passive way what democracy should be like. Rather, children are given the opportunity to participate in constructing a system that exemplifies democracy in action. Students participate in such activities as determining the rules and consequences of classroom interaction, may participate in determining portions of the curriculum, and may be included in various aspects of program evaluation.

2. Students learn to analyze their life situations and to become aware of inequities found in society that have impact on their lives, such as the inequality of pay for equal work found between individuals from different groups or the assumption that an education automatically improves one's life experience. Ogbu cites a position that summarizes this issue:

    > White people have always felt that they are superior to all other groups. And when the minority people begin to protest and challenge this superiority complex the white people begin to shout the slogan of "law and order." But the only solution to the problem, you say, is education. Education will do it. All right, now you take my wife. She has four years of college and yet she can't get a job. Now education is not the only answer. It is one of the answers but not all the answer.[30]

3. Attaining knowledge alone, however, is not sufficient. Students also learn social action skills so they are better prepared to put their knowledge and concerns into action in the political, economic, or social arenas. Only then can significant change occur with the potential to impact large numbers of people.

4. Finally, attempts are made to encourage groups to coalesce such that the efforts of smaller groups become concentrated and strengthened in their fight against

discrimination and oppression. It is then that a large social movement can form. That is, when large numbers of people come together in their efforts to promote or resist change in society, formal organizations may be born. The civil rights and feminist movements of the past few decades resulted in the formation of many organizations that direct their efforts and make significant change.

The Mitchell Typology

Over the years, a number of writers have analyzed the wide variety of multicultural education programs developed in the 1960s and 1970s and have categorized them in ways that might help us understand their purposes and practices. Cameron Mitchell, for example, provides a slightly different typology than do Sleeter and Grant. Writing clearly about the assumptions, expectations, and practices of various multicultural education programs, he argues that most if not all of such efforts fall into one of the following three categories of models.[31]

Models of Cultural Understanding

This approach emphasizes improving communication among various ethnic and cultural groups. Proponents of these models assume that the United States is a culturally diverse nation-state in which the presence of cultural diversity has helped create a powerful society through the contributions of all Americans, no matter what their background. The schools, however, have not promoted this view of American society, with the result that prejudice and discrimination against particular racial and ethnic groups exist. In order to remedy this situation, schools and teachers should "positively endorse cultural diversity and foster an appreciation and respect for 'human differences' in order to reduce racial tension and estrangement of minority groups in the schools and in society."[32]

In this approach, all social and ethnic groups are assumed to be relatively "equal" in worth, and ethnic identity is thought to be "a matter of individual choice or preference—the language of the shopping mall"[33] or the banquet table. Proponents of these models advocate eliminating racial and sexual stereotypes; moving beyond simple awareness of cultural differences in food, dress, and so forth; and emphasizing the development of positive attitudes toward minority and disadvantaged groups. In other words, attitudes should change. Mitchell argues that these programs "take a benign stance towards racial inequality in schooling"[34]; consequently, they focus most of their attention on the development of racial and ethnic harmony.

Expecting that schools will actively promote the cultural enhancement of all students, these programs place primary responsibility on the classroom teacher to provide information and enrichment activities designed to reduce prejudice. Mitchell indicates that these programs have not been very successful in changing attitudes; indeed, in some cases attitudes among white students toward African Americans and other minorities have deteriorated. In part, the lack of success of these programs has been attributed to problems with both content and methods.[35] In addition, these programs may, in fact, foster stereotyping by clustering individuals together on the basis of only one characteristic—race, ethnicity, religion, and so forth. Differences *within* these groups are rarely emphasized.

Models of Cultural Competence

Based on these models, it is not enough to appreciate other cultural groups. What is needed is the ability to understand one's own cultural identity and, beyond that, to become "at home" in more than one cultural system.[36] Advocates believe that traditional assimilationist approaches preserve Anglo dominance and that cross-cultural interaction will assist in the survival of minority language and culture, as well as help decrease discrimination and prejudice.[37] In the cultural competence models, minority students are encouraged not only to be proud of their own heritage but also, in cases in which their background is characterized by subjugation and prejudice, to become fluent in the dominant culture.

Critical of programs designed to remediate so-called cultural deficits, advocates of cultural competence programs argue for inclusive curricula, in which knowledge and values rooted in minority cultures are examined. Mitchell asserts, however, that their twofold approach to cultural identity contains a fundamental contradiction. By affirming minority cultures, these programs challenge the dominant social norms that are promoted in the school. At the same time, by encouraging students to "build bridges" to the dominant culture, often by stressing language adaptation, these programs place students on the road to assimilation.[38]

Models of Cultural Emancipation and Social Reconstruction

These models share with proponents of other models the belief that cultural diversity in the United States is a positive force and that fostering positive self-concepts among minority students is a valuable enterprise. They differ from other models, however, in their focus on the attitudes of teachers and other school personnel and on the culture of the school, which, they claim, suppresses the development of ethnic and racial identity and, thereby, is partially responsible for underachievement and loss of job opportunities among minority students. It is thus incumbent on school personnel to act in ways that will redress past patterns of discrimination and increase educational and job opportunities for minority students.

Criticisms of this model, however, point out that it may be unduly optimistic to believe that improved school achievement based on an inclusive curriculum will translate into better job market opportunities for minority students. Prejudice and discrimination exist outside the school as well as in it, and the school has little power to alter pervasive attitudes in the larger community. In addition, the complexity of school culture itself has not been sufficiently addressed by emancipatory multiculturalists. They tend to ignore the complex social and political relations between the schools and the larger society in which they are embedded. Issues of policy formation, decision making, trade-offs, and the building of alliances for specific reformist initiatives have not really been addressed by multicultural reformers. For these reformist educators, educational change hinges almost exclusively on the reorganization of the content of the school curriculum.[39]

It might be of value for you to revisit the goals of this book, which were presented in Chapter 1. How do each of the approaches to multicultural education meet the goals listed there? Does the integrative model proposed in this book go beyond the approaches presented in this section? What sort of model would *you* build in regard to an education that addresses diversity?

THE OUTCOMES OF
MULTICULTURAL EDUCATION

Student Outcomes

Since the early part of this century, social scientists have known that children as young as 3 years of age are able to differentiate human physical characteristics, such as skin color.[40] Children also, from about age 5, make attributions about others based on their skin color, associating black as having negative value and white as having positive value.[41]

Banks provides a comprehensive survey of the effects of multicultural education on the racial attitudes of children.[42] Positive effects of multicultural education efforts have been observed through the use of a variety of strategies: curriculum units and courses developed around specific ethnic and/or cultural groups (e.g., African American History)[43]; multiethnic readings in the social studies; the integration of multicultural activities into social studies, English, and reading[44]; the use of multiethnic readers in the language arts program[45]; and the particular instructional strategy that is used.[46] For instance, studies in cooperative learning rather consistently suggest that positive racial attitudes can result among students of different ethnic groups when they use cooperative learning activities.[47] The lessons learned from the cooperative learning studies suggest that the content taught may not be as important as how it is taught and how the concepts are communicated to students, parents, and the community.[48]

In general, studies conducted since the 1940s have demonstrated that curriculum interventions can have a positive impact on student attitudes. However, the results of such studies have not been consistent. Some possible reasons for such inconsistent findings include the nature and structure of the intervention, the duration of exposure, individual student characteristics, such school characteristics as degree of cooperation versus competitiveness, the characteristics of the community in which the school is located, and aspects of the individual teachers.[49] There is also a need to analyze the long-term effect of such interventions.

Program Outcomes

It is instructive to reflect on the very different outcomes of the different mandates for equal educational opportunity legislated in the 1960s and 1970s. Why, for example, did PL 94-142 take root, while bilingual education programs and antisex discrimination policies have had less success? While a number of factors may be involved—economic recession, a resurgence of nativism, a backlash against feminism—the success of PL 94-142 and its later amendments is due largely to the actions of vocal parents and other advocacy groups supporting individuals with disabilities. Such advocacy on the part of parents, especially, has also led to an increasing awareness of the importance of community and family involvement in schools and classrooms.

The decade of the 1980s saw a powerful resurgence of the academic (as opposed to the social) mission of schools. That is, in the 1980s the primary function of schooling was seen as the transmission of knowledge rather than the transformation of society. Today, as people begin to understand the magnitude of the demographic changes taking place in the United States, schools are once again being viewed as potential agencies of assimilation, not just for exceptional (handicapped and gifted) students but also for minority culture groups, the lower socio-economic classes, and females. In short, the reality of social and demographic change is forcing schools to reexamine both their academic and their social missions and, in the process, to acknowledge that these two missions cannot be separated. Many teachers and administrators are coming to the realization that curricula that are not attuned to the life experiences, values, and cognitive styles of the student population have little hope of producing desired academic outcomes.

The meaning of the concept of equal educational opportunity is also a problem. For some, it means an *equal chance* to participate in acquiring an education. To them, the government's responsibility is to open doors, not to follow students into schools and classrooms to see that they receive fair and equal treatment. If students cannot, or will not, do whatever is required to obtain a good education, it is unfortunate, but neither the school nor the community has an obligation to do anything about it. In contrast, some believe that equal educational opportunity means an *equal share* in education. Responsibility for effective education lies principally with the government and the school. If students cannot or will not do what the school requires, schools must be restructured in such a way that they can and will. Public educational policy should focus on the outcomes of schooling, and measures should be taken to ensure that most, if not all, students receive the benefits of a good education.

Ironically, demographic and institutional change, historically used to support assimilationist arguments for using schools to socialize the young, may eventually provide the impetus for more pluralist approaches to schooling. Indeed, educational policy may be shaped as much by the numbers of culturally and economically different students sitting in the nation's classrooms as by the changing nature of the global job market.

Americans simply cannot afford to let one-third to one-half of their children "fall through the cracks." Clearly, the attitudes that underlie any changes in American schools will be critical to the kind of changes that are made and to the success with which they are instituted. If schools separate students according to race, ethnicity, religion, social class, health, sexual orientation, or disability, they will simply be repeating the past. Remediation, tracking, and cosmetic programs, such as Black History Month and Women's History Month, often result in further isolation and segregation, not in integration. If, on the other hand, schools approach educational reform with a positive attitude toward differences—that is, with the attitude that different perspectives born of different experiences offer a richer, more complete view of reality—then schooling may become an integrative experience built around inquiry-oriented learning communities.

Active Exercises

The fact that this nation is a nation of immigrants is a central theme of this chapter. The following exercise from *Human Diversity in Action: Developing Multicultural Competencies for the Classroom*[50] complements this chapter well:

Activity 7:   Family Tree Exercise p. 38

Accessing the World Wide Web: Resources for Diversity

For more information on the integration of Central High School in Little Rock, the following web sites are recommended:

http://www.centralhigh57.org/1957-58.htm A timeline of events and series of articles describing the high school then and now.

http://www.phila-tribune.com/092997-OE.htm "The Little Rock Nine: 40 Years Later," a commentary from the *Philadelphia Tribune.*

http://www.usis.usemb.se/usa/blackhis/ltrock A web site containing a large number of articles on all aspects of the integration of Central High School, including the role of the media and interviews with many of those involved in the issue.

For information on the Taino, both historically and in the present, a good source can be found at:

http://hartford-hwp.com/Taino/index.html

For more information on the Freedmen's Bureau and its role in the education of black children in the South, see the following:

http://www.nara.gov/nara/legislative/house_guide/hgch14f.html Records of the House of Representatives, Committee on Freedmen's Affairs, 1866–1875.

http://www.digizen.net/member/stjohns/c_grove.html A history of Clinton Grove school in Prince George's County, Maryland.

Material about the Supreme Court case, *Plessy v. Ferguson*, including excerpts from the actual decision, can be accessed at:

http://oyez.nwu.edu/cases/cases.cgi?case_id=307

Interesting information about the development of the common school and the Catholic school controversy in the mid-nineteenth century can be found at the following address:

http://sun1.iusb.edu/eduweb01 History of American Education Web Project; click on Common School Period of American Education, 1840–1880.

For a historical timeline, photographs, and written memories of immigrants, see:

http://www.teleport.com/~billf/Internet_Lesson_Plans/Ellis.Island/Ellis.Island .html The Ellis Island web page.

Additional background on the definition of multicultural education, as well as issues associated with it, can be found at:

http://www.ncrel.org/sdrs/areas/issues/educatrs/presrvce/pe300.htm

References

1. Robert Frost, "The Gift Outright," in *The Witness Tree* (New York: Henry Holt, 1942), p. 1.41.1.
2. Much of the material in this case study was taken from a timeline on the "History of Little Rock Public Schools Desegregation" and other articles on World Wide Web pages

regarding the incident in Little Rock. See, especially, http://www.centralhigh57.org/1958-58.htm.

3. D. A. Brown, *Bury My Heart at Wounded Knee* (New York: Holt, Rinehart & Winston, 1970), p. 1.

4. L. Dinnerstein and D. M. Reiners, *Ethnic Americans: A History of Immigration and Assimilation* (New York: Harper & Row, 1975).

5. Ibid., p. 2.

6. Eugene F. Provenzo, Jr., *An Introduction to Education in American Society* (Columbus, OH: Charles E. Merrill, 1986), pp. 90–91.

7. Rodman B. Webb and Robert R. Sherman, *Schooling and Society,* 2nd ed. (New York: Macmillan, 1989), p. 524.

8. Nancy Hoffman, *Women's True Profession* (Old Westbury, NY: The Feminist Press and McGraw-Hill, 1981), pp. 90–197.

9. Quoted in Meyer Weinberg, *A Chance to Learn: A History of Race and Education in the United States* (New York: Cambridge University Press, 1977), p. 46.

10. J. E. W. Wallin, *The Mental Health of the School Child: The Psychoeducational Clinic in Relation to Child Welfare* (New Haven, CT: Yale University Press, 1914).

11. F. Koestler, *The Unseen Minority: A Social History of Blindness in the United States* (New York: David McKay, 1967).

12. William A. Hunter, ed., *Multicultural Education Through Competency-Based Teacher Education* (Washington, DC: American Association of Colleges of Teacher Education, 1975), p. 17.

13. Cited by Rupert Trujillo in "Bilingual-Bicultural Education: A Necessary Strategy for American Public Education," in *A Relook at Tucson '66 and Beyond,* report of a National Bilingual Bicultural Institute (Washington, DC: National Education Association, 1973), p. 21.

14. Israel Zangwill, *The Melting Pot* (New York: Macmillan, 1909), p. 37.

15. James Bank, *Multiethnic Education: Theory and Practice,* 2nd ed. (Boston: Allyn & Bacon, 1988).

16. Ibid.

17. Cited in Pamela L. Tiedt and Iris M. Tiedt, *Multicultural Teaching: A Handbook of Activities, Information, and Resources,* 3rd ed. (Boston: Allyn & Bacon, 1990), p. 9.

18. Ibid.

19. Title IX of the Education Amendments of 1972.

20. Anne O'Brien Carelli, "What Is Title IX?" in *Sex Equity in Education: Readings and Strategies* (Springfield, IL: Charles C Thomas, 1988), p. 85.

21. Editorial in the *Albuquerque* (New Mexico) *Tribune,* "Two Language Teaching," 19 May 1975, p. 54.

22. Rudolph B. Schmerl, "The Student as Immigrant," in *Teaching in a Multicultural Society* ed. Dolores E. Gross, Gwendolyn C. Baker, and Lindley J. Stiles (New York: The Free Press, 1977), p. 45.

23. American Association of Colleges for Teacher Education, "No One Model American," *Journal of Teacher Education* 24, 4 (winter 1973): 264–265.

24. James B. Boyer, "The Essentials of Multi-Culturalism in the Context of Teacher Education Research: A Projective Overview," paper prepared for the 1979 Conference on Exploring Issues in Teacher Education: Questions for Future Research, University of Texas at Austin, 1979.

25. Carol Shakeshaft, "A Gender at Risk," *Phi Delta Kappan* 67, 7 (March 1986): 499.

26. James A. Banks and Cherrie A. McGee Banks, eds., *Handbook of Research on Multicultural Education* (New York: Macmillan, 1995); Carl A. Grant, ed., Gloria Ladson-Billings, contributor, *Dictionary of Multicultural Education* (Phoenix, AZ: Oryx Press, 1998).

27. Christine Sleeter and Carl Grant, "An Analysis of Multicultural Education in the United States," *Harvard Educational Review* 57, 4 (November 1987): 421–444.

28. Christine Sleeter and Carl Grant, "Educational Equity, Education That Is Multicultural and Social Reconstructionist," *Journal of Educational Equity and Leadership* 6, 2 (1986): 105–118.

29. Ibid.

30. J. Ogbu, *The Next Generation: An Ethnography of Education in an Urban Neighborhood* (New York: Academic Press, 1974), p. 99.

31. Cameron Mitchell, *Multicultural Approaches to Racial Inequality in the United States* (Baton Rouge, LA: Louisiana State University, 1989), typescript.

32. Ibid., p. 13.

33. Ibid., p. 10.

34. Ibid., p. 12.

35. Ibid., p. 16.

36. Ibid., pp. 19–20.

37. Ibid., pp. 20–21.

38. Ibid., pp. 22–23.

39. Ibid., pp. 30–31.

40. E. Frenkel-Brunswick, "A Study of Prejudice in Children," *Human Relations* 1, 3 (1948): 295–306.

41. Ibid.

42. James A. Banks, "Multicultural Education: Its Effects on Students' Racial and Gender Role Attitudes," in *Handbook of Research on Social Studies Teaching and Learning,* ed. James Shaver (New York: Macmillan, 1990).

43. D. W. Johnson, "Freedom School Effectiveness: Changes in Attitudes of Negro Children," *The Journal of Applied Behavioral Science* 2, 3 (1966): 325–330.

44. O. L. B. Shirley, "The Impact of Multicultural Education on Self-Concept, Racial Attitude, and Student Achievement of Black and White Fifth and Sixth Graders," Ph.D. dissertation, The University of Mississippi, 1988.

45. J. Litcher and D. Johnson, "Changes in Attitudes Toward Negroes of White Elementary School Students after Use of Multiethnic Readers," *Journal of Educational Psychology* 60, 2 (April 1969): 148–152.

46. R. Slavin, "Cooperative Learning: Applying Contact Theory in Desegregated Schools," *Journal of Social Issues* 41, 3 (1985): 45–62.

47. Ibid.

48. Banks, op. cit.

49. Ibid.

50. Kenneth Cushner, *Human Diversity in Action: Developing Multicultural Competencies for the Classroom* (New York: McGraw-Hill, 1999).

CHAPTER 3

Culture and the Culture-Learning Process

CHAPTER OUTLINE

EXPLORING THE CONCEPT OF CULTURE
THREE VIEWS OF CULTURE
    Anthropology
    Sociology
    Cross-Cultural Psychology
THE CULTURE-LEARNING PROCESS
    What Is Learned: The Sources of
        Cultural Knowledge
    How Culture Is Learned: The
        Socializing Agents
    When Culture Is Learned
SOME RESULTS OF SOCIALIZATION
    Ethnocentrism
    Perception

    Categorization
    Stereotypes
    Some Limits on Socialization
UNDERSTANDING CULTURAL DIFFERENCES
    Variations in Cultural
        Environments: Returning to
        Grover's Corners
    Variation in Cultural Attributes,
        Socializing Agents, and Cultural
        Learners
ACTIVE EXERCISES
ACCESSING THE WORLD WIDE WEB:
    RESOURCES FOR DIVERSITY
REFERENCES

Cultures are dramatic conversations about things that matter to their participants.

Robert Bellah

If we, as teachers, are to engage in the "dramatic conversations about things that matter" with our students, it is helpful to analyze the way we define *education*. Clearly, *education*—defined as teaching and learning—is a broader term than *schooling*. Indeed, one of the difficulties we all encounter in talking about education at all is that it is pervasive in human life. Not often emphasized, however, are the actual settings, apart from schools, in which education occurs and the precise nature of teaching and learning in those settings, yet it is in these settings—particularly in the home, the neighborhood, and the house of worship—that we acquire the language, knowledge, attitudes, and values that let us engage in the dramatic conversation called culture. It is in these settings that we develop the cultural identities that we take with us to school.

Giroux and Simon speak directly to the importance of teachers understanding their own cultural identities and those of their students:

> By ignoring the cultural and social forms that are authorized by youth and simultaneously empower and disempower them, educators risk complicitly silencing and negating their students. This is unwittingly accomplished by refusing to recognize

the importance of those sites and social practices outside of the schools that actively shape student experiences and through which students often define and construct their sense of identity, politics, and culture.[1]

By way of clarifying these ideas, let us set up a "thought experiment"—a community we can enter in our imaginations, to consider the educational implications of living there. In this experiment, we will posit an imaginary, freestanding (not a suburb), medium-sized town of about sixty thousand people—let's call it Grover's Corners, after the town in the famous American play *Our Town,* by Thornton Wilder.[2] Conditions in such a town will vary, depending on its ethnic and religious composition, its economic base, and its location (is it in New England? the Deep South? the Midwest? the mountain states of the West? the Southwest? the Northwest?) The size of Grover's Corners is also a factor to consider. If it were a city of several hundred thousand (or millions) or a village of several hundred (or thousand) people, conditions might be different. In our thought experiment, Grover's Corners may assume a variety of characteristics; play along with us, and let's see what we can learn.

Grover's Corners: A Thought Experiment and Case Study

To begin with, our imaginary Grover's Corners is a geographical community in the sense that it is a town. It has city limits; it has a mayor and a city council. It has its own set of laws, as well as being under the jurisdiction of its county (or parish), its state, and the nation. Equally important, it has a fairly good-sized river, which runs through the middle of the town, a fact that the residents acknowledge by using the terms north side and south side.

Grover's Corners has a wealthy residential section, a number of middle-class neighborhoods, and at least one poor section. It has some manufacturing industry, a number of churches, and a synagogue, as well as a mosque and a Buddhist temple. It has several day care centers, a museum, a relatively large public library with several branch libraries, a television station, several radio stations, and a daily newspaper. There are two hospitals—one Catholic—and several "neighborhood" medical drop-in centers. It has department stores, discount stores, bars, neighborhood convenience stores, and numerous commercial and service businesses. It has a municipal park and a Class A professional baseball team with its own ballpark, a YM/YWCA, a welfare department, a children's services department, and a juvenile reformatory for boys. It has a community theatre, several malls, and a downtown business district. It has an adequate number of lawyers, doctors, dentists, accountants, architects, and other professionals. It has both public and private elementary and high schools and a public middle school. In addition, let's put in a community college.

Within the geographical community that is Grover's Corners, there are also educational communities—groups of people who are actively engaged in instruction (formal and informal) and learning, as well as the organizations and settings in which deliberate and systematic teaching and learning occur. It is in these educational communities that the dramatic *conversations of culture take place—in particular families, particular neighborhoods, particular businesses, particular religious settings, and particular voluntary associations. Thus, the particular combination of settings in Grover's Corners "sets the tone," so to speak, of the community itself and of the educational messages—both coherent and conflicting— available there to its people.*

Let's say, for the sake of the experiment, that Grover's Corners is in upstate New York and is a largely Protestant town (of all denominations, including three good-sized black churches). There is also a considerable number of Catholic families, enough to support several churches, a hospital, two elementary schools (north side and south side), and a high school (north side). There are relatively small groups of Jewish, Islamic, and Buddhist families.

We will say, further, that it is a largely white, working- and middleclass town. The African Americans who live there have been there for fifty years and comprise about 12 percent of the population. Most migrated there from the Deep South during and after World War II to work in the town's small factories. Let's further suppose that these industries are suffering from severe competition, both domestic and foreign. Business is not good, and all the residents of Grover's Corners are fearful that many jobs could be lost, thus creating a depressed economic situation for all income-producing businesses.

As in all communities, the cultural conversations of Grover's Corners have their roots in the economic, religious, social class, and family life of the town. The education received by an individual growing up in Grover's Corners depends, in large part, on the ethnic, religious, social class, and occupational character of the individual's family and the character of the housing and neighborhood in which the individual lives, works, and plays. These factors—as well as others, such as the individual's age, health, and the family size and composition—have a great deal to do with the access he or she has to a broad or narrow range of educational resources, both within and outside of the school.

Let us look, now, at four 16-year-old high school students who live in Grover's Corners. What cultural conversations do you think have meaning for them?

Michael Williams is an African American who has lived his entire life with his grandmother and grandfather (retired and at home), his mother (an assembly line worker at the light bulb factory), his aunt (a cleaning woman at the museum), two brothers, and a sister in a house on the northeast side of town. He doesn't know who or where his father is. His older brother is in the local reformatory for drug-related crimes. His family regularly attends the A.M.E. Church. As a child, Richard played basketball at the neighborhood house near his home and continues to help out there with younger children. He attends the public North High School and is in the college prep academic program, where he earns excellent grades. He has a steady girlfriend. He is a member of the high school golf team, which practices at the local golf course; is on the school newspaper staff, which is advised by an editor of the Grover's Corners newspaper; and works after school and on weekends at the golf course.

Toni Catalano lives in a pleasant ranch house on a cul-de-sac on the south side of town. She is the youngest of a large, extended Italian Catholic family. Although she attended Catholic parochial school through the eighth grade, she currently attends the public South High School, where she is majoring in business subjects, planning to become a secretary—perhaps in one of the local banks. Her family has always been very involved in the church, and she gained a considerable amount of attention (not all of it positive) when she became the first alter girl at St. Mary's. Two of her aunts are nuns; one of them, Sister Rita, is a missionary in Central America. One of her uncles is a priest in a church in a neighboring town and disapproves heartily of her aunt's being in Central America. Nevertheless, her family keeps in close contact with Sister Rita, and Toni corresponds with her frequently—sometimes by e-mail. In school, Toni earns reasonably good grades, is on the cheerleading squad, and is a scorekeeper for the wrestling team. She dates a number of boys, mostly athletes, and works on weekends at the nearby Dairy Queen.

Steven Chang lives in a large and comfortable house on The Hill (the west side of town) with his parents and a younger sister. His father is a lawyer, and his mother, an artist, is in charge of the adult volunteers (called docents) at the museum, where Steve sometimes works as a guide for special exhibits. His family does not belong to any religious group. He attends a private high school for boys, where he struggles a bit for average grades and is a member of the tennis and debate teams. As a child, Steve played Little League baseball, belonged to the Boy Scouts, and traveled extensively in the United States and Asia with his family. He doesn't date much, and when he does it is usually with girls who are children of his parents' friends. He takes karate lessons every week, and he participates in formal demonstrations of the martial arts. He is not certain he wants to go to college, much to his parents' dismay.

Shameka Collins is a member of only three African American families on her street, which is on the south side of town. Her parents are divorced, and she lives with her mother, who works as a bookkeeper for a local department store. She sees her father, who lives in another state, only sporadically. She has an older brother who is stationed on a nuclear submarine, presently on duty in the Persian Gulf. As a child, Jennifer was a Girl Scout for a while but dropped out. She has gone to Sunday school at the local Presbyterian church all her life. After school and on Saturday, she works at the main branch of the public library downtown, saving most of the money she makes for college. She does not have either the time or the inclination to date much, but she does find time to go to all the exhibitions at the museum and to all the local community theatre productions. Once, she even had a small part in a play there. Since she and her mother are alone, they spend as much time together as possible. Her mother has taught her to sew, and she makes most of her own clothes. She worries about leaving her mother alone when she goes to college and is trying to decide whether or not to attend the local community college for two years before actually leaving home. Because she takes advanced placement courses in high school, she will be eligible for courses at the college in her senior year and will probably become a student there. She thinks perhaps she will become a doctor.

Each of these students, life-long residents of Grover's Corners, partic- ipates in a particular pattern of educational life, out of which has emerged a cultural identity. As with most Americans, their cultural knowledge, beliefs, attitudes, and values are multiple—none identifies with a single cultural group—yet their cultural/educational patterns are different, and sometimes surprising.

Can you put yourself in Grover's Corners?

EXPLORING THE CONCEPT OF CULTURE

One of the greatest difficulties people have when beginning to explore concepts related to culture and culture learning is that of agreeing on what it is they are talking about. This chapter will look closely at the concept of culture and the culture-learning process (how we acquire a cultural identity). We will begin by looking at some definitions of *culture,* as well as some of the analytical concepts devised by social science scholars in their attempts to understand cultural differences among groups of people and among individuals. This discussion will set the stage for subsequent analysis of the cross-cultural interactions that occur in the context of schools.

Culture is studied by many disciplines, including anthropology, sociology, education, psychology, business, and the military. If you were to peruse the literature of these various disciplines, looking for the concept of culture, you would find literally hundreds of definitions. Some of these definitions are more useful than others as we examine how culture influences the teaching-learning process. What all of these definitions seem to have in common is the idea that *culture* refers to a human-made part of the environment, as opposed to aspects that occur in nature. Culture determines, to a large extent, our thoughts, ideas, ways of interacting, and material adaptations to the world around us. We will explore this notion in greater detail in the following section as we look at insights and practice from the disciplines of anthropology, sociology, and cross-cultural psychology.

THREE VIEWS OF CULTURE

Anthropology

A review of the anthropological literature would uncover many definitions of the word *culture,*[3] each of which attempts to answer the question, What do all cultures have in common? Some try to answer this question by examining the functions or purposes of culture. Webb and Sherman, for example, describe culture in a functional way:

> Cultures solve the common problems of human beings, but they solve them in different ways. . . . Each provides its people with a means of communication (*language*). Each determines who wields power and under what circumstances power can be used (*status*). Each provides for the regulation of reproduction (*family*) and supplies a system of rules (*government*). These rules may be written (*laws*) or unwritten (*custom*), but they are always present. Cultures supply human beings with an explanation of their relationship to nature (*magic, myth, religion,* and *science*). They provide their people with some conception of time (*temporality*). They supply a system by which significant lessons of the culture (*history*) can be given a physical representation and stored and passed on to future generations. The

representation usually comes in the form of dance, song, poetry, architecture, handicrafts, story, design, or painting (*art*). What makes cultures similar is the problems they solve, not the methods they devise to solve them.[4]

One can also understand culture in terms of the assumptions or ideas inherent in the concept itself. Four of these seem particularly important.

Humans Construct Culture

We begin with the notion that human beings are born with fewer biological instincts (e.g., breathing, swallowing) than any other species. This means that we are born relatively helpless and remain so for a considerable amount of time, longer than any other organism in the animal kingdom. Unlike most of the animal world, we are not biologically "programmed" so that we automatically know how to use our environment to find food and shelter. In short, we do not know how to survive without other people to care for us and to teach us. Therefore, humans must discover ways of interacting effectively both with their environment and with themselves. They must learn how to *construct* the knowledge, including rules of living, that will enable them to survive. This knowledge, the manner in which it is presented (in the family, in the neighborhood, in literature, and so on), and the meaning it has for us is called culture.

Thus, the concept of culture usually refers to things (both physical and mental) that are made or constructed by human beings, rather than to things that occur in nature. When you look out over a body of water, for instance, neither the water itself, the undeveloped beachfront, nor the horizon is considered culture. These are naturally occurring components of the environment. How we *think about,* and what we *do* with, the natural environment, however, is usually dependent on culture. Thus, in the United States, a beachfront, such as Miami Beach, has been viewed as a good place to build condominiums, piers, a boardwalk, and a marina. In another culture, this same beachfront might be regarded as a sacred space, with as little human intervention as possible allowed.

The physical artifacts of mainstream American culture are expressions of our underlying knowledge about, attitudes toward, and values about a part of the natural environment. Other expressions of our culture are our behavioral patterns—for example, our tendency to litter our oceans and beaches with various kinds of waste. Traditional Native American societies, on the other hand, have an entirely different view of the natural environment. Rather than seeing themselves as controllers of nature, many Native Americans believe strongly that human beings are an integral part of the natural world. Since in their view we live within rather than outside of nature, they believe we should not interfere with it too much. This is an interesting example, because it shows not only that different sociocultural groups perceive the world in very different terms but also that cultural beliefs and attitudes can and do change. Western peoples are now beginning to see the damage they have caused to the environment and to consider not only ways to "clean it up" but also ways of rethinking the basis of the relation of human beings to nature.

Culture Is Shared

Culture is not only constructed; it is *socially constructed* by human beings in interaction with one another. Cultural ideas and understandings are shared by people who recognize the knowledge, attitudes, and values of one another. Moreover, they agree on which cultural elements are better than others. That is, cultural elements are usually arranged in a hierarchy of value, which can also change over time. Mainstream American attitudes about children's place in the economy provide a good example. Before the middle of the nineteenth century, children in the United States were regarded as economic assets to their families and to the community. That is, they worked, not only on the farm or in the shop, but also often outside the family for money that went to help support the family. Zelizer makes a distinction between the "useful" and the "useless" child in talking about the change that occurred during the last half of the century:

> By 1900 middle-class reformers began indicting children's economic cooperation as unjustified parental exploitation, and child labor emerged for the first time as a major social problem in the United States. . . . By 1930, most children under fourteen were out of the labor market and into schools.[5]

This is another instance of the changing nature of cultural ideas. The notion that children "do not belong" in the labor market, and that parents whose children bring income into the family may be exploiting them, has become a highly valued idea in our society, but it is one that is relatively new. In contrast to early nineteenth-century families, we believe that children should be in school when they are young. Moreover, when we encounter families that do send their children out to work, there is a sense that they are doing something wrong. Thus, in contemporary mainstream U.S. culture, until children are in mid-adolescence, we place a greater value on the "useless" (nonworking) child than we do on the "useful" one who works. Indeed, although many find ways around it, we have in this country legal restrictions on the age at which children can be employed.

In nearly all instances, this shared cultural identification is transmitted from one generation to the next. One exception to this cultural transmission process, however, can be seen in the case of deaf persons whose primary language is a manual system, ASL (American Sign Language) in North America. Although most deaf persons have hearing parents, the deaf normally form strong ties to their own community and tend to marry a deaf partner. Thus, cultural transmission in this instance is deferred until entry into the deaf community occurs through instruction in schools for the deaf and through a network of social clubs, theatre, political organizations, and publications. For some young people, their first enculturation into the deaf community may come through enrollment at the world-famous Gallaudet University, which provides schooling from preschool levels through college.

Culture Is Both Objective and Subjective

A third common assumption about culture is that it is composed of two kinds of elements: objective and subjective.[6] The objective components of culture consist of the endless variety of physical artifacts that people produce, from the language they speak to the clothes they wear, the food they eat, and the unending stream of decorative and ritual objects they create. These are the tangible, visible aspects of people's lives and are what are more commonly thought of when considering cultural differences. Subjective components of culture, on the other hand, are the invisible, intangible aspects of culture, including attitudes, values, norms of behavior, learning styles, and hierarchy of social roles—in short, the *meaning* that more objective components of culture have for individuals and groups. In this respect, culture can be likened to an iceberg—only 10 percent of the whole is seen above the surface of the water. It is the 90 percent of the iceberg that is hidden that most concerns the ship's captain, who must navigate the water. Like an iceberg, the most meaningful (and potentially dangerous) part of culture is the invisible, or subjective, part, which is continually operating at the unconscious level to shape our perceptions and our responses to those perceptions. It is this aspect of culture that leads to most intercultural misunderstandings and is where our emphasis in multicultural or intercultural education should focus.

Culture Is Nurtured

A final assumption about culture is the idea that it involves nurturing and growth, similar to the nurturing of plants. In the case of humans, however, the growing process involves teaching the young, both formally and informally. Thus, to *encul-turate* a child is to help that child become a member of his or her social groups. In the United States, that may mean helping a child negotiate the various cultural perspectives found among the social groups in which he or she participates.

Culture is also related to growth through the fine arts (music, dance, literature, and the visual arts), as well as through social behavior. A "cultured" person is one who has been nurtured (helped to grow) by participation in such activities. However, observation tells us that it is people of comfortable circumstances who most frequently have the time, energy, and inclination to devote to such pursuits. Thus, the notion of an elite (high-status) group enters into the picture.

The idea of culture as "belonging" to an elite group also carries with it the notion that this kind of "high culture" has more value than what we might call "folk" culture. In part, this idea has its roots in the late nineteenth century, when Western anthropologists first developed their ideas from the study of so-called primitive peoples. Comparing these civilizations with their own, more technological societies, they saw differences that were perceived not simply as differences but as deficits. Warren's 1873 textbook on physical geography introduced its readers to the "races of man" in the following manner:

> The Caucasian race is the truly cosmopolitan and historical race. The leading nations of the world, those who have reached the highest state of civilization and possess a history in the true sense of the word, belong to it. It has, therefore, not improperly been called the active race; while the others, embracing the uncivilized or half-civilized peoples, have been termed the passive races.[7]

Such quasi-evolutionary theories of culture have even been invoked to "explain" disabilities. Down syndrome, for example, is named for John Haydon Langdon Down's "ethnic classification," according to which individuals with "mongolian" features, whatever the "race" of their parents might be, represented "regression" to a more primitive state of evolutionary development. Tragically, before the discovery of its chromosomal basis in the 1950s, a newborn with Down syndrome was often described as a "throwback," as were infants with a variety of congenital anomalies.

Western anthropologists' notion of cultural evolution was directed mainly at other (non-Western) societies. At the top of the cultural hierarchy were the highly "civilized" peoples, mostly the Europeans who popularized the concept. At the bottom were the more primitive "savages," or "natives." Everyone else was placed in between and was thought of as having the potential to climb up the cultural ladder.

Inherent in this and other cultural models was the anthropologists' assumption that the natural progression of culture is upward. Indeed, the idea of a hierarchy of cultures existed well before anthropology was even accepted as a scientific discipline. In 1824, half a century before Warren wrote his textbook, Thomas Jefferson wrote:

> Let a philosophic observer commence a journey from the *savages* of the Rocky Mountains, eastwardly towards the seacoast. These he would observe in the earliest stages of association, living under no law but that of nature, subsisting and covering themselves with the flesh and skins of wild beasts. He would next find those on the frontiers in the *pastoral stage,* raising domestic animals to supply the defects of hunting. Then succeed our own *semi-barbarous* citizens, the pioneers of the advance of *civilization,* and so in his progress he would meet the gradual shades of *improving* man until he would reach his, as yet, most improved state in our seaport towns. This, in fact, is equivalent to a survey, in time, of the progress of man from the infancy of creation to the present day.[8]

Jefferson's categories foreshadow those of the early anthropologists. In many ways, our thinking has not moved very far beyond this framework. Books with such titles as *Affable Savages*[9] and commonly used terms—such as *developed* and *under-developed nation,* or First World versus Third World—perpetuate the idea of cultural movement toward something perceived as "better" or more "civilized." Moreover, the direction of this movement is generally toward a culture that looks a great deal like our own. While these ideas are largely discredited among modern anthropologists, they continue to exist in the minds of most Americans when contrasting U.S. society with other societies, particularly those that are less technological.

Traditionally, Americans have expected their schools to socialize all students into traditional Euro-American, upper- and middle-class culture, generally referred to as "the best of Western civilization." While it is true that great art, beautiful music, and meaningful literature have been given to the world by Western peoples, it is equally clear that Western contributions do not represent all that is great and beautiful in the world.

Sociology

Anthropologists are not the only social scientists who have been concerned with the idea of culture. Sociologists also study culture, but from a slightly different angle. Rather than thinking of culture in terms of whole societies, they are more likely to think of it in terms of various competing social groups within a society. Sociologists have developed a number of concepts that are useful when discussing cultural pluralism. Some of these terms are used interchangeably and often cause confusion. Five terms commonly used to describe social groups that share important cultural elements, but are smaller than a whole society, are *subculture, microculture, minority group, ethnic group,* and *people of color.*

Subculture

A subculture is a social group with shared characteristics that distinguish it from the larger cultural group or society in which it is embedded. Generally, a subculture is distinguished either by a unifying set of ideas and/or practices (such as the corporate culture or the drug culture) or by a demographic characteristic (such as the adolescent culture or the culture of poverty).[10]

Microculture

Microculture also refers to a social group that shares distinctive traits, values, and behaviors that set it apart from the parent macroculture of which it is a part. Although the terms *microculture* and *subculture* are often used interchangeably, *microculture* seems to imply a greater linkage with the parent culture. Microcultures often mediate (interpret and transmit) the ideas, values, and institutions of the larger political community.[11] Thus, for example, the family, the workplace, or the classroom can be thought of as a microculture embedded in the larger culture of the neighborhood, the business, or the school. These larger macrocultures are themselves embedded in larger regional, national, or professional cultures. Thus, a particular entity, such as the school, may be simultaneously a macroculture (the culture of the school as a model of society) and a microculture (the culture of the particular school).

Minority Group

A minority group is a social group that occupies a subordinate position in a society. Wagley and Harris define a minority group as one that experiences discrimination and subordination within a society, is separated by physical or cultural traits disapproved of by the dominant group, shares a sense of collective identity and common burdens, and is characterized by marriage within the group.[12] However, characterizing minority groups based on these criteria sometimes leads to confusion and inaccuracy. For example, women are often referred to as a minority group, because they are thought to be oppressed, even though they constitute more than half the general population and do not, as a rule, marry within their group. Similarly, when students who are African American, Native American, or Hispanic constitute a majority of the population in a particular school, the school is often referred to as a "majority-minority school."

Ethnic Group

An ethnic group is composed of people who share a common heritage. When asked to complete the statement, "I am . . ." using as many descriptors as possible to define themselves, the statements that reflect identification with a collective or reference group are often indicative of one's ethnic identity. When one responds that she or he is Jewish, Polish, or Italian, that person is identifying with people who share a common heritage, history, celebrations, and traditions and who enjoy similar foods and might speak a common language other than English. A sense of peoplehood, or the feeling that one's own destiny is somehow linked with others who share this same knowledge, reflects identification with an ethnic group.

People of Color

The term *people of color* refers to nonwhite minority group members but reflects recent demographic realities of the United States. People of color refers to such groups as African Americans, Mexican Americans, Puerto Ricans, and Native Americans and is preferred over *ethnic minority,* because these groups are, in many schools and communities, the majority rather than the minority.

As the United States and its schools grow increasingly complex with respect to cultural difference, many voices are beginning to criticize the use of collective terminology, such as *people of color.* These voices call for an awareness and understanding of specific ethnic, racial, religious, and other groups. In this effort, it is recognized that the term *Hispanic,* for example, is only an umbrella term for a number of Spanish-speaking ethnic groups, including Puerto Rican, Spanish, Salvadoran, Mexican, and many others. Similarly, the term *Native American* is an umbrella term for an enormous variety of tribal identities (more than 400 officially recognized by the Bureau of Indian Affairs) and includes the indigenous people of Alaska and Hawaii. Clearly, these groups can be as different from one another as they can be from the mainstream society.

When school programs are instituted to increase awareness and understanding of specific groups, they are called *group-specific* approaches and stress information about a particular group of people, usually identified by a single characteristic, such as race, ethnicity, religion, or gender. While these approaches have much to offer, several problems are associated with them. First, while attending to differences between one group and another, they still do not attend to important differences *within* groups. Consequently, they tend to give the impression that all people identified as belonging to a group (all Mexican-Americans, all Jews, etc.) are alike. This is clearly not the case. Second, because these programs usually focus on students of certain *samples* of the larger group (e.g., *urban* African Americans, *white* middle-class girls, Navajo *who live on reservations*), they may promote stereotypes. Third, group-specific programs, because of their intentionally narrow focus, cannot attend to the wide array of differences that collectively control the teaching-learning process.

Cross-Cultural Psychology

In contrast to the group-specific approach to understanding diversity is another, more inclusive approach that attempts to deal directly with the complex nature of cultural phenomena. Called a culture-general approach, it derives mainly from principles developed in the field of cross-cultural psychology and training. While cross-cultural psychologists share with anthropologists and sociologists a general definition of *culture,* they are mostly interested in the effect of culture on the *individual.* In addition to describing how culture affects an individual, they have also been developing a variety of training strategies to help individuals anticipate and deal effectively with problems that may arise in intercultural interaction. Figure 3.1 illustrates the major focus of anthropologists, sociologists, and cross-cultural psychologists.

Group-Specific vs. Culture-General Frameworks

It is important to understand the distinction between group-specific and culture-general knowledge. A *culture-general* concept is one that is universal and applies to all cultural groups, as seen in the following example.

The way an individual "learns how to learn" depends on the socialization processes used by his or her culture. That is, learning style is related to socialization processes. This very general statement can be regarded as a cultural "universal." It doesn't tell us anything about an individual's preferred learning style, but it does tell us that everyone has one and that it is formed by socialization experiences. Thus, knowing that socialization experiences vary from culture to culture, it follows that learning styles also vary between cultures. Such a culture-general concept is valuable to teachers in that it warns them of the possibility that there will be many variations in learning style among their students, perhaps as many as there are cultural

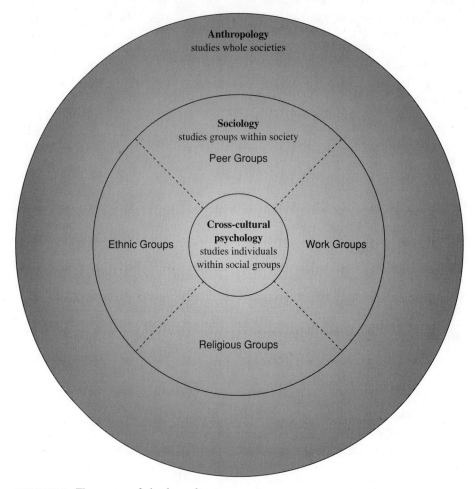

FIGURE 3.1. Three ways of viewing culture.

groups represented in their classroom. So warned, a teacher presiding over a multi-cultural classroom would be alert for signs of learning style differences and would attempt to develop alternative lesson plans or instructional approaches that match these differences.

A *group-specific* concept, on the other hand, is one that applies to a specific cultural group. For example, both Hawaiian and Native American children histori-cally have acquired most of their knowledge, values, and attitudes about the world through direct participation in real-world events. Their teachers were usually other members of their family or tribe who were also participating in those events. Thus, direct participation, or *in-context learning,* became their familiar and preferred learning style.

Contrast this against the more formal schooling given to most urban and subur-ban white middle-class children. These children are sent to a captive learning envi-ronment (school), where specially trained teachers who are usually total strangers use books and other abstract learning tools to provide indirect, or *out-of-context,* learning about real-world events. In a classroom where both cultural groups are present, the teacher should anticipate learning style differences (culture-general knowledge), try to assess the culture-specific learning styles that are present, and adapt instruction accordingly.

In short, teachers in multicultural classrooms need to have both culture-general and group-specific knowledge. That is, they need to know that certain cultural universals (e.g., learning style differences) are at work in every multicultural classroom and then to gather—through observation, inquiry, and study—the particulars of those variations, so that they can plan and deliver instruction that is appropriate to *all* their students. To focus solely on group-specific knowledge, which is always based on *samples* taken from a target culture, is to ignore both individual differences within that group and the cultural universals that cut across groups. Likewise, to focus solely on culture-general knowledge is to ignore the differences that separate groups and that provide a map for assessing and adapting instruction.

Themes from Cross-Cultural Psychology

Cross-cultural psychology also offers teachers the following set of themes, or principles, that can be used to study cross-cultural interactions in the classroom.[13]

1. *People tend to communicate their cultural identity to others in the broadest possible terms.* For instance, on meeting someone for the first time, you may communicate many things about yourself—for example, your age, your nationality, your ethnic group, your religious affiliation, where you grew up, and the nature of your family. At other times, you may describe your status at work or in the community, your health, your social class, or the way you have come to understand your gender. Each of these sources of cultural identity carries with it associated rules for behavior. We offer such information to new acquaintances because, by doing so, we give them cultural clues regarding what to expect from us and how to interact with us. People have multiple "cultures" influencing them at various times. Every one of us may thus be considered multicultural.

2. *Because we are all multicultural, our cultural identity is always changing.* As our environmental circumstances and group associations change, we adapt our cultural identity and behavior accordingly. For example, in certain circumstances, our gender-related knowledge and beliefs may be predominant; at another time, our religious beliefs; at still another, our ethnicity. Thus, our multicultural nature leads to behavioral variations that are sometimes difficult to understand and appreciate.

3. *While culture is complex and variable, it is nevertheless patterned.* Culture helps individuals make sense of their world and, thereby, to develop routinized behavioral patterns to fit different environments. Such common phrases as "the culture of the organization," "the culture of the community," and "the culture of the society" refer to the fact that culture is not patterned simply for an individual but also for a setting, a community, or a society as a whole. When viewed from the outside, these patterns can appear quite complicated and difficult to understand, yet each of us moves quite easily among the cultural patterns with which we are familiar. When confronted by someone whose behavior is *not* familiar, it is the responsibility of the outsider to listen, to observe, and to

inquire closely enough so that the patterns of that person (or social group or society) become evident and understandable. To do so decreases the possibility of misunderstanding and conflict and increases the possibility of new and useful understanding and appreciation.

4. *Interactions with other cultures can be viewed as a resource for understanding.* Culturally different encounters help prepare individuals to deal more effectively with the complexity that is increasingly a part of their lives. In short, the number of cultural variables we learn to accommodate will determine our ability to navigate within a fast-moving, ever changing society.

5. *Behavior should be judged in relation to its context.* This means that observable behavior cannot be understood apart from the context in which it occurs. Seen outside its context, another's "different" behavior can, at best, seem meaningless and, at worst, profoundly misinterpreted. Contextual inquiry allows us to be more accurate in our judgments of others. Consider the example of an 11-year-old boy who became rowdy and disruptive in the classroom every day about 2:00 in the afternoon. Inevitably, the teacher sent the child to the office, where he was promptly sent home. Defined in terms of the middle-class cultural context of the school, this was definitely a troubled child, and he was so labeled by nearly all the adults in the building. Eventually, however, an astute counselor recognized a pattern and did some inquiry. It turned out that the mother's boyfriend came home every day about 2:45, often quite drunk and abusive. In his rage, the boyfriend frequently abused the mother. The boy, quite accurately understanding the cultural pattern of the school, figured out that his misbehavior would result in his being sent home and that, if he was sent home by 2:30, he would arrive before the boyfriend did and thus be able to protect his mother. Thus, the so-called troubled boy's behavior makes sense, and he becomes something of a hero because he has found a way to protect his mother. Again, without full knowledge of the context, behavior is often meaningless or badly misinterpreted.

6. *Persons holding a multicultural perspective continually strive to find common ground between individuals.* In a sense, we must strive to be bifocal. That is, we must be able to see the similarities among people, as well as their differences. While it is the differences that tend to stand out and separate people, it is precisely in our similarities where a common meeting point can be found. A multicultural perspective permits disagreement without anyone necessarily being wrong. If culture in all its complexity is understood as an individual's attempt to navigate the river of life, then cultural differences can be understood simply as pragmatic acts of navigation and can be judged accordingly. In this view, cultural differences become tolerable and the we-they or us-them debate is avoided. There are no winners and losers. We are all in this together. Either we all win—or we all lose.

THE CULTURE-LEARNING PROCESS

As previously stated, individuals tend to identify themselves in a broad manner and in terms of many physical and social attributes. For example, a young man might identify himself as an attractive, athletic Asian American who intends to be a doctor and live in upper-class society. It is important to note that others also identify individuals according to these attributes and that interactions among individuals are often shaped by such identifications. Incorporated into Figure 3.2 are twelve sources of cultural knowledge that research indicates influence teaching and learning. Who learns what, and how and when it is learned, will be briefly described in the following sections and further illustrated and discussed in later chapters.

What Is Learned: The Sources of Cultural Knowledge

Race

Race is a very amorphous term. Biologically speaking, it refers to the clustering of inherited physical characteristics that favor adaptation to a particular ecological area. However, *race* is culturally defined in the sense that different societies emphasize different sets of physical characteristics when referring to the same race. In fact, the term is so imprecise that it has even been used to refer to a wide variety of

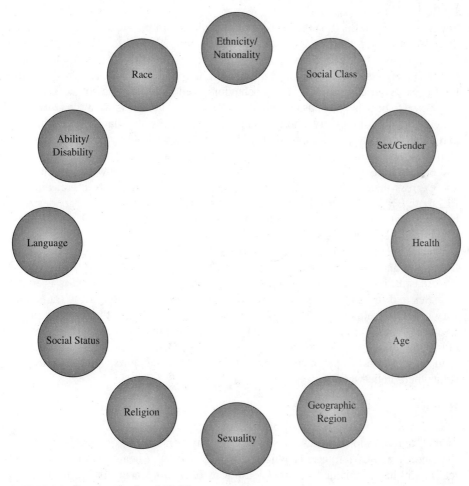

FIGURE 3.2. Sources of cultural identity.

categories that are not physical—such as linguistic categories (the *English-speaking race*), religious categories (the *Jewish* race), national categories (the *Italian* race), and even somewhat mythological categories (the *Teutonic* race).[14] Although *race* has often been defined as a biological category, it has been argued that race as a biological concept is of little use, because there are no "pure" races.[15] Furthermore, as Yetman notes, "Many groups possess physically identifiable characteristics that do not become the basis for racial distinctions [and] . . . criteria selected to make racial distinctions in one society may be overlooked or considered insignificant or irrelevant by another. For instance, in much of Latin America skin color and the shape of the lips, important differentiating criteria in the United States, are much less important than are hair texture, eye color, and stature. A person defined as black in Georgia or Michigan might be considered white in Peru."[16] Thus, race is an important characteristic, not because of its biology but because of its cultural meaning in any given social group or society. In the United States, race is judged largely on the basis of skin color, which some people consider very meaningful and use as a criterion for extending or withholding privileges of various kinds.

Sex/Gender

Sex is culturally defined on the basis of a particular set of physical characteristics. In this case, however, the characteristics are related to male and female reproduction. Cultural meanings associated with gender are expressed in terms of socially valued behaviors (e.g., nurturing the young and providing food), which are assigned according to sex. Such culturally assigned behaviors eventually become so accepted that they come to be thought of as natural to that sex. Thus, gender is what it *means* to be male or female in a society, and gender roles are the sets of behaviors thought by a particular people to be "normal" and "good" when carried out by the assigned sex.

In all sociocultural groups, gender includes knowledge of a large set of rules and expectations governing what boys and girls should wear, how they should act and express themselves, and their "place" in the overall social structure. Further, Elizabeth Beardsley notes that any social or psychological trait can be "genderized" in favor of one sex or the other.[17] Thus, in the dominant society of the United States, active traits, such as aggressiveness, are genderized in favor of males and against females, while more passive traits, such as submissiveness, are genderized in favor of females and against males.

As is the case with cultural definitions of *race,* the specific set of traits assigned to males and females may vary by society. And, within a society, these traits may vary by ethnic, class, or religious group. For instance, on a continuum of submissiveness to men (a norm in U.S. society), many African American girls might fall closer to the *less* submissive end of the scale, many Hispanic girls might fall closer to the *more* submissive end, and many European-American girls would probably be somewhere in between.

Health

Health is culturally defined according to a particular group's view of what physical, mental, and emotional states constitute a healthy person. The "expert" opinion of the medical profession usually guides a society's view of health. Although a medical model has dominated cultural definitions of *health,* most disabilities (mental retardation, deafness, blindness, etc.) are not judged in terms of this model's norms.

Thus, it is possible to be a healthy blind or retarded person, nor would a person with cerebral palsy be considered "sick."

In the United States and most of the industrialized world, the prevailing health system is almost totally biomedical. However, alternative systems, such as acupuncture, holistic medicine, and faith healing, are available, and the acceptance of alternative systems varies widely both within and between social groups.[18] In other societies (e.g., China), what we deem "alternative" medicine may, in fact, be the dominant model, and our ideas of biomedicine may be operating at the fringes. The cultural meanings associated with health depend on which model, or which combination of models, an individual or family group accepts. For example, a 4-year-old Russian child, who recently immigrated with her family to the United States, suddenly suffered a high fever and flu symptoms. The child's nursery school teacher, who was European-American and middle class, wanted the family to take the child to the doctor immediately for an antibiotic. The child's grandmother, on the other hand, who was the family expert on medical matters, prescribed a traditional treatment: the child should be put to bed and surrounded by lit candles, and family members should engage in prayer. In this case, the grandmother was the final authority, and the child got better.

Ability/Disability

As with definitions of *health, ability* and *disability* are culturally defined according to society's view about what it means to be physically, emotionally, and mentally "able." The categories of "ability" and "disability" refer to a wide variety of mental and physical characteristics: intelligence, emotional stability, impairment of sensory and neural systems, and impairment of movement. The social significance of these characteristics may vary by setting as well. For example, the terms *learning disability* and *learning disabled* are primarily used with reference to schooling and are rarely used outside of school. Indeed, it may be that the current emphasis on learning disability in American schools is primarily a reflection of a technologically complex society's concern about literacy. In developing nations, specific learning disabilities among those who are otherwise unimpaired are of little concern. In fact, this "condition," as a category of exceptional individuals, is nonexistent in most of the world.

The cultural meaning of ability and disability is related to both the needs and the public perception of the *ability* or *disability* itself. For example, the "culture of the Deaf" "needs" a shared, rule-bound system of communication (sign language), as well as shared traditions and values among its members. However, the public acceptance of deaf individuals is far less positive than for those who are gifted. This can be seen in the privileges accorded each group in schools. Thus, school experience might enhance the self-esteem of a gifted student while threatening that of a student who is deaf. In the United States, the reaction to ability/disability hovers closely around a socially defined norm: we favor bright individuals but often exclude those who show evidence of extreme intelligence; we favor those who "overcome" their disabilities but often exclude those who cannot.

Social Class

Social class is culturally defined on the basis of the criteria on which a person or social group may be ranked in relation to others in a stratified (layered) society. There is considerable debate about the criteria that determine social class. Some identify class membership primarily in terms of wealth and its origin (inherited or newly earned). Other commonly used criteria include the amounts of one's education, power, and influence.[19]

Class structures vary widely among societies and social groups in terms of their rigidity and their importance to one's life chances.[20] In some societies, such as Britain and India, the class structure is fairly rigid and largely determines the opportunities one will have. In these societies, one is truly "born into" a particular social class and tends to remain there. In others, the structure is not so rigid; although one may be born into a particular social class, it is expected that one may move up by virtue of one's achievements. Societies also vary according to the value placed on "leaving" one's social class. In the United States, upward mobility is a value; in Britain, it is not as valued. The consequences of these attitudes are not always salutary. In the United States, for example, if individuals do not succeed in "moving up," the perception may be that something is "wrong" with them.

Social class differences are also tied to one's social expectations and cultural tastes. For example, to exhibit the childrearing practices, speech, and general tastes of the upper classes in such matters as dress, food, and housing can affect one's social image and, thereby, one's chances for upward mobility.

Ethnicity/Nationality

Ethnicity is culturally defined according to the knowledge, beliefs, and behavior patterns shared by people with the same history and the same language. Ethnicity carries a strong sense of "peoplehood"—that is, of loyalty to a "community of memory."[21] It is also related to the ecological niche in which an ethnic group has found itself and to adaptations people make to those environmental conditions.

The category of nationality is culturally defined on the basis of shared citizenship, which may or may not include a shared ethnicity. In the contemporary world, the population of most nations includes citizens (and resident noncitizens) who vary in ethnicity. While we are accustomed to this idea in the United States, we are sometimes unaware that it is also the case in other nations. Thus, we tend to identify all people from Japan as Japanese, all people from France as French, and so forth. Similarly, when American citizens of varying ethnic identities go abroad, they tend to be identified as "American." A tragic example of this misconception is the recent history of ethnic warfare in what used to be called Yugoslavia. Americans, in general, are unaware of the role that ethnicity may play in dividing people. Most of the conflicts that occur across the planet are the result of long-held ethnic strife and do not cross national boundaries.

Religion/Spirituality

Religion and *spirituality* are culturally defined on the basis of a shared set of ideas about the relationship of the earth and the people on it to a deity or deities and a shared set of rules for living and moral values that will enhance that relationship. A set of behaviors identified with worship is also commonly shared. Religious identity may include membership in a worldwide organized religion (e.g., Islam, Christianity, Judaism, Buddhism, Taoism) or in smaller (but also worldwide) sects belonging to each of the larger religions (e.g., Catholic or Protestant Christianity or Conservative, Reformed, or Hasidic Judaism). Religious identity may also include a large variety of spiritualistic religions, sometimes called pagan or Goddess religions, often but not always associated with indigenous peoples in the Americas and other parts of the world. Like ethnicity, religious affiliation can engender intense loyalty, a sense of belonging or community, and pride in a shared history. Because religious identity involves one's relationship with the earth and with forces perceived to be greater than oneself, the cultural meaning of *religion* is often expressed in terms of a rigid sense of righteousness and virtue that is linked to a belief in salvation or the possibility of an eternal life after death. It is thus often an extremely powerful determiner of behavior.

Geographic Location

Geographic location is culturally defined by the characteristics (topographical features, natural resources) of the ecological environment in which one lives. This includes the characteristics of one's neighborhood or community (rural, suburban, urban) and the natural and climatic features of one's region (mountainous, desert, plains, coastal, hot, cold, wet, dry). It has been argued that, in the United States, one's regional identity functions in the same way as one's national heritage.[22] Thus, southerners, westerners, and midwesterners are identified and often identify themselves as members of ethniclike groups, with the same kinds of loyalties, sense of community, and language traits. This is also the case in countries in other parts of the world.

The cultural meanings of geographic location are expressed in terms of the knowledge one has of how to survive in and use the resources of a particular area. This includes knowledge of what foods are "good" (and how to grow and harvest them), how to protect oneself from the natural elements and common dangers of the locality, and how to spend one's leisure time. It is important to note that this kind of knowledge also applies to the type of community one lives in. It is commonly acknowledged, for example, that "city people," "country people," and "suburban people" can be quite different from one another. The nature of that difference stems, in part, from their familiarity with and knowledge about how to live in a particular kind of community with particular resources and dangers.

Age

Age is culturally defined according to the length of time one has lived and the state of physical and mental development one has attained. Chronological age is measured in different ways by different social groups and societies. Some calculate it in calendar years, others by natural cycles (such as phases of the moon), and still others by the marking of major natural or social events.

Mental and physical development is also measured differentially, in much the same way and under many of the same circumstances as health is determined. Most humans view such development as a matter of "stages," but the nature and particular characteristics of each stage may differ widely. In most Western societies, for example, age cohort groups are usually identified as infancy, childhood, adolescence, adulthood, and old age. "Normal" development markers include the acquisition of motor and language skills (infancy and childhood), the ability to understand and use abstract concepts (childhood and adolescence), and the ability to assume responsibility for oneself and others (adolescence and adulthood). In other societies, these cohort groups differ. For example, in many non-Western societies, the cohort group we define as adolescents does not exist at all, and the classifications of childhood and old age are longer or shorter.

The cultural meaning of age is usually expressed in terms of the abilities and responsibilities attributed to it. Thus, in the United States, childhood is prolonged (hence, the category of adolescence) and adult responsibilities are not expected until at least age 18, if not age 21 or beyond. In other societies (and in the United States prior to the twentieth century), childhood is shorter, and adult responsibilities are assumed at younger ages.

Sexuality

Sexuality is culturally defined on the basis of particular patterns of sexual self-identification, behavior, and interpersonal relationships.[23] There is growing evidence that one's sexual orientation is, in part, a function of one's innate biological characteristics.[24] Culturally speaking, sexuality is tied to a number of factors: sexual behavior, gender identity (both internal and external), affiliation, and role behavior. Like health, sexuality has a variety of orientations. Because sexuality is frequently linked to one's deepest, most meaningful experiences (both religious and interpersonal), persons who deviate from socially approved norms are often socially ostracized and sometimes physically abused or even killed. This is currently the case with homosexuality in the United States, where the prevailing view of sexuality is bimodal: only male and female are identified as possibilities. In other societies, additional possibilities are available. The Lakota Sioux, for example, approve four sexual orientations: biological males who possess largely masculine traits, biological males who possess largely feminine traits, biological females who possess largely feminine traits, and biological females who possess largely masculine traits. The role of the female-identified male in Lakota society is called *berdache* and is accorded high honor as possessing multiple traits and characteristics. Berdache tend to be teachers and artists, and, if a berdache takes an interest in one's child or children, it is considered to be an advantage.

Language

The cultural definition of *language* is "a shared system of vocal sounds and/or non-verbal behaviors by which members of a group communicate with one another."[25] Language may be the most significant source of cultural learning, because it is through language that most other cultural knowledge is acquired. There are those who consider language and the category systems available in language *the* determiners of culture.[26]

Considerable research on the relation of brain function to language gives evidence that human beings are "hard wired" for language development at a particular stage in brain development.[27] That is, children who are in the company of other people appear to be "programmed" to learn whatever spoken language or sign system is used around them. Children even appear to invent their own language systems, complete with syntactical structures,[28] if no other language is available. It may also be that this "program" decreases in power (or disappears altogether) at a certain point, helping explain why it is more difficult for older children and adults to acquire a new language. Language is meaningful in terms of both its verbal properties (what we "name" things, people, ideas) and its nonverbal properties (its norms regarding interpersonal distance, meaningful gestures, and so forth). Because language literally represents reality, the types and meanings of verbal and nonverbal behavior in any society or social group reflect their experience with their surroundings and the ways in which they interact with it. More than any other characteristic, language is a window into another person's life.

Social Status

Social status is culturally defined on the basis of the prestige, social esteem, and/or honor accorded an individual or a group by other social groups or by society.[29] Social status cuts across the other categories, since every social group or society appears to construct hierarchies of honor, prestige, and value with which to "sort out" its members, often on the basis of such attributes as race, age, gender, and ability. In some cases, social status varies with social class; in many other cases, however, social class does not explain one's status in a social group or society. Thus, persons may occupy a high place in the class system in terms of income and power but not be accorded prestige or honor. The children of a newly wealthy family who can afford to send them to Harvard, for example, may have little prestige among the sons and daughters of inherited wealth. Similarly, there may be people accorded high status in the society who occupy relatively low class positions. In U.S. society, many entertainers and sports figures fit this description. Social status is normally expressed through social roles. Thus, status assigned to one's gender may determine the role one plays in any situation; one's health status may determine the role one plays as a "sick" person; one's social class status may determine the role one plays as a member of the upper, middle, or working class.

While there is some overlap among these twelve attributes of culture, the important point to remember is that each of them is culturally defined by a particular society or social group. The cultural identity of all individuals—their knowledge, attitudes, values, and skills—is formed through their experience with these twelve attributes. Such experience is gained through contact with socializing agents, such as one's family, church, workplace, and peer group, as well as the various mass media. These socializing agents can be thought of as "transmitters" of cultural attributes. It is through these socializing agents (depicted in Figure 3.3) that individuals acquire such cultural knowledge as defined by race, ethnicity, gender, language, and social class.

How Culture Is Learned: The Socializing Agents

It is important to understand that we acquire the specific knowledge, attitudes, skills, and values that form our cultural identity through a variety of socializing agents that mediate the sources of cultural knowledge and give them a particular "cultural spin." Thus, one's understanding of race, gender, social class, disability, age, sexuality, and so forth depends in part on their interpretation by the families, schools, neighborhoods, peer groups, workplaces, churches, and communities that one affiliates with at a particular time. Each of these socializing agents has its own slightly different interpretation of a particular cultural attribute, which it passes on to its members.

In contemporary social life, some socializing agents, such as families and peer groups, operate face-to-face, while others, such as the mass media, use technology to operate from a distance. Television, VCRs, and the recording industry, for example, exert significant influence on the self-perceived identity of many young people.

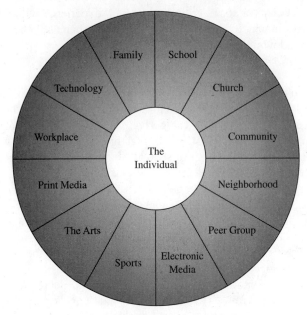

FIGURE 3.3. Socializing agents that transmit culture.

Referred to by some as the "third educator" (following family and school), television influences young peoples' acquisition of basic language and visual and aural skills. It also influences their ideas of "appropriate" dress, language, attitudes, and values. These media lessons not only affect young people's "picture" of themselves but also affect the picture that adults have of them.

The media also teach about older people. The visual image of the woman who has "fallen and can't get up" describes older people as weak, helpless, and slightly hysterical—in need of a product that will alert a caretaking agency that she needs help. Conversely, commercials for vitamins for older adults often depict them as active people—hiking, swimming, traveling—no doubt as a result of taking the promoted vitamins. Because we live in a nation that is growing older, one can expect more commercials defining older people as active rather than passive.

Other technological tools, such as computers and microwave ovens, appear to exert significant influence on our notions of time. Teachers and other human service providers have noticed, for example, that, over the past twenty years or so, both children and adults exhibit a shorter attention span. People seem to have become accustomed to receiving information and accomplishing tasks in shorter periods of time and are unwilling or unable to persevere in tasks that take a long time.[30]

Other socializing agents of note include the performing and visual arts and—in the United States, at least—sports. These are widely available carriers of cultural messages that help shape people's attitudes, values, and behavior. The aesthetic value of design, language, music, dance, and theatre, as well as ideals of moral and ethical behavior, are presented through the arts, and such behavioral ideals as good sportsmanship, personal achievement, and competition are taught through sports. It is also true that other qualities may be taught through these media; violence, for example, is an increasing part of movies, television, and sports. The contemporary nature of national sports teams as bottom-line businesses comes increasingly into competition with our professed value of "sportsmanlike" competition.

Figure 3.3 provided a visual overview of how cultural knowledge is filtered by a variety of socializing agents to individuals through experience. Although sources of cultural knowledge (race, language, sexuality, etc.) are universal and appear in all cultures, the socializing agents (family, schools, media, etc.) that transmit them vary considerably from one culture to another. In most industrialized societies, for example, a wide variety of socializing agents bombard people daily, often with contradictory messages. In agriculturally oriented societies, on the other hand, a few primary socializing agents (e.g., family and gender group) may share the bulk of the culture-filtering process. As a result, individuals in different cultures develop very different worldviews.

When Culture Is Learned

One way to begin to understand how individuals acquire cultural knowledge, attitudes, values, and skills from the social groups with whom they have meaningful contact is to look closely at the concept of socialization. From the point of view of the outside observer (including such people as sociologists and anthropologists, who use the term more than most people), socialization is "the imposition of social patterns of behavior."[31] These patterns include the acquisition of a particular language, the knowledge of social roles and role behavior, and understandings of all aspects of the physical and social environment and normative behaviors toward it. Berger and Berger note that "the socialized part of the self is commonly called identity."[32]

There is some consensus that the processes of socialization occur at three stages of life: (1) primary socialization, which involves the socialization of infants and young children by families and other early caregivers; (2) secondary socialization, which, in most contemporary societies, involves the neighborhood, the religious affiliation, the peer group, and the school, as well as television and other influences that surround and come into the home; and (3) adult socialization, which involves the socialization of adults into roles, settings, and situations for which they may have been unprepared by primary and secondary socialization (for example, taking a new job, marrying, moving to a new area, or becoming a parent).[33] These stages of the socialization process are not entirely discrete but, rather, interact with one another in our lives. What we learn as children can be reinforced or modified (for good or ill) by what we learn as we grow up and have more experiences. In each of socialization's three stages, the purpose is to teach the learner the habits of mind and action that will make him or her a loyal and functional member of a particular group. The use of the word *habits* in this context is important, for it points to another aspect of socialization, which is that the learner should internalize socially approved patterns of behavior, so that he or she will voluntarily—and with little thought or effort—think and behave in an appropriate manner.

One important aspect of the internalization of knowledge, beliefs, attitudes, values, and behaviors is that the process by which they are acquired is, in a sense, a secret. Most people remember very little about their own socialization, the assumptions they make about the world, what has conditioned them, and the various cultural patterns that have become so ingrained in their makeup as to become nearly invisible.

Primary Socialization: Cultural Similarities

Most people share some aspects of primary socialization that are common to all or most Americans, at least those who have been born here and speak English as a native language. Consider, for example, the rules they have learned about eating. When food is put before most Americans, they expect that it will be placed on a plate or in a bowl on a table at which they expect to sit on chairs. Once seated, the American automatically reaches for utensils called forks, knives, and spoons; cuts meat with the forks in the left hand and the knife in the right hand (except for left-handed folks); and then switches the fork to the right hand to carry the food to the mouth. In the same situation, a British person expects the plates, bowls, table, and chairs; cuts meat with the fork and knife in the same hands as an American; but then does *not* switch the fork to the right hand but continues to use it in the left hand. In the same situation, a Japanese person may expect that the food will be placed on a low table, at which he or she will kneel, and the utensils used to carry food to the mouth will be two long, slender wooden or plastic implements that many Westerners call chopsticks. In all cases, the people eating will not consciously think about these expectations and behaviors; they will simply expect and do them because they are "right," "appropriate," and "proper."[34] Within this general "American" set of rules for eating (as within any large nation-state), however, are many variations. How formally we set our tables, how many utensils we use, whether our plates are served for us or we serve ourselves (and how many plates we use), what kinds of food we eat, what we commonly use as a beverage (water, milk, wine, soda or pop, coffee, tea) and whether we bring the beverage to the table in its original container or in a pitcher, all depend somewhat on the region in which we live; the ethnic, social class, and religious origins of our parents; our ages; and so forth. No matter what the particulars of our personal and family "rules" for eating, however, we believe they are "normal," partly because we have internalized them.

Another example of both the secret nature of primary socialization and the degree to which knowledge acquired through primary socialization is internalized concerns the way people learn to speak English. Do you remember how you learned to talk? If you took another language in school, perhaps it was difficult for you—but your *own* language, now that was easy! Or so it seems. It might, however, be very difficult for you to teach a non-English speaker to correctly pronounce the sentence "Can you tell me the time?" when that person might more easily say, "Can you dell me the dime?" What might you tell him or her about English that would correct the pronunciation? How would you teach someone to make the correct sounds? If you have determined that a little puff of air passes out of the mouth when the "t" sound is made in such words as *tell* and *time* that is not passed in words beginning with the letter *d,* you are on the right track to discovering the secret. Correct speakers of English aspirate their stops; that is, some air passes out of the mouth when they speak such letters as *t, p,* and *k.* We call this a secret because, while most of us do this quite regularly and easily, you probably are not able to describe it to others. This practice has become so much a part of your behavior that you take it for granted; it must be consciously thought about in order to describe it to others. This is not the end of the secret, though. If you think about it, you will realize that English speakers aspirate their stops only at the beginning and in the middle of words, not at the end. We do not aspirate the t in *hit, bit, and cat.*

That you have obviously learned these rules is quite clear; you use them all the time. How these rules were learned, however, is considerably less clear. They were probably not taught in formal sessions with your parents or by reading appropriate language texts. Indeed, you may not have been able to talk about them at all, because you did not have the language you needed, such as "aspirate" and "stops." Rather, these rules are typically learned by trial and error as part of our learning to speak our native language. This particular language pattern is often hidden from us, as are its results. The same is true for other aspects of cultural learning; they, too, can be conceived as patterns that are hidden from our conscious thought and behavior.

Few people receive formal education in how to be an appropriate member of any particular cultural group. Rather, people are culturally socialized by observing others, through trial and error, and by continuous reinforcement. In other words, cultural knowledge, such as the "rules" for speaking and eating, are learned through experience, not cognitively. Consequently, it becomes difficult for many people to speak comfortably about the cross-cultural problems they might encounter. One of the difficulties people may face in their intercultural encounters, then, is that they feel uncomfortable or unsure in a given situation *and are unable to talk about the problem.* Thus, they may try to avoid situations in which they feel discomfort— certainly *not* one of the long-term goals of multicultural education. A reasonable goal of multicultural education, then, is for people to become more knowledgeable and thus conversant about the issues at play in cross-cultural interaction.

Secondary Socialization

Perhaps the most important source of secondary socialization in most people's lives is the school. It is in school that individuals are often introduced to ideas and values that differ from those they acquired at home. In fact, one of the purposes of education is to "liberate" individuals from the narrow confines of their primary socialization—in a sense, to expand their cultural identities. The difficulties of this process of alteration, however, should not be minimized, especially when the cultural knowledge, beliefs, values, and skills of the school are in conflict with those of the home. Still, teachers often find themselves attempting to serve as "change agents" of their students' cultural identities.

The main goal of most school socialization in the United States traditionally has been to teach the "rules" of middle-class attitudes, values, and behavior. This cultural socialization to the middle class is no less a secret than the varied cultural socialization of individual families. The school, like the family, does not make cultural socialization explicit; it is simply taken for granted as "normal." Thus, few people ever take a formal course in the variations of cultural knowledge that exist, and they almost never examine their own cultural patterns in contrast to others. Few ever learn why they behave the way they do or why they think many of the things they think. Fewer still ever evaluate the assumptions they make. People thus generally lack the concepts and vocabulary with which to talk about these things, yet cultural patterns taken as "given," along with the assumptions, beliefs, and behavior associated with them, often guide us, whether we are aware of it or not.

There is yet another aspect of socialization that must be analyzed: the power of early socialization when viewed from the "inside." It is certainly true that, as we grow up and meet people outside of our childhood social groups, we learn that there are many ways to interact with the physical and social environment. As children, however, we experience the imposition of patterns of socialization as absolute.[35]

There are two simple reasons for this absoluteness: (1) the power of adults in relation to young children and (2) the ignorance of any other possibilities.[36] Berger and Berger describe the nature of this experience in the following way:

> Psychologists differ in their view as to whether the child experiences the adults at this stage of life as being very much under his control (because they are generally so responsive to his needs) or whether he feels continually threatened by them (because he is so dependent upon them). However this may be, there can be no question that, objectively speaking, adults have overwhelming power in the situation. The child can, of course, resist them, but the probable outcome of any conflict is a victory on the part of the adults. It is they who control most of the rewards that he craves and most of the sanctions that he fears. Indeed, the simple fact that most children are eventually socialized affords simple proof of this proposition. At the same time, it is obvious that the small child is ignorant of any alternatives to the patterns that are being imposed upon him. The adults confront him with a world—for him, it is *the* world. It is only much later than he discovers that there are alternatives to this particular world, that his parents' world is relative in space and time, and that quite different patterns are possible.[37]

SOME RESULTS OF SOCIALIZATION

Ethnocentrism

Because of the absoluteness with which the child experiences socialization, he or she may begin to share the human tendency to view the world from his or her own perspective and may begin to believe that his or her way is certainly the *best* way. This belief is called *ethnocentrism* and is an almost universal result of socialization. Thus, using our example of eating behaviors, when confronted by someone from Bangladesh who eats with his or her fingers, most Americans will consider such behavior not as simply different but as *beneath* or *lesser than* their own. While a certain degree of ethnocentrism binds people together, it can also become a serious obstacle when those who have internalized different ideas and behaviors begin to interact with one another.

One major expression of ethnocentrism is a strong *resistance to change*. People resist change under the best of circumstances, as illustrated in the story of the Wheat Religion people in Chapter 1. If people believe that their way of doing things is best and if they have the power to choose to continue in familiar ways, why should they change? Consider the case of the United States and the adoption of metrics. At this time, *all* other countries of the world have adopted the metric system as their primary means of measurement. The United States is the only country to hold on to something its citizens feel is very dear to them, despite the difficulties it causes travelers, manufacturers, and others who must interact in a variety of ways with people from other nations.

While these examples may seem relatively innocuous, other examples of ethnocentric behavior are not. There is, for example, the current insistence on the part of many educators and politicians that we need to "strengthen" a Eurocentric curriculum in our schools on the grounds that a curriculum based on "the best of Western civilization" is the most valuable preparation any student could have. However, there is increasing interest among some to consider alternate perspectives. The growing debate over Afrocentric curriculum efforts is, for example, one that should be examined quite closely. Similarly, there is increasing pressure to use national, standardized, paper-and-pencil, computer-scored testing, on the grounds that it is "objective" (a Western idea) and, therefore, fair. The point is that having the power to choose whether or not you will adapt to new ways of thinking about and doing things is an important factor in how one exercises one's ethnocentric beliefs.

Another result of socialization is that we learn to literally *perceive* the world and to *categorize* information about people and things in our environment in particular ways. Perception and categorization are both cognitive processes that are shaped by socialization.

People receive millions of bits of information every day through their senses. To think that people can respond to every piece of information is expecting too much; a person's physical and emotional systems would be overwhelmed. Because of the need to simplify things, people organize their world into categories; into each category, they put items that share similar characteristics. People then generally respond to the category to which an individual item belongs.

Perception

Perception is the stimulation of the sense organs: that is, what people report seeing, hearing, feeling, tasting, and smelling. While no two people have exactly the same physiological structure and, therefore, no two people perceive stimuli identically, those with healthy nervous systems tend to perceive similar things in the environment in similar ways. Physicists, for example, tell us that the human eye can distinguish more than 8 million colors, as distinguished by variations in wavelength. There is no practical reason, nor is it humanly possible, to consider all these fine variations of shade and hue, let alone to react to each individual color. Individuals, therefore, need a schema with which to group colors. The most familiar to you is probably the one based on the spectrum in which red, orange, yellow, green, blue, indigo, and violet are the major colors. When asked about the color of the sky, a Westerner's response typically is "blue." A sapphire is blue, oceans depicted on a map are blue, and robins' eggs are blue. Grass, however, is green, as are the leaves of most trees and the inside of a kiwi fruit.

In traditional Japanese language, however, the term "aoi" refers to colors that span blue and green wavelengths. When asked the color of the sky, a Japanese individual's response would be "aoi." When asked the color of grass, the response would again be "aoi." How would you explain this? Certainly, the entire Japanese population is not color-blind. Rather, whereas Euro-Americans have learned to place these stimuli into different schemata, traditional Japanese have learned to place them in the same one.

Categorization

Clearly, sense perception alone is not sufficient. We also need to make sense out of the busy world around us. This is the point at which people use schemata. Another term for such schemata is *category,* and categorization is the cognitive process by which human beings simplify their world by grouping similar stimuli. That meaning usually is given definition by cultural knowledge acquired through socialization. What kind of categories we use, how narrow or broad they are, and what meanings are attached to them are all shaped by culture and acquired through socialization. A good example of the relation between perception and categorization can be found in the case of the dog: how people perceive the animal and how they have learned to respond to the stimuli. While all people "see," or perceive, the dog in a similar way, they think about it differently. Most Westerners think of dogs as pets, companions, and, in some cases, as important members of their families. A traditional Muslim, on the other hand, confronted by the same creature, would consider the dog a filthy, lowly animal and something to be avoided at all costs—similar to the reaction a North American might have to a pig. Some Filipinos or Pacific Islanders, on the other hand, may place a dog in the category of food. It is not uncommon to find dog meat as part of the human diet in many parts of the world.

The concept of a *prototype image* is a critical one in the analysis of categories. For most categories that humans create, there is one set of attributes or criteria that best characterizes the members of that category. In other words, there is a clear example of what the category encompasses. This becomes a "summary" of the group and is what is most often thought of when the category is mentioned. For instance, when asked to think about a bird, a certain prototypic image comes to one's mind. For most readers of this book, the prototypic image of a bird might be a creature about 8 or 9 inches long (beak to tail feathers), brown or perhaps reddish, that has feathers, flies, and nests in trees. The image conjured up probably is not of a turkey, a penguin, an ostrich, or even a chicken. For someone socialized in or near the jungles of South America, the prototypic image of a bird might be larger and more colorful, since those birds that we call exotic (e.g., parrots) are part of their everyday world. However, robins, parrots, and penguins have all the critical attributes that characterize members of the bird family; they all have feathers, beaks, and hollow or lightweight bones, and they all lay eggs. Teachers must examine what their own prototype image of a student is and how they will respond to those who do not fit neatly into this image.

Stereotypes

Categories help people simplify the world around them. That is, people put stimuli that have common characteristics into one category and then respond to the group. People do not, for instance, respond to each and every chair or table when they walk into a room but refer to them in their broader context of chairs, tables, or furniture. People respond in a similar manner in their interactions with people. *Stereotypes* are examples of categories of people. Socially constructed categories designed to simplify the identification of individuals who are in some way "other" frequently become negative stereotypes associated with groups. In this case, the processes of perception and categorization combine with ethnocentrism to create a potentially harmful situation. Although any cultural group may teach its members to categorize other groups either positively or negatively, most stereotypes end up as negative labels placed on individuals simply because they are members of a particular group.

In the most general sense, the word *stereotype* refers to any summary generalization that obscures the differences *within* a group.[38] Stereotypes obtain their power by providing categories that appear to encode a significant amount of information in a concise manner and help us avoid having to pay serious attention to all the sensory data available around us. Negative stereotypes also enable us to keep our ethnocentric ideas intact by preventing us from "seeing" contradictory evidence before our very eyes. For example, it is much easier and quicker to think of all girls as stereotypically "weak" and/or "passive" than it is to notice that at least some of the girls in our classroom are stronger and more aggressive than some of the boys. Indeed, if we do notice such a thing, we tend to label those girls as "unfeminine," thus helping us avoid the larger task of accurately differentiating one girl from another and allowing us to maintain a cultural value that teaches that boys are supposed to be strong and aggressive, while girls are not. Stereotypic conceptions of others can be acquired through both early and later socialization and are powerful insofar as they promote group solidarity and ethnocentric beliefs.

Some Limits on Socialization

While perception and categorization both depend, in part, on the cultural knowledge and meanings associated with the physical and social environment in which a child is socialized, and while early socialization is a powerful factor in the development of identity, it is also the case that the power of socialization has limits. Three of these are particularly important to educators. First, socialization is limited to some extent by the nature of the child as a physical organism. For example, while an infant or a very young child can learn any language and any particular pattern of living, it is not the case that any child can be taught beyond his or her biological limits. Socialization to color wavelength categories, for example, may be limited by color blindness to red and green. Similarly, socialization to musical sounds will not necessarily produce an operatic singer. However, sensory limits in one area may be, and often are, compensated for by increased attention to other senses, as in the case of people with hearing limitations.

Second, because socialization is an unending process that is never completely finished, its powers of control are never absolute. Because a child is socialized according to one set of patterns (language, situational behavior, understanding of role, categorization) does not mean that he or she cannot learn new patterns. The extension of socialization beyond one's childhood knowledge is one of the chief purposes of formal schooling.

Third, socialization is limited in its power, because human beings are not simply passive recipients of socialization but always act on that socialization. Individuals resist or reject accepted norms, they reinterpret accepted norms, and they create new kinds of normative behavior. Thus, socialization can be seen not as an all-powerful force that totally molds the human creature but, rather, as a transactional process through which individuals are shaped but not totally determined. Your future students might become Nobel Prize winners, shuttle astronauts, or famous inventors.

Each of these limits on socialization is a resource on which educators can build. However, as John Dewey noted repeatedly, the most effective learning takes place when it begins with what the child already knows and moves on from there.[39] Thus, it is important for teachers to understand not only the nature and purpose of cultural socialization in general but also the specifics of the cultural patterns to which they and their students have been socialized.

UNDERSTANDING CULTURAL DIFFERENCES

Variations in Cultural Environments: Returning to Grover's Corners

Figure 3.4 summarizes our discussion of the culture-learning process and points up its complexity in multicultural societies, such as the United States. Although the sources of cultural knowledge are the same for all societies, each society—indeed, each community—varies considerably in the number and character of its socializing agents. Thus, in a relatively simple society, such as the Maasai of Kenya, the sources of cultural knowledge shown in the model will be transmitted through very few socializing agents—most notably, the family and members of other families in the community. Because these families have nearly every aspect of life in common, there is likely to be little conflict in the way the various attributes of culture (e.g., age, sexuality, social status) are transmitted to the individual in such a society. The

FIGURE 3.4. The culture-learning process.

same, by the way, can be said of very small towns and villages in the United States, particularly in very poor areas, such as Appalachia, or widely separated regions— such as the broad expanses of the Great Plains in Montana, where contact with the wider society may be limited, even in terms of radio and television.

In complex, multicultural societies such as the United States and many other industrialized nations, however, most individuals interact daily with a vast array of socializing agents, each of which puts a slightly different spin on each of the cultural attributes. For example, one's place of worship is likely to have a significantly different view of sexuality than one's peer group or one's favorite television program. One wonders, for instance, if, in Grover's Corners, Toni Catalano finds a discrepancy in the teachings of her Catholic upbringing and the sexual ideas to be found on most contemporary sitcoms and soap operas. This daily interaction with a variety of socializing agents, each of which may have a unique interpretation of the cultural attributes, means that individuals are bombarded with a variety of conflicting cultural messages.

Furthermore, individuals are not simply passive recipients of incoming messages. Once a message is received, each individual interprets and acts (or not) on its content according to his or her own personality and prior experiences. This interactive aspect of culture learning is depicted in the model in Figure 3.4 through the directional arrows, which connect the individual to various socializing agents and, through them, to the universal cultural attributes. How, for example, can we account for the fact that Steven Chang, the child of well-to-do, professional parents, does not seem to want to go to college? In another instance, how do we account for the fact that Michael Williams, an African American child of a working-class family, spends a lot of time playing not basketball but golf? In short, culture learning is a two-way process in which individuals are both forming and being formed by incoming cultural messages. In many ways, no two individuals construct their world in the same manner.

Perhaps another example would be helpful. Gollnick and Chinn describe two hypothetical women who live in New York City and are thirty years old, white, middle-class, Italian American, and Catholic.[40] One woman identifies very strongly with her Italian American heritage and her church but not very strongly with her age group, her class status, her gender, or her urban life. The other woman defines herself as a feminist, enjoys her urban life, and is conscious of her age but does not pay very much attention to her ethnic background, her religion, or her social class. The significance of these patterns lies not in each woman's self-definition but in the attitudes, values, knowledge, and behavior that such definition entails. Thus, the first woman may spend more time with family than with nonrelated friends, may be a member of a right-to-life group, might choose wine rather than Perrier, may be knowledgeable about and participate in Italian ethnic organizations, and is likely to understand, if not speak, Italian. The second woman may find her most intimate companions among women's groups; be prochoice in her stand on abortion; choose to live in the city, despite the possibility of living in a small town or the country; and—if she does not have children—hear her biological clock ticking. This example illustrates how individuals operating in relatively similar settings with relatively similar environmental demands and socializing agents can develop distinctly different cultures. Perhaps you can begin to imagine how different groups and individuals operating in different settings with differing environmental demands and using different sets of socializing agents can develop distinctly different cultures. Using the model presented in Figure 3.4 can help you recognize the multitude of factors that enter into the cultural identity equation.

In addition, consider that each of the three spheres in Figure 3.4 can spin, so that every cultural attribute can be filtered differently by each of the socializing agents and can result in a variety of personality types. For instance, a passive-reflective individual would interact with the many incoming cultural messages differently than would a volatile, nonreflective person. You can begin to see how complex culture learning can be; how variable individuals can be in the manner in which they receive, process, and act on the various influences they encounter; and how these messages can be transformed into differing behavior and belief patterns. While one might suggest that, in reality, an infinite number of cultural formations are possible, our model is restricted to three parts; with a little practice, anyone can begin to use it as a diagnostic tool for analyzing any multicultural situation.

Despite this enormous potential for variation among individuals and within groups, there are similarities, or generalizations, that can be made about groups of people, and we will be referring to these generalizations throughout this book. People tend to use information that may or may not be reflective of all individuals within a group, so we must always be cautious when using group-specific information to discuss whole groups, because there will always be individuals who do not fit. Individual differences between two people who belong to the same group may be greater than between two people who belong to different groups. Generalizations differ from stereotypes about people, and this point must be kept in mind. Generalizations refer to information that is supported by research and that apply to a large percentage of a population or group. Stereotypes, on the other hand, refer to unsupported information that blurs specific knowledge about others. Such stereotypes would, for instance, "say" that Steven Chang *must* get very good grades because he is Chinese and that Shameka Collins *ought to* be more interested in a secretarial job because she is black. Clearly, such stereotypes are in error, as life in Grover's Corners demonstrates.

Variations in Cultural Attributes, Socializing Agents, and Cultural Learners

Building a positive attitude toward differences requires a sophisticated way of looking at diversity. Much of the educational research on individual differences related to culture rests on three assumptions. First, it is assumed that there is a standard, or an ideal, against which "difference" can be seen, measured, or understood. In this society, people who are white, middle-class, Protestant, English-speaking, healthy, physically and mentally typical, heterosexual, and male are said to make up the dominant cultural group. This "ideal" is, of course, a stereotype, much like the stereotypes of other cultural groups. It is important to note, however, that in the United States this particular stereotype refers to people who are socially privileged[41] by virtue of birth characteristics over which they have little or no control. They are also educationally privileged in that their preschool socialization tends to "fit" them for schooling, which is based on middle-class attitudes and values. One unfortunate consequence of belonging to this model group is that its members don't have to think of themselves as just one of many groups, each with its particular pattern of characteristics. Because they constitute the model group, they fit into perceived societal norms and thus do not have to think about their cultural patterns much at all (see the discussion of "white privilege" in Chapter 9).

Second, any deviation from this normative group is the very definition of difference. If one speaks only Spanish rather than English, is Asian rather than white, is Jewish rather than Protestant, is female rather than male, is homosexual rather than heterosexual, is working-class rather than middle-class, is chronically ill or has a disability rather than is healthy or typical, one is likely to be perceived as different, and this difference is seen as a deficit to be overcome.

Finally, research on difference assumes that, by studying large groups of children with certain characteristics defined as "different," we will know a great deal about all children who possess some or most of these characteristics. There are at least two serious problems with this assumption, however. One is that, while most research looks at only one characteristic at a time (e.g., gender or social class), no one ever "belongs" to just one group. Every individual, for example, simultaneously belongs to gender, social class, and ethnic groups. These "single-characteristic" studies have looked for central tendencies, ways in which the children in each particular group are the same. It may be that this tendency to focus on one narrow point is problematic and may encourage stereotypes. In and of itself, such stereotypes are oversimplifications that tend to ignore the diversity of such things as behavior differences that exist within a group.

While this kind of single-characteristic research has taught us a great deal, it does not enable us to focus on differences within groups, only on differences between groups. Furthermore, it compares groups according to only one characteristic. Thus, it does not help us understand how various characteristics (gender, social class, ethnicity, disability, etc.) combine to form individual personalities and learning styles. For example, to be a deaf American who uses American Sign Language (ASL) with other deaf people but uses English in interacting with hearing persons, as Tom Humphries notes, is " to be bicultural and bilingual. This is just for starters. To be a deaf sign language user *and* African American, Hispanic, Asian/Pacific Islander, or American Indian in the United States is to be multicultural."[42]

Second, such research is most often statistical and tends to be interpreted by practitioners (and the public) in more global terms than its results warrant. If, for example, 65 percent of a given group of girls are found to be less successful at math than a comparable group of boys, the tendency is to believe that *all* girls are less successful at math. Although this generalization is not warranted by the research, it tends to become "true" in the minds of many and to influence their behavior toward girls. Similarly, educators' attitudes and practices regarding students with disabilities have too often been based on broad labels (classifications), such as mental retardation, learning disability, and behavior disorder, all of which obscure wide individual differences.

In this book, we will try to avoid this problem of group stereotyping by looking at the universal connections between culture and learning. These connections are universal in the sense that they seem to apply to all people no matter what their group affiliations. Figure 3.2 illustrated the sources of cultural knowledge that, when mixed together, form the cultural identity of *all* groups and individuals. These attributes are, for the most part, societal designations that have little meaning for the individual, except as experienced through various socializing agents, such as the family, church, neighborhood, and peer group. In other words, one acquires a cultural identity within the larger society through one's experiences with a variety of daily socializing agents.

What teachers must understand is that cultural-learning patterns vary considerably both between and within various cultural groups. In subsequent chapters, we will describe in more detail some of the ways in which differences in cultural learning may lead to misunderstanding and conflict in schools and classrooms. We will also try to show how these differences can be used as a positive resource in learning community classrooms. For now, we encourage you to play with the model. Ask yourself what the universal attributes mean to you in view of your own life experiences and which socializing agents have accounted for your understanding of them. Do the same for others who are close to you—that is, for family members and friends.

These are the kinds of questions we will be asking in the remainder of the book about students, teachers, parents, and school administrators. With the help of the stories incorporated for illustrative purposes and the cases presented for analysis, you should gradually become a sensitive and skillful teacher of *all* children, not just of those whose cultural background matches your own, for, as we have seen in Grover's Corners, when a person *seems* to be quite different from you, by virtue of membership in a different race, class, or religion, they may share some important cultural aspects with you. Even when an individual *seems* to have many cultural aspects in common with you, they may, in fact, be quite different in some important ways.

Active Exercises

The following exercises from *Human Diversity in Action: Developing Multicultural Competencies for the Classroom*[43] may be used to illustrate ideas in this chapter:

Activity 2: Aspects of My Own Cultural Upbringing, p. 10

Activity 3: Childhood Experiences, p. 14

Activity 4: Understanding Cultural Complexity, p. 16

Activity 8: Who Am I? p. 41

Activity 9: The Culture Learning Process, p. 44

Activity 10: How Culture Is Learned: The Socializing Agents, p. 58

Accessing the World Wide Web: Resources for Diversity

For more information on American Sign Language (ASL) and the culture of the deaf, the following web sites are useful:

http://rs6-svr-8.ucl-0.bcc.ac.uk/UCL-Info/Divisions/Library/RNID/hist.html
A web page of deaf culture history and a reading list.

http://faculty.mgc.peachnet.edu/divisions/dst/cyber/deaf.html A web page maintained by a former teacher at Gallaudet University—the most famous of colleges for the deaf—this page has multiple links to sites about deaf culture, language, and schools, as well as entertainment and special interest group resources for the deaf.

http://www.aslinfo.com/deafculture.html This page also has multiple links to information about deaf culture, as well as to good information about American Sign Language (ASL).

To get some idea of what is often meant by *high culture,* or "the best of Western civilization," the following sites are indicative:

http://www.metmuseum.org The Metropolitan Museum of Art, New York City.

http://www.metopera.org/home.html The Metropolitan Opera home page.

For greater knowledge about specific cultural groups, a comprehensive site on the nature of a variety of world cultures, religions, and beliefs is:

http://home.miningco.com/cultures

Other web sites concerned with African Americans, Hispanic, Asian American, and Native American history and culture are:

http://www.watson.org/~lisa/blackhistory A database of African American history.

http://www.soemadison.wisc.edu/IMC/afrocentrism.html A database related to Afrocentrism and schooling.

http://literacynet.org/text/lp/hperspectives/hispcult.html Material on Hispanic history and culture designed for K–12 teachers and students; see, especially, links to "Surface Culture" and "Deep Culture."

http://www.ilt.columbia.edu/k12/naha/index.html An excellent web site for researching a wide variety of aspects of Native American history and culture.

http://www.cetel.org Provides links to Asian American history web sites, Asian American historical documents, and books about Asian American history.

The field of cross-cultural psychology may be somewhat unfamiliar to you. For more information, the following sites may be useful:

http://www.fit.edu/CampusLife/clubs-org/iaccp The web site of the International Association of Cross-Cultural Psychology, this page provides links to information on the association's journal and a number of books published by association members.

References

1. Henry Giroux and Roger Simon, *Popular Culture: Schooling and Everyday Life* (Granby, MA: Bergin and Garvey, 1989), p. 3.
2. Thornton Wilder, *Our Town* (New York: Avon, 1957).
3. See, for example, Alfred L. Kroeber and Clyde Kluckhohn, *Culture: A Critical Review of Concepts and Definitions* (New York: Vintage Books, 1963).

4. Rodman B. Webb and Robert R. Sherman, *Schooling and Society,* 2nd ed. (New York: Macmillan, 1989), pp. 49-50.

5. Viviana A. Zelizer, *Pricing the Priceless Child: The Changing Social Value of Children* (New York: Basic Books, 1985), pp. 61, 97.

6. Harry Triandis, *The Analysis of Subjective Culture* (New York: Wiley-Interscience, 1972).

7. D. M. Warren, *An Elementary Treatise on Physical Geography* (Philadelphia: Cowperthwait, 1873), p. 86.

8. Cited in Roy Harvey Pearce, *The Savages of America: A Study of the Indian and the Idea of Civilization* (Baltimore: Johns Hopkins University Press, 1965), p. 155.

9. Francis Huxley, *Affable Savages* (New York: Viking Press, 1957).

10. Brian M. Bullivant, "Culture: Its Nature and Meaning for Educators," in *Multicultural Education: Issues and Perspectives* (Boston: Allyn & Bacon, 1989), p. 28.

11. James A. Banks, "Multicultural Education: Characteristics and Goals," in *Multicultural Education: Issues and Perspectives* (Boston: Allyn & Bacon, 1989), p. 7.

12. Cited by Christine L. Bennett in *Comprehensive Multicultural Education: Theory and Practice* (Boston: Allyn & Bacon, 1990), p. 42, from a discussion in J. R. Feagin, *Racial and Ethnic Relations* (Englewood Cliffs, NJ: Prentice Hall, 1978), p. 11.

13. Paul Pedersen, *A Handbook for Developing Multicultural Awareness* (Alexandria, VA: American Association for Counseling and Development, 1988).

14. Norman R. Yetman, ed., *Majority and Minority: The Dynamics of Race and Ethnicity in American Life,* 5th ed. (Boston: Allyn & Bacon, 1991), p. 3.

15. Ibid., p. 3.

16. See Julian Pitt-Rivers, "Race, Color, and Class in Central America and the Andes," *Daedalus,* vol. 92, no. 2, 1967, for different interpretations of skin color, eye color, lip features, etc. As cited in Yetman, op. cit.

17. Elizabeth Beardsley, "Traits and Genderization," in *Feminism and Philosophy,* ed. Mary Vetterling-Braggin, F. A. Elliston, and Jane English (Totowa, NJ: Littlefield, 1977), pp. 117–123.

18. Ibid.

19. Gilbert and Kahl, for example, suggest that, in the United States, individual or family income is the central variable from which other opportunities follow. For instance, income generally controls the neighborhood in which one lives. This determines, to a great degree, the educational experience one has, in school and outside of it. The education one has then influences one's profession or occupation, which determines the prestige one obtains, and so forth. D. Gilbert and J. Kahl, *The American Class Structure: A New Synthesis* (Homewood, NJ: Dorsey, 1982).

20. Max Weber, *The Theory of Social and Economic Organization* (New York: The Free Press, 1957).

21. Robert N. Bellah, Richard Madsen, William M. Sullivan, Ann Swidler, and Stephen M. Tipton, *Habits of the Heart: Individualism and Commitment in American Life* (New York: Harper & Row, 1985), pp. 152–155.

22. Yetman, op. cit., p. 3.

23. Gregory M. Herek, "On Heterosexual Masculinity: Some Physical Consequences of the Social Construction of Gender and Sexuality," *American Behavioral Scientist* 29, 5 (May-June 1986): 570.

24. S. LeVay and D. H. Hamer, "Evidence for a Biological Influence in Male Homosexuality," *Scientific American* 270 (May 1994): 44–49.

25. Donna M. Gollnick and Philip C. Chinn, *Multicultural Education in a Pluralistic Society,* 3rd ed. (New York: Macmillan, 1990), p. 211.

26. See, for example, Edward Sapir, *Culture, Language and Personality* (Berkeley: University of California Press, 1949); Benjamin Lee Whorf, "Science and Linguistics," in

Everyman His Own Way: Readings in Cultural Anthropology, ed. Alan Dundes (Englewood Cliffs, NJ: Prentice Hall, 1968); and Lev Semenovich Vygotsky, *Thought and Language* (Cambridge, MA: MIT Press, 1962).

27. Noam Chomsky, *Cartesian Linguistics* (New York: Harper & Row, 1966).
28. Ibid.
29. Peter L. Berger and Brigitte Berger, *Sociology: A Biographical Approach* (New York: Basic Books, 1972), p. 127.
30. Robert J. Cottrell, "America the Multicultural," *American Educator* 14, 4 (winter 1990): 18–21.
31. Berger and Berger, op. cit., p. 51.
32. Ibid., p. 62fn. Berger and Berger tentatively attribute the first use of the concept of identity in this sense to Erik Erikson.
33. Nicholas Abercrombie, Stephen Hill, and Bryan S. Turner, *The Penguin Dictionary of Sociology* (New York: Penguin Books, 1984), p. 201.
34. For an interesting children's book that discusses the manner and mores of eating, see Ina Friedman, *How My Parents Learned to Eat* (Boston: Houghton Mifflin, 1984).
35. Berger and Berger, op. cit., p. 51.
36. Ibid.
37. Ibid., pp. 51–52.
38. Richard Brislin, *Understanding Culture's Influence on Behavior* (Ft. Worth, TX: Harcourt Brace Jovanovich, 1993).
39. John Dewey, *Democracy and Education* (New York: The Free Press, 1966). Orig. published, 1916.
40. Gollnick and Chinn, op. cit., p. 16.
41. For a fuller explanation of privileges that accrue to people who are associated with the dominant group, often without their being particularly aware of them, see Peggy McIntosh, "White Privilege," *Creation Spirituality* (January-February 1992), pp. 33–35, 53; and Gary R. Howard, "Whites in Multicultural Education: Rethinking Our Role," Phi Delta Kappan 75, 1 (September 1993): 36–41.
42. Tom Humphries, "Deaf Culture and Cultures" in *Multicultural Issues in Deafness,* (ed.) K. M. Christensen and G. L. Delgado (White Plains, NY: Longman, 1993): 3–16.
43. Kenneth Cushner, *Human Diversity in Action: Developing Multicultural Competencies for the Classroom* (New York: McGraw-Hill, 1999).

CHAPTER 4

Classrooms and Schools as Cultural Crossroads

CHAPTER OUTLINE

SCHOOLS AND CLASSROOMS: WHERE
    CULTURES INTERSECT
    Student Culture
    Teacher Culture
    School Culture
    Teachers as Cultural Mediators
    Reshaping of Cultural Identity
A MODEL OF CROSS-CULTURAL
    INTERACTION
    State One: Understanding
      Emotional Responses in
      Intercultural Interaction
    Stage Two: Understanding the
      Cultural Basis of Unfamiliar
      Behavior

    Stage Three: Making Adjustments
      and Reshaping Cultural Identity
APPLICATION OF THE CULTURE-
    GENERAL MODEL
    Commonalities Among Groups
    Differences Within a Group
    Critical Incidents at Alden High
ACTIVE EXERCISES
ACCESSING THE WORLD WIDE WEB:
    RESOURCES FOR DIVERSITY
REFERENCES

It is often hard to learn from people who are just like you. Too much is taken for granted. Homogeneity is fine in a bottle of milk, But in the classroom it diminishes the curiosity that ignites discovery.

Vivian Gyssin Paley

Schools, in particular, are cultural crossroads in a society where distinct but overlapping student, teacher, and school cultures intersect. This chapter will examine what occurs when people from different cultures come together, as they increasingly do in our globally oriented pluralistic societies. We will then take an in-depth look at a culture-general model for understanding intercultural interactions. We will take an intercultural perspective and draw from the work of cross-cultural psychologists, who, more than any other group, have been developing practical strategies to help people understand and navigate the tricky waters of cross-cultural interaction. Finally, we will look at this model in action and will apply this model to the analysis of some common cross-cultural situations found in school settings.

SCHOOLS AND CLASSROOMS:
WHERE CULTURES INTERSECT

Within the important limitations of economic circumstance, most people choose the neighborhoods in which they live and the places in which they work, shop, and spend their leisure time. In schools, however, as nowhere else in American society, people of many different backgrounds are forced to come together in close quarters for significant periods of time. The following sections will examine the various cultures, student, teacher, and school, that come together in the context of the school. Next we will examine the role of the teacher as a cultural mediator who is responsible for developing a cooperative learning community within this potentially chaotic setting.

Student Culture

Students, perhaps more than most social groups, represent and exhibit the greatest diversity in American society. Not only do students reflect the cultural identities of their families (ethnicity, religion, social class, etc.) but they also define themselves by creating their own in-school groups. It is a cultural universal that all people identify others into one of two major divisions: those with whom they identify and wish to spend their time (called in-groups) and those from whom they keep a respectable distance (known as out-groups). In-group formation in school can be based on many criteria, from the more potent cultural identities already discussed (e.g., ethnicity, race, gender) to the relatively fluid but no less important unifying features of academic groups (e.g., biology club, French club), special interest or skill groups (e.g., choir, football), and groups that are, from the point of view of most adults, less desirable but nonetheless purposeful, such as gangs. It should be relatively easy for you to construct many examples of the various student cultures that can be found in schools. Typically, individual students gain a certain school identity from participation in these groups. These microcultures within the school operate in ways similar to those of the macroculture outside of it. Individuals learn appropriate rules of interaction, modes of communication, expression of values, and so forth. And, as with larger groups, such as nation-states, membership in these in-school microcultures (gangs, chess club, choir) often brings exclusion from other microcultures (other gangs, sports teams, band).

Teacher Culture

Teachers make up the other dominant social group within the school; however, unlike the diversity found within the student population, teachers are a relatively homogeneous group. Indeed, a disturbing reality, given the increasing heterogeneity of students in public schools, is the relative cultural homogeneity of the teaching force. In the United States, about 92 percent of the teaching force are European American, and two-thirds are female.[1] Even with recent efforts to recruit underrepresented groups into the teaching profession, it is projected that well into the twenty-first century even more new teachers will be female and white. This statistic is not surprising. Most teachers in the United States have always been female and white, at least since the early part of the nineteenth century. However, this statistic raises interesting issues about the cultural and economic backgrounds of teachers in contrast to those of students.

The fact that a large proportion of our teachers is female is related to the power structure of schools. While it is true that teachers have a good deal of authority in their classrooms, it is not true that they have much authority in the schools. For example, teachers are only just beginning to have something to say about school policy and about the curriculum they are expected to teach. While reasons for this may vary, an important one has to do with the way in which large numbers of women entered the teaching profession in the 1830s and 1840s. Prior to that time, the person behind the schoolroom desk was a schoolmaster, a man. However, after about 1830, the growth of industry began providing more and more lucrative jobs for men, leaving teaching vacancies in the classroom. At the same time, the common school movement was evolving across America, opening up additional teaching positions. Conveniently, it was determined that women, who were "natural mothers" and therefore possessed the knowledge, skills, and talents needed to deal with young children, must also be "natural teachers." The elementary school was projected as an extension of the home and the teacher an extension of the mother. The fact that women would work for about one-third of the wages paid to male teachers was also a significant factor in their employment in American schools.[2]

Given the history of their entry into the profession, female teachers have never had the status that male teachers once had. Unfortunately for all teachers, the low status of female teachers has become associated with teachers more generally. Administrators, who have greater authority, higher pay, and higher status, are mostly European-American men. Thus, in our society, schools have become organized in such a way that leadership and policy are very often the exclusive province of white, male administrators.[3]

School Culture

Both schools and the teachers who inhabit them are, to a large extent, "culture bound," and the culture they are bound to is the dominant culture of European-American, middle-class society, which is only one of the many culture groups in the United States. One purpose of public schooling has always been to transmit the cultural beliefs, values, and knowledge affiliated with the dominant group to those in the next generation. The danger, of course, is the ethnocentric tendency of most people, teachers included, to believe that their own cultural tradition represents the "best" way. Too often, the perceptions of both power and virtue combine to lessen the chance that white, middle-class teachers will make a real effort to understand the cultural differences that direct the lives of many of their students. At best, many of these teachers are predisposed to regard diversity as interesting; at worst, they are likely to regard it as a deficit. Teachers seldom go to their classes with the notion that diversity is an exciting and enriching phenomenon. Sara Lawrence Lightfoot, a professor of education at Harvard and someone who has committed her professional life to understanding and assisting with issues of diversity in schools, describes many good teachers as wishing that the diversity they see in September will somehow fade away as the class becomes a group.[4]

Teachers as Cultural Mediators

The cultural interplay between teachers, students, and their school produces a context within which significant culture learning can occur. In a sense, teachers must become *cultural mediators* in their classrooms. Teachers must not only become aware of the multitude of ways in which culture influences the classroom context but also actively engage students in learning about and more effectively accommodating cultural differences. Thus, the specific cultural knowledge and skills that teachers must acquire and exhibit also become content that is taught to the students in their charge. Students, too, must learn how culture is formed and how to understand and handle the many intercultural interactions they are certain to encounter.

Throughout this process, it is imperative that teachers and students understand that a certain amount of adjustment and discomfort may occur. It is good to remember that when we as individuals are confronted by someone who looks, behaves, or thinks differently than we do, we suddenly become aware that our way of doing things may not be the only one. Such a confrontation often affects us at an emotional level—we may feel anxiety, uncertainty, and discomfort. Lacking a vocabulary to describe most cross-cultural differences, and wishing to avoid discomfort, individuals may choose to avoid further interaction with those who are different from themselves. Such avoidance behavior merely perpetuates the cycle of discomfort, mistrust, and ignorance.

These feelings often characterize teachers whose students are different from themselves, and perhaps different from the value and behavior norms of the school. From the school's point of view, such students are often perceived as having deficits that need to be overcome through remedial action. Such actions are often punitive to students, involving exclusionary practices, such as tracking and negative labeling (e.g., "at-risk" students, "learning disabled"). Since most of us do not have a wide variety of experience with cultural patterns other than our own, deliberate instruction in culture, including acquiring a language in order to talk about its patterns, substance, and behavioral results, is one way to create a dialogue concerning differences. Such strategies help us truly understand ourselves and others.

Reshaping of Cultural Identity

It would be easy for teachers to give in to discouragement and try to find a school in which the students were like themselves. Indeed, studies of cross-cultural experiences suggest that there is often a predictable pattern of adjustment when interacting with people one perceives as different from oneself. Using studies of international travelers, cross-cultural psychologists found that people generally experience four marked phases during their adjustment to an intercultural setting.[5] If the experiences people have were placed on a graph, with one's emotional experiences along the vertical axis and time across the horizontal axis, the resulting image would appear as a *U*. Hence, this description of the process of adjustment, or reshaping of one's identity, is called the *U-curve hypothesis* (see Figure 4.1).

Initially, most people are intrigued and perhaps even enraptured by the prospect of an intercultural experience. They have some preconceived ideas of what the new culture will be like and how they might integrate into the new setting. In some

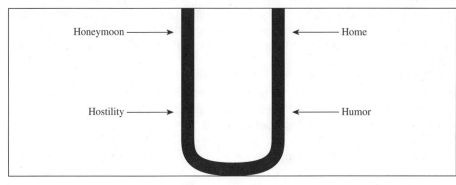

FIGURE 4.1. U-curve hypothesis.

cases, they do not initially perceive that the experience will be much different from experiences they have had in the past. Often they are excited at the idea of moving to a new place, of "starting a new life." In this stage, individuals enter what has been appropriately termed the *honeymoon phase,* in which things are new and fresh; there are new people to meet, new ways of interacting, new foods to eat, new ideas to consider—nothing could be better!

After some time, however, when people begin to get a sense that what looks different really *is* different, and that those differences are important, the constant demand to adjust to new stimuli and to function well in a new setting may become too difficult to accept. Most people react to the stress by entering a state of *hostility* and begin to move down the left side of the *U.* In this phase, people generally attempt to cope with three problems: (1) other people's behavior does not make sense to them, (2) their own behavior does not produce the expected results, and (3) there is so much that is new in the environment that they have no ready-made answers to the questions that may arise.

There are many examples of similar adjustment curves in the psychological literature. Beginning teachers and new students moving into the culture of a particular school, for instance, face a double challenge. Teachers must adapt simultaneously to the culture of the surrounding community and to that of the teaching profession, which, of course, has a culture of its own. In the school context, new teachers must integrate themselves into the norms and attitudes of both a well-established teaching staff and their students, who bring with them the norms of diverse communities. During the hostility phase, new teachers, like new arrivals in any new culture, may become so frustrated by their inability to make sense of their new world that they begin to react in an aggressive, perhaps hostile manner. At the same time, new students must also adjust to the school culture, which may be very different from their home and neighborhood cultures, as well as to the behavioral and academic expectations of schooling and the many possible student microcultures within the school. During the hostility phase, students may become so frustrated that they give up, act up, or drop out.

At this point, a critical choice must be made: remain and learn how to function effectively within the new setting or allow the frustrations to build and eventually retreat from the unpleasant situation. In this phase, those most likely to succeed in their new setting begin to confront their new cultural environment. They learn to cope with embarrassment, disappointment, frustration, anxiety, and identity problems, while beginning to learn the subjective culture of the new environment.

Once this culture-learning stage begins, people typically begin to emerge from this reactive, hostile phase and enter the third phase, just up the right-hand side of the *U*. Often referred to as the *humor phase*, this is a positive step toward reshaping one's own cultural identity. On reaching the humor phase, people begin to understand more of the new culture and can begin to laugh at some of their earlier misconceptions and mistakes. In this phase, by the way, they also can begin to truly understand the humor (e.g., jokes, puns) of the new culture.

Finally, people who succeed in altering their own cultural identities to include the new experiences climb the final leg of the *U* and enter the phase called *home*. In this phase, individuals are able to interpret the world and interact with others, both from their own perspective and from the perspective of that which had been alien to them before. A major change occurs in the ability to process information and to understand the world in ways similar to those of people who are different from oneself. The individual now shows indications of becoming more genuinely appreciative of differences, as the world now seems reasonable and acceptable from more than one point of view.

Most individuals require a significant amount of time before they can develop the in-depth understanding that is required for them to live and work effectively and comfortably with people from other cultural backgrounds. Some suggest that this period may be as long as two years, with full immersion, and when one speaks the local language. In terms of bilingual learners for whom English is not the primary language, often there are two periods of adjustment. On one level, children may learn to speak English relatively quickly and within one year may be quite fluent—on a surface, or an objective, level. That is, non-English speakers may quickly be able to communicate effectively with other children on the playground and in free time; however, when these children are given standardized tests of educational achievement, they do not do as well. A secondary, deeper level of linguistic competence is at play. That is, it may take students between five and seven years to attain the level of linguistic competence in a second language that is typically required in schools. Clearly, if acquiring a cultural identity through primary socialization requires full immersion in a culture over a long period of time, it stands to reason that reshaping one's cultural outlook as a result of secondary socialization will also take considerable time.

In Chapter 3, Figure 3.4 provided a visual overview of how the various sources of cultural knowledge are acquired by individuals through interaction with the many socializing agents they encounter. Although the sources of cultural knowledge (e.g., race, language, sexuality) are universal and appear in all societies, the socializing agents (e.g., family, school, media) that transmit them vary considerably from one society to another. In most industrialized societies, for example, a wide variety of socializing agents bombard people daily, often with contradictory messages. In agriculturally oriented societies, on the other hand, a few primary socializing agents (e.g., family and gender group) may share the bulk of the culture-transmission process. The result is that individuals with different cultural patterns develop very different worldviews.

Robert's Induction Year Problem: A Case Study

Robert had just completed a degree in science education at a large midwestern university and was excited about the prospects of teaching in one of the area high schools. All through his teacher preparation, he had been encouraged to pursue the sciences as an area of specialization. He had often heard about the shortage of science teachers and thought he might have an edge in terms of employment. Robert felt confident that he would obtain a position in a high school not too far from where he had grown up and gone to school. This had been his dream ever since his own high school years.

When Robert finally graduated, however, the employment situation was quite different. The teaching market in the immediate area was not as fruitful as he had been led to believe, so, when school districts from the West Coast came to recruit teachers at his university, Robert found himself seriously considering the possibility of relocating. After all, he did want to teach, and he felt well prepared for any classroom situation.

When offered a position at Alden High School near Los Angeles, Robert gladly accepted and eagerly made plans to move west. Alden High is an urban school of approximately 1,600 students in grades 9 through 12. Approximately 30 percent of the students are Latino, 30 percent African American, 20 percent European American, and 20 percent Asian, Pacific Islanders, or Middle Eastern. Most students come from families at or below the poverty level. There is a large vocational program with more than half of the juniors and seniors enrolled. Approximately 25 percent of the faculty is a mix of Latino and African American; the rest are European American.

Alden has an aging faculty with an average age of 43. Last year, the principal, Mr. Henderson, was unable to hire any teachers of color. This year he was able to attract four new African American faculty members among the new teachers. Robert was one of three European Americans hired this year. He was excited about his first teaching situation and confident that he would be successful.

A few months after the start of the school year, Robert knew that he was confronting a reality far different from the one he had imagined. He felt unprepared for the student diversity he faced every day, and he had no idea how to help students address what he felt were most basic educational needs. He was unaccustomed to the variety of languages and dialects spoken by students, had little understanding of what went on in students' lives outside of school, and struggled daily to present class lessons that motivated and involved students. To top everything off, Robert found himself in the middle of significant racial strife.

In January of the previous year, Mr. Henderson had met with the African American teachers at their request. They had had many concerns, ranging from insufficient minority representation on the teaching and coaching staffs to the way white teachers were dealing with students of color. They had felt that most white teachers did not appreciate the need for the proposed Martin Luther King recognition activities; they had been disappointed at the lack of white response to a request for donations to the United Negro College Fund; and they had felt a negative response to Black History Month activities and other efforts to make the curriculum more culturally sensitive.

As a result of this meeting, a Human Relations Committee was formed. This volunteer group planned and organized a two-day race relations institute. The results of the workshop were disastrous. Instead of improving race relations in the school, the situation became worse. A group of white teachers sent around a list of possible themes for the coming school year that were perceived as racist by the African American teachers. A group of concerned black teachers and parents sent letters to community leaders and higher-level administrators, voicing their concern. Once parents of the Latino students became aware of the situation, they started demanding equal attention to address the needs of their children. Not only the African American students but also the Latino and Asian American students became increasingly alienated from school-related activities.

In March of last year, Mr. Henderson met with the equal opportunity officer in the district and with a racially mixed group of teachers. While concerns were aired, none of the problems was solved. A discussion was begun, but, as Mr. Henderson put it, "We have a long way to go. We definitely have some white teachers who are insensitive to the needs of others, as well as some African American teachers who perceive the white teachers as racist. I'm not quite sure how to begin addressing the students' needs, except to say that we will continue to bring the various parties together to address whatever needs arise. I only hope people will stay with me for the long haul."

Robert was quite uncomfortable attending faculty meetings, and the spinoff was affecting his classroom interactions. He was frustrated, unsure of what was really going on, and uncertain if he could remain in such an environment. He began to question seriously the preparation he had had and wondered how anyone could teach in such a stressful situation.

For years researchers from cross-cultural psychology have searched for a framework that could be used to analyze, understand, and improve intercultural interactions. Recently, Cushner and Brislin developed a framework for understanding the dynamics of any cross-cultural encounter between individuals with different cultural patterns.[6] The approach is grounded in the recognition that people have similar reactions to their cross-cultural encounters, regardless of the setting or the person with whom they are interacting, regardless of the role they adopt, and regardless of their own cultural background. Figure 4.2 illustrates three psychological stages through which individuals usually proceed when immersed in an intercultural encounter.

Stage 1	Stage 2	Stage 3
Emotional Arousal	Understanding Unfamiliar Behavior	Personal Adjustment and Growth

FIGURE 4.2. Stages of intercultural encounters.

Research suggests that these stages are universal, regardless of the shape or content of a cultural pattern. Consequently, anyone participating in an unfamiliar, cross-cultural encounter can use this analytical model as a tool for assessing a situation. While most people try to do this informally, using whatever bits and pieces of relevant experience they may have, a general assessment model provides a more systematic and effective means for doing this.

Because the model in Figure 4.2 is deliberately general, its usefulness lies in its adaptability to any cross-cultural encounter. It allows one to capture the *experience* of cultural differences from a variety of perspectives (emotional, informational, and developmental) and to offer frameworks within which specific problem situations can be addressed. However, it does not go beyond its diagnostic purpose—that is, it does not offer prescriptive courses of action in dealing with difference. Such approaches are not only impossible, but they are unethical, given the complex realities of today's classroom. It is the individual student or teacher, empowered by culture-general knowledge, who must propose solutions to the specific problems and issues that arise. The discussion that follows provides a more in-depth examination of each stage in the culture-general framework, and the critical incidents at the end provide an opportunity to apply this framework.

Stage One: Understanding Emotional Responses in Intercultural Interaction

In any intercultural encounter, people's emotions are quickly aroused when they meet with unpredictable behavior on the part of others or when their behavior does not bring about an expected response. It is important to note that the nature and strength of these emotional reactions often surprise the people involved. This is often the case with students of color who do not anticipate the differences between their own cultural patterns and that of the school. It is also the case for teachers who find themselves in a school or classroom context that is significantly different from their prior experience. Recognizing and accommodating the strong emotional responses people are certain to have when involved in intercultural interactions is critical to negotiating them successfully. Figure 4.3 identifies the emotional responses most commonly experienced by people confronting an unfamiliar culture. A brief description of these responses follows.

Anxiety

As individuals encounter unexpected or unfamiliar behavior on the part of others, they are likely to become anxious about whether or not their behavior is appropriate. Children and teachers in new schools, individuals in new jobs, and families in new communities all experience a degree of anxiety as they attempt to modify their own behavior to fit new circumstances. Such feelings may be powerful, while their cause (cultural differences) may be unaltered. Feelings of anxiety may result in a strong desire to avoid the situation altogether, and individuals sometimes go to great lengths to do so, all the while rationalizing their avoidance behavior on other grounds.

Ambiguity

When interacting with those who are culturally different, the messages received from the other people are often unclear, yet decisions must be made and appropriate behavior somehow produced. Most people, when faced with an ambiguous

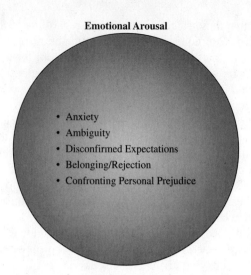

Emotional Arousal

- Anxiety
- Ambiguity
- Disconfirmed Expectations
- Belonging/Rejection
- Confronting Personal Prejudice

FIGURE 4.3. Emotional responses in intercultural interaction.

situation, try to resolve it by applying culturally familiar criteria. For example, it is quite common, when giving instructions to individuals who are just beginning to speak English, to ask them if they understand what has just been said. In an attempt not to seem ignorant or impolite, such individuals often respond in the affirmative and act in ways consistent both with their (perhaps incomplete or mistaken) understanding of the message and familiar behavioral strategies. However, their later behavior may reflect only partial understanding of the message or an inappropriate response. Because the new intercultural situation may not fit familiar criteria, this is often an ineffective strategy.

The uncertainty of ambiguous situations may be the most critical element in the development of anxiety and is one of the more important factors in cross-cultural misunderstanding. People who are effective at working across cultures are known to have a high tolerance for ambiguity. That is, in situations in which they do not have full understanding of what is going on, they are skilled at asking appropriate questions and modifying their behavior accordingly.

Disconfirmed Expectations

Individuals may become upset or uncomfortable, not because of the specific circumstances they encounter but because the situation differs from what they expected. Despite our recognition that differences are all around us, we have a tendency to expect others to think and behave as we do. Thus, when involved in intercultural interactions, most people are surprised and disconcerted when others do not respond in expected ways. An example is a child who consistently looks at the floor when being spoken to by an adult, rather than looking the adult in the eye. This reaction sets up a cycle in which unexpected behavior is attributed both negatively and inaccurately (this student isn't paying attention and is disrespectful) according to preconceived notions of what is "right," or correct, and further actions (the student is scolded for showing disrespect), based on such negative or inaccurate attributions, do not produce the intended result (the student continues to look at the floor). This is often very upsetting for all parties involved.

Belonging/Rejection

People need to fill a social niche, to feel that they belong and are at home in the social milieu in which they find themselves. When they are immersed in an intercultural situation, this sense of belonging is difficult to achieve, because they don't know the "rules" of behavior in the new situation. Rather, people may feel rejected as "outsiders," and, when this sense of rejection is strong enough, they may become alienated from the situation altogether. For example, students who feel alienated from the classroom or school are more likely to become discipline problems and have difficulty paying attention to classroom work. Similarly, teachers who work with youngsters very different from themselves may feel alienated from their students and their students' families and may respond with an undue exercise of power or with burnout.

Confronting Personal Prejudice

Finally, when involved in intercultural interactions, one may be forced to acknowledge that previously held beliefs about a certain group of people or certain kinds of behaviors may be inaccurate or without foundation. Such a revelation may result in embarrassment or shame. It may also require a basic change in one's attitudes and behavior toward others. And, since change is difficult even in the best of circumstances, people often continue to harbor their prejudices even when faced with contradictory evidence. Making the cognitive shift can be very demanding— but it is essential.

Stage Two: Understanding the Cultural Basis of Unfamiliar Behavior

In addition to accommodating their feelings, the parties in an intercultural encounter need to understand the cultural influences that have shaped one another's knowledge about the world. Individuals typically try to understand another person's behavior according to their own cultural knowledge base. Put another way, since most people do not have extensive experiences with people who think and act differently than they do, they tend to interpret another's behavior in terms of their own cultural frames of reference. We see what we expect to see and, with incomplete information or inaccurate knowledge, we may make inappropriate judgments about a situation.

Let's go back to the student who consistently looks at the floor when being spoken to by an adult. Some children from certain ethnic groups (e.g., Mexican American, African American) are taught to demonstrate respect for elders or persons in authority by avoiding eye contact; hence a child who is being spoken to by an adult avoids gazing into that person's eyes. On the other hand, European American children (and most of our teachers) are taught to look a person of authority directly in the eye. Imagine the outcome of an interaction involving a Mexican American or African American child being addressed by a European American teacher. The child, as he or she may have been taught, looks away from the gaze of the teacher, thereby demonstrating respect. The teacher, expecting eye contact as a sign of respect, interprets the child's behavior as communicating, "I am not listening to you," or "I do not respect you." This incorrect judgment may result in a reprimand, in response to which the child attempts to show respect by continuing to look away. Without the teacher's understanding the cultural basis for this behavior, future interactions may be in serious jeopardy.

- Communication and Language
- Values
- Rituals
- Situational Behavior
- Roles
- Social Status
- Time and Space Orientation
- Relationship to the Group

FIGURE 4.4. Analyzing unfamiliar behavior.

The individual skilled in intercultural encounters learns to seek alternative explanations of unexpected behavior, rather than simply interpreting such behavior according to his or her own cultural framework. The question, Why is this behavior occurring? precedes the question, What is the matter with this child?

As discussed in Chapter 3, there are many aspects of cultural knowledge, each of which reaches the individual through a network of socializing agents. Regardless of the complexity of this socialization process, the resulting knowledge base gives us satisfactory explanations of our world and tells us how best to interact with the people around us. Within this cultural knowledge base, however, the following kinds of knowledge are likely to differ across cultural patterns (see Figure 4.4).

Communication and Language

Communication differences are probably the most obvious issues that must be overcome when crossing cultural boundaries. With language, this is the case whether the languages involved are completely different (e.g., Japanese, Kiswahili, English, American Sign Language), are similar in root but not in evolution (e.g., French, Italian, Spanish), or are variations or dialects of the same language (e.g., French, French-Canadian; English, Ebonics). In any case, it is difficult to learn a second or third language. In addition, nonverbal communication customs, such as facial expressions and gestures, differ across cultural patterns, so that what a particular gesture means to one person may mean something very different to someone with another cultural pattern.

Values

The development of internalized values is one of the chief socialization goals in all societies. Values provide social cohesion among group members and are often codified into laws or rules for living: for example, the Ten Commandments for Christians and Jews or the Hippocratic Oath for doctors. The range of possible values with respect to any issue is usually wide, deeply held, and often difficult to change. For example, in the dominant culture of the United States, belief in "progress"is highly valued and almost religious in character. A teacher holding that value may have a very difficult time interacting with the parents of a young woman, who seem not to value her academic potential. The young woman's parents may believe that she should assume the traditional role of wife and mother after high school, rather than seeking a college education. The teacher, on the other hand, may believe that the young woman should "look to the future" in another way, "change with the times," and "make progress" for herself. These are not small differences.

Rituals

All social groups develop rituals that help members meet the demands of everyday life. Such rituals vary in significance from the rubbing of a rabbit's foot before a stressful event to the intricate format of an organized religious service. The difficulty, however, is that the rituals of one social group may be viewed as silly or superstitious by members of other social groups. Increasingly, children from a wide variety of religious and cultural backgrounds bring to school behaviors that are often misunderstood and labeled "superstition." Native American spirituality, for example, often includes rituals involving the personification of natural objects, such as trees, rocks, and animals. Such personification is usually viewed as superstition by those who have been brought up with a scientific and technological mindset. Or consider the case of the preschool teacher in Chapter 3 who learned that one of her children was being treated for an illness through rituals involving lighted candles and prayer.

Situational Behavior

Knowing how to behave appropriately in a variety of settings and situations is important to all people. The "rules" for behavior at home, school, work, sporting events, and so forth are internalized at an early age. Such rules can be easily "broken" by one who has internalized a different set of rules for the same setting or situation. A child, for example, who has learned that learning is best accomplished by quiet and intense observation is likely to run afoul of a teacher who believes that learning is best accomplished by active participation with others in class.

Roles

Knowledge of appropriate role behavior, like that of situational behavior, may vary from role to role and group to group. How one behaves as a mother or father, for example, may be different from how one behaves as a teacher. Similarly, the role of mother, father, or teacher may vary among sociocultural groups. Furthermore, role patterns change over time, as is the case now as middle-class mothers are increasingly also working mothers, necessitating considerable alterations in the role of "being" a mother. Indeed, this change in middle-class motherhood brings it into closer correspondence with the pattern that has long been established by working-class mothers.

Social Status

All social groups make distinctions based on various markers of high and low status. Social class and social status are both the results of stratification systems whose role assignments may vary considerably from group to group. The role of the aunt in the African American community, for example, has a much higher status than it does in middle-class, European American society. Often, the aunt of an African American child bears considerable responsibility for the well-being of that child. Middle-class, European American teachers, unaware of this status and relationship, when confronted by a proactive aunt, may believe that the child's mother is somehow shirking her responsibilities.

Time and Space Orientation

Differences in conceptions of time and space may also vary among social groups. In addition to differences in the divisions of time (e.g., a week, a crop harvest), groups vary in the degree to which time is valued. It is common for European Americans, for example, to value punctuality, since that is seen as an expression of respect. However, measures of time and their value may be much more elastic in nonindustrialized societies, where work is less synchronized. Similarly, the ease and comfort of one's position in space vis-á-vis other people may vary. How close one stands to another when speaking and the degree to which one should stand face-to-face with another are both subject to cultural variation.

Relationship to the Group

All people sometimes act according to their individual interests and sometimes according to their group allegiances. The relative emphasis on group versus individual orientation varies from group to group and may significantly affect the choices one makes. In the dominant culture of the United States, for instance, individualism is highly valued. Schools traditionally have reinforced this value through emphasis on "doing one's own work," the ability to "work independently," and the recognition of "individual responsibility." However, other social groups, such as the Japanese, place much greater emphasis on group behavior, group solidarity, and group helpfulness and well-being. For them, it is often considered wrong to stand out, to be independent, to "rise above" the group.

Stage Three: Making Adjustments and Reshaping Cultural Identity

As a result of prolonged intercultural interaction, an individual may experience personal change. That is, an individual's way of perceiving the world, processing those perceptions, and viewing themselves and others may alter. Typically individuals who have had significant intercultural experiences become more complex thinkers. This is, of course, one of the central goals of multicultural education, since it enables people to handle more culturally complex stimuli, to be more accurate in their interpretations of others' behavior, and thus to deal more effectively with the differences they encounter. As individuals continue to have intercultural experiences, they become less culture-bound and more understanding of how others perceive the world. Such individuals can now "see" from another's point of view; they are more complex thinkers and can handle a greater variety of diverse information. They are also less likely to make inaccurate judgments or attributions, because they are more likely to inquire into puzzling beliefs and behavior, thereby improving their understanding. Think back to the example of the gaze-avoidance behavior in the interaction between the European American teacher and the Mexican American or African American child. The interculturally knowledgeable teacher understands

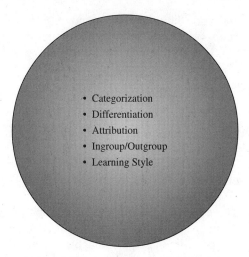

- Categorization
- Differentiation
- Attribution
- Ingroup/Outgroup
- Learning Style

FIGURE 4.5. Ways of processing information.

the meaning that underlies the child's gaze-avoidance and more accurately judges the child to be listening and demonstrating respect. While even people who have considerable intercultural experience may have limited knowledge of the content of a particular cultural knowledge base, they do know that all people process information in similar ways, and they are willing to investigate the outcomes of such processes. Several important ways of processing information are listed in Figure 4.5, each of which can be investigated by the participants in intercultural exchanges.

Categorization

Since people cannot attend to all the information presented to them, they create categories for organizing and responding to similar bits of information. Cultural stereotypes, for example, are categories usually associated with particular groups of people. People involved in intercultural interactions often categorize one another quickly, according to whatever category systems they have learned. Examples of this kind of categorization are old/young, rich/poor, friend/enemy, native/foreigner, and healthy/disabled. The context within which people categorize each other also influences the categorization process. Recall the earlier example in Chapter 3 of the boy who was sent home from school before the end of each day. From one perspective, the boy was categorized as a troublemaker. Once the context of the situation was better understood, the boy was seen as a hero, doing whatever he could to help protect his mother. Of particular importance is the fact that category systems and their meanings not only differ from group to group but also are rarely neutral in value. Thus, placing another in a particular category may also place that person in a more or less valued position (e.g., to be "learning disabled" is usually considered to be in a less valued position than not to be "learning disabled").

Differentiation

Information related to highly meaningful categories becomes more refined or differentiated. As a result, new categories may be formed. Such refinement, or differentiation, is usually shared only among people who have had many experiences in common (e.g., doctors) and, thus, may be unknown even to those whose background, apart from occupation, is similar. A good example of this process is the way in which high school students differentiate their peers into groups, such as "brains," "nerds," "jocks," etc. While a similar type of differentiation may occur in most high schools, the particular categories and their meaning may differ considerably.

Attribution

People not only perceive others according to familiar categories, but they also make judgments about others based on the behavior they observe and its meaning in their own social milieu. They judge others, for example, as competent or incompetent, educated or naive, well-intentioned or ill-intentioned. Psychologists call these judgments attributions[7] and tell us that, within about seven seconds of meeting someone new, initial judgments are made. These initial "sizing-up" judgments, once made, are usually resistant to change. Human judgments, however, are fallible, and certain judgment errors occur repeatedly in human thought. One of these, called the *fundamental attribution error*, describes the tendency people have to judge others on different sets of criteria than they apply to themselves, particularly with respect to shortcomings. Thus, if I fail at a given task, I am more likely to look to the situation for an explanation: it was too hot, someone else was unfair to me, the task was too hard. If I observe someone else fail at a task, I am more likely to explain the failure in terms of the other person's traits: she is lazy, he is stupid, she is uncaring. This tendency is even more prevalent when individuals with different cultural patterns interact, because there is likely to be an abundance of unfamiliar behavior which is misunderstood. Given the speed with which people make judgments and the probable lack of intercultural understanding, attribution errors abound in intercultural situations. Couple this with the tendency people have to form categories (and, sometimes, negative stereotypes about people), and you can see how a very detrimental, complex situation can evolve.

Ingroups and Outgroups

People the world over divide others into those with whom they are comfortable and can discuss their concerns (ingroups) and those who are kept at a distance (outgroups). Based on initial categorization and differentiation, as well as on continuing interaction, individuals may identify one another as potential members of their own ingroup or as members of an outgroup. Those entering new cultural situations must recognize that they will often be considered members of an outgroup, will not share certain ingroup behavior and communication, and thus will be kept from participating in certain ingroup activities. A really good, if somewhat mundane example of this is the situation experienced by a substitute teacher who is, by definition, an outsider in the culture of the classroom and school.

Learning Style

Sometimes called *cognitive style*, a learning style is one's preferred method of learning and is very much a matter of cultural pattern difference. How (and what) one perceives, the categories into which one places sensory stimuli, and whether learning is preferred through observation, listening, or action are all, in part, based on cultural patterns. For example, as they grow up, some children who are native Hawaiian or Native American learn from a variety of individuals, both adults and other children. They may also participate in much group learning; that is, children may learn and practice a skill with other children, not necessarily on their own. These children's preferred learning style (the way in which they have learned how to learn) may be more group-oriented than that of their European American counterparts, who have a tendency to learn how to learn in a more individualistic manner. Such children may not achieve as well in traditionally oriented classrooms as they might in cooperative learning situations. While learning styles are partly the result of strengths and weaknesses in sensory perception (one's hearing is more acute than one's vision, for example), cultural patterning may teach a child to attend to certain kinds of stimuli, rather than to others.

APPLICATION OF THE
CULTURE-GENERAL MODEL

At this point, you may appreciate the potential of the culture-general model but not know how it can be applied in your daily interactions. The main value of such a model is that it allows people to build a common, culture-related vocabulary that can be used to analyze intercultural interactions in a variety of contexts. That is, it provides a tool whereby people can more accurately judge the nature of the interactions they are reading about, witnessing, or participating in. For example, in the following paraphrased discussion of Mexican Americans found in Farris and Cooper's book *Elementary Social Studies: A Whole Language Approach*, specific themes of the culture-general model are designated in italics. Following this example from the literature are a few cases for your analysis.

> While tremendous diversity exists within the Mexican American culture, some generalities about the traditional Mexican American experience can be made. To begin with, there is strong identification with the family, the community, and the ethnic group at large (*belonging, relation to the group, ingroup/outgroup distinctions*). Individual achievement readily encouraged in many Anglo-American children is not stressed. Rather, achievement for the child means achievement for the family (*social status, relation to the group, roles*). Parental involvement in the education of Mexican American children is important to attain success. Because parents provide a positive support system every attempt should be made to inform parents of their child's progress. Both sending work home as well as accepting items from the home in school helps to strengthen the necessary home-school relationship (*belonging, roles, values, learning styles*).
>
> Mexican American culture typically encourages cooperation rather than competition as is typical in Anglo-American culture. As a result, many Mexican American children may find the typical reward structure of schools confusing and frustrating. Teachers may find greater success when motivation is applied to group activity rather than for personal gain such as a letter grade (*relation to the group, learning styles*).
>
> Mexican Americans also tend to be sensitive to the emotional needs of others. Strong interpersonal relationships should be expected. As such, teachers should encourage children to help one another (*belonging, learning styles, relation to the group*). Mexican American children are also more likely to use both verbal and nonverbal means to call a teacher's attention. This may explain their reluctance to ask a teacher for help or to pose a question; their actual request may have been nonverbal (*communication and language use, attribution*).

The Mexican American humanistic orientation extends well beyond the nuclear family. Extended family actively includes *primos,* or cousins with the same last name but no blood relationship; *tocayos,* or namesakes, those with the same first name; *concunos,* or brothers-in-law; *cunadas,* or sisters-in-law; and the very important *padrinos,* or godparents, *ahijados,* or godchildren, and *compadres,* or natural parents to the godparents. All of these individuals (and others) may play significant roles throughout the individual's life (*roles, ingroup/outgroup, relation to the group, belonging, categorization*).

In such an extended family, status and role relationships are rigidly defined. Younger children defer to older children, and females often defer to males. Respect for parents is expected, regardless of one's age. Sexual roles are well-defined, with females having responsibility for the condition of the home and the raising of children. Males, having higher status, are primarily the wage earners (*roles, class and status, categorization*). There is also a strong obligation to the family. Teachers should keep this in mind when hearing that students have responsibilities such as caring for younger children after school or working in the family business (*values, relation to the group, roles*).

Finally, among Mexican American families there exists a strong orientation and identification with Mexican-Catholic ideology. This powerful force reinforces their value system, many of their daily actions, and their respect for parents, family, and tradition (*rituals, values, belonging*).[8]

Commonalities Among Groups

In the example in the previous section, at least eleven culture-general themes were evident, perhaps you identified others. Used in this manner, the culture-general model can help both students and teachers find commonalities among the cultural differences they encounter. For example, some aspects of the Mexican American experience are similar to those of other ethnic experiences, and some are different. Some aspects may be similar to those of your own experience, while others are different.

Viewed in the broadest terms possible, the goal of this model goes beyond simply negotiating cross-cultural interactions or adapting one's teaching in order to accommodate culturally diverse learning styles. Its search for commonalities among people of all cultures offers the possibility that all individuals in a pluralistic society will feel sufficiently similar that they can confront differences without going through the hostility stage that was shown in Figure 4.1. In short, an awareness of similarities—kinship feelings, for example—can motivate people to learn about and appreciate differences. Thus, the model offers a way to go beyond tolerance, which often means "letting people alone," to begin to build a truly multicultural society.

Differences Within a Group

The foregoing discussion presented two dimensions in which the culture-general model is useful: (1) in building a common vocabulary around differences and (2) in using those concepts to analyze group-specific information. The information about traditional Mexican American culture provided an example of using the model across ethnic/nationality boundaries, differences that are most commonly thought of as "cultural differences." It also allowed us to look for commonalities among specific cultural ideas and practices. A third dimension of difference is also made more visible by using the culture-general model, and that is in identifying and analyzing differences within a specific cultural group. Such differences as social class, geographical location, sexual orientation, and religion are not always easy to see but may, in fact, be important differences in the way individuals perceive the world, interact with one another, and approach learning. Questions raised by a consideration of these kinds of differences can lead to inquiry about, for instance, whether or not *particular* Mexican American children are Catholic, whether or not *particular* Mexican American children have learned to operate in a cooperative manner, or whether or not *particular* Mexican American children identify strongly with their extended families. Research has shown, for example, that some of these cultural attributes may diminish in successive generations of Mexican American families. To automatically assume that such characteristics will occur in all children and adults of Mexican American descent is to stereotype all individuals who belong to a particular ethnic group and to run a grave risk of misinterpreting observable behavior.

Critical Incidents at Alden High

It is time to apply the culture-general model to the analysis of some cross-cultural situations. Only by doing so is it possible to understand the degree to which culture influences teaching and learning in schools. We will examine the kinds of incidents that might occur in the fictitious school called Alden High School, which you read about earlier in the chapter. You should realize, however, that the incidents reported here could easily occur in most schools in the United States.

Let's go back to the case study and take a close look at Robert's induction year. Stop at this point and look closely at some of the culture-general themes that may be at play. It seems obvious that this is a highly charged, emotional situation for many of the people involved. To begin with, Robert must reconcile the reality of this situation with his early expectations. Thus, Robert is clearly experiencing a case of *disconfirmed expectations*. Robert must begin to understand the real situation and adjust his behavior according to what is, rather than to what he expected.

He is also faced with a considerable amount of *ambiguity* in his new situation. While he is enthusiastic about the challenge of an urban teaching experience, he is unprepared for its specific dimensions. Such a situation promises to elicit a high degree of ambiguity. Robert is aware that certain actions are expected but unsure of what those actions are or how to begin to learn them. At another level, Robert is certainly experiencing a high degree of *anxiety* as he strives to integrate into the faculty at Alden High. Such ambiguity and anxiety, while common, must eventually be negotiated if Robert is to be effective in his new setting. Hopefully, as Robert begins to build closer relationships with other teachers and gain a better understanding of his students, his emotions will come under control and he can begin to feel as if he *belongs* in this setting.

Robert's situation represents only one of many ambiguous situations that might arise in such a diverse setting as Alden High. Let's now look at some other situations that could conceivably occur there.

Andre's Role Problem

Andre is a 23-year-old, first-year social studies teacher hired along with Robert. African American and from a middle-class background, Andre has always prided himself on knowing a lot about people at all socioeconomic levels and from many ethnic groups. Andre began the year with the intent of relating especially well to the African American students. He intends to show them that he is really one of them and understands their needs.

While walking down the hall on his first day in school, Andre sees a group of black males standing near a wall of lockers. They are wearing typical casual clothes—jeans, t-shirts, and sneakers. Andre is dressed in slacks, shirt, tie, and sport coat. Andre greets the group with a hearty "What's happening, bro?" The students look at him and continue with their own conversation. Andre tries to strike up a conversation by asking about any good rap groups in the school, saying that he has done some "bad rappin" himself. The boys eye him up and down, then slowly move on down the hall. Andre is puzzled. He had thought that they would respond to his approach and would see him as a "brother."

The next day, Andre sees the same group again and begins to approach them. Seeing him coming, one of the group steps forward and quite sarcastically says, "Hey, bro! You be down in Room 104 [the teacher's lounge], not in my face!" Then the group walks away. Andre does not understand the group's obvious hostility and rejection.

Why do you think the students rejected Andre's attempts to be friendly? There are many possible explanations for this situation. One, the group may have felt that Andre's clothes were too "different." They couldn't relate to this "different-looking" adult (*outgroup, categorization*). Two, Andre's use of Black English may have been incorrect in this particular time and place, and may have labeled him in their eyes as a "phony"—someone who couldn't be trusted (*communication, outgroup*). Three, it is possible that Andre came on too hard to these particular students and that he was seen as pushy and was rejected because of it (*role*).

Using the culture-general framework to analyze the situation suggests another possible explanation. The group may not have accepted Andre because they saw him as an outsider, regardless of his race or his language. Andre was still a teacher in the eyes of these students (*role, status*), and one they did not yet know. Andre was categorized by the students in a different way than he would categorize himself— that is, as an outgroup member rather than the ingroup member he expected to be (*categorization*).

It is important to identify the criteria that others use to form categories and, thus, the meaning attributed to those groups. Although Andre may have been fairly close to their age and talked their talk, he was still seen as an adult teacher, an authority figure who could not be trusted, at least at the outset. As a teacher, he should not have expected to be included as one of their group. Their response told him that he should be in Room 104, that he was a teacher and should have acted like one. New teachers are usually eager to be accepted by students. This is normal, especially as they may not be far removed from the lives and concerns of high school students themselves. Given time, Andre can establish the rapport he wants, but he must do so in his role as a teacher.

Joao's Identity Problem

Joao is a teenager from Providence, Rhode Island, who was sent to live for two years with his aunt and uncle, who live near Alden High School. This is the first time that Joao has been away from his family, who emigrated from Portugal when he was a child. His family is strongly united and feels a deep pride in its Portuguese heritage. Joao has heard that the school has a reputation as being a place where students from different backgrounds get along well together, so he has not been worrying about being the only Portuguese in the student body. He has looked forward to attending his new school.

During Joao's first week in school, he discovers that several members of the faculty view him as belonging to a group of students who speak Spanish. A few teachers greet him in Spanish, and one suggests he join a club mainly for Central American students. Joao is surprised and resentful that these teachers just assume he is Hispanic. During his second week, a teacher gives him a notice to take home to his uncle; it is in Spanish. Joao startles the teacher by loudly protesting, "Please try to remember; I'm Portuguese!"

Many different issues may be at play in this situation. First, Joao might have felt some dislocation at being sent to live with his aunt and uncle in the first place. His sense of unity with his family in Providence was very strong, and it is reasonable to suppose that he missed them very much (*belonging*). Second, Joao had been attending schools in Providence in which many other students were native Portuguese. The idea of going to school with students from other ethnic and cultural groups—but no Portuguese—although initially interesting, might also have been somewhat frightening (*ingroup/outgroup*). It is also possible that Joao's parents had kept him under such tight discipline that he had never learned much self-discipline. Thus, his first experience of living away from home may have been so demanding that he was unable to control himself.

At another level, Joao was obviously upset about being identified as a member of a cultural group other than his own (*categorization, values*). Proud to be a native Portuguese and having shared this pride with other Portuguese students in Providence, he couldn't adjust to being viewed as a Spanish speaker from Mexico or Central America. In addition, being used to teachers who recognized the Portuguese language and culture, he was perhaps shocked to find teachers who did not (*disconfirmed expectations*).

The teachers meant to be helpful to Joao, of course. They no doubt thought of him as coming from one of the Spanish-speaking countries, because they needed to fit him quickly into one of the ethnic and cultural categories already familiar to them. Since the Portuguese language is similar enough to Spanish that Joao could understand the teachers when they addressed him in Spanish, they found it convenient to categorize him with the other Spanish-speaking students.

Rosita's Alienation Problem

Rosita Gomez arrived in the United States two months ago from El Salvador, an orphan being sponsored by a European American, middle-class family. Before her arrival, her American parents went to

Alden High School and provided the administrators and faculty with information about her situation. To make her adjustment easier, a number of teachers organized a group of students to act as sponsors for Rosita. The students were to teach her about the school and community and to help her with transition problems, as well as to offer friendship.

During the past two months, the appointed students have helped Rosita in school and have been friendly to her. They have encouraged her to become involved in student council and to attend after-school extra-help sessions whenever she needed to. Rosita, though, has often been left out of students' social activities, such as parties, group movie dates, and volleyball games, and she thinks she is being treated as an outcast. She feels lonely and afraid and complains to her American parents and school counselor about her feelings. This confuses the Alden High students and teachers very much, as they have tried hard to make Rosita feel at home. How might you explain this situation?

It is possible that Rosita, having had a major transition in her life recently, is magnifying the situation. Perhaps the circumstances are such that she is experiencing what is commonly referred to as "culture shock." However, *culture shock* is a very generalized term that refers to an overall reaction to a complex series of events; the term isn't very useful when analyzing specific situations. There is something more specific going on here.

It is also possible that the students do not really like Rosita and are trying to have as little to do with her as possible. The appointed students may feel put upon by their teachers and are thus taking it out on Rosita. However, the students are having what appears to be extensive contact with Rosita in school. If they did not like her, they would probably forego school contact as well.

Viewed through the culture-general model, it is possible that Rosita's predicament can be understood in terms of ingroup behavior. In every culture, there exist ingroups, people who are comfortable with one another, share similar values and casual language, and seek each other's company. Ingroups allow people to share their concerns, laugh and joke about problems as a way to reduce tensions, and generally just let their hair down. The students in this situation represent such an ingroup. Rosita has left her own ingroup behind in El Salvador and needs to reestablish herself as part of a new ingroup. The students, however, do not see Rosita as being part of their ingroup, at least not yet. She would not understand most of their jokes, does not share their intimate and extensive knowledge of other students and teachers, and could not enter into their conversation easily. The students, thus, do not invite Rosita to share in their social activities. Not belonging to an ingroup, Rosita feels like an outcast (*belonging*) and is missing the support system so needed during her difficult transition to a new culture.

Rema's Communication Problem

Rema, a 16-year-old girl from Lebanon, came to the United States just one year ago. Although she still has some difficulties in speaking and writing English, her language skills are sufficient for her to be academically successful at Alden. Midway through the eleventh grade, Rema was achieving *B*s and *C*s in all of her classes, including Andre's social studies class.

Actually, social studies is Rema's favorite subject, and Andre continually remarks to others about the breadth and depth of her reading. Rema reads voraciously and does not limit herself to materials studied in class. She keeps up on international news and reads literature in two languages.

Andre is concerned, however, about Rema's test scores. When the class takes a multiple-choice, true-false, or fill-in-the-blank test, Rema's grades are usually among the highest. When the class is assigned an interpretive essay, however, Rema's grade is always much lower. Andre has said many times, "Rema just never really gets to the point; she tries to talk about everything at once." Despite repeated efforts to remedy this writing problem, Rema continues to write confusing analyses.

There are many ways to explain Rema's writing performance. It is possible that she lacks the basic writing skills and vocabulary necessary to compose lengthy compositions of this kind. However, her overall academic performance indicates that she is competent in English vocabulary and writing. Her problems with written expression are probably not due to technical deficiencies.

It is also possible that Rema has misunderstood or misinterpreted the main elements of the work she is studying. But having read works of equal breadth and depth on her own, it is unlikely that Rema is unable to analyze and appreciate what she is reading.

Alternatively, Rema may not be able to think clearly under the pressure of tests. However, this does not seem to be the case in objective tests; she shows no particular "test anxiety." Thus, Rema's problem seems to lie elsewhere.

Analyzed from the standpoint of cultural differences, however, it is possible that Middle Eastern and North American modes of learning, thinking, and communicating are very different. In many cultures, including Arab countries, communication is accomplished through associations. Everything that is associated with an idea is considered relevant when thinking about or communicating a concept. Such communication may seem highly indirect to a European American, who typically gets right to the point and reasons in a systematic, step-by-step fashion. In contrast, a Middle Easterner often makeas many loops while communicating a point. In short, when viewed in terms of her native culture, Rema's highly associative compositions demonstrate both her knowledge of the subject and her overall intellectual ability. Once Rema and her teacher are aware of these culturally different writing styles, they can take some practical steps to improve the situation.

Kaye's Communication Problem

Issues of communication affect dialogue among teachers as well. Kaye Stoddard is in the middle of her first year as assistant principal at Alden High. Kaye is an energetic person who encourages staff input concerning school policies and curriculum. She encourages staff participation through periodic surveys and group discussions at staff meetings. Lately, however, Kaye has been disturbed about the dearth of input she is receiving from Latino teachers. She is particularly interested in their ideas, since so many of the school's students are Latino. Although she has solicited feedback from everyone, most of her information comes from the European American teachers. How might this situation be explained?

One simple explanation for this lack of participation might be that the Latino teachers do not want to interact with Kaye because she is non-Hispanic. However, there is no indication that this is the case. The entire school population is mixed, and such a situation would make it difficult for the Latino teachers to limit their interactions with non-Latinos. Also, there is no indication that Kaye feels she is the target of hostility.

It is also possible that the European American teachers dominate the Latino teachers, giving them little chance to express their opinions. Again, however, there is no indication that this is the case. Nor is there any indication that the Latino teachers are indifferent concerning the subjects Kaye includes in the surveys and meetings. Like other professionals, most teachers have strong opinions about their workplace.

A more probable explanation can be found in culturally different communication styles. Kaye has taken an impersonal approach to eliciting opinions, whereas the Latino teachers may favor a personalized approach. Latino culture strongly emphasizes the affective side of interpersonal relationships. Personalized contact is, thus, very important to many Latino teachers. Although Kaye is genuinely interested in the opinions of all her teachers, she has approached them impersonally through her written surveys and large-group staff meetings. The Latino teachers might respond more easily if approached individually or addressed personally at a meeting. At the same time, many Latinos feel strong affiliation with the group (*relation to the group, individualism vs. collectivism*), and the Latino teachers might respond even more enthusiastically if they were asked for their ideas and opinions together in a small group.

Each of these critical incidents explores several of the many possible cultural issues always at work in diverse settings, such as Alden High School. They illustrate ways in which classrooms and schools function as cultural crossroads, as places where infinite variations of cultural knowledge, beliefs, values, and skills meet and are forced to interact. In this chapter, we have presented a culture-general model that offers a language and concepts that provide a common framework for all such interactions, no matter what their variation. Perhaps you would like to analyze experiences you have had that might be understood in light of the culture-general model. See if you can think of some.

In Part Two of this book, we will be focusing on longer case studies, in which teachers, students, administrators, parents, and others also experience cross-cultural interactions of various kinds in contexts of changing ideas of good practice in schools. Remember as you read on that there is never any "one best answer" to the issues that arise. Indeed, an understanding of the complexities of cultural diversity suggests that, in many instances, the idea of a single "best solution" is not only impossible but also inimical to a culturally pluralistic environment. In short, teachers must learn to feel comfortable with, appreciate the possibilities of, and negotiate effectively in ambiguous situations.

Active Exercises

The following exercises from *Human Diversity in Action: Developing Multicultural Competencies for the Classroom*[9] complement this chapter well:

Reading 11: "Understanding Misunderstanding: Barriers to Dealing with Diversity," p. 64

Activity 12: Adjustment to Change, p. 68

Activity and Reading 13: "A Culture-General Framework for Understanding Intercultural Interactions," p. 71

Activity 14: Critical Incident Review, p. 86

Activity 15: Observing Cultural Differences, p. 130

Activity 16: Learning About Others, p. 133

Activity 24: Writing Your Own Critical Incidents, p. 158

Accessing the World Wide Web: Resources for Diversity

For more information on cross-cultural communication, see the contents of the booklet *Cross-Cultural Communication: An Essential Element of Effective Education*, by Orlando L. Taylor, at:

www.nwrel.org/cnorse/booklets/ccc/

For a quick reference for the definition of terms widely used when speaking about issues in multicultural education, see the *Diversity Dictionary* of the University of Maryland at:

http://www.inform.umd.edu/EdRes/Topic/Diversity/Reference/divdic.html#Q

Another university site that has numerous links to pages of interest with respect to specific cultural and culture-general issues is the UCLA Diversity Page, which can be found at:

http://latino.sscnet.ucla.edu/diversity1.html#AsA

References

1. Center for Education Statistics, *Digest of Education Statistics* (Washington, DC: U.S. Government Printing Office, 1987).
2. Nancy Hoffman, *Women's True Profession: Voices from the History of Teaching* (New York: The Feminist Press, 1981), p. xix.
3. Myra H. Strober and David Tyack, "Why Do Women Teach and Men Manage? A Report on Research on Schools," *Signs: Journal of Women in Culture and Society* 5, 3 (Spring 1980): 494–503.
4. Sara Lawrence Lightfoot, in an interview with Bill Moyers as part of the *World of Ideas* series, American Broadcasting Corporation, 1989.
5. Gregory Trifonovitch, "Culture Learning–Culture Teaching," *Educational Perspectives*, 16, 4 (1977): 18–22.
6. Kenneth Cushner and Richard Brislin, *Intercultural Interactions: A Practical Guide*, 2nd ed. (Thousand Oaks, CA: Sage, 1996).
7. F. Heider, *The Psychology of Interpersonal Relations* (New York: John Wiley & Sons, 1958).
8. P. J. Farris and S. M. Cooper, *Elementary Social Studies: A Whole Language Approach* (Madison, WI: Brown & Benchmark, 1994).
9. Kenneth Cushner, *Human Diversity in Action: Developing Multicultural Competencies for the Classroom* (New York: McGraw-Hill, 1999).

Multicultural Teaching in Action

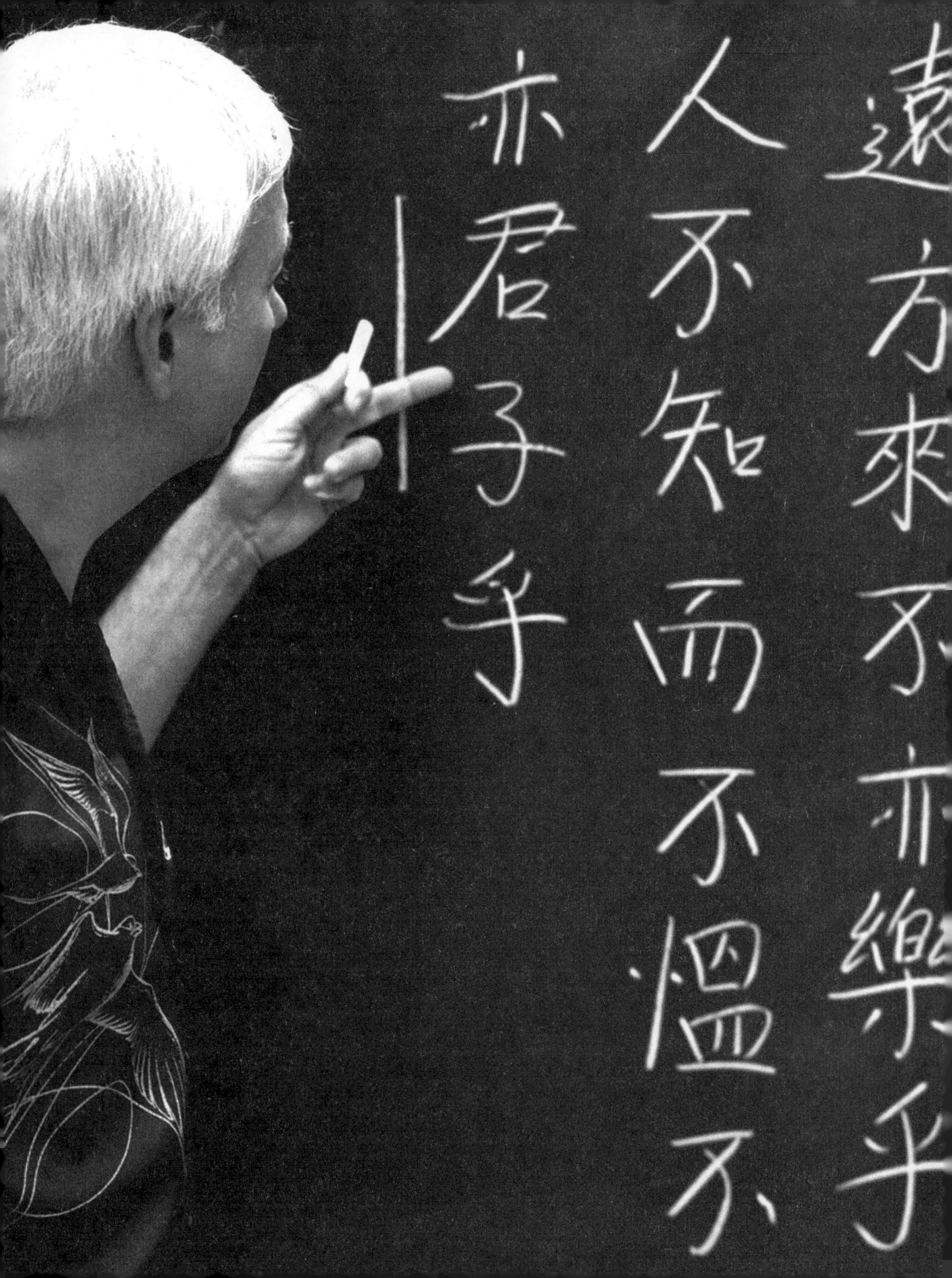
遠方來不亦樂乎
人不知而不慍不、
亦君子乎

Developing Learning Communities:
Language and Learning Style

CHAPTER OUTLINE

CHARACTERISTICS OF A LEARNING
    COMMUNITY
RATIONALE FOR LEARNING COMMUNITY
    CLASSROOMS
    Pedagogies: Old and New
    Roles: Old and New
    Place of Content Knowledge: Old
      and New
    Assessment: Old and New
PERSPECTIVES ON LANGUAGE ACQUISITION
    Language and the Family
    Institutional Aspects of Language
PERSPECTIVES ON LANGUAGE VARIATION
    Verbal Communication

    Nonverbal Communication
CULTURE, LANGUAGE, AND
    LEARNING STYLE
    Components of Learning Style
    Origins of Learning Style
    The Relation of Language and
      Learning Style to Culture
    Communication Style
    Bilingual Education
SOME REFLECTIVE QUESTIONS
ACTIVE EXERCISES
ACCESSING THE WORLD WIDE WEB:
    RESOURCES FOR DIVERSITY
REFERENCES

We are living in a new age which itself is defined by the fact that challenges we face do not respect any conventional boundaries. They don't respect geographical boundaries and they don't respect old definitions.

Richard F. Celeste

Language and Learning Style in a Learning Community Classroom: A Case Study

It is 4:00 P.M. on a Friday afternoon in mid September, and Martina Chandler stands by the windows in her third-floor classroom, watching the sun glinting off San Francisco Bay. Typical of many high school classrooms, this one is a large rectangle, with a chalkboard on one end, windows along one side, and a variety of furniture and equipment for student use. Unlike many high school classrooms, however, the space in this room is organized for active work rather than for passive listening. Most of the furniture is adaptable to many uses: low, three-shelf bookcases on wheels can be moved around to create a variety of spaces; individual desks have been replaced by several round tables with moveable chairs that can accommodate four or five students at a time; individual carrels made of large boxes that fold up when not in use can be set up on small tables or on one long table, so that students can work or study alone; learning center areas for various purposes can be created and recreated from a number of bright plastic "orange crates" also on wheels. Also in the room is a large, cushioned porch rocker inherited from Martina's grandmother. Even Martina's desk is lightweight and movable when required by the classroom activities.

In addition, the walls are covered with maps, posters, and pictures from around the world. One striking poster has the Greek, Hebrew, Cyrillic, Spanish, Japanese, Arabic, French, and English alphabets side-by-side in bright colors. Another has a variety of drawings of students engaged in different styles of learning—reading, talking to one another, writing, building, singing, and dancing. Still another displays a "language tree," which shows the roots of the world's major languages.

Now that the last student of the day has left, Martina is thinking about the progress her students have made in the first two weeks of school. Although she has five classes, she is particularly interested in her tenth grade English class, which has shown strong interest in setting class goals for the year and in deciding how they are going to achieve them. They have caught the spirit of the learning community classroom earlier than her other classes and seem to be enjoying themselves a great deal.

Unlike some teachers in her school, Martina has chosen to teach heterogeneous classes. The twenty-four students in the tenth grade English class come from backgrounds that vary by family income, ethnic heritage and country of origin, religion, native language, past school achievement, and race. Martina views this variation as potentially enriching for herself and her students. It is very important to her that the class becomes a community of learners in which the sociocultural and linguistic backgrounds of all her students are known, appreciated, and used.

Prior to the beginning of school, Martina began assembling her usual set of student files by looking up her student's official records in the school office. She recorded her students' full names, their birthdays, their parents' occupations, and any information available concerning their English-language abilities, as well as their abilities in languages other than English and their ninth grade achievement scores. From this information, she knew that this class was more linguistically diverse than others she had taught. Also, for the first time, she was going to have a deaf student and her interpreter in class. Martina was fairly certain that differences in the cultural and language backgrounds of these students would mean differences in their learning styles and personal interests. To aid her planning, she made up a variety of charts that let her see the demographic composition of the class at a glance. (See Tables 5.1 and 5.2.)

TABLE 5.1 Tenth Grade English Class: Gender/Ethnicity/Religion

123

CHAPTER 5
Developing Learning
Communities:
Language and
Learning Style

	Ethnicity	Religion
Males		
Tomas	Mexican American	Catholic
Ricardo	Mexican American	Catholic
Tran	Vietnamese	Buddhist
Peter	Japanese American	Methodist
Yoshi	Japanese American	Shinto
Ritchie	African American	Conservative Baptist
Dontae	African American	Nonaffiliated
Jacques	Haitian American	Catholic
Joe	Bohemian American	Nonaffiliated
Steve	Hungarian American	Catholic
Abdul	Kuwaiti American	Muslim
Females		
Grace	Mexican American	Catholic
Rosita	Mexican American	Catholic
Maria	Puerto Rican American	Presbyterian
Juanita	Mexican American	Catholic
Wei-Ping	Chinese	Methodist
Komiko	Japanese American	Shinto
Elaine	Japanese American	Baptist
Houa	African (Niger)	Muslim
Anna	German American	Catholic
Natasha	Russian American	Jewish
Kate	Scottish American	Presbyterian
Hannah	Scotch Irish American	Assembly of God
Tammy	Scotch Irish American	Nonaffiliated

The First Week: Exploring Names and Languages

Since beginning school two weeks ago, Martina has devoted much of her classroom time to activities designed to help her students get to know one another and to begin forming a classroom community. At the end of the first class, Martina asked her students to talk with their parents about the origins of their first and middle names and what nationality their names represented. She also asked them to find out if their names had a special meaning in another language. "Tomorrow," she announced, "we will begin interviewing one another for the Class Bulletin Board."

When her students came to class the next day, Martina used a technique she had read about to form the students into pairs.[1] She had the students line up around the room according to their birthdays and then asked each student to be a partner to the student who had a birthday closest to him or her. When partnerships were established, she handed out the following list of questions for students to use in interviewing one another:

1. What is your name? What do you like or dislike about your name?
2. What do you know about how you got your name? Were you named after someone else? Who named you?
3. Are there members of your family who have the same name?
4. Do you have any friends who have the same name as you do?
5. Are there any famous people who have the same name as yours?
6. Are you at all like any of these people who have the same name as yours?
7. Does your name have any other meaning?
8. Was your name originally in another language? Was it spelled differently in that language? Does it have a special meaning in that language?
9. What does your family call you? Do you have a nickname?
10. What do you like to be called?[2]

The class spent about fifteen minutes interviewing one another. Then Martina asked them to "introduce" their partners to the class by telling what they had learned. While each student was talking, she listened carefully and took notes. At the end of each "introduction," Martina took a

TABLE 5.2 Tenth-Grade English Class: Social Class (*Based on Parents' Occupation*)

Name	Father's Occupation	Mother's Occupation
Poor (25 percent)		
Jacques	Migrant laborer	Migrant laborer
Hannah	Not available	Waitress
Joe	Merchant seaman	Waitress
Dontae	Not available	Not available
Tammy	Not available	Cleaning lady
Juanita	Farmhand	Wife and mother
Working Class (29.2 percent)		
Tran	Truck farmer	Truck farmer
Tomas	Not available	Office worker
Maria	Restaurant cook	Waitress
Komiko	Merchant seaman	Data entry worker
Grace	Not available	Secretary
Rosita	Salesman	Teacher's aide
Steve	Longshoreman	Not available
Middle-Class (33.4 percent)		
Ritchie	Minister	Nurse
Wei-ping	Architect	Wife and mother
Yoshi	Computer specialist	Teacher
Peter	Banker	Social worker
Natasha	Teacher	Professor
Elaine	Store manager	Store clerk
Anna	Teacher	Teacher
Kate	Doctor	Nurse
Ricardo	TV videographer	Day care director
Upper-middle Class (8.4 percent)		
Houa	Diplomat	Wife and mother
Abdul	Oil company executive	Wife and mother

snapshot of each student and repeated the student's name. Class ended before they finished, and Martina told them they would complete the "introductions" the next day.

On Wednesday, after the introductions and picture taking were completed, the students were asked to hand in the notes on their question sheets. Then the class spent the rest of the period discussing the number of different languages, accents, and dialects represented in the class. One exercise that all the students liked was to pronounce aloud the following words:

greasy	here	car	bath	dog
get	aunt	because	idea	park
house	fit	Mary	were	right
fire	sorry	log	child	

The students were surprised to discover that, although everyone spoke at least some English, all of them also spoke dialects, some of which were regional and some of which were social in their origin. Anna and Mrs. Thomas (the deaf student and her interpreter) also participated by signing each of the words and talking about how the signs developed and how they might be used in sentences.

The students also considered English words that have been borrowed from other languages. Divided into groups of four and using one of the several dictionaries and other reference books in the room, students first tried to guess and then looked up the derivation of the following words:

algebra	Arabic
gingham	Malay
chocolate	Nahuatl (Native American)
khaki	Hindi
linen	Old English
safari	Arabic (through Swahili)
home	Old English
klutz	Yiddish
prairie	French
zombie	Congo
seersucker	Persian
skunk	Algonquian (Native American)
satin	Chinese
shampoo	Hindi
kimono	Japanese
piano	Italian
tycoon	Japanese

boondocks	Tagalog (Philippines)
smithereens	Irish
gorilla	West African (through Greek)[3]

Martina was pleased that the students had become so interested in the subject of "word borrowing" that they were determined to develop a "Borrowing Dictionary" to leave with Martina for her other classes. By Friday of the first week, the pictures of all the students had been developed, and the class spent the period designing and putting together the Class Bulletin Board. Right in the middle of the pictures, they put a printed sheet that read

A FABLE

In a house there was a cat, always ready to run after a mouse, but with no luck at all.

One day, in the usual chase the mouse found its way into a little hole and the cat was left with no alternative than to wait hopefully outside.

A few moments later the mouse heard a dog barking and automatically came to the conclusion that if there was a dog in the house, the cat would have to go. So he came out only to fall into the cat's grasp.

"But where is the dog?" asked the trembling mouse.

"There isn't any dog—it was only me imitating a barking dog," explained the happy cat, and after a pause added, "My dear fellow, if you don't speak at least two languages, you can't get anywhere nowadays."[4]

Over the weekend, Martina looked at the notes she had made from the students' official files, the notes she had taken in class as the students were introducing one another, and the question sheets that the students had filled out. From these three sources, she developed a chart on the linguistic variability of the class. (See Table 5.3.)

The Second Week: Exploring Learning Styles and Family Stories

The second week, Martina began class by asking students if they knew how they learned best. "They tell me that we're going to get a computer for our classroom soon, and we'll all have to learn how to use it. How many of you are already familiar with computers?" About a third of the class raised their hands. "OK," she said, "what would be the very first thing the rest of you would do in order to go about learning how to use the computer?"

Students answered in different ways. Some said they would get a book on computers or on a particular program and start that way. Others said they would get someone who was familiar with computers to tell them about it first. Still others said there was no way they could learn without sitting down in front of one and actually doing it. Steve and Joe said they would first try to take the computer apart.

Using this short discussion as an introduction, Martina divided the class into four groups, asking each group to look at and discuss the materials on learning style she had placed on their table. At one table were materials on field dependence and field independence[5] (two types of cognition

TABLE 5.3 Tenth Grade English Class: Linguistic Background/Language Proficiency

Name	Native Language/Dialect	Comments
Tran	Vietnamese	Recent immigrant; limited English but able to make himself understood if necessary; also speaks French. Needs help with many words; clever use of gestures to get meaning across. No record of reading or writing scores.
Anna	ASL	Speaks English as a second language; speaks standard English reasonably well; prefers to sign; reading and writing scores good.
Peter	English	Second-generation Japanese American; has some Japanese but uses it only with his grandparents; reading and writing scores fairly high.
Tomas	Spanish/Mexican	Speaks English with a slight Spanish accent; reading scores moderate; writing scores fairly low.
Wei-Ping	Chinese/Mandarin	Speaks standard English well but very formally; does not use vernacular English; reading and writing scores high.
Grace	English	Monolingual in English; speaks standard English reasonably well but uses a good deal of slang; reading scores moderate; writing scores moderately low.
Joe	English	Monolingual in vernacular English; does not appear at all comfortable speaking in front of the class; reading and writing scores moderately low.
Rosita	Spanish	Bilingual in Spanish and standard English; has a pronounced Mexican/Spanish accent; reading and writing scores moderate.
Ritchie	English	Bidialectal in Black English and standard English; seems to be able to switch back and forth easily, depending on whom he's talking to and what he's talking about; reading and writing scores moderately high.
Natasha	Russian	Bilingual in Russian and standard English; speaks well in front of people; reading and writing scores high.
Steve	English	Monolingual in standard English; uses vernacular English mostly; lives with his father and grandmother, who are bilingual in Hungarian and English; reading scores moderate; writing scores moderately low.
Yoshi	English	Bilingual in English and Japanese; is second-generation Japanese and lives near her grandparents, with whom she speaks Japanese regularly; reading and writing scores moderate.
Maria	Spanish/Puerto Rican	Came to United States at 5; fluent English speaker but still speaks some Spanish at home; reading scores moderately high; writing scores moderately low.
Kate	English	Monolingual in standard English; speaks easily and fluently in front of class; reading and writing scores high.
Dontae	English	Monodialectal in Black English; recently moved here from South Los Angeles; has a lot of energy and speaks easily and quickly in his own dialect; reading and writing scores in standard English low.
Ricardo	Spanish	Bilingual in Spanish and vernacular English; speaks standard English with effort; reading and writing scores moderately low.
Hannah	English	Monolingual in vernacular English.

TABLE 5.3 Tenth Grade English Class: Linguistic Background/Language Proficiency *(cont.)*

Name	Native Language/Dialect	Comments
Komiko	English	Monolingual in standard English; third-generation Japanese American; parents do not speak Japanese and she has no one to learn it from; reading and writing scores moderate.
Abdul	Arabic/French	Trilingual in Arabic, French, and standard English; speaks standard English formally; reading and writing scores high.
Juanita	Spanish/Mexican	Bilingual in Spanish and English.
Tammy	English/Appalachian	Monolingual in vernacular rural English; has a strong West Virginia "twang" accent; reading scores moderately high; writing scores low.
Jacques	French	Recent immigrant; speaks vernacular French, some vernacular Black English, some standard English; reading and writing scores moderately low.
Elaine	English	Third-generation Japanese; monolingual in standard English; uses considerable slang; reading scores moderate; writing scores moderately high.
Houa	Tribal/French	Trilingual in her ethnic-group language, French, and standard English; speaks somewhat less formally than other nonnative-born students; reading and writing scores moderately high.

that are at the heart of learning style). At the next table were materials on the need for structure in the learning environment,[6] while at a third table were materials on perceptual modalities (visual, auditory, and kinesthetic approaches to learning).[7] On the last table were materials on a broader-based approach to learning styles called the Learning Style Inventory.[8] After each group had had a chance to discuss the materials, and after a spokesperson at each table had summarized his or her group's materials for the rest of the class, Martina handed out a questionnaire she had designed to help students assess their own patterns of learning. She also pointed out additional books, articles, and materials in the classroom to which students could go for further information.

"I don't want you to think of this as some kind of intelligence test, or that you are 'stuck' with the main learning style you appear to have. All of us use many different approaches to learning all the time, and we are all quite able to learn new ones. The point of thinking about learning style is, first, that it is one more piece of the puzzle that is you and, second, that it will help explain to you why this class may be a bit different from others you have had. It's important to me that everyone in this room learns as much as possible. To do that, we'll always have a variety of ways of approaching knowledge and skills. I'll always encourage you to try out new approaches, as well as to use ways that are familiar and comfortable for you. OK?" The students looked a bit skeptical but more or less willingly answered the questionnaire. The real discussion occurred when they compared their answers with those of others at their tables. It was still going on when the class was over.

129

CHAPTER 5
Developing Learning
Communities:
Language and
Learning Style

For the rest of the week, Martina and her students worked on family stories, building on some of the comments that had come out of the "introductions" exercise on the second day of class. Steve, for example, said that his grandmother always called him "Stefan," which is his name in Hungarian; Komiko commented that the only thing Japanese in her house were her family's names. Martina then introduced the notion of "family stories" as discussed by the author Elizabeth Stone.[9] Stone interviewed over a hundred people from various backgrounds, regions of the country, and ages in order to see if there was a pattern to the influence that family stories had on the beliefs, values, and behavior of individuals. She concluded that family stories give us a sense of our past, of the norms and values held by the family, and, perhaps most important, of the future we might be able to expect by virtue of belonging to a particular family. She tells, for example, of one Irish family in which, because of too much drinking and a curiously morose temperament, many of the males committed suicide before the age of 50—a kind of "tragic O'Connor curse." And a young African American spoke proudly of his Creek Indian ancestors, who burned all their corn as they were dispatched on the Trail of Tears, so that their white oppressors couldn't benefit from their hard work—a story that describes a tradition of self-assertion and bravery in his family.

"Now, what I want you to do," Martina said to her students, "is think about the stories of your family members that you've heard ever since you were little. Many of these stories may be about how your families came to the United States, or about how someone conquered terrible odds to achieve something, or about how your family regards love, courtship, and marriage. Some stories may be very short and some may be quite complex, but all of them usually teach you something about yourself as a member of your first 'culture.' Eventually, we're going to write these stories and share them with the rest of the class. Then, we're going to look at some common characteristics of your stories and of narratives in general. Tomorrow, some friends of mine are coming in to tell some of their family stories, and then we'll start on our own."

Now it was Friday afternoon. The students had heard stories about escaping from Nazi Germany during the Holocaust, about a family in which one ancestor had coined the word robot, *and about a family in which several generations of women had fallen "in love at first sight" and had married because of it. Next week the students will begin their own stories and will help each other by offering critiques and suggestions.*

"Maybe," she thought, "we'll have the computer by then and can actually publish them!"

As the following list shows, Martina Chandler's classroom illustrates a number of strategies both for creating a learning community classroom and for taking advantage of various language backgrounds and learning styles to help her students explore and become more proficient in the English language:

1. She organized her classroom so that she and her students could alter it to fit a variety of activities.
2. In the first two weeks of school, she helped students get to know one another through the "introductions" activity, the Class Bulletin Board, the learning style

discussions, and the family stories. Each of these activities is designed to increase the understanding of the differences and commonalities among members of the class.

3. She got to know students through the use of student files and her own charts.
4. She introduced other adults into the class as storytellers. One can expect that she will continue to include family and community members as well as other school staff in her classroom.
5. She began the process of democratic experience by encouraging the students to develop their idea for a "Borrowing Dictionary" as a collaborative project.
6. She used a variety of teaching methods, including questioning, describing, collaborative learning, and developing "voice," all of which coincide with her initial emphasis on names, individual language backgrounds, and family stories.
7. She used culturally based word exercises and learning style activities to put her students' similarities and differences at the center of the educational enterprise, rather than at the margins. Given the linguistic diversity in this class, she is setting up situations in which such diversity can become a resource rather than a hindrance in the exploration and practice of standard English.
8. Finally, she did all of these things in the context of expanding students' awareness of language and, especially, improving their ability to use standard English. In just two weeks, Martina has provided a number of opportunities for oral and written expression that she can use to diagnose her students' language proficiency and then plan both the content and the pedagogy for the class. The content of the English class—principally reading, writing, and speaking—is not only central to but also enhanced by the approaches and methods she uses.

Martina Chandler's impressive accomplishments during the first two weeks of school are just the tip of the iceberg of what she needs to know in order to accomplish the goals that she and her students set. In addition to the personal knowledge of one another that she and her students now share, Martina also needs three kinds of general language-related knowledge. First, she needs to understand the central role of the family in the acquisition and use of language. Second, she needs to understand how language functions as a communication tool and how it is possible to have variations of that tool. Third, she needs to understand the relationships between one's language tools and one's parent culture and how this relationship influences one's learning style. Each of these dimensions of language will be explored in the sections that follow. We will begin by looking closely at what it means to develop a learning community.

CHARACTERISTICS OF A LEARNING COMMUNITY

Education for democratic citizenship implies active participation in the life of the school and classroom community. What many school people are struggling with is the shift from *adding* these ideas to traditional classrooms to focusing on them as the *basis* for educational practice. In schools and classrooms where students and adults have succeeded in altering their focus, the look, feel, and sounds of classroom life are easily discernable.

First, learning community schools and classrooms are organized for activity. Student work covers the walls of halls and classrooms. There may be an absence of "posted rules carefully outlining what one can or cannot do."[10] Arrangements of classroom furniture and equipment vary according to the work being done in them: easy chairs or sofas for reading and conversation, darkrooms for photography, tables for assembling books and newspapers, tables and counters for scientific work, computer corners, and open spaces for gathering people together. There is a sense of "purposeful clutter in these schools and classrooms. They are places to do things in, not places to sit and watch."[11]

131

CHAPTER 5
*Developing Learning
Communities:
Language and
Learning Style*

Second, everyone present in the school participates in this activity-oriented environment. Young children are eager to show off the books they have written; older students are engaged in activities that range from interviewing older community members to engaging in the scientific inventory of nearby plants and animals. Parents and teachers are often found working together to develop and implement instructional goals.[12] Principals, teachers, parents, and students often work collaboratively on joint projects, such as publishing a newspaper or refurbishing the library. Because of all this ongoing activity, such schools and classrooms are rarely quiet, at least in the traditional sense of a school, in which adults talk and children listen. "Children are doing things, not just watching someone else. These are schools where learning is not a spectator sport."[13]

Third, in learning community schools and classrooms, there is a sense that everyone belongs to the community: students, teachers, parents, administrators, support staff, volunteers, and other members of the broader community outside the school. Relationships among all people are collaborative, and each individual perceives all others as both teachers and learners. In a learning community, each individual is valued: cultural and linguistic identity is affirmed by using what each person brings to school as starting points and building blocks.[14]

RATIONALE FOR LEARNING COMMUNITY CLASSROOMS

Building communities of learners centers on the traditional goal of preparing students to be citizens in a democracy. While not a new idea, citizenship education has sometimes been obscured by an overemphasis on the preparation of students for the workplace. At the core of citizenship education are two tenets: (1) the need to negotiate differences through sharing a common curriculum, and (2) the need for students to learn citizenship by *practicing* democracy. With respect to the need for a common curriculum, John Dewey and his daughter argued in 1915 against the separation of students into academic and vocational tracks:

> It is fatal for a democracy to permit the formation of fixed classes. Differences of wealth, the existence of large masses of unskilled laborers, contempt for work with the hands, inability to secure the training that enables one to forge ahead in life, all operate to produce classes, and to widen the gulf between them. Statesmen and legislation can do something to combat these evil forces. Wise philanthropy can do something. But the only fundamental agency for good is the public school system. . . .

There must not be one system for the children of parents who have more leisure and another for the children of parents who are wage earners. The physical separation forced by such a scheme . . . brings about a division of mental and moral habits, ideals and outlook. . . . A division of the public school system into one part that pursues traditional academic methods, and another that deals with those who are to go into manual labor means a plan of social predestination totally foreign to the spirit of democracy.

The democracy which proclaims equality of opportunity as its ideal requires an education in which learning and social application, ideas and practice, work and recognition of the meaning of what is done, are united from the beginning and for all.[15]

With respect to the need to practice democracy in order to learn democracy, George Wood, in 1992, described the requirements of the democratic life in the following terms:

Fundamentally, democracy requires citizens who participate broadly in informed public decision-making with an eye toward the common good. Citizens must thus be literate, able not only to master the rudiments of reading, writing, and computing, but able to use these tools as ways of understanding the world and making their voices heard in it. We must also know how to find and evaluate information, how to sift through the items that bombard us daily, to sort the useful from the superfluous, and the clearly propagandistic from the approximate truths.

Members of the republic must also have an ongoing sense of community, an obligation to the common good. Citizens should see themselves as members of a community that makes their individuality possible, and they should value and nurture that community. Democracy also requires that we each have courage, that we believe our actions are important and valued, and that we have not only a right, but also an obligation to participate publicly. The democratic citizen is, in sum, the individual who has the intellectual skills and conviction necessary to participate publicly in making the many choices that confront us, in ways that will promote the common good.[16]

One way to provide a common curriculum in which all students practice the required skills of democratic participation is to create communities of learners in which all those involved—students, teachers, parents, administrators, counselors, nurses, and volunteers—actively participate in decisions regarding the educational process.

Pedagogies: Old and New

Much has been written lately about new ways of teaching that are presumed to benefit a greater variety of students. Included in these new ways of teaching are such labels as "interactive learning," "feminist pedagogy," "inquiry learning," "emancipatory curriculum," "critical pedagogy," "discovery learning," "whole language," and "collaborative learning." While there are some "new" aspects contained in these ideas (which will be described in later chapters), in general they can all be grouped in the much more traditional category of "good teaching." Moreover, most of them have been around for a long, long time.

Dialogue, for example, or what is sometimes known as "interactive teaching and learning," is Plato's dialectic in contemporary dress. Discovery learning, or the use of teaching techniques that present students with questions and materials that impel students to active investigation, was the centerpiece of Abelard's teaching in the twelfth century.[17] Critical pedagogy, inquiry learning, feminist pedagogy, and collaborative learning all hearken back at least to John Amos Comenius in the seventeenth century. He believed that understanding was more important than rote learning, that demonstration is more effective than listening to experts, that education should follow the natural development of the student, that students should teach and learn from one another, and that both text material and learning activities should incorporate the student's own experience as a starting point.

133

CHAPTER 5
Developing Learning
Communities:
Language and
Learning Style

What is relatively new in learning community classrooms is not that such varied methods of instruction should exist but that they should exist more or less simultaneously and be exercised by both children and adults. Their emphasis depends on the age of the student, the nature of the subject matter, and the kind of learning activities used. Thus, in a learning community classroom, there is plenty of room for *all* the old methods of dialogue: telling, demonstrating, modeling, and problem posing. In addition, several relatively new ideas about teaching are often incorporated into learning communities. One is that teaching strategies should attend to the development of "voice" among students. That is, teaching should encourage the expression of distinctive beliefs and experiences based on both biological and sociocultural differences. In addition, because learning community classrooms include parents and other community members as part of the classroom community, family or adult literacy may also be a pedagogical goal.

Roles: Old and New

As with pedagogy, the traditional roles of adults and children in learning community classrooms are not so much changed as they are expanded. Thus, the role of teacher as "teller" is expanded to teacher as guide, coach, and sometimes cheerleader! The role of teacher is also expanded to include other adults—parents, administrators, and community members—who provide various types of specialized assistance to the regular classroom teacher. Similarly, the role of teacher is also extended to students, who serve as teachers and critics to one another. The role of learner, like that of teacher, is also expanded in learning community classrooms. Because everyone (teachers, students, administrators, parents, and community members) has unique experiences and specialized knowledge to share, it follows that everyone (adults included) will be a learner as well as a teacher.

Place of Content Knowledge: Old and New

In a learning community classroom, the place and function of content knowledge also vary, although they are certainly no less important than in traditional classrooms. Thus, mathematics, language, history, science, and the arts serve in dual capacities. Sometimes such knowledge is learned as an end in itself. This is the more "traditional" approach to content. At other times, content knowledge serves as a means to another end, such as solving a problem or constructing a new way of looking at the world. This is the "newer" approach to content learning. More often than not in learning community classrooms, subject matter knowledge is acquired in the service of other goals. Thus, if one needs to produce a newspaper, one must know how to use language in intelligible ways. If one is going to measure the amount of rainfall during a storm, one must know about fractions and forms of measurement. Conversely, in traditional classrooms, it is likely that such "subjects" as language and mathematics are taught as ends in themselves, with applications of that knowledge coming later (or maybe not at all). In learning community classrooms, the project or activity often comes first, and the knowledge and skills needed to accomplish the activity become necessary tools in the service of that activity. In this way, students come to appreciate the relevance of subject matter knowledge.

Assessment: Old and New

In traditional classrooms, the assessment of student achievement is largely accomplished through paper-and-pencil testing. Moreover, the results of such assessment are often used to separate (track) students into homogeneous groups, presumably for their own benefit. When standardized commercial tests are used, they indicate to administrators and the community how "well" or "poorly" student, teacher, class, or school is doing in relation to other students, teachers, classes, and schools.

In learning community classrooms, such traditional paper-and-pencil forms of assessment are also used, although for somewhat different purposes. For example, unit tests are used mostly for instructional feedback to individual students, rather than to group them or to provide interim or final grades. In addition, other forms of assessment, including peer evaluation, portfolios, group tests, and self-evaluation, are used. All of these measures are combined when judging what grades a student has earned.

At this point, you might be wondering how the ideas of a learning community classroom are related to the issues of individual biological, psychological, and sociocultural differences discussed in the first four chapters of this book. As an example, let's look at the ways in which one important source of cultural identity—language—might play out in a learning community classroom.

PERSPECTIVES ON LANGUAGE ACQUISITION

It is often said that language is what makes us human. Certainly, language is the primary means for socializing us into our families and our social groups and, through them, giving us our cultural identity.

Language and the Family

Berger and Berger refer to language as the first institution encountered by an individual. This may surprise you if you think of the family as being the first institution, the one that introduces us to language. Looked at another way, however, infants can't know what a family is until they have acquired language.[18] Language *objectifies, interprets,* and *justifies* reality for the child,[19] thus structuring the child's environment. It puts labels on roles (mommy, police officer, teacher, priest) and permits the child to extend those roles into the wider community. It also brings the meanings and values of the wider community onto the small stage of the immediate family. Consider the case of a father in the act of punishing his child:

> As he punishes, he talks. What is he talking about? Some of the talking may just be a way of giving vent to his own annoyance or anger. But, in most cases, much of the talking is a running commentary on the offending act and the punishment it so

richly deserves. The talking *interprets* and *justifies* the punishment. Inevitably, it does this in a way that goes beyond the father's own immediate reactions. The punishment is put in the vast context of manners and morals; in the extreme case, even the divinity may be invoked as a penal authority. . . . The punishing father now represents this system.[20]

135

CHAPTER 5
*Developing Learning
Communities:
Language and
Learning Style*

Institutional Aspects of Language

It might be important here to consider several characteristics that language has in common with other social institutions.[21] First, language is external. It is experienced as "out there," in contrast to the individual's private thoughts or feelings, which, incidentally, are also structured by language and its meanings. Further, when one hears language spoken by another person, that person is speaking according to a particular language *system* that was created neither by the speaker nor the listener. It is external to them both.

Second, language has objectivity; that is, everyone who shares it agrees to accept the norms and conventions of its particular symbol system. Berger and Berger note that "the objectivity of one's first language is particularly powerful."[22] They write:

> Jean Piaget, the Swiss psychologist, tells the story somewhere of a small child who was asked whether the sun could be called anything except "sun." "No," replied the child. How did he know this, the child was asked. The question puzzled him for a moment. Then he pointed to the sun and said, "Well, look at it."[23]

Third, language has the power of moral authority to direct us. As children learn to speak their native language, they are usually excused small lapses in pronunciation and usage. As they grow up, however, the inappropriate use of language may expose them to ridicule, shame, and guilt. Consider the child who speaks a language or dialect different from that of the school, the working-class college student who is expected to engage in polite conversation at a formal reception, and the adult who tries to speak in the rapidly changing vernacular of her teenage children. Not only are these individuals often misunderstood but they are also often the objects of considerable disdain.

Finally, language is historical. It was there before we were born and will continue after we are gone. Its meanings were accumulated over a long period of time by a myriad of individuals now lost forever. Furthermore, language is a living, changing tool, with new words and meanings constantly being added, some for a few days, others for much longer. Some regard language as a "broad stream flowing through time."[24] Berger and Berger write:

> An Austrian writer, Karl Kraus, has called language the house in which the human spirit lives. Language provides the lifelong context of our experience of others, of self, of the world. Even when we imagine worlds beyond this one, we are constrained to put our intimations or hopes in terms of language. Language is *the* social institution above all others. It provides the most powerful hold that society has over us.[25]

Given the power of language to shape us in many ways, it is good to keep in mind that it is not only our "own" language—formal or informal—that has such power. As Gonzalez notes,

There is no such thing linguistically speaking as a good language or a bad language, a superior language or an inferior language. Each language is appropriate for its time, place, and circumstances. All languages are complete in this respect.[26]

PERSPECTIVES ON LANGUAGE VARIATION

In the opening case study, a number of Martina Chandler's classroom activities were designed to show how language varies from one cultural group to another, as well as between individuals within the same group. Likewise, teachers and students sometimes speak different historical languages, but, more often, they speak the same language in different ways. Moreover, teachers and students use both verbal and nonverbal means to communicate significant messages to one another.

Verbal Communication

Human beings are unique in their ability to make sounds that, when joined together in certain ways, can be understood by others. Through an extensive process of evolution, humans have developed the ability to produce, receive, store, and manipulate a variety of symbolic sounds. Human beings, more than any other creature, depend on the production of sound in the form of verbal language as their primary means of communication.

Within any given language, however, vocabulary, pronunciation, syntax (grammatical structure), and semantics (the meaning of words) may differ widely. When Martina's students took turns saying such words as *greasy, fire, log,* and *aunt,* they were able to hear differences in pronunciation. Furthermore, the form in which language is conveyed may also differ—for example, as in sign language, in which syntax is composed of a combination of specific movements of the fingers, hand, and arm, as well as facial expressions. Most people are fascinated to watch this kind of speech, made public in recent years by signers who accompany performances on television or talks by public officials. Martina's students were also very interested in Anna's and Mrs. Thomas's use of sign in class.

As Martina's students interviewed one another and then introduced their partners to the rest of the class, they were able to hear other variations in language as well.

Accents

An accent differs from the standard language only in the way words are pronounced, and it often results from pronunciation habits shared by people from a geographical region. Thus, people with a typical New England accent may pronounce the words *car, far,* and *bar* as if they were spelled *caaa, faaa,* and *baaa.* Similarly, people who have learned to speak English in Appalachia, the South, or the West may have significant differences in the way they pronounce the same words. It is also the case that those whose first language is other than English may have difficulty pronouncing certain English words. Japanese speakers, for example, often have trouble with the letter *l,* and Russian speakers may have difficulty with the letters *w* and *v* as they are used in English words. Note that such speakers may be speaking proper standard English, but with accents.[27] In Martina's classroom,

Hannah and Tammy, who had both moved to California from West Virginia, have the softness and somewhat slurred accent of the West Virginia hills. Yoshi, who speaks both English and Japanese, can imitate her grandparents' Japanese accent as they speak English. Rosita speaks English with a pronounced Spanish accent.

137

CHAPTER 5
*Developing Learning
Communities:
Language and
Learning Style*

Dialects

A dialect is a variation of a "standard" language form that includes differences in pronunciation, word usage, and syntax. Such differences may be based on ethnicity, religion, geographical region, social class, or age. Dialects differ not only in their origin but also in the specifics of their expression. Regional differences, for example, usually involve variations in the pronunciation of vowels (recall the earlier example of people from New England). Similarly, Tammy and Hannah, as well as having Appalachian accents, speak a dialect of English sometimes referred to as "mountain English." Social dialects, on the other hand, are most often distinguished from one another by variations in the pronunciation of consonants, particularly the *th* sound and the sound of the consonants *r* and *l*. Dontae, the young man from Los Angeles, exhibits this language pattern. It is important to remember that regional and social dialects and accents may vary together or be a combination from a number of sociocultural origins, depending on the life experiences of the speaker.[28] Although there are a variety of dialects spoken in the United States, the three most widely known are Ebonics (Black English), rural English, and standard English.

Ebonics. Ebonics (also called Black English or African American Language [AAL]) is a dialect spoken primarily but not exclusively by urban African Americans.[29] Although it is often associated with those who live in low-income communities,[30] it is also spoken by African Americans from a variety of social classes and serves, in part, as an expression of cultural identity.[31] The influence of social class on Ebonics is seen mainly in the ability of Black English speakers to switch back and forth between Ebonics and standard English. Dontae, who speaks Ebonics fluently, has difficulty in switching to standard English and is not certain that he wants to do it. One explanation for the origin of Ebonics is that it is derived from Gullah, a Creole dialect developed by Africans brought to the United States as slaves, which puts English words into a syntax similar to many African languages. Another explanation sees it as a version of a regional English dialect spoken by early English settlers on the East Coast. Gullah is still spoken by some residents of the Sea Islands off the Carolina coast; while many of the distinctive features of Black English are similar to Gullah, Black English is also similar to other dialects spoken by European whites in some rural areas of the United States and England.[32]

Recently, a nationwide debate was sparked when the Oakland, California, school board decided to incorporate Ebonics into its plans to improve student achievement. Although we will speak more about this event later in the chapter, here it is enough to say that much of the controversy was due to the press's misrepresentation of the district's intent. The public was led to believe that students would be taught Ebonics instead of, or in addition to, standard English. The policy, however, never stated that Ebonics would be taught to students, only that their learning would be enhanced when teachers and others recognized and understood Ebonics. In reality, only teachers would be taught Ebonics, enabling them to better understand and communicate with their students.

Rural English. Sometimes called "mountain English," rural English is spoken primarily in Appalachia and is derived from the language of early English settlers in the area. While people from Appalachia are often ridiculed for their speech, some linguists say that mountain English is the "purest" English spoken in the United States, and the closest to the English spoken in Shakespeare's time. It has been preserved, in part, because of the isolation of mountain people, in the same way that Gullah has been preserved off the coast of the Carolinas.

Standard English. It may come as something of a surprise to middle-class European Americans that so-called standard English is also a dialect of the English language. Although the term *standard English* is usually taken to mean the version of the English language most acceptable or most "correct," in fact, there are many varieties of standard English. Gollnick and Chinn, for example, note that "standard English may vary from community to community: 'standard' is what is normative in that community."[33] Moreover, standard English as it is spoken in such countries as Australia, India, Nigeria, and England differs significantly from standard English as it is spoken in the United States.[34] As it is generally used in U.S. schools, *standard English* usually refers to the dialect spoken by educated middle and upper classes and to the formal written and oral English that dominates print and broadcast media.

Bidialectalism

Bidialectalism is the ability to speak two (and sometimes more) dialects and to switch back and forth easily. Examples of bidialectalism are the "country boy" who has become an executive in a large city and switches dialects when he goes back to his hometown and the African American woman who has become a professor and speaks standard English but switches to Black English when speaking informally to African American colleagues, students, and friends. The ability to "code-switch" is often encouraged in schools as a way of enabling youngsters both to broaden their language horizons and to receive the perceived economic and social benefits of speaking standard English. Although research does not support the belief that it is necessary to speak standard English in order to read or write it, it is often the case that prejudice against those who speak nonstandard dialects leads to economic and social discrimination.[35] In Martina's class, Ritchie is able to switch back and forth between Black and standard English easily and does so often.

Sign Language

A form of nonverbal language is the language of signs spoken by the deaf. Several varieties of signed communication exist—notably, American Sign Language (ASL), which is the only sign system recognized as a language; signed English, which translates oral and written English into signs; and fingerspelling (sometimes called the manual alphabet), which literally spells out English words letter-by-letter. Anna acquired ASL in infancy in the same way that her hearing classmates learned oral language. Like other languages, ASL has its own syntax and rhythms. Anna learned to think in it and translates other sign languages and lip reading into it.[36] Closely associated with the culture of the deaf, ASL is the subject of often-heated debate in educational circles. Some believe that all deaf and hearing-impaired children should learn to speak orally, while others believe that signed communication not only is sufficient but also should be universally acknowledged as a complete and legitimate form of communication. In fact, many individuals—both hearing and hearing-impaired—are bilingual in ASL and English. Such is the case with Anna, who has learned to speak oral English but much prefers to use sign.

Like other languages, English and its dialects usually have two sets of norms, one for formal situations and writing and one for informal situations. Thus, one usually speaks informally to one's friends and family but more formally when speaking to strangers or in formal situations. Formal English is also generally used when writing, except, perhaps, in letters to friends or family or in personal journals.

139

CHAPTER 5
*Developing Learning
Communities:
Language and
Learning Style*

Nonverbal Communication

Although sign language is often thought of as nonverbal communication, it is also a form of verbal expression. Nonverbal communication, used by both hearing and hearing-impaired individuals, includes body movements, facial expressions, and a variety of word replacement strategies. It has been estimated that nonverbal communication accounts for 50 to 90 percent of the messages we send and receive.[37] Leubitz has identified four functions of nonverbal communication: (1) it can convey messages; (2) it can augment verbal communication; (3) it can contradict verbal communication; and (4) it can replace verbal communication.[38] For purposes of analysis, three aspects of nonverbal behavior are usually studied: proxemics, kinesics, and paralanguage. It is good to remember, however, that they are seldom used or experienced individually; rather, they combine in various ways with one another and with verbal language to produce the innumerable nuances we take for granted in ordinary communication.

Proxemics

Proxemics is the study of the normal physical distance between speakers when they are communicating with one another. For white Americans, particularly those of northern European ethnic heritage, a comfortable distance between speakers, often called "social space," is about 21 inches.[39] Standing closer than that may be interpreted as hostile or "in your face" behavior, while standing farther away is likely to be interpreted as disinterest or "stand-offishness." In contrast, southern Europeans, Arabs, and Latin Americans normally stand much closer, while African Americans stand farther apart.[40] Since it is so closely linked to cultural norms, the use of social space and other forms of nonverbal communication are not issues we ordinarily think about; rather, they are so much a part of us that they become unconscious behaviors.

Kinesics

Kinesics is the study of body movements, often called "body language," including gestures, posture, facial expressions, and eye contact. Like social space, body language is often involuntary, which accounts for the ability of nonverbal communication to contradict or replace verbal communication. That is, we often "say" with our bodies something opposite to that which we "say" with words, or we communicate attitudes and feelings without the use of words at all. Body language is also closely tied to culture. Indeed, cultural variations in the meaning of particular facial expressions and gestures, as well as the presence or absence of eye contact, can account for serious misinterpretations among people from different cultural backgrounds. Consider, for example, the case of eye contact. African American speakers tend to look more directly at their conversational partner while speaking than while listening, which is the direct opposite of Caucasian Americans. Thus, in conversation, a black listener is likely to look at a white speaker less than the white speaker expects. Likewise, while a black speaker is speaking, both parties in the conversation are likely to be looking at one another more than either expects. Imagine the range of misinterpretations or misattributions that are possible.

Paralanguage

Among the most interesting and least recognized forms of nonverbal communication is paralanguage—vocalizations that are not words. Two categories of paralanguage are distinguished. *Vocalizations* include sounds, such as crying, coughing, laughing, and sighing; the intensity and pitch with which words are expressed; and "vocal segregates," which are sounds that act as word replacements, such as "shhh" and "uh-huh."[41] *Vocal qualifiers* lend meaning to words by means of rhythm, tempo, resonance, and control of articulation.[42] Gollnick and Chinn note that "vocal cues can enable listeners to distinguish between male and female speakers, African American and white speakers, and older and younger speakers, and to distinguish educational level and area of residence within a certain dialect region. A person's social class and status can often be determined based on the vocal characteristics of the individual."[43] Indeed, in the musical *My Fair Lady,* Henry Higgins's almost magical ability to identify a speaker's geographical and social origins is attributable in no small measure to his knowledge of paralanguage.

Such differences in verbal and nonverbal language can lead to harmful misinterpretations in both student-to-student and teacher-to-student communication. When teachers and students belong to the same cultural groups, accurate interpretation is likely to proceed without too much difficulty. When teachers and students come from different cultural groups, however, misinterpretation is likely to be an ongoing problem, unless both are aware of these differences and make an effort to accommodate them.

CULTURE, LANGUAGE, AND LEARNING STYLE

A third important area of language concerns its relationships to culture and learning styles. As we have pointed out, language provides the names for ideas, people, and things that enable us to make sense of the world around us, and it does so at such an early age that it helps structure the very ways in which we think. Thus, the language that students and teachers take with them to school inevitably affects the mental processes by which they perceive, think, solve problems, learn, and approach learning. Language is also both a product and a shaper of culture. The two are inextricably intertwined.

Originally investigated in the 1950s by psychologists interested in perception and other forms of cognition, learning style research in the past decade has become increasingly available to educators interested in the variation they see in patterns of learning. Definitions of *learning style* vary, but the National Task Force on Learning Style and Brain Behavior has adopted the following tentative definition:

141

CHAPTER 5
Developing Learning
Communities:
Language and
Learning Style

> Learning style is that consistent pattern of behavior and performance by which an individual approaches education experiences. It is the composite of characteristic cognitive, affective and psychological behaviors that serve as relatively stable indicators of how a learner perceives, interacts with, and responds to the learning environment. It is formed in the deep structure of neural organization and personality [that] molds and is molded by human development and the cultural experiences of home, school, and society.[44]

Components of Learning Style

Perhaps the most widely used dimension of learning style was also the first to be investigated. Studying variations in perception, Witkin and his colleagues discovered that most individuals could be grouped according to whether they were *field dependent* or *field independent*.[45] An individual who is field independent easily perceives discrete parts, is good at abstract analytical thought, tends to be individualistic and less dependent on others, has less-well-developed social skills, prefers working alone and self-organizes information to be learned, and tends to be intrinsically motivated and unresponsive to social reinforcement. In contrast, an individual who is field dependent (now more often referred to as "field sensitive") perceives globally or holistically, does less well at analytical problem solving, tends to be sensitive to the social environment with well-developed social skills, prefers an observational approach to learning and will accept information to be learned as it is presented, and tends to be extrinsically motivated and responsive to the social environment.[46]

A second dimension of learning style has to do with an individual's *preferred* sensory mode for learning. Although, barring physical disability, all six senses (sight, sound, smell, touch, taste, and movement) are normally open to learning stimuli, some individuals tend to learn most easily and efficiently through one of the sensory modes. There is also some evidence that preferred modes change as a factor of age. Barsch, for example, found that younger children make efficient use of taste, smell, and touch, while older children come to rely on movement, hearing, and vision.[47]

Other variations in learning style include differences in response to the immediate environment, emotionality, social preferences, and cognitive-psychological orientation.[48] Responses to environmental influences include an individual's preference for quiet or noise, bright or soft illumination, and warm or cool temperatures. Emotionality includes such factors as motivation, persistence at tasks, and sense of responsibility, as well as one's response to the structure of a given context. Social preferences are the degree to which the presence of others facilitates learning. Included in this category is the degree to which an individual prefers to work alone, in pairs, in cooperative groups, or with adults. Finally, the psychological dimension includes the tendencies of individuals to be learners who are global or analytic, right-brain or left-brain dominant, and reflective or impulsive.

Origins of Learning Style

Although the exact origins of a person's particular learning style are still a matter of conjecture, it is clear that learning patterns develop from a combination of biological, psychological, and sociocultural (including linguistic) factors. Also, much research indicates that childrearing practices and other forms of socialization are heavily implicated in the development of learning style. Since, as we have seen, language is the medium through which much socialization occurs in the family, it is not unreasonable to surmise that the relation of language to patterns of learning is considerable. In addition, since language is closely linked to culture, learning style differences may be more readily understood if we look at the connections between language, culture, and learning style.

The Relation of Language and Learning Style to Culture

It has been estimated that more than 3,000 languages are spoken around the world—700 in Papua New Guinea alone and more than 1,000 on the African continent. Geography, history, and cultural experience all influence the way a person acquires language, which language that person learns, and what meanings are attributed to words. As we have seen, the family is normally the first mediator of the culture to a growing child. Nevertheless, language and cultural knowledge are inextricably bound together.

Of primary importance in the development of language is the acquisition of vocabulary—the "right" words for ideas, people, actions, and things. But words themselves are arbitrary. Indeed, the very concept of "word" may differ among language groups. The Japanese word *ikimasu,* for example, can mean any of the following English words: I (*you, he, she, we, they*) am (*is, are*) going.[49] A Japanese speaker decides which of these meanings is correct by the context of the conversation. An even more complex concept of "word" can be found in the Yana Indian language in northern California. The word *yabanaumawildjigummaha'nigi* has the following subparts:

ya	=	several people move
banauma	=	everybody
wil	=	across
dji	=	to the West
gumma	=	indeed
ha'	=	let us
nigi	=	we

In English, we might say, "Let us each move to the West," but, as Tiedt and Tiedt note, "Even with the parts of the long word defined, we still do not understand [the Yana word] because we arrange our thoughts differently and do not repeat words as the Yanas did."[50]

Even in the same language, the same words may have different meanings. Consider the word *tip. Tip* can mean to push something over or off an edge. It can also refer to payment for services over and above the stated price. A tip can also be a good idea or suggestion that one person might give another, or it can be a slender point at the end of something. Finally, in some parts of the world, a tip is a garbage dump. Such common English words as *love, bread, chicken, turkey, bat,* and *top* all have many meanings. Linguists have estimated that the fifty most often used words in the English language can produce more than fourteen thousand different meanings.[51]

143

CHAPTER 5
*Developing Learning
Communities:
Language and
Learning Style*

Language also plays a critical role in the maintenance of subgroups within a larger cultural/language group. Recall that ingroup membership is granted to those with whom one feels comfortable and with whom one has perceived similarities. One function of language is to distinguish those who should be considered potential members of the ingroup from those who should not. Language helps us develop a sense of social unity. Thus, a variation from a language "standard" that contributes to a group's sense of identity is nearly as important as the parent language itself.

Language reflects the thought processes of a culture. According to Kaplan, English writing and thinking is linear.[52] That is, the speaker or writer tries to "get right to the point," eliminating reference to issues and topics seemingly irrelevant to the message. The task is to communicate the message quickly and efficiently. Speakers who do not "keep to the task" can be quite frustrating to English listeners, as witnessed by the English colloquialism "He just keeps beating around the bush!" On the other hand, speakers of Semitic languages (Arabic and Hebrew) use various kinds of parallels in their thinking. References to past events, for example, are common and expected. Another important function of verbal communication among Semitic speakers, as well as many others, is the building of personal relationships through language use.

No pattern of communication is "right" or "wrong"; all have evolved to express and satisfy cultural patterns and needs. Some, however, may stress the development of interpersonal relationships more than others. If those interpersonal relationships are not expressed in the message (for example, when an American is speaking with an Arab), the person receiving the message may interpret it in a way that the speaker does not intend. Consider an American discussing plans to meet later in the week. While the American is interested in "nailing down" the time, place, and purpose of the meeting, the Arab intersperses the conversation with questions about the health of family members, the last time the two parties met, and other significant events in the lives of the two conversants. Both speakers are using language for cultural purposes in cultural ways: the American to "get something done" and the Arab to indicate a committed relationship. It would not be surprising, in this instance, if misunderstanding were to occur.

Learning style is also developed, in part, as an expression of culture, since what we attend to and how we attend to it are culturally shaped adaptations to the physical and social environment. Christine Bennett, for example, cites a story told by an Anglo-American speech student who had two experiences that illustrate this point, one with a Hopi Indian and the other with Trukee islanders:

> "Look at those clouds!" I exclaimed one afternoon. "We'll probably have rain later today."
> "What clouds?" my Hopi companion asked.
> "Right there!" I responded in amazement, pointing to obvious puffs of white and gray.
> "All I see is the sky."
> "You mean you really don't see those clouds?"
> "There's nothing there but sky."

Several months later, this same student was in the opposite situation with a group of Trukee fishermen.

> I thought we were lost. There had been no sign of land for hours. My companions tried to reassure me that we weren't lost at all. They read the wave patterns like I'd use a map. All I could see were waves. Even when they pointed to specific signs, I couldn't see anything. Here we were looking at the same body of water. It felt strange to know that I simply could not perceive what they actually saw.[53]

Research has indicated that particular patterns of learning (or learning style) can be associated with particular cultural groups. For example, many African Americans and many females tend to be field sensitive, while many Japanese and Japanese Americans tend to be field independent. It is important to note, however, that *there may be more difference within these groups than between them.* As was pointed out in Chapter 3 (Figure 3.2), a large number of factors can contribute to one's particular pattern of culture, and this holds true for the development of one's language and learning style.

Communication Style

Central to the issue of how we communicate is another set of culturally learned characteristics associated with both language and learning style called *communication style.* Herbert Grossman has written extensively on the subject and his work forms the basis for the following categories and analysis.[54]

Formal vs. Informal Communication

As we have already noted, all languages have sets of norms for both formal and informal communication. However, some cultural groups (and some languages) are much more rigid than others in this differentiation. "Strict codes of communication may be designed to show respect for others, to avoid open demonstrations of conflict and disagreement, or to avoid causing individuals to 'lose face.'"[55] Many Asian students, for example, are shocked to discover how informally American students talk to teachers.

Emotional vs. Subdued Communication

Some cultural groups are concerned more with the sensibilities of other people, while other cultural groups are concerned more with protecting the individual's right to express her or his intense feelings. In the United States, such a distinction can be seen in the African American pattern of emotionally intense speech versus the generally European American pattern of subdued, less emotional speech.

Direct vs. Indirect Communication

Cultural groups vary in terms of their emphasis on frankness and direct communication. Asians and Pacific Islanders, for example, are more likely than Americans to communicate in indirect ways, and Americans are often surprised at the even more direct speech patterns of Russians. One variation of the direct/indirect distinction is the use of poetic or analogous communication. "Educators who prefer direct expression may also mistakenly think that some African American and Hispanic American students who use a more poetic speech pattern are 'beating around the bush,' that they cannot think straight, or that they have communication problems."[56]

Objective vs. Subjective Communication

145

CHAPTER 5
*Developing Learning
Communities:
Language and
Learning Style*

While no culture places an emphasis on total and complete honesty, cultural groups differ on the emphasis placed on accuracy and "truth." To some groups, the need to "save face" and the importance of maintaining interpersonal relationships may be more important than honesty. Nguyen, for instance, writes that

> Falsehood carries no moral structure for a Cambodian, Laotian, or Vietnamese. The essential question is not whether a statement is true or false, but what the intention of the statement is. Does it facilitate interpersonal harmony? Does it indicate a wish to change the subject? Hence, one must learn the "heart" of the speaker through his/her words.[57]

Responses to Guilt and Accusations

Cultural groups also differ in the ways their members respond to accusations of wrongdoing and guilt. For example, European Americans usually respond vigorously to accusations of which they are innocent but show guilt by lowering their eyes and appearing embarrassed. African Americans, on the other hand, tend to lower their eyes as a sign of respect rather than guilt and may feel no particular need to defend themselves against false accusation. It is easy to see that, unaware of these differences, European Americans and African Americans are likely to interpret such signs inaccurately.

A number of other issues fall under the general rubric of communication style, such as cultural and language differences in the way people handle conflict, how and when they avoid blame, what they consider appropriate topics of general conversation, and whether and how they indicate affection. What is clear from the preceding discussion is that teachers must be aware of some of these distinctions in language, learning, and communication styles if they want to interact effectively with their students.

Bilingual Education

Perhaps no other issue pertaining to diversity in American public schools has been as emotional and divisive in recent months as the debates over bilingual education. Two that immediately come to mind both surfaced in California, but they represent a growing backlash against the teaching of students in any other language but English. The first one was the largely symbolic decision (since partially amended) of the Oakland (CA) schools to recognize the use of Ebonics among some of its students and to attempt to use that fact as a tool to improve student performance. At no time did the Oakland Board of Education plan to teach students *in* Ebonics. Rather, the policy was part of a larger effort to "stop blaming children and start demanding more accountability from teachers and administrators in a district where the average grade among African American students is a D+."[58] The approach, rather, was to "train teachers to recognize and respect ebonics as the everday language of many African American students and, instead of declaring them wrong when they use it, helping them translate to standard English."[59] In other words, teachers would *begin* with the students' own language (or, in this case, dialect) in order to take them more effectively toward the understanding and use of the standard English of the typical American workplace. So sensitive are some Americans to the bilingual education issue, however, that something of a firestorm erupted when the Oakland Board announced its plans. What most critics missed was that such an approach was only part of a *process* of teaching standard English, not its aim.

A second major issue arose in California in the state's decision to endorse Proposition 227, which requires California public schools to teach limited-English-proficient (LEP) students in special classes that are taught almost entirely in English. It also shortens the time most LEP students would stay in special classes, normally not longer than one year. Although there are some exceptions to these rules, in general Proposition 227 will effectively eliminate most bilingual education programs in the state. Although one of the arguments against bilingual education is its cost, this initiative will not significantly reduce school spending in California, because the level of state spending for K–12 schools in based on a formula contained in the state's constitution. In addition, the initiative provides $50 million each year for ten years for English classes for adults who promise to tutor LEP students. State costs for this provision will likely reduce expenditures on other school programs.

Given these issues, it is perhaps worthwhile to inquire why people become so upset about bilingual education. Two major factors seem to be at work. The first is whether children will suffer if they participate in bilingual instruction. Advocates for Proposition 227 argued that, although bilingual education began with good intentions in the 1970s, it has failed in actual practice and that Latino immigrant children are its principal victims, as evidenced by their high failure and dropout rates. The assumption is that bilingual education results in students *not* learning to speak, read, and write English and, thus, being injured for life both economically and socially. A subtext of this argument—a fear of overwhelming numbers of *unassimilated* students entering the adult American world—is reminiscent of arguments for assimilationist practices at the beginning of this century (see Chapter 2).

A second, related issue deals with the effects of a bilingual education. The assumption of many parents and teachers is that children cannot achieve as much in a bilingual context. Children, it is thought, cannot cope with the demands of schooling in two languages.

The bilingual education issue is further complicated by the difficulty of defining just who is and who is not bilingual. While someone may be able to speak in two languages, the use of one of those languages may be restricted to a particular setting. One's native language, for example, may be used only at home or among other speakers of that language, while one's second language may be used at school or at work. No definitive cutoff points can be identified that distinguish a monolingual from a bilingual.[60] The 1984 Bilingual Education Act defines limited-English-proficient individuals as those not born in the United States, those whose native language is not English, those from environments in which English is not the dominant language, and the various Native American groups among which languages other than English are commonly used.[61] There are between 3.5 and 5.5 million LEP students in the schools today, less than two-thirds of whom receive the support they need to succeed in school.[62] This is unfortunate, because children's psychological security, their sense of belonging, and their general school adjustment are better when they are able to communicate effectively in the language of the school.

Types of Bilingual Programs

147

CHAPTER 5
Developing Learning
Communities:
Language and
Learning Style

Bilingual education for language minority students has three goals: (1) students should attain high levels of proficiency in the English language; (2) students should achieve academically in all of the content areas in school; and (3) students should experience positive personal growth. To achieve these goals, schools in the United States have adopted one of four general models of bilingual education: submersion, English as a second language (ESL), transitional bilingual education (TBE), and structured immersion. The distinctions among these models are somewhat blurred, but they can be differentiated according to their primary emphases and methods.

In *submersion* programs (which is the general direction mandated by Proposition 227), language minority children are placed in the regular classroom with native speakers of English. This can accurately be described as a "sink-or-swim" approach. Some unexamined myths commonly exist about the effectiveness of the submersion experience. It is quite common to hear such statements as "My grandparents came to this country without speaking a word of English. They received their education only in English, and they didn't suffer." Those who make such statements are probably ignorant of the feelings their ancestors actually experienced. Language use plays a critical role in identity, both for the group and for the individual. Most people have a strong need to use their first language as a means of self and group preservation, particularly for first- and second-generation members.

The Supreme Court decision in *Lau v. Nichols* found submersion programs unlawful. In most instances, *English as a second language (ESL)* programs have replaced the typical submersion approach. In ESL instruction, the student's background and cultural experiences become the focal point for learning English. Children are kept in the regular classroom for most of the day, as in the submersion experience, but they are "pulled out" at various times for English instruction.

In *transitional bilingual education (TBE),* efforts are made to phase out the student's native language while developing facility in English as quickly as possible. The thinking behind such an effort is that, unless children's skill in English develops rapidly, they will soon fall behind their English-speaking counterparts in the regular classroom. In such programs, instruction in the child's first language is gradually withdrawn as his or her facility in English grows.

In *structured immersion* programs, students are taught by teachers who are fluent in the child's native language. While students are allowed to speak in their first language, the teacher usually responds in English. In this way, students receive instruction in subject matter that is comparable to their English-speaking peers while simultaneously learning to speak English.

The distinction between submersion and immersion programs is important. Baker provides a good analogy in differentiating the two.[63] Comparing language learning to learning how to swim, *submersion* embodies the idea of a nonswimmer being thrown into the deep end of a pool. In submersion programs, students are forbidden to use their home language. The entire school program is presented in the majority language. It is assumed that expert users of the majority language who will assist in his or her language development will surround the second-language learner. In reality, however, the second-language learner is likely to have considerable difficulty keeping up with the ideas and interaction of fluent speakers. In *immersion* programs, the student gradually moves from the "shallow" to the "deep" end of the pool. Pupils are allowed to splash about, using their first language while slowly being taught the skills necessary to acquire the second language. Slowly moving into deeper and deeper water, the swimmer eventually learns all four strokes and is able to swim unaided. Similarly, the language student can listen, speak, read, and write in either language as needed. In immersion programs, students are homogeneous in their ability to use the new language; they are all non-swimmers. Slowly, as their ability and confidence grow, children naturally switch to the second language. Successful immersion programs enable children to dive into either language pool equally well.

An Explanation of Bilingual Functioning

Cummins maintains that it is possible to propose a scientifically valid theory of bilingual education,[64] yet many remain frustrated by the indecision and vagueness of American policymakers with regard to bilingual education. Even today, thirty years after passage of the Bilingual Education Act of 1968, agreement has not been achieved on the goals and methods of bilingual education. Even with the various Supreme Court rulings that have arisen from the act, the initial vagueness has not yet disappeared. The *Harvard Encyclopedia of American Ethnic Groups* had this to say:

> The Bilingual Education Act, like most congressional legislation, was passed in response to demands of diverse interest groups and was, of necessity, sufficiently vaguely worded to satisfy advocates with conflicting views. It has no commonly agreed-upon purpose. At a minimum it aimed to use the native tongue of non-English-speaking children for a limited number of years in order to ensure the acquisition of basic skills such as arithmetic and writing. At the maximum its goal was not only the provision of temporary help to children in the process of linguistic assimilation, but also linguistic and cultural maintenance—the preservation of the language and value of foreign culture.[65]

The very ambiguity inherent in bilingual educational policy has been reflected in the arguments of those who were *against* Proposition 227. They argued unsuccessfully that, although there have been some failures in California bilingual education programs, this initiative prevents both the continuation of programs that have been successful and experimentation in new and better ways to teach English to LEP students, all the while eliminating the ability of parents, teachers, and local school boards to choose how their children will learn English.

An additional complication in the bilingual debate is that there is little agreement on a scientific basis for bilingual functioning. Scholars have developed various theories and models to explain this phenomenon. Among them are the balance theory and the thresholds model, which will be considered in the following sections.

Balance Theory. *Balance theory* is intuitively held by many people who assume that any "increase" in one language automatically causes a "decrease" in the second language. Bilingualism, in this case, is conceived of as a set of weighing scales, with one side increasing at the expense of the other. Such an idea assumes that the brain has only so much room for language skills. If a second language is introduced, it is thought to be at the expense of the first language. The consequence of such a situation is lowered proficiency in both languages—in thinking, reading, vocabulary, and knowledge. The analogy of balloons being inflated in the head by the entrance of knowledge and skill is often used. A bilingual person is pictured as having two half-filled balloons, while a monolingual person has one completely filled balloon. This theory assumes that the two languages are kept separate from one another.[66] Unfortunately, this can also be used as an argument against foreign language instruction for English-speaking individuals.

149

CHAPTER 5
Developing Learning
Communities:
Language and
Learning Style

Balance theory has not been substantiated by research. Indeed, Baker says that little or no scientific evidence exists to support the notion that bilingualism weakens cognitive functioning.[67] In fact, the balanced bilingual may have certain cognitive advantages over the monolingual. In addition, bilingual education that fosters two languages to a good level of proficiency has no effect on first-language skills.

Thresholds Model. The *thresholds model* contends that a critical level of competence must be attained in a language before a student can learn to think and develop in that language. This model can be viewed as simultaneously climbing two language ladders.[68] If not enough steps are climbed, the child stays at a lower level characterized by potentially negative cognitive effects. The child reaches the first threshold when age-appropriate proficiency in one language is achieved. The second threshold is reached when the child is relatively balanced and proficient in two languages. At this point, the potential for cognitive gains is great.

Thresholds theory helps explain why in early immersion programs there are temporary lags in achievement when instruction is carried out in the second language. Until the child has mastered the second language to a level that conceptual learning can occur, below average performance can be expected. While the thresholds theory helps us understand why immersion education is successful, it also suggests that minority children taught in their second language, who fail to develop sufficient competency in that language, will not benefit from second-language instruction.[69] The negative effects of this situation are cumulative, with children falling progressively further behind in academic and cognitive skills until their second-language threshold is reached. In other words, if they are not able to think "fluently" in the second language, they cannot learn to think effectively, either. For the monolingual student, failure to master the "new" vocabulary of mathematics and, thus, failure to keep up with classroom instruction is an analogous experience.

Why Bilingual Education Is Important

Consider the U-curve of adjustment presented in Chapter 4. It was noted that it may take up to two years before an individual feels comfortable and is functioning effectively in a new cultural setting. Children may also be able to communicate with teachers and peers at a surface level of fluency in a relatively short period of time— also one to two years. Years of linguistic research, however, has demonstrated that it may take from four to seven years before individuals are able to master the English language to the degree that is required for academic competence. Thus, academic English, which allows children to succeed in school, should be distinguished from conversational or informal English, which can be attained in a much shorter period of time.

Bilingual education, thus, allows students to continue their academic development in such areas as math, science, and social studies during the four to seven years it takes them to master academic English. If students were instructed solely in

English, they would learn the language but never attain competence in the content area of instruction. Instruction solely in English, then, often leaves students further behind their native English-speaking peers. Bilingual education, thus, allows students to maintain their academic standing while they learn a second language. Bilingual education benefits students in other ways as well, as discussed in the following section.

Outcomes of Bilingual Education Efforts

The largest evaluation program of bilingual education is currently being carried out by Collier and Thomas (1996, Office of Bilingual Education and Minority Language Affairs web site, p. 3). In their study of about 42,000 students spanning ten years, they have found that

> When bilingual education students are tested in English, they typically reach and surpass native English speakers' performance across all subject areas after 4–7 years in a quality bilingual program. Because they have not fallen behind in cognitive and academic growth during the 4-7 years that it takes to build academic proficiency in English, bilingually schooled students typically sustain this level of academic achievement and outperform monolingually schooled students in the upper grades.[70]

In 1981, Baker and De Kanter reviewed more than 300 studies of transitional bilingual programs in the United States and abroad.[71] They concluded that special programs in schools *can* improve the achievement of language minority students. However, they found no evidence that any particular program should be preferred by the federal government. The situation is much the same today. Given these findings, Baker suggests that immersion-type programs are preferable to transition programs, as they provide support for the home culture and language.[72] Transition programs imply assimilation into an exclusively English-speaking society. Immersion programs aim to foster bilingualism, biculturalism, and a pluralistic nation. Educators will have to do some deep soul-searching as the debate over immersion or transition-type programs continues. To date, at least twenty-three states in the United States have passed an "English as an official language" law. And, as this book goes to press, Congress is considering similar legislation. This is expected to generate considerable debate concerning bilingual education in the United States.

Bilingual education programs can also produce fully bilingual students who are capable of communicating in English as well as another language—something highly valued in a multicultural/global society. In addition, successful bilingual education programs can produce students with superior problem-solving skills, as they are able to use multiple perspectives more readily.

Ethical Issues in Bilingual Education

There are also ethical and moral issues associated with teaching linguistically diverse students. Martina Chandler, for example, is aware that students who speak another language or who speak dialects of standard English are likely to be stigmatized by other students, as well as by school policies.

It is good to remember that most U.S. schools, and most of the general public, are committed to the proposition that all students learn and perform effectively in a dialect of English called "standard English," which is the dominant social group's language of choice. Therefore, debates about bilingual education and English as a second language revolve as much around issues of cultural domination and subordination as around what is best for individual students. In short, the debate about bilingual education is part of a larger debate about who controls the school curriculum and for what purposes.

Another ethical issue is the degree to which the assessment of student progress is measured by culture-biased tests, which favor students who are already fluent in standard English. It is likely, for example, that a student is quite knowledgeable about a subject matter but cannot express his or her knowledge in the manner required by certain kinds of tests. Similarly, most traditional assessment instruments tend to favor students who are field independent rather than those who are global learners, who are visual learners rather than auditory or kinesthetic learners, and who prefer to work alone rather than in cooperative groups. In recent years, alternative forms of performance-based assessment have been designed that enable teachers to accurately assess progress for those students who do better with other styles of learning. However, such assessments (which will be discussed in a later chapter) are slow in being accepted by the educational establishment. In the meantime, teachers like Martina Chandler must find ways to demonstrate that their students are, in fact, learning effectively according to traditional assessment strategies.

151

CHAPTER 5
Developing Learning
Communities:
Language and
Learning Style

SOME REFLECTIVE QUESTIONS

Clearly, establishing a learning community classroom like Martina Chandler's tenth grade English class is fraught with both difficulties and possibilities. It is likely that Martina, at this early point in the school year, is asking herself the following questions:

1. How am I going to create a democratic, interactive learning community when my students come from such different backgrounds?
2. How am I going to discourage standard English speakers from stigmatizing students, such as Tran and Dontae, whose language differences are often rejected in American schools?
3. How am I going to provide ways in which Anna and Mrs. Thomas can participate fully in the life of the classroom?
4. How am I going to create a classroom environment in which students can teach each other effectively?
5. How am I going to organize instruction so that students with different learning styles can have equal access to the material at hand?
6. If the school wants to put Jacques and Tran in an immersion program, should I argue against it?
7. How many of my students' parents are able and willing to come into the classroom to assist in teaching? How many other community members can I interest in these students?
8. Can my nonstandard-English-speaking students learn to write in standard English without also learning to speak standard English?

Martina has a great deal to think about and do. Her students are just beginning the year and seem eager. What do you think you would do in her shoes?

Active Exercises

The following exercises from *Human Diversity in Action: Developing Multicultural Competencies for the Classroom*[73] complement this chapter well:

Activity 27: Ethnic Literacy Test, p. 172

Activity 28: Learning Styles, p. 186

The following *critical incidents* will also place some of the issues in this chapter in a "real-life" classroom perspective.

The Art Awards Ceremony

Ritchie, one of the African American students in Martina's class, had a strong interest in art, which he typically pursued on his own by visiting museums, reading books, sketching, and painting. Much of his work reflected his African American heritage. At mid-year, Ritchie's family moved across the bay, where he was enrolled in the predominantly white JFK High. He took an art class and was encouraged by his teacher to develop his talent. Ritchie entered several paintings in the school art show, received praise and attention for his work, and went on to enter the all-city show, where he also did well. The longtime principal of his school, a middle-aged Euro-pean American man, Mr. Tarbell, was present at the awards ceremony and was delighted that one of his students received rave reviews and an award. Congratulating Ritchie, he said, "Good work, Ritchie. We are proud to have such a talented black student representing our school. You have an uncanny ability to paint."

Mr. Tarbell was surprised when Ritchie simply walked away from him with no comment.

What do you think is going on in this incident? If Ritchie were to telephone Martina and complain about Mr. Tarbell, how could she best help him understand the situation?

Conversation at Lunch

Ranjani and Sathie are two female students from India who are in another of Martina's classes. They often eat lunch together in the cafeteria, usually by themselves. They are both very pleased to have found another person from their country with whom they can share their concerns. They often have quite animated discussions, in English, giving each other help and advice.

Steve, a Hungarian American student, usually sits nearby. One day, seemingly out of frustration, in the middle of lunch when Martina happened to walk by, he asked, "Why do those two students from India argue so much?" Ranjani and Sathie looked at him in astonishment and did not know what to say. Martina, too, was a bit taken aback by his comment.

How would you best explain the situation?

The Students Balk

Mrs. Allen teaches an elective class, English as a Standard Dialect, which meets just down the hall from Martina. Her students (most of them African Americans, with some Hispanics) have been identi-fied by English teachers and guidance counselors as speaking an excessive amount of nonstandard English. The students and their parents have chosen to take advantage of this special class. A few members of Martina's tenth grade English class take this class as well.

Mrs. Allen's classroom is supplied with library carrels and tape recorders, along with the usual individual desks arranged in slightly cramped quarters at one end of the room. Mrs. Allen went to a great deal of effort to collect copies of written materials from a variety of sources and to make audiotapes for oral work. Each student took a placement test at the beginning of the year and received a binder full of individualized lessons geared to his or her particular needs.

On the days when the class stays together, working from a common textbook, the students concentrate and participate. Other days, when they work individually, they complain, do not do much work, and visit others around the room. The only way Mrs. Allen can get individual work done is to act in a very authoritarian manner, which she is not comfortable doing.

If Mrs. Allen were to approach Martina for advice, how do you think Martina would explain the situation, and what advice might she offer?

From a Fishing Village to a School in Town

Natasha, one of the tenth grade students in Martina's class, is part of a special program to encourage young people to become teachers. One of Natasha's special opportunities is to assist in one of the district's elementary schools two days a week. She has been asked by the classroom teacher to observe a new student, Jimmie, who recently moved to San Francisco from a small fishing village outside Anchorage, where he had spent most of his young life among his father's people, the Tlingits. Before coming to San Francisco, Jimmie had often accompanied his father while he made his living fishing for salmon and hunting for the winter food supply.

Jimmie's mother had taught him at home, and he had pursued his studies on his own with her guidance. When he came to San Francisco, he tested at grade level and was placed with other 9-year-olds in the fourth grade. In social studies, the class was broken into small groups, each having a different topic for group inquiry and presentation. Natasha noticed that Jimmie usually sat quietly at the edge of the group and did not share or discuss with others in the group, even after several meetings, although he did seem to have his report outlined and completed. Natasha approached the classroom teacher, concerned that Jimmie was not doing his fair share of the work.

Why do you think Jimmie was not doing his work? How might Martina help Natasha better understand why Jimmie was not doing his work?

Careful Preparation of Lectures

Robert, an experienced agricultural engineer from New England, felt extremely fortunate to have been invited to spend four weeks north of San Francisco training four groups of young, English-speaking immigrant Mexican-American farmworkers in the use of some new machinery. Each week he taught a different group the use and maintenance of some new farm machinery, which they were excited about using. He had met Martina on a weekend outing and had made frequent trips to the city to spend time with her on weekends. He was having trouble with some of his work and was glad to be able to share his concerns with Martina. As a professional educator, perhaps she could help him improve his teaching.

Robert told Martina that he often spent hours in the instructional lab, constructing diagrams explaining the use of the machines and the maintenance of their parts. He was especially pleased with the diagrams he had made that explained possible problems and actions one should take when a problem occurs. This media, combined with his extensive lecture notes, company operating manuals, films, books, and audio materials, he thought, would certainly assure the success of the program.

Much to his surprise, Robert found this teaching experience to be an extreme struggle, for both himself and his students. The first day seemed to go well, but the remaining four seemed long and drawn out. The students often complained about a lack of understanding. They were restless, talkative, and seemingly uninterested in what Robert had to offer. This really confused Robert, as he had assumed that the students would be eager to learn the use of these machines, which would ultimately improve crop yield.

What do you think is the source of the problem here? If you were Martina, how would you advise Robert?

The Chemistry Lab

Ricardo, a 16-year-old Mexican student in Martina's class, has been in the United States for one year and can speak and understand English well enough to function in school. He has done well in his studies, carrying a 2.5 GPA with his highest grades in literature and history courses. He struggled through the first semester of chemistry, however, with Ds and Fs on most tests, which were based on class lectures. His lab reports salvaged his grade, because they were always of the highest quality—a fact that his teacher, Mr. Thompson, attributed mainly to the influence and help of Ricardo's lab partner, Dave, the best student in the class.

When everyone was assigned a new lab partner for the second semester, Ricardo was paired with Tim, who was failing the course. Ricardo's lab reports, however, continued to be excellent, and Tim's also improved significantly. Mr. Thompson was puzzled by Ricardo's performance.

How might Ricardo's performance in chemistry class be explained?

Accessing the World Wide Web: Resources for Diversity

For more information about learning community classrooms, see the Los Angeles Educational Partnership's Learning Community Program, a project of the LEARN community plan for comprehensive school reform, at:

http://www.lalc.k12.ca.us/laep/lcp/lcphome.html

For a discussion of learning styles, including links to "How People Learn," "What Is Learning Style?" and "Explanation of Learning Styles," see the University of Minnesota Student Handbook at:

http://www.d.umn.edu/student/loon/acad/strat/lrnsty.html

Identify your own learning style by doing several exercises provided. This site is part of a web site of Training Development Canada. It offers four "learning styles": enthusiastic, imaginative, practical, and logical. See how these categories compare with the learning styles discussed in the University of Minnesota Student Handbook.

http://rick.dgbt.doc.ca/~jean/english/lrn_styl.htm

For those interested in learning more about languages and linguistics, and Ebonics, the following web sites will give you a start:

http://www.sil.org/lla/usa_lg.html Languages of the United States; this site is a chart, outlining a wide variety of languages spoken in the United States, as well as the geographical location and number of speakers of this language.

155

CHAPTER 5
*Developing Learning
Communities:
Language and
Learning Style*

http://207.77.90.67/wguide/wire/wire_192276_48622_3_1.html   This site provides material on Ebonics, including the controversy over Ebonics in the schools.

http://www.english.uiuc.edu/English302/ebonresource.html   A listing of resource Ebonics.

http://www.cal.org/Ebonics/   The Center for Applied Linguistics Ebonics Information Page; resources available from the Center for Applied Linguistics.

http://educ.queensu.ca/~qbell/update/tint/postmodernism/ling.html   This site provides a listing of linguistic variations between standard English and Black English. It is part of "A Teacher's Guide to Ebonics," by Mary Camelon and Jennifer Wilson.

For more information on bilingual education, including the controversy surrounding it, the following web sites are helpful:

http://www.ed.gov/offices/OBEMLA/q_a.html   Office of Bilingual Education and Minority Language Affairs, U.S. Dept. of Education, frequently asked questions about bilingual education: "What Is Bilingual Education?" "Does Bilingual Education Work?"

http://www.estrellita.com/~karenm/bil/html   Bilingual education resources on the net.

http://www.nabe.org   National Association of Bilingual Education.

http://www.teachermag.org/context/hotlist/biling.htm   Best of the web articles on bilingual education.

http://www.primary98.ss.ca.gov/VoterGuide/Propositions/227analysis.htm   A web site prepared for the primary elections in California that describes in detail the pros and cons of Proposition 227.

http://www.englishfirst.org/begeneral.htm   Provides arguments *against* the use of bilingual education in the schools, put forth by an organization called English First.

http://www.edweek.org/context/topics/biling.htm   An excellent article from *Education Week* including discussion of California's Proposition 227, an initiative that largely eliminates bilingual education from the state's public schools.

http://caselaw.findlaw.com/cgi-bin/getcase.pl?court=US&navby=case&vol=414&invol=563   A review of *Lau* v. *Nichols*, the 1974 Supreme Court case that has been the foundation of arguments for bilingual education in the public schools.

References

1. Frank Siccone, *Celebrating Diversity: Building Self-Esteem in Today's Multicultural Classrooms* (Boston: Allyn & Bacon, 1995), pp. 14–16.
2. Adapted from "Name Interview Work Sheet," ibid., p. 16.
3. Taken from Jim Carnes, "An Uncommon Language," *Teaching Tolerance* (spring 1994): 56–62; and Pamela L. Tiedt and Iris M. Tiedt, *Multicultural Teaching: A Handbook of Activities, Information, and Resources,* 4th ed. (Boston: Allyn & Bacon, 1995), p. 162.

4. Found in Tiedt and Tiedt, op. cit., p. 168; reprinted from BBC *Modern English* 2, 10 (December 1976): 34.

5. H. A. Witkin, C. Moore, and F. J. McDonald, "Cognitive Style and the Teaching/Learning Process" (American Educational Research Association Cassette Series 3F, 1974); A. Casteneda and T. Gray, "Bicognitive Processes in Multicultural Education," *Educational Leadership* 32 (December 1974): 203–207.

6. D. E. Hunt, "Learning Style and Student Needs: An Introduction to Conceptual Level," in *Student Learning Styles: Diagnosing and Prescribing Programs* (Reston, VA: National Association of Secondary School Principals, 1979).

7. H. Reinert, "One Picture Is Worth a Thousand Words? Not Necessarily!" *Modern Language Journal* 60 (April 1976): 161–169.

8. R. Dunn and K. Dunn, *Teaching Secondary Students through Their Individual Learning Styles: Practical Approaches for Grades 7–12* (Boston: Allyn & Bacon, 1993).

9. Elizabeth Stone, *Black Sheep and Kissing Cousins: How Our Family Stories Shape Us* (New York: Viking Penguin, 1989).

10. George H. Wood, Schools That Work: America's Most Innovative Public Education Programs (New York: Penguin Books, 1992), p. xviii.

11. Ibid., pp. xiii–xiv.

12. Sudia Paloma McCaleb, *Building Communities of Learners: A Collaboration Among Teacher, Students, Families, and Community* (New York: St. Martin's Press, 1994).

13. Wood, op. cit., p. xv..

14. Adapted from Sudia Paloma McCaleb, op. cit., p. xii..

15. John Dewey and Evelyn Dewey, *Schools of Tomorrow* (1915); cited in R. Freeman Butts, *Public Education in the United States: From Revolution to Reform* (New York: Hold, Rinehart & Winston, 1978), pp. 222–223.

16. Wood, op cit., p. xvii.

17. See Harry Broudy, "Historic Exemplars of Teaching Method," in *Research on Teaching,* ed. Nat Gage (Chicago: Rand McNally, 1963), pp. 1–43.

18. Peter L. Berger and Brigitte Berger, *Sociology: A Biographical Approach* (New York: Basic Books, 1972).

19. Ibid., pp. 68–69.

20. Ibid., pp. 69–70.

21. Ibid., pp. 70–75.

22. Ibid., p. 72.

23. Ibid., p. 72.

24. Ibid., p. 75.

25. Ibid., p. 75.

26. G. Gonzalez, "Language, Culture, and Exceptional Children," *Exceptional Children* 40, 8 (1974): 565.

27. Donna M. Gollnick and Philip C. Chinn, *Multicultural Education in a Pluralistic Society,* 3rd ed. (New York: Macmillan, 1990), p. 213.

28. Ibid., pp. 214–215.

29. Tiedt and Tiedt, op. cit., p. 163.

30. Gollnick and Chinn, op. cit., p. 217.

31. Tiedt and Tiedt, op. cit., p. 163.

32. Ibid., p. 164.

33. Gollnick and Chinn, op. cit., pp. 216–217.

34. Tiedt and Tiedt, op. cit., p. 158.

35. Herbert Grossman, *Teaching in a Diverse Society* (Boston: Allyn & Bacon, 1995), pp. 164–166.

36. Gollnick and Chinn, op. cit., p. 212.

157

CHAPTER 5
*Developing Learning
Communities:
Language and
Learning Style*

37. Dean Barnlund, *Interpersonal Communication: Survey and Studies* (Boston: Houghton Mifflin, 1968), pp. 536–537.

38. L. Leubitz, *Nonverbal Communication: A Guide for Teachers* (Skokie, IL: National Textbook, 1973), cited in Gollnick and Chinn, op. cit., pp. 218–219.

39. Gollnick and Chinn, op. cit., p. 219.

40. Ibid., p. 219.

41. Ibid., p. 221.

42. Ibid., p. 221.

43. Ibid., pp. 221–222.

44. J. W. Keefe and M. Languis (untitled article), *Learning Stages Network Newsletter* 4, 2 (summer 1983): 1, cited in Christine L. Bennett, *Comprehensive Multicultural Education: Theory and Practice,* 3rd ed. (Boston: Allyn & Bacon, 1995), p. 164.

45. Herman A. Witkin, *Psychological Differentiation* (New York: Wiley, 1962).

46. Adapted from Bennett, op. cit., p. 168.

47. R. H. Barsch, "The Processing Mode Hierarchy as a Potential Deterrent to Cognitive Efficiency," in *Cognitive Studies: vol. 2: Deficits in Cognition,* ed. J. Hellmuth (New York: Bruner/Mazel, 1971).

48. Rita Dunn, Jeffrey Beaudry, and Angela Klavas, "Survey of Research on Learning Styles," *Educational Leadership* 46, 6 (March 1989): 50–58.

49. Tiedt and Tiedt, op. cit., p. 175.

50. Ibid., p. 176.

51. Larry Samover, Richard Porter, and Meni Jain, *Understanding Intercultural Communication* (Belmont, CA: Wadsworth, 1981).

52. Robert Kaplan, "Cultural Thought Patterns in Inter-Cultural Education," *Language Learning* 16, 1, 2 (1966): 15.

53. Christine Bennett, "Teaching Students as They Would Be Taught: The Importance of Cultural Perspectives," in *Culture, Style, and the Educative Process,* ed. Barbara J. Robinson Shade (Springfield, IL: Charles C. Thomas, 1989), pp. 76–77.

54. Herbert Grossman, op. cit., pp. 172–184.

55. Ibid., p. 173.

56. Ibid., p. 174.

57. L. D. Nguyen, "Indochinese Cross-Cultural Adjustment and Communication," in *Identifying, Instructing and Rehabilitating Southeast Asian Students with Special Needs and Counseling Their Parents,* ed. M. Dao and H. Grossman (ERIC ED 273-068, 1986), pp. 6, 7.

58. Elliot Diringer and Lori Olszewski, "Critics May Not Understand Oakland's Ebonics Plan: Goal Is to Teach Black Kids Standard English," *The San Francisco Chronicle*, 21 December 1996, p. A17.

59. Ibid.

60. Colin Baker, *Key Issues in Bilingualism and Bilingual Education* (Clevedon, UK: Multilingual Matters, 1988).

61. H. Hernandez, *Multicultural Education: A Teacher's Guide to Content and Process* (Columbus, OH: Charles E. Merrill, 1989).

62. Ibid.

63. Baker, op. cit.

64. J. Cummins, "The Influence of Bilingualism on Cognitive Growth: A Synthesis of Research Findings and Explanatory Hypotheses," *Working Papers on Bilingualism* 9 (1976): 1–43.

65. Stephan Thernstrom, *Harvard Encyclopedia of American Ethnic Groups* (Cambridge, MA: Belknap Press, 1980).

66. J. Cummins, *Bilingualism and Minority-Language Children* (Ontario: Ontario Institute for Studies in Education, 1981).

67. Baker, op. cit., p. 171.

68. J. Cummins, "The Influence of Bilingualism on Cognitive Growth: A Synthesis of Research Findings and Explanatory Hypothesis." *Working Papers on Bilingualism* 9 (1976): 1–43.

69. Ibid., pp. 1–43.

70. Office of Bilingual Education and Minority Language Affairs web site, http://www.ed.gov/offices/OBEMLA/q_a.html (1996), p. 3.

71. K. A. Baker and A. A. De Kanter, *Effectiveness of Bilingual Education: A Review of Literature* (Washington, DC: Office of Planning, Budget, and Evaluation, U.S. Department of Education, 1981).

72. Baker, op. cit., p. 85.

73. Kenneth Cushner, *Human Diversity in Action: Developing Multicultural Competencies for the Classroom* (New York: McGraw-Hill, 1999).

Creating Developmentally Appropriate Classrooms: The Importance of Age and Developmental Status

---

CHAPTER OUTLINE

RATIONALE FOR DEVELOPMENTALLY
    APPROPRIATE EDUCATIONAL
    PRACTICES
    Economic Aims for Schooling
    Early Childhood Education and
        Developmentally Appropriate
        Practice
    Constructivist Thought in
        Developmentally Appropriate
        Practice
CHARACTERISTICS OF A DEVELOPMENTALLY
    APPROPRIATE CLASSROOM
    Pedagogies: Old and New
    Roles: Old and New

Place of Content Knowledge:
    Old and New
    Assessment: Old and New
PERSPECTIVES ON AGE AND DEVELOPMENT
    Sensitive Periods and
        Developmental Crises
    Individual Differences and
        Developmental Domains
    The Importance of Developmental
        Knowledge
ACTIVE EXERCISES
ACCESSING THE WORLD WIDE WEB:
    RESOURCES FOR DIVERSITY
REFERENCES

The blunt fact is that the American high school was designed for fifteen- to eighteen-year-olds who were children only beginning their journey to adulthood. It is now filled with young adults of the same age. One does not have to subscribe to a Freudian theory of human development to accept the sharp distinction between the years before and after sexual development. And likewise, one does not need to be a professional psychologist to recognize that the way in which one deals with a prepubescent youngster is quite different from the way in which one deals with one in the early stages of puberty.

Leon Botstein

Age in Developmentally Appropriate Classrooms: A Case Study[1]

It was a coincidence that Sally Dougherty and Tony Stuart—both recent graduates of the same midwestern university—were hired in the same month at Garfield Elementary School in Asheville, West Virginia. What was not a coincidence was that both Sally and Tony had wanted to come back to the Appalachian Mountains, where they had been born.

Settled in waves of people moving westward, Appalachia is ordinarily defined as a set of 397 counties in 12 states, running from southern New York to Mississippi with a population of 18 million people. Its population has been comprised predominantly of a mixture of English, German, Welsh, Scots-Irish, and French, who, on their arrival, met major civilizations of Iroquois and Shawnee in the north and Creek, Cherokee, Choctaw, and Chickasaw in the south.

Historically, Appalachia has been a hiding place for Native Americans, runaway slaves, and whites escaping from indentured servitude in the early colonies, as well as privation and persecution in Europe. Long cut off from the rest of the world by geography, traditional conservatism, economic hardship, and fear, the people of Appalachia have developed a culture that values kinship, independence, and tradition. They tend to distrust and avoid involvement with major social institutions, such as church, state, and schooling. Strangers are often regarded as suspect or with disinterest, including all the outsiders who in recent years have descended on the area in an effort to "fix" it.

Sally and Tony, however, were not outsiders. They knew that out of the pride of independence (some might say the curse of individualism) and the nature of poverty has come a people who are accustomed to making do or doing without, whose experience with the outside world has been largely one of repeated disappointment, who refer to themselves proudly as "highlanders" or "mountain people," and who have produced beautiful folk art in wood carvings, quilts, dulcimer and fiddle music, baskets, and pottery. Indeed, it was because of their sense of loyalty to and admiration for the people and places in which they had grown up that the two young teachers wanted to return to bring the best education they had to offer to a new generation of mountain children.

Garfield Elementary School, with about 350 children in grades K–8, is typical of many elementary schools in the region. Constructed of cement block, it was built in 1968 as part of an effort to "modernize" education. It has twelve classrooms painted in pastel colors, tiled floors, a cafeteria with a kitchen, a library, modern restrooms, dependable heating, and adequate lighting. It serves a number of surrounding communities, has about a 10 percent absentee rate, and has a low budget for books and materials. About 40 percent of its children qualify for free lunches. Most teachers in the school have been there for twenty to twenty-five years, and many are ready to retire. That both Sally and Tony were hired at the same time reflects the fact that several teachers had retired the previous June.

Other changes had occurred before they came as well, perhaps the most important one being the conversion two years previously of the sixth, seventh, and eighth grades into a middle school housed in the same building as K–5. While Sally was hired to teach kindergarten, Tony was hired to teach music to the sixth, seventh, and eighth graders. Although they had known one another slightly in college, neither Sally nor Tony realized that they were going to be teaching in the same school until the week before school began, when they met at the dumpster behind the school. Each was there on the first possible day, getting their rooms ready for the first day of school.

Surprised and excited by their meeting, the two neophyte teachers compared notes.

"I've been planning all summer for this," confided Sally. "I didn't get to see much of the place when I came to be interviewed, but I wanted to get here early so I could arrange my room the way I wanted it. Come and see!"

She practically dragged Tony to her classroom, where she was beginning to organize furniture into activity centers, like those she had used in student teaching. Already discernible was a block area, with several kinds of blocks for construction; a part of the room for active games and other large-muscle activities; a science center, with a terrarium; an area for counting, sorting, and measuring; a listening center; and a quiet area, where children could stretch out with picture books. "I had hoped to have a computer and a sand table," she said, "but maybe I can figure out how to get those later. At least I have a sink in my room for cleaning up after painting, washing hands, and getting water for our classroom pets."

Not to be outdone, Tony was also eager to show off his room. One of the first at their university to graduate with licensure in middle childhood, Tony knew that the whole concept of middle school had been devised in part to allow young people more time to explore before committing themselves to futures foreordained by the type of curriculum they chose to pursue. For this reason, there were a lot of things to explore in Tony's room. He had arranged the usual chairs in a semicircle at one end of the room for choral rehearsals and singing, thereby leaving the rest of the rather large room available for bookshelves, tables, and—his pride and joy—a large workbench, on which were tools and materials for making and repairing musical instruments.

"I got a lot of these from my grandfather," he explained, pointing to the tools. "He makes both hammered and lap dulcimers and knows just about everything there is to know about mountain music. I'm going to have him come in several times this year and help teach the kids how to play and repair them."

"That's great!" exclaimed Sally. Then, thinking about her own situation, she asked, "Is that part of your curriculum? You know, I didn't get to talk with the principal about the philosophy of the school, and my curriculum is certainly laid out without a lot of room for extra stuff!"

"Well, I'm supposed to do both vocal and instrumental music, and many of these kids are already familiar with the sound of dulcimers, even if they don't know how to play them. And I thought that both dulcimers and flutes could be good introductions to other stringed and woodwind instruments. The songs of the mountains are also familiar, and I hope they'll get the kids interested in other kinds of singing."

"Sounds good to me," said Sally as she left to go back to her room. But she was thoughtful. I wonder what these folks will think about 'developmentally appropriate practice,' she said to herself, as she thought about the district's goals, which were clearly spelled out for the "subjects" comprising the kindergarten curriculum, the scope and sequence of which left little to the teacher's, or the children's, imagination.

On the first day of school, it was hard to tell who was more excited, Sally and Tony or the new kindergartners. In the kindergarten room, there were a few difficult separations, and some tears. Although several of the children had had preschool experience, most had not, and this was their first introduction to "the school." Familiarizing herself with background information that was available, Sally had learned that four of the boys were "late starters," kindergarten entry having been delayed based on readiness testing. She wondered fleetingly whether the tests had been accurate assessments. During her student teaching experience, she had witnessed an incident in which a young boy had failed a reading readiness test, although he was fully able to read, because his teacher had never used workbooks or dittos and her students had not had much practice in what she called "the skills test makers want—filling in small dots, sitting for hours, etc." When she had gone to the administrator in charge of the tests with samples of the boy's work and the books he was reading in class, the administrator had again referred her to his test scores, which indicated that he wasn't even ready to learn to read. When she pointed out that there was no reading on the "reading readiness" test, the administrator retorted that perhaps she should spend more time getting her students ready to read than in having them read!

Looking across the hall at the other kindergarten classroom, Sally saw that Mrs. Conrad had already passed out dittoed worksheets to the quietly waiting children seated around five rectangular tables. She also saw a gaily decorated but otherwise empty bulletin board with the words GOOD WORK at the top ready to receive the children's efforts. Sally had been told by the principal that Mrs. Conrad would be a good mentor for her. "She's an excellent teacher," he had said. "She always has things under control, and she has a quiet, friendly manner with the children."

As she invited her charges to look around their room, Sally spent some time observing them as a group. Three other children, two girls and a boy, had "borderline birthdates," but their parents were adamant that they not be held back. Altogether, the group represented more varied ethnicity than Sally had expected, certainly more than she had experienced in her own elementary schooling, with four African American and two Asian American pupils, the latter's families having recently immigrated to the United States. Both were just beginning to speak a little English, and one girl spoke scarcely at all. As Sally quickly learned, she was by no means the only child in the group that it would be difficult to bring out. And that small boy with the sad expression—David: what could be on his mind?

Meanwhile, in Tony's room, there appeared to be a kind of organized chaos. Because Tony was a "special" teacher, his students came to him on a rotating basis. His first group consisted of seventh graders, scheduled for music three times a week, and they were definitely not yet ready to settle into any kind of routine! Remembering his own alarming entry into puberty, Tony grinned at the interplay between boys and girls. Like most young people at this age, the girls were well ahead of the boys in all domains, though most obviously physical development. And, like all pre-teens and early teens, they came in all shapes and sizes and were at diverse points along the road to being grown up, in every sense. He also knew that most had already tried out "adult" behaviors, including sexual and substance-related ones.

Noticing that the students were all clustered around the workbench, Tony went behind it and began to talk with them about what was on the bench. *Might as well begin where they are,* he thought to himself. *Here's where my career begins!*

As the year progressed, Sally's room acquired a variety of children's artwork—some of it not perfect, by any means, and some of it unlike anything anyone had ever seen before, but all of it respected and valued because it had been produced by the children's own imaginations. In one corner was the class fairy tale museum, complete with a gingerbread house, and on a low table was a carousel with photographs of each child riding a horse. By January, there was also a list of rules for the classroom hanging on the wall, developed by the children. Rule #1 was "No smoking," and Rule#2 was "No throwing books at the lights." Mrs. Conrad had commented more than once on the list of rules as being a little silly, but Sally believed that the room was their space as well as hers and that the experience of deciding what rules should be followed by everyone was an important step toward building the sense of community she wanted in her class.

Knowing that play is the young child's work and natural mode of expression, Sally had developed a schedule that balanced child-selected activity in especially arranged interest centers with whole-group circle activities. Following opening circle routines—who was here, who would be helpers, today's weather—she introduced a theme through an intriguing "lesson," based on a story or finger play, after which each child was asked to choose from among various centers where that theme could be pursued in different ways, as she became a "participant-observer," moving from center to center and encouraging children to explore with different media. As new themes were introduced, centers were changed accordingly, but always enabling children to have experiences with language and other modes of expression, quantities and physical attributes, cause-effect relationships, social interactions, and other "curriculum content" appropriate for 5-year-olds. Noting what each child chose, and how each child played, she supported mutual helping and other prosocial behavior, intervening as unobtrusively as possible. Then, bringing the children back to the circle, she returned to the theme, urging them to talk about what they had done, often helping them frame this in the form of a story in which each child was an important character.

Tony also was learning about his students, and, as he was quick to point out to her, he had a much wider range of age to deal with than she did. Even in a single class, students' interests and needs were far from uniform. Furthermore, while Tony had anticipated needing to establish his own authenticity (and authority), the students at first had seemed to him to be compliant but apathetic. After the first week, they had little apparent interest in either the workbench or any of the other activities he had planned. Even their singing of familiar songs had a tendency to be dirge-like. Clearly, he thought, he was failing to "connect" with their concerns, their priorities.

165

CHAPTER 6
Creating
Developmentally
Appropriate
Classrooms: The
Importance of Age
and Developmental
Status

Toward the end of September, a tragic fire in a cabin up in the hills brought them, at least temporarily, out of their lethargy. Two children died in the fire, and one was very badly burned. The family had little money, nothing to wear, and no place to live, except with cousins down the road who already had cramped quarters. Help came from all the communities in the school district: a hundred families met to fell trees and raise a new cabin, provided clothes, and collected money to tide the family over. But the burned child faced months of hospitalization, and her parents were faced with not only medical bills but also the expenses of traveling back and forth to the city in which she was hospitalized, 60 miles away.

As his students continued to talk about the family's plight, Tony got an idea. Perhaps his classes could raise some money for the family themselves by staging a country music fair, performing in a musical review, and selling space for local musicians and craftspeople to sell their wares. Why not?

When presented with the idea, Tony's classes were excited. He formed a grade 6–8 chorus and organized students into groups to write the review, decide on the music, make costumes, build sets, talk with the principal and other community leaders about finding space for the fair, write an article for the local newspaper to publicize the event, take orders from crafts-people for booth space, and attend to all the other details that had to be worked out. After two weeks, most of the school was involved one way or another: other middle school teachers were using the event to teach English, social studies, and math, and even Sally's kindergartners were drafted to help paint large pieces of scenery. The event itself was scheduled to be held just before Thanksgiving in a local church.

The students decided to write a pageant about the history of the community, which enabled them to choose from a wide variety of music—colonial church hymns, patriotic anthems, and 200 years' worth of folk music from many countries that had been adopted and adapted over the years until it became true "mountain music."

Tony found himself stretched to provide enough music history—let alone the music, itself—for the eager students' needs. He very quickly learned whom in the community could be called on to help (his own grandfather, was, of course, one of the first to be asked), and the project became a community effort. Nearly every minute of Tony's time was devoted to advising, guiding, rehearsing, and teaching his students what they needed to know. Everyone had a job (most had several!), and all the students felt they were participating in something important.

A number of youngsters truly "came out of themselves" during the weeks before the event. Tony's favorite was a boy named Tim, a diminutive, prepubescent loner who strove mightily to affect a "grunge" persona. Tim, it turned out, had a talent for limericks that could be set to music. Tim's favorite, his "signature piece," went as follows:

My name is Tim Bandles.

I eat lighted candles.

I eat them for lunch,

I eat them in a bunch.

Oh, how I wish they had handles!

This little limerick was the source of much teasing and giggling among his peers, but it also gave Tim something to call his own; in fact, it provided a name for the combined chorus—The Lighted Candles. "That's good!" exclaimed Tony when the students suggested it. "'Light a candle where you are' is just what we're all doing."

And they were: when the music fair was all over, Tony's students had raised five thousand dollars to help the stricken family.

By the end of that first year, both Sally and Tony were tired. Sally still did not have a computer or a sand table, the district curriculum was still confining, and Mrs. Conrad was still using dittoed worksheets. Tony had a hard time coming up with activities in the second half of the year that were as interesting and exciting as the music fair had been in the first half, and his students were still afflicted with adolescent moods and quick mouths. Still, Sally's students had discovered that school was a happy and productive place to be; that they could, in fact, learn to read; and that first grade was something to look forward to. Tony's students had learned a great deal about the history of Appalachian music and instruments and quite a bit about themselves as caring, collaborating, and capable people, which, as the two teachers agreed, is what developmentally appropriate practice is all about.

RATIONALE FOR DEVELOPMENTALLY APPROPRIATE EDUCATIONAL PRACTICES

Age is one of the two most obvious dimensions of diversity among human beings; clearly, Sally's kindergartners and Tony's "middlescents" are at very different points on the journey to adulthood. In fact, although Tony's specialization of music education is a "multiage" field, his middle school licensure identifies him also as an "age-specialist," as is Sally (whose licensure, in fact, qualifies her to teach children from preschool through grade 3.) Both these novice teachers were fortunate in being assigned to children of an age group, and within a cultural context, for which they felt a particular affinity. They also recognized that, those commonalities notwithstanding, each of their students was a unique person, making his or her own way along that journey.

During the twentieth century, patterns of schooling have been radically influenced by increasing knowledge of distinctive phases of human development. A striking example was the emergence of junior high schools in the 1920s and 1930s, a trend greatly influenced by G. Stanley Hall's *Child Study* movement. Based on questionnaires, interviews, and teacher observations, Hall argued that early adolescence is a particularly vulnerable and malleable period and that schooling for each age group ought to be different from that provided in high schools. The attempt to apply what is known about children's development to school organization is even more sharply reflected in today's middle schools, as well as in primary schools and early childhood centers. In brief, developmentally appropriate practice involves providing learning environments, instructional content, and pedagogical practices that are responsive to the major attributes and salient needs and interests that characterize a given life period, in order to facilitate continuing developmental progress.

However, whatever learners of a given "age and stage" may have in common, the principle recognizes both each child's uniqueness and the diversity of the social and cultural contexts affecting children's socialization. Accordingly, the revised definition statement asserts that

> *Developmentally appropriate practices* result from the process of professionals making decisions about the education and well-being of children based on at least three important kinds of information or knowledge:
>
> 1. *what is known about child development and learning*—knowledge of age-related human characteristics that permits general predictions within an age range about what activities, materials, interactions, or experiences will be safe, healthy, interesting, achievable, and also challenging to children;
> 2. *what is known about the strengths, interests, and needs of each individual child in the group* to be able to adapt for and be responsive to inevitable individual variation; and
> 3. *knowledge of the social and cultural contexts in which children live* to ensure that learning experiences are meaningful, relevant, and respectful for the participating children and their families.
>
> Furthermore, each of these dimensions of knowledge—human development and learning, individual characteristics and experiences, and social and cultural contexts—is dynamic and changing, requiring that early childhood teachers remain learners throughout their careers.[2]

Economic Aims for Schooling

Leon Botstein, president of Bard College, offers the "modest proposal" of *replacing the American high school* and ending secondary education with what is now the tenth grade. If schooling were more *age-appropriate*, he argues, it could be more efficient, as well as far more effective. While his argument is essentially for faith in the potential of the American educational system—for "the language of hope"—his critique of "what's wrong" with the system essentially concerns developmentally inappropriate curriculum and pedagogy. "The challenge," he writes, "is to find ways to engage the early onset of adolescence and its attendant freedoms and habits."[3] If we are able to do that, and to capitalize on the learning potential of younger children, what today's 18-year-olds have imperfectly learned most students can master by age 16, when they can move on to postsecondary academic or technical preparation.

The currently high profile of early childhood education can be attributed to a combination of factors, not the least of which is mounting evidence of the critical importance of early educational experiences. The recognition of such evidence was reflected in Goal 1 identified by The National Education Goals Panel that, by the year 2000, all American children will enter school "ready to learn."[4] However, despite the panel's call for all children to have access to developmentally appropriate preschool programs as an important means for achieving this goal, is there a danger in attempting to meet this goal of placing developmentally *inappropriate* cognitive, perceptual-motor, and social-emotional demands on young children?

Concerned observers cite two sources of danger. The first is an economic view of educational aims—that is, the view that the major purpose of schooling is to prepare students for the workforce. The second, and related, concern emerges from higher education, which is now enrolling many students who might not have gone on to college but now find that a college degree is required for an increasing number of jobs. Such a view begins with the business community and the professorate, and the sequence of attribution goes something like this: employers concerned about workers' literacy skills, and professors concerned about students' "readiness" for college work, blame high school teachers, who attribute responsibility to junior high and middle school teachers for failing to prepare students for the rigors of concentrated academic study. In turn, they think intermediate-level instruction must have been weak, for students lack grounding in the basics (mathematical operations, paragraph construction, reading for meaning, etc.); alas, that is the fault of primary instruction. The ultimate "blame" doesn't stop with the kindergarten teacher (who ought to better ensure children's "readiness" for first grade); it gets passed on to parents. If the ultimate goal is international competitiveness, and if American graduates fare poorly when compared with their counterparts in other industrialized nations, one kind of logic argues for "more! earlier! faster!" And advocates for young children maintain that such logic inevitably results in inappropriate practices that actually impede children's development in the attempt to accelerate it.

169

CHAPTER 6
Creating
Developmentally
Appropriate
Classrooms: The
Importance of Age
and Developmental
Status

Early Childhood Education and Developmentally Appropriate Practice

Although the principle is relevant to all levels of schooling, *developmental appropriateness* emerged as a particular concern in the rapidly growing field of early childhood education. As Rebecca New and Bruce Mallory have summarized, the resulting publication of the National Association for the Education of Young Children (NAEYC), *developmentally appropriate practice (DAP)* was—like many other reform ideas—an important political statement:

> The NAEYC effort was motivated primarily by the need to respond to the increasingly pervasive pressure for early childhood programs to conform to an academic model of instruction typical of programs designed for older children. Throughout the document, there is also evidence of the intent to advocate for the field's longstanding core values of respect for and nurturing of young children as among the necessary means to achieve the democratic goals of a just and compassionate society.[5]

Constructivist Thought in Developmentally Appropriate Practice

While developmentally appropriate practice is not itself a theory of education (or of child development), it reflects a tradition of child pedagogy that, while centuries old, has gained scientific support, largely due to Jean Piaget's highly influential theory of cognitive development. Thus, appropriate practice in early childhood education is often described as based on, or at least congruent with, *cognitive developmental theory*, especially Piagetian theory. Also reflecting the *social constructivist* theory of Lev Vygotsky, DAP is clearly congruent, as well, with the ideas of cross-cultural psychology, which posits that the ways in which individuals construct their worlds are influenced by cultural factors. Leslie Williams describes the pedagogical implications of the theoretical orientation intended by the term *constructivism* in this way:

Children are understood to be active constructors of their own knowledge. Mental activity is enhanced by wide experience with people, materials, and events, through which children form concepts and develop perceptions. Children's skills also are refined through repeated experience. Curriculum is therefore expected to provide multiple opportunities for children's direct and concrete engagement. This view of children's learning places the locus of control of the process within children themselves. Adults are not the pivotal factor in the process. They can provide a conducive setting, but it is the children's inner structures that impel them to learn.[6]

The word *structure* in this context refers to the concepts, ideas, and understandings that children *construct* through their transactions with their social and physical environment. Some scholars call this a "frame," a "lens," or—after Vygotksy—a "scaffold," but all agree that it is through this construction that individuals filter information and make sense of the worlds in which they live.

Thus, from a constructivist perspective, knowledge is "made" by the knower, who (to use Piaget's terms) *assimilates* new experiences within knowledge structures already present and *accommodates* to experiences that do not fit neatly into those structures, as when a small child who knows the class "dog" as four-legged creatures with bushy tails encounters a stub- or pointy-tailed dog . . . or a pony. One 5-year-old, his family newly arrived in the United States from the English Midlands, revealed cognitive structures unique among a playground group in inquiring about a Shetland sheepdog, "Is that a *dog*? Then why does it look like a *fox?*"

Motivation to learn emerges from the fact that children's cognitive structures are continuously challenged, and the child's inherent need to understand—"epistemic curiosity," in philosophical terms—provides the impetus for acquiring new knowledge. Note that this is an *internal* motivating factor and is significantly different from such *external* factors as the praise of adults or the awarding of candy and stickers. Since some conditions are more likely than others to elicit that motivation, the teacher's task is to solve "the problem of the match" between what each child is cognitively and motivationally "ready" to learn and what is made available to the child to learn. (Vygotsky called the range of experiences that are sufficiently challenging, yet manageable, "the zone of proximal development."[7])

While NAEYC's DAP guidelines constitute a virtual manifesto on the uniqueness of the early childhood year, from birth through the primary level of schooling, both the concept of developmentally appropriate teaching and its underlying constructivist theory of learning and knowing are arguably relevant to the instruction of older children, adolescents, and even adults. Many (most?) college students, experiencing a small epiphany of understanding of a concept or an idea, remember that it was introduced in a high school course, but they "didn't get it" then. Many also remember lack of interest and boredom with material already too familiar.

The constructivist view differs from the traditional notion of readiness—used as a criterion for determining when a child should enter kindergarten, move on to first grade, and so on—in that constructivists emphasize that cognitive readiness is not determined simply by biological maturation, a kind of natural "unfolding." Rather, it is an interactional—better, a *transactional*—matter. At any point in time, every individual is "ready" to learn, if learning experiences are at an optimal level of novelty or incongruity. Clearly, what is "optimal" for one learner is not necessarily optimal for another, even among learners of the same age. Though each of us functions within a particular social-cultural context, everyone undertakes what Robert Havighurst[8] called the *tasks* of development as an individual.

171

*CHAPTER 6
Creating
Developmentally
Appropriate
Classrooms: The
Importance of Age
and Developmental
Status*

CHARACTERISTICS OF A DEVELOPMENTALLY APPROPRIATE CLASSROOM

Pedagogies: Old and New

Though they have historical antecedents, constructivist notions gained scientific support and integrity as a coherent theory due to the work of Piaget and other theorists—notably, Lev Vygotsky and Jerome Bruner, both of whom placed greater emphasis than did Piaget on the social-cultural context of children's development.[9]

Constructivist ideas were actually advanced much earlier by a succession of educational theorists and reformers, Comenius in the seventeenth century, Condillac and Rousseau in the eighteenth, Pestalozzi and Parker in the nineteenth, and Dewey in the twentieth. Sharply critical of the old methods used in teaching reading in the schools—memorization based on recitation from the New England Primer—Horace Mann argued that children could best master reading and writing if instruction were guided by, and built on, the child's language base. (Does that sound like today's "new" whole language approach?) Pestalozzi's "object teaching" emphasized the child's experience and perceptions as the basis for organizing knowledge and developing powers of reasoning—a "faculty" the "educational psychology" of his day considered not available to young children.

In Colonel Francis W. Parker's "child-centered" approach, school subjects and practical arts were "correlated" (integrated), as pupils worked eagerly, without coercion or control by the teacher, at their individual and cooperative "jobs." In contrast to the traditional *faculty psychology*, which portrayed the mind as comprised of a number of discrete faculties and pedagogy as mental discipline to strengthen them, Parker viewed children's learning as holistic and, like Piaget, inseparable from development. However, turn-of-the-century classrooms, with few exceptions, such as Parker's Quincy (Massachusetts) System and Dewey's laboratory school at the University of Chicago, and kindergartens (which were still quite separate from public schools), were as described by Larry Cuban:

> Generally, teachers taught the entire class at the same time. Teacher talk dominated verbal expression during class time. Classroom activities revolved around teacher questions and explanations, student recitations, and the class's working on textbook assignments. Except for laboratory work in science classrooms, teachers sought uniformity in behavior. The social organization of the turn-of-the-century classroom, then, was formal, with students sitting in rows of bolted-down desks facing the teacher's desk and chalkboard, rising to recite for the teacher, and moving about the room or leaving it only with the teacher's permission. The academic organization of the classroom hinged upon the whole class's moving as one through the course of study, text, recitations, and homework. Those who worked, succeeded; those who didn't, failed.[10]

Does that picture sound familiar to you? Based on his study of American classrooms from 1880 to 1990, Cuban concluded that teacher-centered instruction continued to be the dominant pattern, although, at the elementary level and in some secondary schools, ". . . a hybrid version of student-centered practices, begun in the early decades of this century, has spread and is maturing."[11] Such practices have included the use of small-group organization, activity centers, projects, more provision for student choice, joint teacher-student planning of learning activities, and the integration of content.

One fairly "mature," and certainly coherent, constructivist model that has recently attracted much interest among American educators is the *Reggio Emilia* approach,[12] named for the town in the Emilia Romagna region of northern Italy where it has been developed over about forty years from post–World War II origins. The distinctive qualities of Reggio Emilia include some familiar ideas. Specifically, learning occurs within the context of an "emergent curriculum," organized around "projects" carried out over extended periods of time (determined by children's activity and choice, rather than adult-controlled time schedules), integrating diverse areas of learning, and eliciting children's *expression*, in all of their "hundred languages,"

> . . . including words, movement, drawing, painting, building, sculpture, shadow play, collage, dramatic play, and music. Leading children to surprising levels of symbolic skills and creativity, the approach takes place not in an elite and sheltered setting of private education, but rather in a municipal system of full-day child care open to all, including children with special needs.[13]

Perhaps the most striking feature of Reggio Emilia may be the most difficult to translate from one cultural setting to another: the view, shared by parents and educators, of the school as an extension of the home. This deeply embedded understanding is a legacy of its origins in a parent cooperative movement that emerged in the region during the years of post–World War II reconstruction. A second distinctive feature perhaps difficult to translate is the valuing—the centrality—of artistic expression. Although this approach was explicitly designed for preprimary schools (ages 3–6) and infant-toddler centers, as with DAP itself and the progressive and "open education" movements, some of the key concepts would seem valid and applicable with older learners:

- A conscious awareness of the important role of physical space, and especially of aesthetic properties of the physical environment, in inviting learning
- Not holding students' motivation and accomplishment hostage to the tyranny of the clock, curriculum guide, or textbook
- The importance of true team collaboration, over time, marked by shared ownership of the educational process, and continued inquiry, on the part of teachers, learners, families, and leaders (principals, supervisors)
- The elimination of artificial compartmentalizations among "subjects" and between science and the arts, knowledge and creativity, effort and enjoyment
- Trust in, and respect for, students, expressed through responsibility combined with empowerment, opportunity to work cooperatively as well as independently, and valuing of diverse modes of expression
- A concept of *development* as a dynamic process, rather than in terms of static "levels"

The shift from the traditional junior high school to the more developmentally appropriate middle school is another example of DAP being put into practice, uniting an understanding of the development of young people with the principles of learning. As each age level seems to have a set of characteristics that make it, in a sense, unique from all others, one of the most marked is that of children who are in the transition between childhood and early adolescence. While administrative organization and grade-level content often seem to be the emphasis at secondary levels of education, as well as in the traditional junior high school, a focus on a broader definition of the needs of the learner is fundamental in the middle school—encompassing the full range of intellectual as well as social, emotional, and other developmental needs. The challenge of middle school education, then, is, as the National Middle School Association states, "to develop an educational program that is based on the needs and characteristics of a most diverse and varied population."[14]

A "true" middle school, according to the National Middle School Association, displays the following "essential elements": (1) educators knowledgeable about and committed to young adolescents; (2) a balanced curriculum based on the needs of young adolescents; (3) a range of organizational arrangements; (4) varied instructional strategies; (5) a full exploratory program; (6) comprehensive advising and counseling; (7) continuous progress for students; (8) evaluation procedures compatible with the nature of young adolescents; (9) cooperative planning; and (10) a positive school climate.

Roles: Old and New

While constructivism (in both its old and new forms) places the student at the center of the learning process and acknowledges that much important learning is done by students entirely on their own or with peers, the teacher's role is of key importance. In the 1997 revision of the NAEYC DAP guidelines, Sue Bredekamp affirms the basic responsibility of teachers, as well as the principle that a child's sense of competence and worth is the essential foundation for learning and development:

> The goal is for teachers to support the learning and development of all children. To achieve this goal, teachers need to know children well and use everything they know about each child—including that individual's learning styles, interests and preferences, personality and temperament, skills and talents, challenges and difficulties. Children are more likely to achieve a positive sense of self if they experience more success than failure in the early school years. The teacher must support a positive sense of self-identity in each child.[15]

If there is one word that best captures the most fundamental change in the teacher's role, the word is perhaps collaboration. Since the field of early childhood education has been a major influence in bringing about a reexamination of the teacher's role, another look at its history may be instructive.[16]

Soon after Friedrich Froebel's notion of "child-gardening" was brought to America by Margarethe Meyer Schurz in the wake of great German immigration, Elizabeth Peabody described the role of "kindergartner" (the term referred to the kindergarten *teacher*) as a partner and adviser for parents in nurturing young children. While kindergartens have been around since the mid nineteenth century, *pre*kindergartens as such have been in existence only about half as long. The common school (long far from "common," considering that most American children received very little instruction and many none at all) enrolled pupils as young as 3 years, but mixed in with their older brothers and sisters, with no provisions for early

173

CHAPTER 6
*Creating
Developmentally
Appropriate
Classrooms: The
Importance of Age
and Developmental
Status*

childhood's uniqueness. "Nursery" schools, such as those Margaret MacMillan started for English children of poor families, as well as kindergartens, spread as a facet of the British, and then the American, Settlement movements, with a particular focus on health and nutritional concerns.

Two other important movements fostered the expansion of early childhood education in the United States: *child study* and *mental hygiene*. G. Stanley Hall, often called the founder of child psychology, was a key influence in both. He influenced the latter by introducing to American intellectuals and professionals psychoanalytic theories of the formative significance of early childhood experiences. Arnold Gesell, Hall's student, led the growth of nursery education, by 1930, in his words, "from a no man's land to an every man's land,"[17] although nursery teachers, like "kindergartners," were invariably women. What Gesell meant was that a broad range of professionals—psychologists, physicians, social workers, public health workers—had become involved. Universities had established laboratory programs, such as Gesell's own "Guidance Nursery" at Yale, as centers for child development research and teacher training. He and other professionals viewed programs for young children as important both in identifying problems early in life so that timely ameliorative measures could be provided and in promoting the healthy development of mind and body.

Though the Great Depression halted the spread of nursery education, when the Second World War called multitudes of women to defense industry work, the Lanham Act created another role for such programs, what we usually call day care. The years since, especially since the 1960s, have witnessed an enormous increase in the need for outside-the-home child care in the United States and other nations, and a developing crisis, certainly for families, but also for providers and policymakers. Parents and child advocates insist that child care must be more than custodial, but is it "education"? Again, in the United States, the NAEYC has joined forces with other major child advocacy groups, the most important was the Children's Defense Fund, in working for policies to ensure that day care is accessible and affordable, while also adhering to high-quality standards of professional nurture and guidance, in the interests of children and, consequently, of society itself. That is, whether provided in a center or in someone's home, child care must be *developmentally appropriate*.

Growth in families' need for child care has led to new discoveries about young children and, consequently, to the redefinition of adult roles. Conventional wisdom in the burgeoning field of child psychology had held that group experiences were of no value for children until at least age 3. But, as necessity truly became the mother of invention, caregivers (and psychologists) discovered that toddlers were quite interested in each other, and even babies were, in their fashion, social creatures. Such discoveries implied a *teacher* role (developmentally appropriate) for adults caring for infants and toddlers, as well as a number of roles (model, partner in parallel play, friend, leader) for very small children. An awareness of the key importance of those latter roles, as they become ever more influential in the course of children's development through and beyond the early childhood years, plainly marks a fundamental difference between old and new. Observations of the ways young children learn from, and with, each other suggested the value of rediscovering Parker's and Dewey's less-teacher-centered and teacher-directed concepts for organizing instruction, for older students, as well, through such strategies as cooperative learning and small-group activity. From birth through all the years of schooling, *learners* have a central role in their own learning and an instrumental role in that of their peers.

175

*CHAPTER 6
Creating
Developmentally
Appropriate
Classrooms: The
Importance of Age
and Developmental
Status*

Early childhood programs, especially Project Head Start and initiatives to support families, such as *Early Start,* emphasize collaborative relationships with families to promote optimal development during the most formative years. The teacher's role has increasingly become a collaborative one in other respects. Rather than being expected to function on their own, teachers can anticipate the support of peers, through building-level planning, problem-solving teams, and actual *team teaching.* Of course, working collaboratively with others—fellow professionals, parents and other family members, and community resource persons—requires its own set of sensitivities and skills.

Place of Content Knowledge: Old and New

As we have seen, DAP means a change in the place of content knowledge in early childhood education that involves the rediscovery of some old wisdom, undergirded by new knowledge about human development. What is often called the "cognitive revolution" in American psychology that began in the 1950s and 1960s brought new respect for young children's intellectual resources, as well as for the potential of early childhood programs to influence the course of development. But it also contributed to an unduly narrow emphasis, raising what Piaget called the "American question": how much can we accelerate the pace of cognitive learning in order to create "smarter" adults?

The discourse concerning DAP is more concerned with *process* than with content, which Bernard Spodek attributes to the fact that "early childhood educators are more concerned with the effects of early childhood education on a child's development than with what a child comes to know as a result of that education."[18] While what Piaget called "social knowledge" (information)—imparted by parents, teachers, *Sesame Street,* and siblings and peers—is important, cognitive development is an active, transactional process, not a passive one. The deductive reasoning basic to mathematical understanding and the inductive questioning that is the hallmark of scientific inquiry are inherent capabilities of young children as they strive to reconcile incongruities and impose structure on their constantly expanding experiential world. In related fashion, literacy learning begins in early childhood—in fact, in earliest infancy—and is fostered to the degree that the child's active and creative use of language and pleasure in its use are encouraged.[19] However, to put basal readers or phonics worksheets in the hands of all 3-year-olds would be developmentally inappropriate. Simply stated, in the constructivist perspective, learners *generate* content knowledge, not just "receive" it.

Assessment: Old and New

When we consider assessment in the context of learners' developmental status, we need to distinguish the various purposes of assessment. Statewide proficiency tests and international comparisons of educational achievement reflect urgent American concerns for accountability and a national effort to identify and maintain educational *standards* as essential for educational reform. "Setting the bar" higher, some argue, will only widen the gap between the more and the less advantaged children and schools, yet, conversely, two decades of research have demonstrated the strong link between expectations and student (and school) performance: *expectancy* becomes a self-fulfilling prophecy.[20] Whatever standards are agreed on for progression through the educational system and ultimate graduation, there must be a means of assessing the status of individual students in terms of those standards. While it may be imperfectly implemented, assessment is certainly essential to educational accountability.

However, the assessment of student progress vis-à-vis performance standards should not be confused with "sorting," a questionable and potentially invidious use of assessment. In the past, assessment was often used to "validate" beliefs about the limited learning potential of children of poor and low-income families and immigrants, children of color, and children with disabilities. Although inappropriate assessment procedures have also been used to identify which children are "ready" for school and which ones are not, the DAP guidelines are explicit about the responsibility of *schools* to be "ready" for all children. As Samuel Meisels has said, screening and assessment should never be used to *close* educational doors for a child, but to open them.[21]

A new view of assessment goes beyond a reliance on narrow and fallible tests in linking knowledge about individual learners with instructional planning and decision making. This view is frequently identified by the term *authentic assessment*. Noting the limited value of traditional, norm-referenced assessment procedures with young children, DAP guidelines emphasize the importance of the observation of children in natural activity contexts, collections of children's work, and ongoing communication with parents "for the purpose of improving teaching and learning."[22]

PERSPECTIVES ON AGE AND DEVELOPMENT

School experiences both profoundly influence and are influenced by people's development as human beings. That statement may seem on the surface so obvious that it scarcely deserves mention. But consider more closely. What is development, and precisely what implications does it have for learning and teaching in schools? David Shaffer summarized, "Simply stated, *development* refers to systematic changes in the individual that occur between the moment of conception . . . and the moment the individual dies."[23] You are probably familiar with important concepts involving patterns of change that humans experience over time, such as "nature vs. nurture," sensitive or "critical" periods, individual differences, and developmental stages and "domains." What implications do such concepts have for schooling?

Sensitive Periods and Developmental Crises

Since critical "systematic changes" occur before schooling begins (indeed, from the moment of conception) as well as afterwards, it may appear that development proceeds relatively independently of formal education. While the so-called nature vs. nurture debate has revolved more around what young children experience at home than what older children and youth experience in school, major social programs, such as Project Head Start, have reflected the belief that that education, especially in the early years of life, can alter the course of children's development. And most people probably believe their own lives have been affected in crucial ways by their school experiences that occurred at a point in their lives when they were particularly receptive, or particularly vulnerable.

While those points of receptivity/vulnerability are an individual matter—associated with a major change in one's family situation, such as parental divorce, separation, or death; one's own or a family member's illness; a move to a new community and a new school; a new friendship; even a certain teacher or coach—some are universal. In Erik Erikson's formulation,[24] the development of *ego identity* is a lifetime enterprise, involving eight stages of psychosocial development, each marked by a conflict to be resolved. The adolescent "identity crisis" is preceded by successive childhood crises, or turning points, emerging from conflicting influences or needs: basic trust vs. mistrust; autonomy vs. shame and doubt; initiative vs. guilt; industry vs. inferiority. Everyone remembers—happily, painfully, or ruefully—their own adolescent years and the changes they brought. For centuries, in fact, adolescence, though not identified as such, was assumed to be the "critical period" for learning, and schooling often didn't begin until then. "Infancy," traditionally the first seven years of life, was accorded little importance.

Individual Differences and Developmental Domains

Developmentally appropriate practice is based not only on age and stage differences but also on another key concept in the psychology of human development: individual differences. Many such differences are culture-related, while others are situational, influenced by circumstances in a person's life and quite idiosyncratic. Wide variations, even within cultures, are to some degree attributable to "built-in" factors, certainly biological heredity. Arnold Gesell, well known for his detailed descriptions of nearly universal characteristics of infants, children, and youth that are virtually "programmed" in humans, as in other species, asserted that, "no two infants were ever born alike."[25] While the nature side of "nature vs. nurture" involves both common (maturational) and highly idiosyncratic (hereditary) influences, development involves their subtle interaction with a host of environmental influences—many cultural and many specific to the individual. All the many characteristics, or "traits," that distinguish everyone's unique personality reflect an interactive mix of biological and environmental influences. That is true of even some physical attributes, such as skeletal structure, although others (e.g., eye color) are entirely biologically influenced.

Human development proceeds on many fronts, often referred to as developmental domains, such as motor, cognitive, language/communication, social/emotional. The notion of "domains" in some ways involves arbitrary distinctions, for babies, children, youth, and adults are whole beings, not just composites of discrete parts. Language development, for example, is virtually inseparable from cognitive and social development. During the "critical period" for language acquisition—the first three years of life—it is mightily influenced by sensory and motor development, but language can be analyzed on the basis of domain-specific concepts—phonology, morphology, syntax, semantics, and pragmatics. Appropriate educational practice requires knowledge of such concepts and patterns of change associated with major domains. It is not developmentally appropriate to expect

177

CHAPTER 6
Creating
Developmentally
Appropriate
Classrooms: The
Importance of Age
and Developmental
Status

3-year-olds to cut expertly with scissors or to "know" (in the adult sense) what clouds are, for 5-year-olds to be physically inactive for extended periods or to argue the merits of a bicameral legislature, or for 10-year-olds to do grueling labor or to solve algebraic equations.

Since "milestones," such as first words and independent walking, and transitions from one stage to another are reached by different children at different times, it is necessary to be aware of normal ranges of variation in the timing and sequencing of developmental changes. Such variations are attributable to many factors, including gender, geography (e.g., climate), genetics, specific environmental influences, and differential cultural values and expectations. For some children, such as a child who is blind or one who has cerebral palsy, developmental processes may differ *qualitatively*, rather than quantitatively, from their typical peers. It makes no sense to say, for example, that a child who cannot see has "delayed" visual development or that a child with cerebral palsy who cannot walk independently has "delayed" motor development. The first learns to complement functional vision with other sensory information more than do most children; the second may accomplish mobility with the aid of adaptive equipment, such as a wheelchair.

The Importance of Developmental Knowledge

What should teachers know about children and adolescents in order for their instruction to be developmentally appropriate? Until the latter half of the nineteenth century, most American and European teachers and school officials knew very little, for not much attention was paid to the unique features of successive stages. In some common schools, children as young as 3 were instructed along with older students, even adolescents, seated on hard benches inappropriate for all, awaiting their turn to recite. As age-grading supplanted such arrangements, however, instruction could be more age-appropriate, but it rarely took into account individual variations; pupils who deviated considerably from the norm presented problems that were addressed through grade repetition, "ungraded classes," and classes for "unrulies" (forerunners of special education classes, discussed in Chapter 7.)

The child study movement, while promoting more positive awareness of differential rates of development among children, mainly inspired more age-appropriate practices, such as the introduction of the junior high school. From the child study tradition, through the work of Gesell and his associates, a generation of aspiring teachers trained in the 1940s and 1950s also learned about the "terrible twos," "trusting threes," and general attributes characteristic of successive "ages and stages." What they didn't learn about development was the extent to which, and the ways in which, it is influenced by *experience* and the wide variability among children that can be expected within each of the successive stages. Nor did they learn about the variability associated with diverse cultural norms, expectations, and values.

Stage theories of human development emphasize the universality of developmental milestones and manifestations of defining attributes of successive stages. In addition to Gesell's normative descriptions, some well-known theories have focused on personality development (those of Sigmund Freud, Anna Freud, Erik Erikson), others on cognitive development (the theories of Jean Piaget), language (those of Noam Chomsky), and moral development (those of Lawrence Kohlberg).

Many underlying potentialities may emerge in much the same way among the world's children; however, they may be differentially valued, and expressed, in different cultural settings.

179

CHAPTER 6
Creating
Developmentally
Appropriate
Classrooms: The
Importance of Age
and Developmental
Status

One instance involves the notion of *independence*, or autonomy, and developmental domains labeled on assessment scales as "self-help," "adaptive," or "social-emotional." Rebecca New, noting aspects of the Reggio Emilia early childhood approach that may be culture-specific, comments on a standard routine children in American day care centers quickly learn: how to put on one's jacket when it's time to go home or for outdoor play by flipping it, arms in sleeves, over one's head. While this may require concentration, and involves occasional mistakes, the pleasure in accomplishment and sense of mastery youngsters experience are apparent in their expression. "Few Italian 2-year-olds have been taught how to put their coats on unassisted," she notes, for "adults . . . enjoy the opportunity to assist children, even as they encourage children to also help one another.[26] This example illustrates a difference in culturally valued independence vs. cooperation that is expressed in various ways. What implications do such differences have for developmentally appropriate expectations concerning children?

As previously noted, the concept of developmentally appropriate practice (DAP) emerged in a political context, with a certain "agenda," of establishing consensus concerning the uniqueness of early childhood, defined as the first eight years of life. But developmental appropriateness, at least as defined in DAP, cannot be the sole determinant of *educational* appropriateness, in the early childhood years or beyond. The guidelines, as they were originally formulated and generally understood, may have been insufficiently responsive to diverse cultural values, a concern addressed in the revised version of DAP. For example, Leslie Williams contrasts widely shared Native American traditions of interconnectedness, interdependence, and respectful listening with DAP's original strong emphasis on individualism, independence, and overt expression of language.[27] The constructivism underlying DAP's guidelines has thus been criticized as ethnocentrically narrow, inadvertently legitimizing social and educational inequities by expressing a preconceived and prescribed version of what is developmentally appropriate.

A broader *social constructivism*, on the other hand, implies a more inclusive and collaborative perspective of educational practices that not only "considers" family and culture but also recognizes their primacy in the lives of children and respects children in both their uniqueness and their interconnectedness. In the Reggio Emilia educational approach, for example,

> . . . the child is understood as having not only needs but competencies and rights as well. . . . Implicit in this view is the recognition of the child's embeddedness in a family, a community, a culture, and a society. It is thus the responsibility of the teachers, in active collaboration with parents and other members of the community, to acknowledge and respect those rights, to identify and understand those competencies, and respond collectively to those needs. In order to fulfill this role, teachers in Reggio Emilia become researchers in their own classrooms, regularly making and sharing hypotheses about learning and development rather than reifying existing conceptions. . . .[28]

There are, in fact, different "constructions" of what constructivism entails, ranging from those that encompass applied behavior analysis and direct instruction to those that consider *teaching* "a dirty word"[29] (in the sense that it connotes adult direction and management of children's learning). Exclusive commitment to any doctrinaire approach in teaching risks blinding a teacher to the differences among students at any particular stage of development or level of schooling. In its essence, constructivist teaching recognizes that learning, though it occurs in and is supported by social contexts, is an individual affair. Developmentally appropriate practices are those that respond to each student's uniqueness.

Active Exercises

The following exercises from *Human Diversity in Action: Developing Multicultural Competencies for the Classroom*[30] complement this chapter well:

> Activity 9: The Culture Learning Process, p. 45
>
> Activity 10: How Culture Is Learned, p. 58

Accessing the World Wide Web: Resources for Diversity

The concept of *developmentally appropriate practice* (DAP) has been associated specifically with the education of infants, toddlers, and young children and has been championed by the National Association for the Education of Young Children. However, it is relevant to the education of learners of any age. You may wish to contact any of a number of web sites, in addition to that of NAEYC. You may also wish to access information concerning educational reform and to think about how those efforts consider the developmental characteristics and needs of children and youth.

> *http://www.naeyc.org/text/about/position/daptoc.htm*   This web site summarizes NAEYC's position statement on developmentally appropriate practice, adopted by the organization's Governing Board in July 1996.
>
> *http://www.cmu.edu/hr/child-care/position.html*   This web site summarizes the application of developmentally appropriate practice in child care settings.
>
> *http://ericps.ed.uiuc.edu/eece/pubs/digests/1997/dunn97.html*   This ERIC Digest web site summarizes research findings concerning the application of developmentally appropriate practices in education.
>
> *http://www.icyber.com/excell/bktnq.html*   Contact this web site for information about ten recent research studies reporting the effectiveness of developmentally appropriate practices in kindergarten and the primary grades.
>
> *http://www.negp.gov/webpg50.htm*   This web site summarizes and explains the eight National Education Goals identified by the National Education Goals Panel.
>
> *http://www.negp.gov/WEBPG20.htm*   This web site summarizes progress at the national and state levels toward achievement of the National Education Goals.
>
> *http://ericps.ed.uiuc.edu/readyweb/s4c/sreb-gsr/cur-ass*   This web site, which summarizes a report titled "Getting Schools Ready for Children: The Other Side of the Readiness Goal," focuses on developmentally appropriate curriculum and assessment; it is instructive with respect to the developmental

appropriateness of Goal One of Goals 2000, which is that all children will enter school ready to learn.

http://www.angelfire.com/mo/drmtch/ Contact this web site for research and other information concerning middle school education.

181

CHAPTER 6
*Creating
Developmentally
Appropriate
Classrooms: The
Importance of Age
and Developmental
Status*

References

1. The setting for Garfield Elementary School and elements of Sally Dougherty's classroom have been taken from a true story related by George Wood about a first grade classroom in southern Ohio in *Schools That Work: America's Most Innovative Public Education Programs* (New York: Penguin Books, 1992), pp. 9–12.

2. Sue Bredekamp and Carol Copple, eds., *Developmentally Appropriate Practice in Early Childhood Programs,* rev. ed. (Washington, DC: National Association for the Education of Young Children, 1997), p. 9.

3. Leon Botstein, *Jefferson's Children: Education and the Promise of American Culture* (New York: Doubleday, 1997), p. 85.

4. NEGP (National Education Goals Panel), *Profile of 1994-95. State Assessment Systems and Reported Results.* (Washington, DC: Author, 1996).

5. Rebecca S. New and Bruce L. Mallory, "Introduction: The Ethic of Inclusion," in *Diversity and Developmentally Appropriate Practice: Challenges for Early Childhood Education,* ed. Bruce L. Mallory and Rebecca S. New (New York: Teachers College Press, 1994), p. 1.

6. Leslie R. Williams, "Developmentally Appropriate Practice and Cultural Values: A Case in Point," in Mallory and New, op. cit., p. 158.

7. L. Vygotsky, *Mind in Society: The Development of Higher Psychological Processes* (Cambridge, MA: Harvard University Press, 1978).

8. Robert J. Havighurst, *Developmental Tasks and Education*, 3rd ed. (New York: David McKay, 1972).

9. Unless otherwise noted, the source consulted for the historical background information discussed in this chapter is Philip L. Safford and Elizabeth J. Safford, *A History of Childhood and Disability* (New York: Teachers College Press, 1995).

10. Larry Cuban, *How Teachers Taught: Constancy and Change in American Classrooms, 1890–1990,* 2nd ed. (New York: Teachers College Press, 1993), p. 37.

11. Ibid., p. 272.

12. Carolyn Edwards, Lella Gandini, and George Foreman, eds., *The Hundred Languages of Children: The Reggio Emilia Approach to Early Childhood Education* (Norwood, NJ: Ablex, 1993).

13. Ibid., pp. 3-4.

14. National Middle School Association, *This We Believe* (Columbus, OH: National Middle School Association, 1992), p. 4.

15. Sue Bredekamp, "Developmentally Appropriate Practice: The Early Childhood Teacher as Decisionmaker," in Bredekamp and Copple, op. cit., p. 40.

16. See Lillian Weber, *The Kindergarten: Its Encounter with Educational Thought* (New York: Teachers College Press, 1969) for an excellent analysis of the impact of the Progressive movement on the philosophy and goals of the American kindergarten.

17. Arnold Gesell, "A Decade of Progress in the Mental Hygiene of the Preschool Child," *The Annals of the American Academy of Political and Social Sciences* 151 (1930): 143.

18. Bernard Spodek, "Early Childhood Curriculum and Cultural Definitions of Knowledge," in *Issues in Early Childhood Curriculum,* ed. Bernard Spodek and Olivia N. Saracho (New York: Teachers College Press, 1991), p. 1.

19. See recommended guidelines of the Early Childhood and Literacy Development Committee, International Reading Association, in Richard Vacca, Jo Anne Vacca, and Margaret Gove, *Reading and Learning to Read* (Boston: Little, Brown, 1987), p. 65.

20. Botstein, op. cit.

21. Samuel J. Meisels, "Testing Four- and Five-Year Olds: Response to Salzer and to Sheppard and Smith," *Educational Leadership* 44, 3 (1981): 90–92.

22. Bredekamp and Copple, op. cit., p. 17.

23. David R. Shaffer, *Developmental Psychology: Childhood and Adolescence*, 3rd ed. (Pacific Grove, CA: Brooks/Cole, 1993), p. 4.

24. Erik H. Erikson, *Childhood and Society*, 2nd ed. (New York: Norton, 1963).

25. Arnold Gesell, "Human Infancy and the Ontogenesis of Behavior," *American Scientist* 37 (1949): 529–553, 548.

26. Rebecca S. New, "Culture, Child Development, and Developmentally Appropriate Practice: Teachers as Collaborative Researchers," in Mallory and New, op. cit., p. 72.

27. Williams, op. cit.

28. Williams, op. cit., p. 158.

29. Karen R. Harris and Steve Graham, "Constructivism: Principles, Paradigms, and Integration," *Journal of Special Education* 28, 3 (1994): 233–247.

30. Kenneth Cushner, *Human Diversity in Action: Developing Multicultural Competencies for the Classroom* (New York: McGraw-Hill, 1998).

Creating Inclusive Classrooms: The Health Dimension and the Ability/Disability Continuum

CHAPTER OUTLINE

RATIONALE FOR INCLUSIVE CLASSROOMS
CHARACTERISTICS OF AN INCLUSIVE
   CLASSROOM
   Pedagogies: Old and New
   Roles: Old and New
   Place of Content Knowledge: Old
     and New
   Assessment: Old and New
PERSPECTIVES ON HEALTH AND THE
   ABILITY/DISABILITY CONTINUUM
   The Health Dimension

The Ability/Disability Continuum
What Is "Exceptionality?"
Historical Perspectives on
   Special Education
The Important of Collaboration
What Does "Flexibility" Involve?
Ethical Issues
ACTIVE EXERCISES
ACCESSING THE WORLD WIDE WEB:
   RESOURCES FOR DIVERSITY
REFERENCES

*Wow! I would love to be able to show yesterday to others and say, THIS is inclusion! . . .
I really enjoyed visiting Tim's class. . . . It's good to see him in the classroom
environment, so mature and confident.*

A parent

Schools That Include All Students: A Case Study

*Located in an affluent suburb of a large midwestern city, Burlington Ele-
mentary School serves the children of middle- and upper-middle-class
families.[1] The community is a relatively conservative one, but it wants
what is best for its children and is willing to pay for it. Inspired by a state
initiative encouraging schools to develop alternative "models" to include
students with disabilities in the regular school program, Burlington's faculty, with the administration's blessing, developed a proposal designed to
enhance the educational opportunities of all students.*

185

In its first year, the program focused on including primary-age children with specific learning disabilities in regular classrooms. Planning for this was accomplished through regular meetings of the participating teachers and a special educator, who was present in each inclusion classroom during the seventy-five minutes scheduled daily for the Language Arts block, the area of greatest difficulty for most of the "identified" students.

By the fourth year of the project, all Burlington students with disabilities, including significant delays and multiple impairments, as well as disabilities requiring less intensive intervention, were being served in nine "inclusion classes." These classes comprise typical pupils experiencing no particular difficulties, pupils considered "at risk" for learning or behavior problems, and pupils with identified disabilities, ranging from mild to severe. For each student eligible for special education, the specific goals and related services identified in the student's IEP are implemented within the context of regular classroom activity. While joint planning is continuous, each Inclusion Team meets once a month to review progress and consider needs to modify the strategies. In addition, all teams come together for periodic Building Inclusion Meetings, joined by the school psychologist, counselor, speech/language pathologist, art and physical education teachers, and librarian.

While all nine classes reflect a common philosophy and use the same basic strategy of collaboration and individualized adaptation, each is a unique community in many respects, including the specific needs presented by its members with disabilities. One variable is the amount of time each day a special educator is physically present, sharing in ongoing instruction. That is determined by varying the degrees of support and of curricular and instructional adaptation needed by individual students, which also determines class size, the ratio of typical students to those with special needs, and whether an aide is assigned to the teacher, or to individual students, throughout the day. Related services are integrated within ongoing class routines (e.g., physical therapy in the context of physical education, occupational therapy in art and other activities), except where certain objectives (e.g., self-care for a child with cerebral palsy) suggests the need for brief, unobtrusive "pull-out" by a therapist.

Carol is enrolled in a first grade classroom on a full-time basis. Although Carol's IEP indicates a label of "multihandicapped," she is an accepted and integral part of Mr. Beeman's classroom. The supports and services she needs have also become an integral part of the classroom routine; that is, as Carol needs assistance, everyone knows that the support is needed and will be provided, sometimes by the classroom aide assigned to that role, sometimes by Mr. Beeman or by another student.

On this particular day, the class is learning about units of measurement. Working in small, cooperative learning groups, the children are engaged in a variety of tasks, including determining how many "hands" it takes to measure the length of a doorway, or how many "knuckles" it takes to measure the length of a table. Today's lesson also involves walking heel-to-toe across the room to determine its length and width in "feet." As Mr. Beeman is providing directions for this part of the lesson, he notes that Carol will be unable to participate as the other children will because she requires a wheelchair to move across the room. Without missing a beat, he interests the class in another unit of measurement. He instructs the students in the group with Carol to place a piece of tape on the wheel of her chair and determine the number of rotations required as she moves from one side of the room to the other.

The students view this simply as another part of their lesson on units of measurement, while Carol is happy to have yet another opportunity to participate in the ongoing activities of her classroom. Despite the apparent inspired brilliance of Mr. Beeman's response, he gives it little thought and moves on to engage students in other explorations. In his view, he provides assistance Carol needs, not because of her label or goals on her IEP but simply so Carol can participate along with her learning group. "Isn't that what being included should be?" he reflects. "It's no big deal."

Carol's parents have been gratified by her teachers' willingness to regard her as just another one of the students. Prominent in her file is the letter they wrote last year to the principal:

Watching my daughter go off to kindergarten was the beginning of a new adventure. The anticipation of riding the "big yellow school bus" and entering a world of all new learning was thrilling! She was filled with excitement and energy. As the school year progressed, each day brought much joy. She loved making new friends and learning new skills. Carol's confidence and willingness to learn is only enhanced by the surrounding of real life with real children of all walks of life. It has been fulfilling to watch her grow in a classroom where the teacher reaches out to all the children's potential. All children deserve to discover their abilities and develop their talents regardless of their circumstances. It has been a positive . . . experience for Carol to be given the opportunity to expand her mind in an exceptional classroom . . . where all children are invited and encouraged to pursue their academic and social challenges. . . [and] where the teachers know the importance of developing the whole child and including all children.

Since teachers' participation has been voluntary, some negotiation has been involved. Speaking to an interviewer from a nearby university, Elizabeth Sims, a first grade teacher with nineteen years of experience, recalls being "very apprehensive" when Sheila Marks, a special education colleague, approached her. "She assured me it would be fun and listed the benefits: a full-time aide's help with running off papers and monitoring recess, a hand-selected class with fewer children, specials such as art and gym at the time we would choose, and the largest classroom in the building. After listening to her litany, being one who does not say no easily, I agreed."

Mrs. Sims continues, "It was a wonderful decision. I have truly enjoyed being in this total inclusion classroom. I am a teacher who has done a 360-degree turn! I always felt 'those children' needed to be in a class by themselves with teachers who were trained to meet their needs. I saw no benefit to including them in regular classes and felt a disservice was being done to the typical child. Now, I see the advantages far outweigh the disadvantages. The children are accepting of differences and very helpful to each other, typical or special needs. I also feel the special needs child tries more challenging things when seeing what their peers can do."

187

CHAPTER 7
Creating Inclusive
Classrooms:
The Health
Dimension and the
Ability/Disability
Continuum

"The fact that there are two teachers is great. (Two heads are better than one!) We have come up with some fantastic projects and ideas while putting our heads together. I find I really need to be organized because we plan on Wednesday for the following week. I must have everything planned and run off so Sheila is able to adapt the material for the children with special needs. Flexibility is also a must! There are times when the best laid plans must be changed because something is not working correctly. Although this is a necessity in an inclusion classroom, I've always felt flexibility must be present in a typical classroom as well. I really have not had to change the program I have always used, except with Sheila's help to adapt it to make sure the child with special needs is being reached."

Margaret Burns, a kindergarten teacher, also stresses the importance of flexibility, in combination with collaboration. As her reflections on the matter of balance make clear, her concern is for all the children in her class. "My elementary education background, with one 'overview of special needs children' class," she says, "gave me little specific knowledge of the population that this program might serve. As it has turned out, my preparation as a regular teacher, combined with the expertise of the specialist I'm privileged to work with, has created an effective and positive learning environment for all of the children."

"Our class is composed of twenty typical children and four with disabilities identified as 'low-incidence.' The teaching team includes me, the special education specialist, a kindergarten aide, and two student teachers for part of this year. There are several critical factors responsible for the success of this type of program. Perhaps the most basic is having a team of teachers with the same philosophy and vision for all of the children being served. Hands-on time with the children is fundamental, especially at the kindergarten level, where every child has immediate needs; therefore, a workable teacher-pupil balance is essential. The specifics of this number vary, as do the profiles of the children from year to year. Having a special educator with broad-based knowledge and experience on the team has been instrumental in making this program successful. Perhaps our greatest strength as a team is the flexibility visible every single day in our classroom. Knowing that our bottom-line is meeting the emotional and educational needs of each of our students gives us the freedom to exchange roles, modify plans, and adapt as situations warrant."

"One necessity is a small enough enrollment to accommodate all the typical and special children being served, the extra adults that are routinely present in the classroom, and the eventuality of special equipment that children may need. For example, this year one of our students went progressively from braces, to a total lower body cast and wheelchair, then to crawling on his stomach, and, finally, to an unassisted walking gate. Particularly during the time he was using the wheelchair, our space was taxed to the limit. Also, it is important to keep the number of children slightly low, so that flexibility is maintained to accommodate additional children as the year progresses if the need arises. It is unfair to assume, because an 'extra teacher—the specialist' is present to specifically meet and modify for special needs that the dynamics of an inclusion classroom

are just the same as any regular classroom. We feel that they are not, but they can be positive if they have been planned for appropriately."

"It is critical to the success of inclusion, in my opinion, that the class be truly a representative sample of a normal population distribution. Placing many identified children in one room and calling it 'inclusion' would defeat its most important purpose—to be a model for the world we live in outside the school walls. Indeed, we've had wonderful feedback from parents of children without disabilities. Listen to this one from the parents of two boys, both of whom have been in inclusion classrooms:"

189

CHAPTER 7
Creating Inclusive
Classrooms:
The Health
Dimension and the
Ability/Disability
Continuum

"Our fourth grade son was in a homeroom with several multiple-handicapped children last year. This school year our first grade son has been in an inclusion room. Both boys have had wonderful learning experiences as a result of this. They have been able to be involved directly on a day-to-day basis with special children. We as adults have not been exposed to this! Imagine how great it has been for their learning environment to know that not all people are alike. Everyone has special gifts and at such a young age my children have been able to realize this! I think it has brought out in them responsibility, increased sensitivity to others, and a sense of pride in being involved with these special children. As parents we have been very pleased with the inclusion environment for all these reasons. Our children are receiving an excellent education, both scholastically and socially."

"And here's another," Ms. Burns says, waving a second letter:

"We thought being in an inclusion class would be a great experience for Shana, but we didn't realize to what extent. Her acceptance of the disabled children in the class, we feel, is far beyond her years and extends to the typical children as well. Being a part of this class has given her more self-confidence and a chance to make friendships she may not have had the opportunity to do. Being in this inclusion atmosphere has greatly added to her education. We only wish our other children had this opportunity."

Elementary children are not the only ones to benefit from inclusive classrooms in the Burlington schools. In the past two years, such classrooms have been developed at both the middle and high schools.

Marty, for example, is in the seventh grade. For anyone who has spent any time in a middle school, the definition of normal *may be difficult. In Marty's school, 800 students between the ages of twelve and fifteen are grappling with the everyday developmental tasks of adolescence.*

Because he had entered school before the inclusion program was implemented, Marty spent most of his elementary school years in a self-contained class with other similarly labeled children. It had often been believed "necessary" to implement behavior management plans in response to his displays of inappropriate social behaviors, especially his incessant drooling and frequent bathroom accidents. A significant amount of professional time was invested in ensuring that Marty made it to the bathroom according to a prescribed schedule. When Marty entered middle school, his educational program underwent significant changes, since he was included in regular classes for most of the school day. Interestingly, within a short time, Marty's drooling practically disappeared, and he began to show a much greater interest in monitoring his own bathroom schedule—with very positive results.

One of the intended byproducts of being included in regular educational settings is involvement in the ongoing social milieu of the school and the community. This outcome was truly realized for Marty the day he was "hanging out" with other students in the school lobby after lunch. It seems that he and several of his "regular" friends were taken to the office when an exchange of taunting and teasing with members of the opposite sex escalated. The assistant principal determined that every member of the group involved would be subject to a "sentence" in the in-school suspension program, but neither Marty's resource teacher nor his parents viewed this event negatively. In fact, they were excited that he was an integral member of the group of students being disciplined. Welcome to adolescence, Marty!

Similarly, students in the high school also participate in inclusive classrooms. James, now 17, spent much of his childhood in segregated residential facilities and "special schools," but, within the past three years, his life has undergone a dramatic change: James went to live in a foster home and was given the opportunity to attend a "regular" high school, enrolled in "regular" classes.

One of the first assignments in his Public Speaking class required the recitation of a poem, which presented a challenge for James, since he does not read. He also has difficulty maintaining conversation, due to a tendency to repeat phrases or sentences spoken by the individual with whom he is conversing, which a clever teacher turned into a teaching strategy. The poem selected for James was recorded on tape by another student, who left a lengthy pause on the tape between each line and stanza. When the time came to recite, he was given the tape recorder and a set of headphones. When the voice on the tape recited a line into James's ears, he repeated it flawlessly. This continued until he had recited the entire poem. As he finished reciting, the entire classroom erupted into applause and cheers, his classmates relishing the success James had achieved and sharing in the joy of his accomplishment.

RATIONALE FOR INCLUSIVE CLASSROOMS

From its inception, a fundamental characteristic of American schooling has been its intended inclusiveness, across social boundaries of gender, class, and—belatedly—race. Today the term *inclusion* refers to the practice of including another group of students in regular classrooms, students with chronic health problems and those with physical, developmental, or emotional disabilities.

The argument for inclusion has both a philosophical and a legal basis. Philosophically, proponents of inclusive classrooms believe that communities of learners are, by definition, inclusive communities—cohesive groups with common goals, each of whose members is a unique individual, different from every other member but sharing with every other member the characteristics that distinguish the age (e.g., middle school), affinity (e.g., computer club), or other basis for forming that particular community. All members have their individual contribution to make, and each derives his or her own benefits from membership.

191

CHAPTER 7
Creating Inclusive
Classrooms:
The Health
Dimension and the
Ability/Disability
Continuum

The philosophical basis of inclusive education does not rest on the manifestly wrong notion that everyone is the same as everyone else. It rests, instead, on the principles that heterogeneity within a group is both unavoidable and desirable and that differences in ability—to read printed material or use braille, to speak or use sign, to walk or use a wheelchair, to acquire and master skills rapidly or slowly, to express thoughts with pen and paper or with a keyboard—are not marks of greater or lesser worth.

Another key philosophical basis for inclusive education is the concept of *normalization,* an idea that emerged in work with persons with mental retardation in the Scandinavian countries in the 1970s. It was originally defined as "making available to all mentally retarded people patterns of life and conditions of everyday living which are as close as possible to the regular circumstances and way of life of society."[2] Subsequently extended to all areas of disability, normalization means that the lives of exceptional individuals, of any age, should be characterized as much as possible by the same kinds of experiences, daily routines, and rhythms as those of persons who do not have disabilities.

For a person living in an institution, rather than with a family in the community, that implied radical changes in practice—a shift from institutional care to community-based services, such as group homes and supported employment. This principle also has had important implications for exceptional children and youth in school, not in suggesting they do not need supportive services but concerning *how* assistance is provided. The idea is to provide whatever adaptations are needed as unobtrusively as possible, ensuring that the student can participate in all classroom experiences, and in the same manner as everyone else.

While philosophical principles transcend the letter of the law, civil rights legislation represents their expression in public policy. In the legal sense, an inclusive classroom is one from which no "otherwise qualified" student, who would ordinarily be a member, has been *excluded* because of a disability, if the student's needs can be addressed through "reasonable accommodations."

Those key phrases were contained in two pieces of civil rights legislation. First, Section 504 of the 1973 Rehabilitation Act, which prohibited discrimination based on disability on the part of agencies receiving federal funds (including public schools), extended to the private sector by the Americans with Disabilities Act (ADA) of 1990.[3] As a practical matter for schools, that means no *a priori* policies can be adopted consigning pupils who have, have had, or have been thought to have a certain "type" of disability to a certain "type" of program. It means that pupils with impairments affecting major life functions cannot be deprived of access to learning opportunities by architectural or attitudinal barriers and that all pedagogical decisions, including placement, must be based on individual, rather than categorical, considerations. This legal protection from discrimination affects pupils who are not eligible for special education (including many with special health care needs, but no difficulties in learning), as well as those who are.

The other legal cornerstone of inclusive education is the principle of *least restrictive environment* (LRE), expressed in Public Law 94-142, federal legislation reauthorized in 1990 as The Individuals with Disabilities Education Act (IDEA).[4] While recognizing a continuum of potential placements, this principle states that, to the maximum extent appropriate, students with disabilities must be educated in a regular classroom, with nondisabled peers, and must be removed from such settings only if the student's needs cannot be met there, even with supportive aids and services. Moreover, each student's individual education program (IEP) must include a statement of the extent to which the student will participate in regular education and an explanation of why any needed services cannot be provided in a regular class. While this law, like Section 504 and the ADA, was most compellingly based on the need to prohibit *exclusion,* in this instance of children from public schooling, its intent was also to promote the *inclusion* of exceptional children in the learning experiences shared by other children. The clear intent of Congress was to ensure that each student found eligible received specialized instruction and related services (e.g., speech, physical, occupational therapy; adapted physical education; counseling; adaptive equipment or technology; etc.) appropriate to his or her needs, in the most normal setting considered feasible for that student.

While the legal basis for inclusion has not changed—nondiscrimination and LRE—changes in language educators, advocates, and the exceptional individuals themselves use reflect philosophical changes. *Mainstreaming,* a word often used in the 1970s, implied movement *out* of a special placement, most often for limited periods of time, and into regular school experiences—the "mainstream." In the 1980s, reflecting the legacy of the Civil Rights Movement, the word on the lips of many educators and parents was *integration,* sometimes merely physical, preferably social, but rarely instructional.

Like societal inclusion, inclusive education implies the fully shared participation of diverse individuals in common experiences. As one might expect, this concept is interpreted somewhat differently by different people and, therefore, is implemented with varying degrees of inclusiveness. The most straightforward interpretation of *full inclusion,* which many endorse as the standard, is that a pupil should attend the school she would attend if she did not have a disability, with her neighbors and siblings, and should be enrolled with whatever group or groups of learners she would be part of if she did not have a disability. A key proviso is that any needed supportive aids or services should be provided, including those requiring the direct service or consultative expertise of specialists, so that special education is defined as a *service*, not a *place*.

Students with and without disabilities are intended to benefit from participation in inclusive classrooms. Perhaps the greatest benefits are the positive self-esteem of all the students and the fact that more students have their needs met than in a conventional classroom. The special education student doesn't experience the stigma and confusion associated with the daily journey to a "special" room for "special" instruction. The day is less fragmented and the student doesn't feel left out. Also, special education teachers have hands-on experience with their interventions, applying them to real, daily learning situations, and can make more precise changes in those interventions as they are needed. With a co-teaching situation, there is always a teacher available to help a student. Also, co-teaching provides two perspectives on any situation and increases creativity in teaching.

While the preceding discussion gives a sense of what inclusion in this specific sense means, it is likely to raise questions in a teacher's, or prospective teacher's, mind about how, or even whether, it works. Inclusive schools and classrooms do not just happen, nor do they require each teacher to be "all things to all students." Some of the major ideas reflected in the case study considered here are based on legal requirements, but most derive from or are congruent with emerging principles and practices in general pedagogy and in the way Third Wave schools operate.

One fundamental idea is an old one, as we noted, that a major purpose of schooling is to prepare the young for citizenship in a democracy, which is also a heterogeneous society. Another is relatively new: that the young must be prepared for successful participation in a global economy. The fact that the adult world children will enter is not one in which everyone is like themselves has important implications for the learning experiences a child with a disability or health impairment, or one without, ought to have. The former will not live in a society comprised only of other people with cerebral palsy, mental retardation, autism, dyslexia, diabetes, and so forth; the latter will not live in a society comprised only of people who do not have these conditions or characteristics. Related to that societal reality is another that can be seen in any school and in any classroom: even if it were desirable to eliminate heterogeneity in a group of learners by putting anyone who is "different" in another group, it is impossible, for every group is necessarily heterogeneous; *all* children are "different."

193

CHAPTER 7
Creating Inclusive
Classrooms:
The Health
Dimension and the
Ability/Disability
Continuum

Another major idea emerging in general pedagogy, *collaboration*, involves new kinds of teacher-specialist relationships and team models, more mutually supportive school-family relationships, and new awareness of the important role of interactions among learners. Each of these sets of relationships is multifaceted. For example, Marlene Pugach and Lawrence Johnson have described four roles—*supportive*, *facilitative*, *informative*, and *prescriptive*—underlying the relationships of adults within schools.[5] While the IDEA legislation implies such relationships with respect to the education of students with disabilities, the idea of collaboration goes beyond the legal requirements:

1. The law requires only multidisciplinary participation in assessing a student's current functioning and in planning and monitoring the student's IEP, but *collaboration* suggests continuing *interdisciplinary teamwork* on the part of regular and special educators and other specialists in implementing the student's program.
2. The law requires parents' informed consent prior to multifactored evaluation, participation in developing the IEP, and right to procedural due process in the event of disagreement; *collaboration* suggests going beyond these bare legal requirements to ensure that a student's IEP reflects the family's concerns and priorities, that a student's home and school expectations and experiences are mutually supportive, and that professionals respect the primacy and continuing influence of families on children's development.
3. The law requires that students with disabilities be educated as much as is appropriate with peers who do not have disabilities; *collaboration* implies optimizing the potential benefits for both by fostering positive classroom interactions and creating opportunities for students to respect and learn from each other and to develop feelings of group identification.

CHARACTERISTICS OF AN INCLUSIVE CLASSROOM

While policy requirements have a critical role in determining how students with disabilities are educated, it is also the case that, as in all aspects of schooling, other factors, such as research findings, influence pedagogical practices. It might be a good idea to step back and summarize some contrasts between the old and the new, bearing in mind that, in one sense, everything before PL 94-142—now called IDEA—was enacted is "old," yet what is "new" continues to emerge.

Pegagogies: Old and New

While traditional methods of teaching are incorporated in pedagogies for inclusion, a major influence on inclusive pedagogy is *constructivism,* a way of understanding students' learning as a process of cognitive development influenced, but not controlled, by adult instruction. Constructivist perspectives are fundamental to current conceptions of developmentally appropriate practices for young children, but they are also reflected in current discussions of elementary, middle school, and even high school curriculum and instruction, especially in the areas of literacy, mathematics, social studies, and science. Is all genuine and meaningful learning, although externally influenced (by family, peers, teachers, and textbooks) internally motivated and internally organized? And, if so, is that true of some, but not all, learners? Beliefs about *how* children learn are key determinants of *what* is taught.

This issue is critical with respect to the pedagogy of inclusion, because special education, strongly influenced by both a medical model of treatment and a behavioral model of learning, has traditionally placed great emphasis on skill acquisition, through training strategies used by teachers and therapists. The assumption has been that, while most children "naturally" learn important skills, such as language skills, and generalize what they have learned to new situations, children with delayed development, or disabilities for which they must learn to compensate, require more direct adult intervention.

While this is far from a simple issue, considering the wide variation among children with disabilities, such distinctions have certainly been unduly emphasized; generally speaking, children with disabilities, and children with health impairments, are more *like* other children in the way they learn, and in what they need to learn, than they are *different* from their peers.

Moreover, some constructivist practices were actually introduced or readily adopted by special education pioneers, such as S. G. Howe, Edouard Seguin, and early educators of deaf children. Seguin, Maria Montessori, and Ovide DeCroly were convinced the experiential methods they developed working with children with mental retardation, based on faith in every child's ability and motivation to learn, should be extended to the instruction of all children.[6] Even given that some learners require more adult direction and adult-imposed structure than others, that clearly is also true of many who do not have disabilities. Arguably, the diverse needs present in any group of learners can be accommodated more effectively within constructivist approaches to teaching than those that assume all pupils learn the same things at the same pace. This individualized approach represents an important legacy of special education.

Roles: Old and New

The most dramatic difference between old and new affecting the education of children with disabilities is that today most live at home with their families and attend public schools. That implies fundamental changes in the roles of both families and educators, as well as critical changes in their relationships. Moreover, the increasing number of students with disabilities who participate to some degree in regular education suggests fundamental changes in the roles of both special and regular educators, and in *their* relationships. To appreciate the significance of both, it may be helpful to consider other contrasts between the old and new roles of regular and special educators.

195

CHAPTER 7
Creating Inclusive
Classrooms:
The Health
Dimension and the
Ability/Disability
Continuum

The special educator of the past was, indeed, a specialist, not only as a special educator but as a teacher of a specific "category" of students. As children were segregated, so, too, were their teachers. Early special educators were trained in residential schools, following a medically oriented, preceptor model, which was quite unlike the preparation their counterparts were provided in normal schools. Even as preparation for both moved to degree-granting colleges and universities, special and general educators were most often prepared separately, taught different content by different instructors. Like the separate structures in schools, those barriers have been gradually receding.

Except in schools for deaf students, which have a strong pedagogic tradition, the special educator was a clinician, albeit a junior one, increasingly likely to be a woman, as Seguin insisted, "supervised by a competent physician."[7] In school and clinical settings, special education teachers were (and are today) members of teams, collaborating with (or carrying out the recommendations of) psychologists, sometimes physicians and/or social workers, and physical, occupational, and speech/language therapists. In medical settings—hospitals, rehabilitation centers, and residential treatment facilities—the team was often led by a physician; in schools, by a school psychologist or special education supervisor. Since team members were expected to work together, each applying his or her own expertise, the model was referred to as *multidisciplinary*. To the extent that diverse perspectives on the child as patient or client were integrated into a unified plan (which was difficult, since members had been trained in their respective disciplines in relative isolation from each other), teams increasingly evolved an *interdisciplinary* approach. While in clinical settings a social worker often provided the only link teachers had with parents, that was less true in schools, where home-school cooperation and consistency were often seen as critical. A more integrated *transdisciplinary team* model has recently emerged, most notably with young children, characterized by *role exchange* and *role release*, whereby professionals share and synthesize perspectives on an ongoing basis.[8]

Like their fellow team members, then, and quite unlike regular education teachers, special educators were imbued with a clinical orientation influenced more by a medical than an educational model. Just as their preparation was relatively distinct from that of elementary and secondary teachers, they often worked in relative isolation from other teachers, in classrooms located "next to the boiler room" (as many recall), their pupils often transported separately and using the playground at separate times, as well as eating lunch in their classroom with their teacher, rather than the cafeteria. Like their students, many special educators perceived themselves as outsiders; in fact, they were more likely to be accountable to a central office supervisor, or "inspector," than to the building principal.

Regular educators, for their part, were often the first line of identification of children experiencing difficulty in school, as well as those who might be gifted. Their principal role vis-à-vis exceptional students, then, was identifying "suspected" problems and, as the law stipulates, attempting to address such problems within the regular classroom, referring a student to be considered for a multifactored evaluation, with parents' informed consent, only if such attempts were not successful. However, the continuum of possible school arrangements, mandated since 1975, implied that most exceptional pupils would have varying degrees of involvement in regular education, either "pulled-out" for special help or provided supportive aids and services in the mainstream.

Place of Content Knowledge: Old and New

As suggested in the foregoing discussion, *what* was to be learned has long been a key issue in special education, and it is a key issue in discussions of inclusion. Generally, content issues have involved the same fundamental question, posed by Herbert Spencer, that has been raised for all learners: what knowledge is of most worth?[9] In the case of blindness, deafness, and other physical impairment, the answer to that question was knowledge that can enable one to be maximally independent and self-supporting as an adult, which historically meant a central role for training in a trade. While their societal role shifted from instruction to containment, facilities for persons with mental retardation and epilepsy were also intended originally to be training schools, a designation that was maintained even as though residents were "trained" based on the expectation of lifelong institutionalization. As the day class model pioneered in Europe was introduced in the United States, at first in the form of ungraded classes for relatively undifferentiated low achievers, the goal of economic self-sufficiency implied the need for pupils with mild retardation to develop habits that would make them reliable workers, as well as good citizens. Consequently, the distinctive curricular tradition that emerged in special classes focused on relatively generic, and social, employability skills. With extension of schooling under the "zero exclusion" mandate of PL 94-142, a "criterion of ultimate functioning" was advanced as the basis for curriculum for students with severe disabilities, including severe cognitive disability. This criterion means that what is taught must be age-appropriate, future-oriented, functional, and community-referenced.[10]

The advent of the concept of specific learning disabilities, which today comprises more than half the special education enrollment (encompassing many pupils who previously would have been designated as having mild mental retardation), brought a greater focus on differential instructional strategy than on curricular content. Based on an educational diagnostic profile showing specific areas of strength and of difficulty, or *intraindividual differences*, an individual plan of remediation or compensatory instruction could be devised for each pupil, usually within the context of the standard curriculum. This distinctive feature, individually tailored instruction, was subsequently mandated for all eligible students with disabilities, through the IEP, which specifies individual annual goals and short-term objectives for each area in which a student is to receive special education. While not required by federal law, in some states an IEP and other provisions are required for students identified as gifted.

Assessment: Old and New

With respect to children with disabilities, assessment has both a general and a specific meaning. While emerging trends in educational assessment (general) are relevant for all learners, two assessment concerns (specific) have unique importance: the

197

CHAPTER 7
Creating Inclusive
Classrooms:
The Health
Dimension and the
Ability/Disability
Continuum

determination, as a result of assessment, of eligibility for special education services and the determination of how accountability for those services is demonstrated. The former concern also pertains to possibly gifted and talented students, but, for those with "suspected handicaps," the IDEA requires that, to be eligible for special education services, a pupil must have a disability (as defined in the law) that adversely affects educational functioning. Such determination cannot be based on only one measure or one criterion but is based, instead, on a multifactored evaluation, conducted with informed parental consent by appropriately qualified, multidisciplinary professionals, using appropriate and nondiscriminatory procedures.

While the IDEA broadly defines criteria for each "category," individual state standards may specify what types of assessment must be carried out, such as medical or psychological evaluations. In the case of gifted and talented programs, mandated in some states but not in others, local districts often stipulate certain criteria and identification processes. In both cases, norm-referenced, standardized tests (e.g., IQ tests) play an important role but must be used in combination with other appropriate procedures (e.g., criterion-referenced tests of academic skills, teacher reports and ratings).

With respect to outcome as well as process, the IEP is an accountability document. It states what services the pupil will be provided and, for each goal listed, the evaluation procedure that will be used and who is responsible. These two key functions reflect the legacy of a medical and a behavioral model, the former in such concepts as *screening* (to identify indications of need for thorough diagnostic evaluation) and *diagnosis*, the latter in stipulating that objectives must be stated in the form of observable, measurable behavior. While medically oriented diagnostic evaluation may be essential in determining eligibility, it has limited value as a guide to the individualized instruction that is the hallmark of special education.

Although the term *diagnostic/prescriptive teaching,* a legacy of the medical model tradition, has been closely associated with special education, more instructionally relevant types of assessment have been developed. Moreover, whether special learning difficulties are believed to reflect underlying process differences (e.g., in information processing or visual-motor coordination) or viewed as specific skill deficiencies to be identified and remediated, the most useful types of assessment are criterion-referenced, rather than norm-referenced. That is, the purpose is to ascertain a pupil's current status and progress on the basis of age or stage expectations (*developmental assessment*); the school's or state's curricular expectations (*curriculum-based assessment);* systemic observation of functioning in the classroom (*behavioral assessment*); skill acquisition (*task-analytic assessment*); or the accomplishment of the skills required to function in present and/or future environments (*ecological assessment*).

For young children, diagnostic profiles are often based on developmental domains, as described in Chapter 6. For older students and those with severe or multiple impairments, diagnostic profiles often are based on functional domains—that is, important life functioning areas, such as work and leisure skills. For children with visual impairments, assessing how the child uses his or her vision, orients in space, and progresses in achieving independent mobility are critical assessment concerns. For those with hearing impairments, the use of residual hearing or of compensatory (hearing aid augmentation, lipreading) or alternative (sign language) communication modes is critical. In both instances, progress in communication and literacy, as well as in general curricular areas, are continuously assessed. For children with impaired mobility or communication, specific assessment concerns involve possible needs for adaptive equipment or procedures.

While every student is unique, some have differences that require adaptations or certain support services in order to receive an appropriate education, as required under federal law. Can these be provided within normal classroom settings, in which they learn side by side with "typical" peers? That is the challenge of inclusive education.

PERSPECTIVES ON HEALTH AND THE ABILITY/DISABILITY CONTINUUM

The Health Dimension

Although certain forms of disability may involve greater vulnerability to health problems (for example, many people with Down syndrome tend to experience cardiac difficulties and middle ear and upper respiratory infection), health is a dimension encompassing everyone. Some disabilities, such as spina bifida, may involve *health services* (most often, catheterization). A child with cerebral palsy may have significant motor, sensory, communication, and possibly cognitive impairment yet experience no health problems, while a child with no such involvement may experience chronic asthma. While most of us enjoy reasonably robust good health most of the time, all of us will at some times in our lives experience debilitating illness. Some of us, were it not for anticonvulsant or other forms of medication, special diet, or other adaptations, would experience continuous, significant disruptions in our daily lives or the impairment of the critical life functions of self-care, working, and school attendance. For some, supplemental oxygen, kidney dialysis, and adaptations to make it possible to take in nourishment or eliminate waste are essential to those life functions. Children with leukemia or other forms of cancer may experience times of great fatigue; those with sickle cell disease may experience times of excruciating pain.

While they represent a very small proportion of students eligible for special services, children with significant health care needs are often a matter of concern in discussions of inclusion. Actually, a great many American children, estimated at more than one in ten, experience a chronic illness, although the number with relatively severe conditions is much less. However, that number has certainly risen, due to a number of factors: interventions that sustain life in utero and enable newborns at very low birth-weight and with other biological risk factors, such as respiratory distress, to survive; medical advances in bringing certain childhood diseases into remission during the vulnerable first year of life; marked increases in drug-affected pregnancies; and HIV transmission to newborns. Given these factors, in 1987 an estimated 1 to 2 percent of all surviving American newborns had conditions implying special health care needs.[11]

While some conditions involve *established risk* (that is, the condition is known to involve lasting impairment), much more often the future of a newborn at *biological risk* (e.g., very young gestational age at birth, very low birth-weight) cannot be reliably predicted, for much depends on the quality of nurture the child will have. While

199

CHAPTER 7
*Creating Inclusive
Classrooms:
The Health
Dimension and the
Ability/Disability
Continuum*

many of the great numbers of children born each year who were prenatally exposed to alcohol, crack or powder cocaine, or other drugs continue to have special needs, biology is not destiny. These and other biological factors interact in subtle ways with environmental ones—most crucially, the quality of attachment and caregiving.

After a brief period of time in the neonatal intensive care unit, a still tiny infant is likely to go home, dependent on life support equipment parents need to manage as they attempt to normalize the baby's, and their own, lives. While many young children soon cease to be technology-dependent, some continue to need a respirator, perhaps, or to require nasogastric or gastrostomy tube feeding. While the term *medically fragile* may be inappropriate, considering the struggle a child may need to put forth, some children who require no special adaptations to support life functions may be particularly susceptible to infection, experience debilitating allergies, or have other special health care needs throughout their school careers, perhaps throughout their lives.

The notion that children with special health care needs require special educational arrangements had its origins in efforts to contain the spread of tuberculosis as "fresh air" classes were established, the first in the United States in Providence, Rhode Island, in 1908. While "open air" schools in Europe were often located in the mountains or forests, like the adult sanitoriums, many of those in the United States were in the large cities, where the disease was epidemic, sometimes on a tenement roof. (Tragically, little effective intervention was done in the reservations and boarding schools established for Native Americans, where tuberculosis decimated tribal populations.) In the eastern states, siblings of infected children were often removed to "preventoria." Where children were thus gathered, hospital schools were provided, school districts collaborating with charity groups and health agencies to provide instruction, mild exercise, and rest. Generally, as public health measures worldwide were brought to bear, segregation strategies to halt the spread of tuberculosis became less necessary. However, the special class or special school model established in response to tuberculosis was adopted for children with other health care needs, such as heart defects.

Also, for children experiencing lengthy hospital stays for any of a number of reasons, the convention of establishing a hospital school, introduced in Europe, was adopted in the growing number of pediatric hospitals, or pediatric units in general hospitals. Increasingly, the operation of such schools was also assumed by public education, especially in large metropolitan communities. For many children believed unable to manage the physical demands of school attendance, whether hospitalized or at home, public education established tutoring for "homebound and hospitalized children."

The health needs of children and youth have changed with the presumed "conquest" of tuberculosis, poliomyelitis, and a number of diseases, such as smallpox, scarlet fever, and diptheria, to which children had been particularly vulnerable. And so have philosophies of medical care. Extended periods of hospitalization are now rare for children (as for adults); while that has been influenced by the crass realities of cost and insurance coverage limits, it also reflects awareness of the importance for children to experience conditions of growing up that are as normal as possible. Most children who in times past would have been excluded, either by formal policy or assumed dependency, weakness, or vulnerability, now go to school with their siblings, neighbors, and friends.

What are the implications for inclusive education? First, we should remember three basic, and obvious, principles: (1) we can all expect to experience serious health problems at some time in our lives, for they are part of the universal human condition; (2) serious health impairment in children is certainly not a new phenomenon, historically speaking, evidenced in epidemics and pandemics of the past, to which children were especially vulnerable; and (3) a health problem is, for a child or an adult, certainly not a person's only identifying characteristic or need.

No doubt our own vulnerability helps explain an element of fear, particularly of contagion, that in antiquity focused on leprosy, a century ago on tuberculosis, then on poliomyelitis, and today on AIDS, although other conditions (e.g., hepatitis B) are much more readily transmitted than the HIV virus. Today all school personnel are strongly advised to adopt *universal health precautions* to lessen the risk of any form of infection, of oneself or of pupils, especially if there is possible exposure to blood or any body fluids. The need for such precautions is not affected by whether or not a school adopts an inclusive education philosophy. While, understandably, contagious disease is feared, it is conquered not by avoiding it, ignoring it, or blaming the victim. That is certainly the message of AIDS awareness.

Another source of fear has to do with a different type of vulnerability, implied by inappropriate terms such as *medically fragile.* Teachers neither want a child to be endangered nor themselves to be vulnerable to self-imposed guilt feelings or even to a lawsuit, should a pupil in their charge incur injury or even die. As with many human fears, these are best allayed by information, the availability of appropriate resources and supports, and, most important *personal experience.* That seems to be the case whether a child has a condition that, is actually life-threatening or has no chronic special health care needs *per se* but significant physical impairment. A fourth grade teacher participating in an inclusion project in Virginia spoke of "fear of the unknown. . . . You're afraid they might hurt you or you might hurt them." Rachel Janney and her co-authors, reporting on the success of that project, summarized:

> Teachers who initially had been hesitant to get involved (22 of the 26) judged that their original fears and expectations were based on inaccurate perceptions about the integrated student's needs and abilities. By getting to know the students with disabilities on an individual basis, they had gained knowledge of the student's unique abilities and a new perspective on disabilities in general. "I guess we just really had never thought about them being 'normal.' They really are," explained the junior high math teacher in District C. These general education teachers' attitudes toward integration also had been changed by finding that it was personally and professionally rewarding to work with the integrated students, a sentiment expressed in these words by the high school physical education teacher in District A: "These kids seem to appreciate you a lot more . . . and that's a little pat on the back for the teacher."[12]

The Ability/Disability Continuum

Ability/disability and health are distinct dimensions. Excepting conditions, such as muscular dystrophy, that entail high risk for health problems, they do not necessarily overlap. People who are in any way "exceptional" with respect to ability/disability—such as those with cerebral palsy or a hearing loss or those who are intellectually gifted or intellectually impaired—are not necessarily "exceptional" with respect to health. Like anyone else, they experience health problems. As stated, the inclusive classroom is one in which class members *include* some who are considered exceptional on either of these two dimensions; they have not been *excluded* because of their exceptionality.

201

CHAPTER 7
*Creating Inclusive
Classrooms:
The Health
Dimension and the
Ability/Disability
Continuum*

What Is "Exceptionality?"

Defining childhood exceptionality is a circular affair, for exceptional children and youth are those eligible for special educational services, which in turn are services provided for exceptional pupils. However, this definition restricts the scope of human differences we are considering here to

- Sensory differences (vision and hearing)
- Other physical differences (e.g., those affecting mobility or other voluntary control of motor activity, vitality, and such basic life functions as eating)
- Communication differences (speech and language)
- Cognitive, or intellectual, and information-processing differences
- Emotional and behavioral differences

Federal guidelines under IDEA delineate thirteen disability "categories" based on the preceding dimensions (e.g., *deaf* is distinguished from *hard of hearing*, some children are both deaf and blind or are otherwise multiply impaired, *autism* and *traumatic brain injury* are now distinct categories, etc.). Explicit definitions of each are important, since the allocation of financial resources is involved, and schools must ensure that eligible pupils receive the services to which they are entitled. However, since many such differences occur along a continuum (e.g., cognitive, social-emotional, communication, etc., as discussed in Chapter 6), differentiating exceptionality from normality in the course of children's development is often a matter of judgment and somewhat arbitrary. While some disabilities, and some special health care needs, involve qualitative differences that must be considered and addressed, most exceptional children have the same needs, interests, and concerns their "typical" peers have, and the same right to public education.

Historical Perspectives on Special Education

Horace Mann believed the goal of education as preparation for citizenship in a democracy applied to all children. Accordingly, Massachusetts's compulsory attendance law of 1851 explicitly encompassed "crippled" children, and Boston's Horace Mann School was named in recognition of Mann's efforts to provide day classes so that deaf children could live at home and interact with hearing children. His staunch ally, Samuel Gridley Howe, was nineteenth-century America's most influential special educator. Though he founded the world-renowned Perkins Institute and was an important figure in their spread, he saw institutions for persons with disabilities only as a "last resort." "The practice of training . . . blind and [deaf] children in the common schools" he wrote, ". . . will hardly come in my day; but I see it plainly with the eye of faith and rejoice in the prospect of its fulfillment."[13]

Special education's history is studded with tales of pioneers such as Howe, the first to teach a pupil who was both deaf and blind; Jean-Marc Gaspard Itard, the physician who taught Victor, the "wild boy of Aveyron"; and Edouard Seguin, who defied prevailing wisdom by undertaking to instruct pupils who were thought unable to learn and fated to be beggars, dependents, or even a threat to society. The historical record also reveals that the key breakthroughs were often made by persons who themselves had disabilities. Arguing that in blindness lay a key to understanding human reason, the Enlightenment philosopher Diderot advised that, to understand blindness, one must consult blind persons.

Special education emerged in the context of social reform, inspired by the belief in natural rights and individual worth and the conviction that, through education, every person can contribute to society. Valentin Hauy, who founded the world's first school for blind students in Paris in 1784, heeded Diderot's counsel and learned from his first pupil how reading could be accomplished through touch. Since then, the pantheon of "greats" in this field has included such blind individuals as J. W. Klein, Louis Braille, Helen Keller, Thomas Cutsworth, and Robert Irwin. We alluded in previous chapters to the critical role deaf persons have had in gaining recognition of deaf culture and the legitimacy of signed languages. While deaf education has had hearing pioneers, their own "teachers" were their deaf pupils, some of whom, such as Laurent Clerc, themselves became influential leaders.

In important respects, special education began as a "rescue mission," for in 1860 nearly two-thirds of the countless "unfortunates" who languished, untaught and uncared for, in American almshouses were children with sensory or other physical impairments or mental retardation. By the 1870s, state Boards of Charities, supporting the work of local charity groups and benevolent societies, had undertaken a major "child-saving" effort, organized nationally as the National Conference of Charities and Corrections. In some families of more privileged circumstance, parents advocated for schooling for their children, a tradition that since has been pivotal in bringing about major policy reforms.

While the most urgent concern of nineteenth-century reformers was to provide proper care and some form of instruction, the goal then, as now, was maximum independence and integration in society. However, as attitudes toward deviance became less accepting, that goal was for a time abandoned for many children with mental or physical abnormality, such as epilepsy. While nineteenth-century facilities were often called asylums, they were intended as schools, in the United States as extensions of the common schools. But they were "training schools," using a highly utilitarian pedagogy to enable pupils to become, as much as possible, able to support themselves through certain prescribed trades, such as boot-making.

Specialized instruction began its gradual move into the common schools at the beginning of this century. At the same time, school officials, pressed by such Settlement leaders as Lillian Wald and Jane Addams, were struggling to meet the challenge of pupil diversity, compounded by massive immigration from southern and eastern Europe. Special classes were a facet of a more general "diversification" effort: "steamer classes" to expose immigrant youngsters to the English language (which led to programs for children with actual speech impairments); classes for "unrulies"; "fresh air" schools for pupils with tuberculosis or who were "physically weak" (which led to classes for children with other health impairments); and "ungraded classes" for those who "just didn't fit" (from which classes for pupils with mild retardation evolved). Excepting deafness and blindness, and speech training for "young stammerers," "special" pedagogy was secondary to the perceived need to separate pupils who were different as a way of making schooling more manageable.

203

CHAPTER 7
Creating Inclusive
Classrooms:
The Health
Dimension and the
Ability/Disability
Continuum

While the early programs were centralized residential facilities, they represented an important step in enabling children with disabilities "to share in the blessings of education" (as Howe eloquently persuaded the Massachusetts legislature in 1848).[14] By the first decades of the twentieth century, day classes had increasingly become a component of the common school. The first public school program for blind children, in Chicago, involved them in many ways with seeing peers, a model emulated in other cities. In rural areas, since blindness was a low-incidence impairment (compared, for example, with specific learning disabilities), many children, even those using braille, were enrolled in regular classrooms, receiving periodic assistance from itinerant specialists. Many schools made "reasonable accommodations" for pupils with other physical impairments long before that was legally mandated. But, as American attitudes toward "differentness" became less accepting, special education increasingly took the form of a system-within-a-system, separately administered and often separated physically from "regular" classes. It seemed as though schools sought to manage pupil diversity by trying to make it go away—that is, by segregating students who "didn't fit" and excluding altogether children who "didn't fit" in special classes.

By the 1930s, as schools adopted IQ testing, the basis for separating those who had difficulty learning presumably became more "scientific," but their instruction was distinguished from regular instruction mainly because it was provided in somewhat smaller groups, comprising pupils of various ages: urban versions (in most instances) of the one-room schoolhouse. However, curricula emphasizing *life skills* necessary for adult living emerged in these programs. For children with physical impairments, chronic health problems, and (by the 1960s) emotional and behavioral problems, special pedagogy was truly an afterthought, decidedly secondary to the medically oriented *treatment* focus. Until the parent-led learning disability movement gathered force in the 1960s, special education was more likely to mean "special place" than special pedagogy. And, with the implementation of systematic exclusionary policies, the place was often likely to be somewhere other than public school—home, an expensive private facility if parents could afford it, or an institution.

Even as special education expanded, however, most children and youth with special needs, who were not excluded from schooling altogether, were "included in the mainstream" because their problems had not been identified or services were not available. For those who had difficulty learning, and those who were exceptionally capable, there was a downside. A pupil who needed more time, or much less time, than others or one who could succeed only with some adaptation in the way material was presented or assignments could be completed often paid a considerable price for being treated like everyone else. In 1975, a watershed year from the standpoint of social policy, The Education of All Handicapped Children Act (PL 94-142, re-authorized in 1990 as PL 101-476, The Individuals with Disabilities Education Act [IDEA]) required schools to identify all students whose disabilities adversely affected their educational functioning and to provide them—excluding none—with a Free Appropriate Public Education (FAPE). But, even earlier, some special educators (and parents) questioned whether special education must mean special placement, while many regular educators (and parents) were concerned about students experiencing difficulties but who were not eligible for special education. In the 1920s, a few leaders, such as Leta Hollingworth, were concerned also that gifted children were not being challenged to realize their potential.[15]

The law defined *appropriate* on the basis of the IEP developed for each student, stipulating that the student's educational placement must be in the LRE. Subsequent amendments extended these provisions to children as young as 3; added a family-focused early intervention component for infants and toddlers; stipulated a required *transition plan* (by age 16) in anticipation of a student's leaving school and entering the adult world; clarified definitions; and distinguished two forms of disability (autism and traumatic brain injury) from other forms.

The Importance of Collaboration

Mutual understanding and mutual respect are essential elements in any true collaboration. The Burlington teachers agreed that the special and regular educators should acknowledge that both have specialized knowledge and skills but that their perspectives and knowledge bases may differ. For example, it is important for the special educator to recognize that regular educators' instructional and behavior management techniques can be effective in working with students with special needs. They must also understand that teachers in regular classrooms must respond to the needs of many students in rapid fashion and that having a student with disabilities does not relieve the teacher of responsibilities to the other students. Thus, the teacher cannot devote disproportionate time and attention to any one student and that some techniques that may be successful in a separate special education class may not be appropriate for the regular classroom environment.

At the same time, the regular educator should strive to understand that the special education consultant may be responsible for supporting many students in a variety of settings and therefore have a limited amount of time to devote to each student. Further, the regular education teacher must realize that it is unlikely that a new intervention strategy will have an immediate effect and that a fair trial is needed before judging it ineffective. Acknowledging that students differ in the extent of instructional adaptations they need, regular classroom teachers should understand that many adaptations the consulting teacher recommends will be extensions of regular education techniques. They should also maintain familiarity with each exceptional student's IEP, sharing responsibilities with the consultant for determining how goals and objectives can be reinforced during the course of classroom activities.

The Burlington teachers developed the following set of principles to guide their communication and collaborative team functioning:

1. Establish a communication system.
2. Discuss each placement together.
3. Assist each other in individualizing instruction.
4. Work together to adapt subject matter.
5. Share materials.
6. Assist each other in adapting evaluative procedures.
7. Exhibit flexibility, dedication, reliability, organization, imagination, energy, initiative, and enthusiasm.
8. Involve others by sharing plans and ideas.
9. Seek support and suggestions from others.
10. Set realistic goals.

11. Work to improve interpersonal relations.
12. Be happy and proud about working with students with special needs.
13. Remember that presenting a positive attitude will change attitudes about inclusion both inside and outside the school.

205

CHAPTER 7
Creating Inclusive
Classrooms:
The Health
Dimension and the
Ability/Disability
Continuum

What Does "Flexibility" Involve?

The Burlington teachers often use the word *flexibility* in describing their inclusion program. While flexibility is important in any teaching situation, as they note, it is critical to the success of the inclusion of students whose learning characteristics and needs may require adaptations, both planned and spontaneous, in the instructional program. Classroom adaptations to accommodate differential individual needs among *all* students can be delineated in terms of four basic parameters: curriculum materials, instructional strategies, classroom organization, and behavior management.

Within the context of the regular curriculum, instructional materials and experiences can be adapted in a wide variety of ways. Following are a few examples the Burlington teachers suggested:

- In identifying fractions, provide recipes that include measurements and have students identify all the fractions on the recipe.
- In identifying time on the hour and the half-hour, help students develop a personal schedule, showing daily activities matched to a clock face showing the time of the activity.
- In adding two columns of numbers and regrouping, practice balancing a checkbook or compile a shopping list with prices, using a calculator to add.
- In taking a spelling test, have students practice identifying functional words.
- In identifying U.S. presidents, have students practice keyboarding skills by locating the letters of presidents' names.

Adaptations in instructional strategies include:

- The way instruction is delivered, such as in the use of visual aids, learning centers, cooperatively structured activities, cooperative learning, small-group instruction, and auditory aids.
- The way the learner can demonstrate knowledge, such as oral vs. written response; pictures; the computer; augmentative communication devices, such as picture boards, tape recorder, language master, calculators.
- The number of items the learner is expected to complete, such as spelling words and math problems.

Adaptations in classroom organization can be made in:

- The skill level, problem type, or rules on how the learner may approach the work, such as using calculators, using a computer, simplifying task directions, changing rules to allow for participation, breaking tasks down to sequential steps, and providing more planned opportunities to achieve success.
- The amount of individual instruction with a specific learner, such as the use of peer partners and teaching assistants.
- The time allowed for learning, task completion, or testing, such as extra time to practice new skills, individualized timelines for work completion, and flexible class schedules.

In regard to behavior management, adaptations can be used to anticipate and prevent inappropriate or disruptive behavior, such as:

- A student's participation may involve assisting with visual aid equipment while some other students are being instructed.
- Students can take on the teacher role by sharing a favorite activity or interest.
- Goals or outcome expectations while using the same materials can be individualized—for example, the language arts activity of diagramming a sentence can be for some students a verbal language activity of hearing and speaking in full sentences.

As a way of conceptualizing variations in individual students' needs for instructional adaptation and/or curricular modification, the Burlington teachers devised a continuum of "levels," each defined by a question for the team to resolve through discussion.

Level I. What can the student learn in the regular program of instruction with the same performance standards as nondisabled peers?

Level II. What can the student learn with nondisabled peers, but with adjustments in performance standards according to the student's needs as identified through curriculum-based assessment?

Level III. What can the student learn with adjustments in pacing, method of instruction, and/or special materials or techniques provided with consultant support to the teacher?

Level IV. What can the student learn with adjustments in pacing, method of instruction, and/or special materials or techniques provided jointly with regular and support or ancillary staff?

Level V. What can the student learn with adjustments in the content of the classroom curriculum to be taught jointly by regular and special support or ancillary staff?

Level VI. What classroom curriculum content must be modified significantly and taught by special staff?

Level VII. In what situations is some or all of the content of the classroom curriculum inappropriate for this student? What alternative curriculum program will be used to provide for this student's educational needs?

Ethical Issues

As we noted, federal legislation does not mandate *inclusion*, as defined earlier in the chapter, although it does forbid *exclusion*. The legal basis for inclusion continues to be the least restrictive environment (LRE), the requirement that education occur "as much as appropriate" in a regular classroom setting, with supportive aids and services, as may be needed. Some professionals, organizations, and parents have reservations about any concept that could be interpreted to mean "one size fits all," especially if legislators and school officials construe inclusion to mean less costly services. (While individual needs differ widely, the average cost per year of educating a student with disabilities is, on average, about twice the cost of educating other pupils, only a part of which is provided through IDEA.)

The American Federation of Teachers, in fact, called for a "moratorium" on inclusion until it can be assured that the kinds of supports (resource specialists and classroom aides) and other provisions (such as manageable class size) are provided in all schools. But advocates compare such proposals to calls for a moratorium in the course of the Civil Rights Movement, until all white Americans fully "accepted" their African American fellow citizens. And, in both situations, should the crucial years of childhood, for both minority and majority children, be allowed to pass irretrievably, while their elders await optimal conditions?

What percentage of children with disabilities is currently included in regular classrooms? Based on data compiled for the U.S. Department of Education's annual report to Congress, 73 percent of students with mental retardation still receive their instruction in separate classes or even separate schools. Although about 70 percent of all students with disabilities receive at least some instruction in regular classes, less than 30 percent are fully included. Resource room arrangements represent the most frequent type of placement, especially for pupils with learning disabilities, by far the largest group, whereby the pupil is either pulled-out for certain purposes, or mainstreamed in for selected subjects or activities.[16]

This may seem to offer the best of both worlds—normalizing experiences supplemented by more intensively individualized instruction by specialists. But Joanne Yatvin, a superintendent, found that many students dislike "being sent 'down the hallway' to learn." Moreover,

> When students return to their classrooms, their regular teachers, believing that they have had their daily dose of "special education," feel little need to modify other instruction during the rest of the school day. Under such a system, students get far less instruction than they would if they were grouped with their peers, by age and interest, in regular classrooms with teachers who knew that they had to modify instruction for everyone.[17]

Many educators, parents, and persons with disabilities themselves maintain that, if the society of the twenty-first century is to be an inclusive one, in which human differences are recognized and celebrated, it must begin with inclusive schools and classrooms. They point out that it is not inclusion that needs to be justified but, rather, separation, even for part of the school day. That is precisely what the IDEA legislation requires: a child with a disability may not be removed from the regular classroom unless it has been demonstrated that *that child's* needs cannot be met within the regular classroom, even with supportive aids and services. Policies and practices that segregate children on the basis of a categorical label, whether the label refers to ability/disability, health, or race, are in violation of the U.S. Constitution.

Can every child with special needs receive an individually appropriate education without having to be segregated in a special place? Can these students still get the services they need? What about the "typical" students? As such questions are debated, in local schools, such as those cited in Burlington, many teachers, in collaboration with parents, are making inclusive education a reality. From such examples, the Advocacy Board for the Center on Human Policy at Syracuse University has developed the following statement:

207

CHAPTER 7
*Creating Inclusive
Classrooms:
The Health
Dimension and the
Ability/Disability
Continuum*

Inclusion Means

1. Educating all children with disabilities in regular classrooms regardless of the nature of their disabling condition(s).
2. Providing all students enhanced opportunities to learn from each other's contributions.
3. Providing necessary services within the regular schools.
4. Supporting regular teachers and administrators, such as providing time, training, teamwork, resources, and strategies.
5. Having students with disabilities follow the same schedules as non-disabled students.
6. Involving students with disabilities in age-appropriate academic classes and extracurricular activities, including art, music, gym, field trips, assemblies, and graduation exercises.
7. Students with disabilities using school cafeteria, library, playground, and other facilities along with non-disabled students.
8. Encouraging friendships between non-disabled and disabled students.
9. Students with disabilities receiving their education and job training in regular community environments when appropriate.
10. Teaching all children to understand and accept human differences.
11. Placing children with disabilities in the same schools they would attend if they did not have disabilities.
12. Taking parents' concerns seriously.
13. Providing an appropriate individualized educational program

Inclusion Does Not Mean

1. "Dumping" students with disabilities into regular programs without preparation or support.
2. Providing special education services in separate or isolated places.
3. Ignoring children's individual needs.
4. Jeopardizing students' safety or well-being.
5. Placing unreasonable demands on teachers and administrators.
6. Ignoring parents' concerns.
7. Isolating students with disabilities in regular schools.
8. Placing students with disabilities in schools or classes that are not age-appropriate.
9. Requiring that students be "ready" and "earn" their way into regular classrooms based on cognitive or social skills.[18]

Perhaps the most important ethical issue involved in inclusion, however, is the degree to which it can have a positive effect on an individual student and the degree to which educators are committed to seeing that positive effects occur. Consider the case of Stevie as it is described by his parents:

> Stevie ends each day by asking if it's a school day tomorrow. When it is, he picks out his clothes promptly for the next day so that he won't be late. We believe that his eagerness reflects his joy in being included in a kindergarten classroom, just like every other child in his neighborhood. In so many ways, Stevie is just like all of the other children. But he does face extra challenges due to his diagnosis of Down syndrome. We recognize that Stevie's learning style and ability do differ

209

CHAPTER 7
*Creating Inclusive
Classrooms:
The Health
Dimension and the
Ability/Disability
Continuum*

when compared with his typically developing peers. What we have found critical, though, is not the differences in style and ability but the desire to do what his peers are doing. We believe that this desire is shared by all children. And for Stevie, this desire becomes his greatest source of motivation and, thereby, his success.

In an inclusive classroom, Stevie's classmates become his positive role models. In the past six months, Stevie has made considerable progress in his academic and fine motor skills. He is now able to write his name with minimal prompting, count to five with meaning, and begin to identify the beginning letters of words by their sounds. His speech, self-help, and social skills continue to improve because he wants and expects to interact with the other children. Probably one of the most important benefits of an inclusive classroom is that our life is just *more normal*. As parents, we volunteer in the classroom and participate in school-sponsored events, just like every other parent. Thus, we are constantly talking to other parents about mutual parenting concerns. For Stevie's younger brother, it gives him the opportunity to follow the footsteps of his big brother, just like other siblings do. And, for Stevie, he has *friends*. Stevie's friends include classmates who are both typically developing and others who have special needs. This, too, we believe will become the norm for all children because of inclusion. Thus, inclusion leads us to focus our attention on the *child* first and his disability second. Stevie needs that focus. We will always strive to maintain it.

Active Exercises

The following exercises from *Human Diversity in Action: Developing Multicultural Competencies for the Classroom*[19] complement this chapter well:

Activity 17: What Does It Feel Like to Be Excluded? p. 134

Activity 23: The Student with Special Needs, p. 155

Activity 25: The Triad Model, p. 159

Activity 27: Ethnic Literacy Test, p. 172

Accessing the World Wide Web: Resources for Diversity

There are numerous resources for students, professionals, and parents concerned with educational and other issues affecting children and youth with special needs. You may want to contact these web sites for more information about children with disabilities and inclusive education.

http://www.nichcy.org/   The web site of The National Information Center for Children and Youth with Disabilities is an excellent source.

http://www.ed.gov/offices/OSERS/   This is the web site of the Office of Special Education and Rehabilitation Services, the branch of the United States Department of Education that administers federal special education and related programs and services for children and youth with disabilities.

http://www.hood.edu/seri/serihome.htm   This web site, for Special Education Resources on the Internet, links to sites on issues relating to a wide range of specific areas, such as autism spectrum disorder, attention deficit/hyperactivity disorder, speech and language impairments, as well as inclusive education.

http://www.cec.sped.org/ericec.htm

http://cec.sped.org/ericec/abouterc.htm   The ERIC Clearinghouse on Disabilities and Gifted Education (ERIC EC) is one of sixteen federally funded clearinghouses in the ERIC system; these web sites are helpful guides for searching the ERIC Information System for digests, fact sheets, and other references concerning children with disabilities, as well as children who are gifted, and their education.

http://www.cec.sped.org/   This is the web site of the Council for Exceptional Children (CEC), the largest professional organization the focus of which encompasses all aspects of education and other services for children and youth with disabilities, as well as gifted children and youth, and their families.

http://www,usdoj.gov/crt/ada/

http://www.usdoj.gov/crt/ada-home.htm/   These web sites are sources of information on the Americans with Disabilities Act (ADA).

http://www.TASH.ORG   This is the web site of TASH (formerly The Association for Persons with Severe Handicaps), an international organization whose mission emphasizes advocating opportunities for and the rights of persons with disabilities, especially severe disabilities, including full educational and societal inclusion.

http://www.healthy.net/pan/cso/cioi/ACCH.HTM   This is a web site for the Association for the Care of Children's Health; providing member and services information.

http://ericps.ed.uiuc.edu/npin/reswork/workorgs/careof.html   This is also a web site of the Association for the Care of Children's Health; it describes resources for professionals who work with parents of children with special health care needs.

References

1. The case study in this chapter is a composite, reflecting the experiences of children, parents, and educators in two communities, both acknowledged in the Preface. Appreciation to the educators, who, with parents' consent, provided material for this case study is repeated here. The names of all children and adults are pseudonyms.
2. Bengst Nirje, "The Normalization Principle," in *Changing Patterns in Residential Services for the Mentally Retarded,* rev. ed., ed. R. B. Kirgel and A. Shearer (Washington, DC: President's Commission on Mental Retardation, 1976), p. 231. Also see Wolf Wolfensberger, *The Principle of Normalization in Human Services* (Toronto: National Institute of Mental Retardation, 1972).
3. Vocational Rehabilitation Act of 1973 § 504, P L 93-112, 29 U.S.C. § 794 (1983); Americans with Disabilities Act of 1990, 42 U.S.C. § 12101 (1990).
4. Individuals with Disabilities Education Act of 1990, PL No. 101-476, 20, U.S.C. §§ 1400-1485 (1990, re-authorized in 1995).
5. Lawrence Johnson and Marlene Pugach, *Collaborative Practitioners, Collaborative Schools* (Denver: Love, 1995).
6. The source for this and subsequent historical information in this chapter is Philip Safford and Elizabeth Safford, *A History of Childhood and Disability* (New York: Teachers College Press, 1995).

211

CHAPTER 7
Creating Inclusive
Classrooms:
The Health
Dimension and the
Ability/Disability
Continuum

7. Edouard O. Seguin, *Report on Education (U.S. Commissioner on Education at the* Vienna *Universal Exhibition)* (Washington, DC: U.S. Government Printing Office, 1880).

8. For a detailed explanation and discussion of collaborative team strategies, see Beverly Rainforth, Jennifer York, and Cathy Macdonald, *Collaborative Teams for Students with Severe Disabilities: Integrating Therapy and Educational Services,* 2nd ed. (Baltimore: Paul H. Brookes, 1997).

9. Herbert Spencer, "What Knowledge Is of the Most Worth?" in *Education: Intellectual, Moral & Physical* [Essays, 1854-1859] (Patterson, NJ: Littlefield, Adams, & Co., 1963), pp. 21–96.

10. See Martha Snell, ed., *Instruction of Students with Severe Disabilities,* 4th ed. (New York: Macmillan, 1993).

11. Surgeon General's Report: U.S. Department of Health and Human Services. *Children with Special Health Care Needs: Campaign '87* (Washington, DC: U.S. Government Printing Office, 1987).

12. Rachel E. Janney, Martha E. Snell, Mary K. Beers, and Maria Raynes, "Integrating Students with Moderate and Severe Disabilities into General Education Classes," *Exceptional Children* 61, 5, (1995): pp. 425–439.

13. Laura E. Richards, *Letters and Journals of Samuel Gridley Howe, the Servant of Humanity* (Vol. 2). (Boston: Dana Estes & Co., 1909), p. 56; p. 25.

14. Samuel Gridley Howe, *Report of Commission to Inquire into the Conditions of Idiots of the Commonwealth of Massachusetts* (Boston: Senate Document No. 51, 1848).

15. Leta S. Hollingworth, "Provisions for Intellectually Superior Children," in *The Child: His Nature and His Needs,* ed. Michael V. O'Shea (New York: The Children's Foundation, 1924), pp. 277–299.

16. U.S. Department of Education, *Annual Report to Congress on the Implementation of the Education of All Handicapped Children Act* (Washington, DC: U.S. Government Printing Office, 1991).

17. Joanne Yatvin, "Flawed Assumptions," *Phi Delta Kappan* 76, 6 (1994): 482–484.

18. Center on Human Policy: Inclusion (Inclusion in Education: A Choice for Your Child), *Newsletter, TASH: The Association for Persons with Severe Handicaps* 20, 9 (1994): 27.

19. Kenneth Cushner, *Human Diversity in Action: Developing Multicultural Competencies for the Classroom* (New York: McGraw-Hill, 1998).

Developing a Collaborative Classroom: Gender and Sexual Orientation

CHAPTER OUTLINE

RATIONALE FOR COLLABORATIVE
    TEACHING AND LEARNING
CHARACTERISTICS OF A COLLABORATIVE
    CLASSROOM
    Pedagogies: Old and New
    Roles: Old and New
    Place of Content Knowledge: Old
      and New
    Assessment: Old and New
PERSPECTIVES ON GENDER AND
    SEXUAL ORIENTATION
    Sex Role Socialization
    Sex Role Socialization in the
      Middle Class
    Masculine and Feminine Behavior
PERSPECTIVES ON SCHOOLS AS
    SOCIALIZING AGENTS

    Sex Role Stereotypes in School
    Recent Studies
PERSPECTIVES ON GENDER AND
    SCHOOL CULTURE
    Productive and
      Reproductive Processes
    Gender and European American
      Values in Traditional
      School Culture
    Gender and School Rules
    Homophobia and School Culture
    Ethical Issues
SOME REFLECTIVE QUESTIONS
ACTIVE EXERCISES
ACCESSING THE WORLD WIDE WEB:
    RESOURCES FOR DIVERSITY
REFERENCES

Prejudices, it is well known, are most difficult to eradicate from the heart whose soil has never been loosened or fertilized by education; they grow there, firm as weeds among rocks.

Charlotte Brontë

Gender and Sexual Orientation in a Collaborative Classroom: A Case Study[1]

It's the beginning of April in Spokane, Washington, and Tom Littleton's combined biological/environmental science class is in full swing. The twenty-seven juniors and seniors in the class are working together in twos, threes, and fours at a variety of tasks—putting together a large display unit, cataloging leaf and bark samples at the two stone-topped lab benches, looking at water samples under a microscope, taking notes from a well-illustrated

213

botany book, and working at a computer in the corner. Three adults who come into the class regularly—Steven's father, a journalism teacher, and a staff member from the local Environmental Protection Agency—are working with some of the students while Tom moves from one group to another watching, listening, answering questions, and giving advice.

Since school started in late August, these students have turned the classroom into what they call a working land lab. Its purpose is to study the ecological characteristics of the land, water, plants, and animals that make up a wooded plot of ground behind the school. They have taken and tested water samples for toxic chemicals, tested the soil for its chemical compounds, identified and cataloged all the trees and plants (including several rare species), and noted the presence of animal and bird life. In short, they have developed a "map" of the ecological system in this area and have come to understand the living relationships existing there. In the process, they have decided to formally request that the School Board set aside this land as a nature preserve for use by students and members of the community.

The project began somewhat haphazardly last summer, when several of the students noticed that the creek running through the property looked cloudy. When school started, they asked Tom about it and he showed them how to take and test water samples. Since then, the creek area not only has become the catalyst for teaching and learning the subject matter in Tom's class but also has provided an opportunity to accomplish other worthwhile goals. As the school year ends, the class is preparing displays of their findings and writing a report they intend to present to the School Board in May. The report contains their recommendations for establishing the nature preserve. On one long wall is a hand-lettered chart that says

---

Natural History Perspectives: Goals

- To appreciate the universality of change and the dynamic processes of the physical and biological sciences
- To obtain a personal standard of scientific literacy that allows for a reasonable assessment of the local and global condition in terms of economic, social, legal, and applied science concepts
- To achieve the ability to distinguish between science, personal opinion, and pseudoscience through inquiry, investigation, research, and interpretation of data

---

Next to this chart on the same wall is a brightly colored poster of flying geese, with a printed text superimposed on the drawings. It reads

---

Lessons from Geese[2]

1. As each bird flaps its wings, it creates an "uplift" for the following bird. By flying in a *V* formation, the whole flock adds 71 percent greater flying range than if the bird were to fly alone. The lesson to be learned is that people who share a common direction and sense of

---

community can get where they are going quicker because they are traveling on the thrust of one another.

2. Whenever a goose falls out of formation, it suddenly feels the drag of trying to fly alone and quickly gets back into formation to take advantage of the "lifting" power of the bird immediately in front. The lesson to be learned is that, if we have as much sense as a goose, we will stay in formation with those who are headed where we want to go. We should be willing to accept their help and give them ours.

3. When the lead goose gets tired, it rotates back into the formation and another goose flies at the point position. The lesson to be learned is that it pays to take turns doing the hard tasks, and sharing leadership. People, like geese, are interdependent.

4. The geese toward the rear honk to encourage those up front to keep up their speed. The lesson to be learned is that we need to make sure our honking from behind is encouraging, not something else.

5. When a goose gets sick, wounded, or shot down, two geese drop out of formation and follow it down to help and protect it. They stay with it until it is able to fly again or dies. They then launch out on their own, with another formation, or catch up with the flock. The lesson to be learned is that, if we have as much sense as geese, we, too, will stand by each other in difficult times as well as when we are strong.

Seeing that all the students are occupied and that no one seems to have a question at the moment, Tom moves over to his small, crowded desk, sits down, and takes a spiral-bound notebook out of one drawer. The same drawer also contains portfolios that document the accomplishments of individual students. Tom's notebook is a reflective journal in which he notes observations of students, details the work they are all doing, and records ideas for future teaching. In a way, the journal is Tom's portfolio, his assessment of himself as a teacher in this class. "One of the great things about this class," he thinks, "is that, as the year goes by, the students need me less and less. They really are learning to work together and to solve their own problems."

When the year began, Tom had two major objectives apart from, although related to, the curriculum. The first was to systematically encourage the girls in this class to participate actively, to put forth their ideas and speculations willingly, and to be outwardly as well as inwardly proud of their accomplishments. For several years, he had been encouraging ninth and tenth grade girls to take this class, and this year the class was nearly half female. Tom thought that a science class might be the perfect place for girls to exercise their collaborative skills. After all, discoveries in science are nearly always the result of a group effort involving scientists, lab technicians, social scientists, and often students. The process of actually doing science, he thought, should be a particularly fitting one for girls, who were usually socialized to collaborate with others. Unfortunately, he also knew that girls were often guided away from scientific and technical classes by parents and counselors who believed that girls were less suited to such subjects. He knew that girls (and boys) usually thought that science and math were "male" activities.

His second goal was to fully integrate three students from the fairly large Gypsy community that lived in Spokane. These students, Steven, Rebecca, and Ian, had been part of a long-term effort by the Spokane schools to build relations of trust between the schools and Gypsy (or, more accurately, Romani) parents. Because of a long history of persecution by the wider community in both Europe and the United States, these Gypsy parents were hesitant about sending their children to school.

Steven and Rebecca had been in school since they were 7; Ian moved to Spokane when he was 10. All three began school in a program especially designed to accommodate cultural factors within the Gypsy community, such as its close family structure, its respect for age, the fact that it is a highly male-dominated society, and its trait of being highly resistant to change. Also, Gypsy children are expected to assume responsibility in the community at an earlier age than European American middle-class children and are, thus, somewhat more mature than their age-mates.

Some aspects of the program are very different from traditional school practice. For instance, because it is a male-dominated society, boys have to be served lunch first, and female teachers are expected to wear "female" attire—dresses and skirts. Because Gypsy parents are afraid for their children, phones have to be installed in every classroom, so that parents can have direct access to teachers and to their own children regarding after-school activities. Because the community's goal is English literacy but not cultural literacy, the classrooms are explicitly not assimilationist. Because change is feared on a deep level, bus drivers have to keep the same routes, and teachers have to stay with the same children. Because respect for elders has to be maintained, illiterate parents cannot be taught along with their children but need separate instruction, younger children cannot serve as tutors for older children, and teachers are expected to be over 30. Teachers also need to be flexible regarding school goals and schedules to allow for participation in community events and rituals.

While Gypsy children had originally been separated from other children in this program, its goal is to eventually build enough trust in the Gypsy community that they would allow their children to be placed in regular classrooms. Steven, Rebecca, and Ian had gone into regular classes when they began the ninth grade. At this point, the three are still inclined to stay together, but Tom has noticed that they all had become deeply involved in the work of the land lab and that even Rebecca had seemed willing to venture forth with a suggestion now and then.

As Tom leafs through his notebook and watches the students at work, scenes from the past several months float through his mind. He remembers the first day of class, when he introduced the students to the concept of prediction by doing an exercise called a Future's Window. In this activity, students divide a piece of paper into quarters and label the top half "Self" and the bottom half "World." The left side of each half is labeled "5 years," while the right half represents "20 years" into the future. Students are then asked to make at least five entries in each quadrant, things they expect themselves to have accomplished or to be dealing with in five years and in twenty years, and things they expect the world to be confronting in five and twenty years. Students do this activity at first by themselves and then with two or three others. They have about ten minutes to come up with a compilation of the groups' responses to the activity, after which the whole class discusses what they have generated.

217

CHAPTER 8
Developing a
Collaborative
Classroom: Gender
and Sexual
Orientation

Tom remembers that the list generated by this class was typical:

Self

5 Years	20 Years
In college	Well into my career
Own a car	Have a graduate degree
Married	Married, with children
Have a good job	Travel overseas
Live on my own	Own a business
Have a good stereo	Own a vacation home
Graduated from college	

World

5 Years	20 Years
More pollution	Still polluted
Increase in AIDS	Cure for AIDS
Many conflicts and war	World War III
Increase in crime	World hunger still a problem
Homelessness still a problem	Still many people without homes and work
Nuclear arms in the hands of terrorists	Nuclear explosions in a few places on the planet
Spread of antibiotic-resistant viruses	Criminals more sophisticated
Another Chernobyl-like disaster	
Increase in global warming	

He also remembers that, like most students this age, this class had a hard time realizing that there is a connection between their own lives and the life of the larger community and world. He also remembers that not one of the Gypsy students contributed to the discussion and that only one girl said anything at all. How different they are now!

Tom's eyes glance at a page in his journal and he recalls the day, about a month after school started, when he saw Steven's mother standing in the hall, watching the class through the partially open door. He invited her in and she came, somewhat hesitatingly, saying that she only wanted to see that Steven and the other two Gypsy students were all right. Tom didn't know at the time that she had been one of the first parents involved in the Spokane outreach to Gypsy children. In fact, it had been Steven's mother and grandmother who had been primarily responsible for convincing the Gypsy community that "those school people" could be trusted with their children.

Tom also remembers the day that all his careful work to create collaborative working relationships in the class was almost destroyed. For several months, Tom had noticed that many of the students had been avoiding one of their peers, a young man named Kurt. Although he was not overtly excluded from participation in class activities, the boys interacted with him only when necessary and did not include him in the informal conversation and laughter that was often a part of their group work. One rainy Saturday morning in November, Tom had taken Kurt with a group of other boys out to the land area behind the school to finish identifying and tagging trees. In dividing the group into pairs, Tom put Kurt with Jimmy, who immediately objected, saying he would rather work with two other boys. Not paying too much attention, Tom told him that, since the work would be accomplished much faster if they divided up and since it was raining and they all wanted to get inside, he'd appreciate it if Jimmy would just go along with Kurt and get to work. He was totally unprepared for Jimmy's loud reaction: "I'm not going off alone with that fag, and you can't make me!" There was a dead silence in the group. All eyes were down except Jimmy's, who stared defiantly at Tom. Tom looked around the group and said, "OK, guys, I guess there is something more important going on here than cataloging trees. Let's go into the school and see if we can sort this out." Somewhat reluctantly, the boys followed him into their classroom, where they spent the rest of the afternoon talking about what had happened and what they were going to do about it. Tom had told them two things: (1) he was not going to tolerate homophobic (or any other kind of) name-calling, and (2) since it seemed likely that homosexuality has a biological basis, hating a person because of sexual orientation was a lot like hating someone because he or she had brown eyes, was left-handed, or was very tall. Thinking about it now, Tom knew that the discussion didn't change the boys' minds and hearts all at once—homophobia is too emotional and too strong for that. But the air was cleared, and, in fact, several of the boys were intrigued to learn that sexual orientation was not a simple matter of sexual choice. Afterwards, there was no more name-calling, and Kurt's expertise with the computer earned the admiration of his classmates. He even wrote some programs that enabled the class to classify their data more easily. Although Jimmy was still obviously antagonistic toward Kurt, and Ian and Steven looked at him now and then with some distrust, most of the class seemed to accept him as just another member of the class and several became his good friends.

Tom remembers many other incidents during the year: the day the students finally settled on the three basic goals of the class, which were now hanging on the wall; the time Rebecca's father joined them on one of their field explorations and told them the name and habits of every bird they saw; the excitement generated by a group of four girls who were the first to identify the source of the cloudy water; the time Eric told Penny she should take the notes in a class meeting because she was a girl; the arguments and the discoveries made by each student in collaboration with others. It was certainly not a perfect year, but it was a good one.

And now they were almost ready to present their case to the School Board. Tom didn't see how they could fail. In fact, he thought, even if the School Board refuses to act on its request, nothing could stop their interest in their project now.

Tom Littleton's class and its land lab provide numerous examples of a collaborative and gender-sensitive classroom in action. It also illustrates the importance of dealing effectively with nonacademic problems that threaten the existence of a learning community atmosphere. Key elements of a collaborative learning environment that are evident in Tom's classroom include the following:

219

CHAPTER 8
*Developing a
Collaborative
Classroom: Gender
and Sexual
Orientation*

1. Students are encouraged to work together on a project they helped design. During the year, each student has an opportunity to work with others on a variety of tasks that are part of a larger group goal.
2. The use of collaborative teaching and learning encourages the girls in the class to think of themselves as equal partners in the group endeavor.
3. Other adults (teachers and parents) are encouraged to bring their own expertise and experience into the classroom for students' benefit.
4. By combining his own knowledge with that of collaborating teachers, Tom is able to show how solving real-world problems requires integrating knowledge from a variety of subject areas. His nature study project requires measurements and calculations (math); report writing (English); consideration of social, political, and economic issues (social studies); and the preparation of drawings and displays (art).
5. Students are actively involved in setting their own goals and in planning strategies for accomplishing them.
6. Students have learned how specialized tasks, such as testing water and writing the results of the tests, are interdependent subgoals that are part of a larger, more holistic goal.
7. Students have learned that their individual successes depend, in part, on the successes of those with whom they are working.

As he reflects on the goals he set for this class, particularly those related to gender and cultural difference, Tom Littleton realizes that he needs more than biological and environmental knowledge: he needs a firm grasp on the basis of collaborative teaching and learning. Furthermore, he realizes now how closely related such things as gender and cultural difference are to both in-school and out-of-school learning. In the following section, we will discuss collaborative learning, gender, sexual orientation, and education from a variety of perspectives, including the differences between collaborative and traditional teaching and learning, the importance of socialization to gender role, the relation of middle-class values to the creation of gender identity, and the role of the school as a gender-socializing agent.

RATIONALE FOR COLLABORATIVE TEACHING AND LEARNING

The rationale for collaborative teaching and learning rests on many of the same ideas as the rationale for democratic communities of learners and developmentally appropriate and inclusive classrooms. In addition, support for increasing collaboration in schools and classrooms emerges from two other major sources.

First, as it becomes clear that we are members of an interdependent global economic and political community, many theorists suggest that we must learn to live cooperatively with one another, rather than continue to engage in the kinds of destructive competition that produce hunger, disease, and war. As the world's population increases, such issues as access to natural resources, food, and human problem-solving power become critical ones. Choices between competing for such resources, which has been a major cause of war, and sharing them, which means cooperative efforts at problem solving, must be made. Some of the traditional values espoused by the mainstream culture in the United States (e.g., individualism, materialism, an emphasis on technology) may be intensifying rather than ameliorating the major problems that we must confront (e.g., preservation of the environment, increasing poverty, and loss of community). Solutions to such complex social problems demand collaboration and cooperation.

A second and very different source of support for collaborative classrooms emerges from thirty years of research on gender and on the degree to which boys and girls have different experiences in school. Such research suggests two important points: (1) girls and women tend to focus on preserving relationships, while boys and men tend to focus on principles of behavior,[3] and (2) girls and women tend to learn more effectively when collaboration rather than competition is central to the teaching-learning process.[4] This research will be discussed in more detail later in this chapter. The point to be made here is that gender researchers have developed instructional models based on classroom collaboration and cooperation, rather than on competition, and that these models are currently available for classroom use.

Both of these rationales for collaborative classrooms suggest a shift away from the values of individualism and competition, which are so deeply woven into both our political and economic culture and the school curricula which transmit that culture. While teachers and the school curriculum are not the only means of socializing youngsters, they are critical elements in helping them attain the understanding and skills needed to live cooperatively and comfortably with others.

CHARACTERISTICS OF A COLLABORATIVE CLASSROOM

Fortunately, teachers, parents, and supporting school personnel are beginning to recognize both the opportunity and the obligation they have to effect change in this direction. The characteristics of collaborative classrooms can be described as follows.

First, while competition is not absent from collaborative classrooms (nor should it be), cooperation and collaboration are woven throughout both instructional and evaluative processes. Similarly, while group activities and group performance are clearly in evidence, individual acquisition of knowledge and skills and individual performance are still stressed. Indeed, one of the primary goals of collaboration is the enhancement of individual learning. In U.S. schools, competition has often been blindly equated with rigor and quality, both of which are regarded as exemplifying American values of hard work and individual achievement. When a competitive environment threatens classroom equity, however, it becomes problematic. Clearly, we need both. As John Goodlad has pointed out, "Equality and quality are the name of the game. These two concepts will frame dialogue, policy, and practice regarding schooling for years to come."[5]

Second, collaborative classrooms involve teachers and other school personnel, parents, and other community members working together to plan and implement instructional goals. In traditional schools, teaching is often a lonely activity involving little or no interaction with other adults. This is unfortunate on many accounts, not the least of which is that, in order to grow professionally, teachers must work in collaboration with others. By observing other teachers in their classrooms, teachers gain new ideas, fresh strategies, and new perspectives on their professional lives.

Third, because teachers in collaborative classrooms work closely with other adults in the school, many of whom have different areas of expertise, lessons and other activities tend to benefit from the integration of different disciplines and skills. Students, thus, begin to see connections between the subjects they study and their own learning goals.

221

CHAPTER 8
Developing a
Collaborative
Classroom: Gender
and Sexual
Orientation

Fourth, collaborative classrooms also extend beyond the school—most obviously, to the home. Often referred to as "parent involvement," interest in home-school collaboration initially emerged from concerns about increased student failure and dropout rates among minority groups, particularly immigrant families, many of whom were unfamiliar with the culture and practices of American schools. In truly collaborative classrooms, however, the involvement of parents is perceived as central to effective education, not as a response to difficulties in an otherwise effective schooling system. In short, parents are regarded as the child's first and continuing teachers, and as such, are natural partners in a collaborative relationship with classroom teachers.

Finally, in collaborative classrooms, students cooperate with one another in planning their activities. Students may be organized (or organize themselves) in project teams or in dyads and triads, depending on the nature of the work to be done. The assumption here is that students bring to school useful knowledge from a variety of backgrounds and experiences and that they are competent to assist one another in acquiring new knowledge.

Pedagogies: Old and New

Traditionally, schools have sponsored a variety of collaborative activities. One thinks, for example, of sports teams, choirs, dramatic productions, school newspapers and yearbooks, not to mention a wide variety of social and fund-raising activities carried on by students and teachers. Each of these activities requires the skills of teamwork, cooperation, and interdependence. However, each of these is also either cocurricular or extracurricular.

In collaborative classrooms, the teaching processes and strategies so necessary to co- and extracurricular activities are applied to the very heart of schooling itself—that is, to the formal curriculum. Teachers find themselves working together to plan units and often teach in teams. One excellent example of this is a middle school in which four teachers have 100 students. During the course of the school day, one teacher may be working with all 100 students while the other three meet to plan future lessons. Or each teacher may be working with 25 students on separate aspects of a unit. The possible combinations of teachers and students, as well as the possible uses of time, are broad.

One of the most widely known pedagogical strategies found in most collaborative classrooms is called "cooperative learning." Like other instructional strategies, cooperative learning encompasses a variety of instructional techniques. In general, cooperative learning environments are characterized by what is called *positive goal interdependence*. That is, individuals share the same group goals, and members of the group are accountable to one another. In short, the group sinks or swims as one, working in concert to attain a particular instructional goal. Group cohesiveness, thus, is paramount.

In discussing his interest in cooperative learning, Kagan relates some findings from his early research on children's play in Mexico.[6] One finding that intrigued him was that children from rural parts of Mexico were more cooperative with one another than were their peers in urban settings. Somewhat bothered by this finding, Kagan extended his work to look at cooperation and competition among children in other parts of the world. What he discovered appears to be nearly universal and has to do with differences between students who live in rural and urban areas. That is, worldwide, regardless of the continent or culture, children in urban environments are more competitive than their rural counterparts. This finding, coupled with the fact that the world is becoming increasingly urban, raised considerable concern in Kagan's mind. Out of fear that the social character of the nation and world would become increasingly competitive, Kagan began exploring ways to help reverse the children's tendency to become more competitive with age. He found that using cooperative teams in the classroom, often referred to as cooperative learning, worked quite well.[7]

Slavin identified two factors that seem to account for the effectiveness of cooperative learning.[8] The first is that cooperative groups must work to achieve a group goal that cannot be mastered unless each member performs his or her assigned task. The second critical factor is that each individual in the group must still be held accountable for learning the required content. That is, members must work together to make certain that all have mastered the assigned content and have earned satisfactory grades or other forms of recognition. The group's success depends on each individual's learning the required material. Evidence of group success might be seen in the sum of the individual member's test scores or in the presentation of a group report. In other words, each individual in the group must have differentiated tasks whose successful performance is critical to achieving the group goal. Secondary characteristics of cooperative learning include an emphasis on face-to-face interpersonal interaction, the development of social skills, and group reviews that help members analyze how well they are functioning.

Cooperative learning groups may be used to teach specific content (information or skills), to ensure the active cognitive processing of information during a lecture, or to provide long-term support and assistance for academic progress.[9] Basically, any assignment in any curriculum area for a student of any age can be accommodated through cooperative learning.

It is important to emphasize that cooperative learning does not imply either devaluation of individual contributions or lack of individual accountability. Instead, when individuals of diverse cultural backgrounds and differing physical characteristics have the opportunity to work together in pursuit of a common goal, the barriers of stereotyping that prevent people from knowing each other as individuals are likely to be broken down. Friendships are more likely to form. Individual accountability is explicitly addressed in cooperative learning strategies in either or both of two ways: task specialization or the determination of group scores for team assignments.[10]

Task specialization, or the assignment of a specific subtask to each member of a team or group, is particularly effective in ensuring that students with disabilities, for example, contribute significantly to the group effort. In some instances, a student with a disability may be uniquely able to carry out a certain task, because students with physical, academic-cognitive, or emotional-behavioral differences are also people with *abilities*. Thus, not only can the self-image and identity of students with disabilities be enhanced, but all students can, through first-hand experience, realize this fundamental truth.

223

CHAPTER 8
Developing a
Collaborative
Classroom: Gender
and Sexual
Orientation

By far, the greatest number of students identified as handicapped, based on definitions of Public Law 94-142, can be described as academically handicapped—that is, they experience difficulty with some (specific learning disability) or most (mentally retarded) areas of academic learning. Clearly, traditional, competitive classroom organization contributes to negative peer attitudes toward low-performing students. Thus, the mere presence of these students in the regular classroom cannot in itself realize the potential of mainstreaming. In Slavin's words,

> If mainstreaming is to fulfill its potential to socially integrate handicapped children, something more than the usual instructional methods is needed. If the classroom is changed so that cooperation rather than competition is emphasized and so that academically handicapped students can make a meaningful contribution to the success of a cooperative group, acceptance of such students seems likely to increase.[11]

The corollary to collaborative learning, of course, is collaborative teaching, which refers to interactions among students who are teaching one another, to interactions between teachers and students, and to interactions between teachers engaged in collaborative efforts. In classrooms where collaboration is the norm, teachers do some of the talking, but are not necessarily the center of attention, even the majority of the time. Students work in teams, discuss issues, engage in group problem solving, and help one another understand the material at hand. Teachers and other adults work with students by encouraging them to inquire, to reflect, and to share and modify ideas.

Roles: Old and New

As in other types of classrooms we have discussed, the traditional roles of teacher as teller and student as listener change in a collaborative classroom. Rather than always being the "expert," the teacher often acts as "coach," encouraging and assisting students to complete the assigned tasks. Students also serve as coaches for one another and sometimes find themselves acting as "experts" in particular areas. One of the most obvious examples of this phenomenon is the native Spanish, French, or German speaker in a foreign-language classroom. There are, however, many other ways in which students of all ages can provide expert knowledge and/or skills to their fellow students. For instance, the child who actively uses the computer at home, or one who has a well-developed skill in playing a musical instrument, can become active as a peer-tutor in these areas.

One of the most important role changes in a collaborative classroom, however, is that of parents. In traditional elementary classrooms, parents ordinarily serve in various "motherly" capacities, such as providing goods for a bake sale, bringing treats on birthdays, and acting as planners for holiday celebrations. Parents also are expected to ensure that homework assignments are completed and to attend open houses and parent-teacher conferences. In traditional middle and high school classrooms, the role of parents is often limited to these last functions.

In many collaborative classrooms, however, parents (and even grandparents) are central to the instructional program, helping make and implement curricular and instructional decisions. For example, parents may take an active role in elementary reading instruction by organizing various small-group activities. Or parents may work with small groups of students in math-related activities, thus providing greater opportunity for children to be actively engaged in classroom content.

It is not always easy to encourage such collaboration, however. Indeed, McCaleb has explored various reasons for the lack of parental involvement, particularly among nondominant groups.[12] One reason she offers for a lack of involvement among minority parents centers on the perceived inequality between students from non-standard-English home environments and students from the dominant culture. She argues that most young children, understandably, identify strongly with their families—their primary teachers. If students happen to come from families with minimal or no schooling, or if the educational experience of parents differs significantly from that which is normally experienced by the American middle class, children quickly sense the contradictions between their home and school lives. Seeing many books at school, for example, and few at home, they may begin to question their own potential for educational success. A similarly negative self-attribution may be made by parents if they, in turn, believe that they have little to teach or share with their children. In Hawaii, however, a successful curricular innovation involves grandparents and other community elders, who regularly enter elementary classrooms to teach children Hawaiian culture and language from their traditionally oral approach.

Greenspan, Niemeyer, and Seeley[13] conducted a study of how principals perceive parental involvement in school affairs. They cite four reasons for the lack of parental involvement in schools.

1. *A significant transient population.* Many schools have children whose families move frequently, thus forcing their children to attend new schools.
2. *Alienation between the home and school.* Social class differences, for one, tend to separate families from teachers and administrators. Such differences, they suggest, may be accentuated by racial factors. Most of the principals interviewed for the study, however, concurred that poor parents were just as concerned about education and wanted the same things for their children (a good education, good behavior, respect for authority) as other parents. What they did not understand was how to assist their children in attaining these goals.
3. *School-generated problems.* In some instances, teachers and other school staff are simply insensitive to the needs and problems of students and their families.
4. *Disintegration of the family.* The authors inferred this from the large number of children who seem to be cared for by adults other than their natural parents.

McCaleb, on the other hand, suggests that the perceived "broken family" issue might be a classic case of misunderstanding and misattribution. She suggests that such nonparental caring arrangements do not represent a disintegration of the family but, rather, a reinterpretation of the concept of "family," since many of these families consist of an extended network of caregivers.

To summarize, in collaborative classrooms, parents and other community members share with teachers and other school staff the responsibility for educating children. This partnership model views parents as resources and contributors to the education of their children and helps integrate the school and the community. Cummins agrees with these suggestions when he proposes that changes in schools will only take place when the relationships of power begin to change and the voices and concerns of parents and the community are heard and acted on.[14]

Place of Content Knowledge: Old and New

225

CHAPTER 8
Developing a
Collaborative
Classroom: Gender
and Sexual
Orientation

As we have said, in collaborative classrooms where teachers, parents, other school personnel, and students are working together, the boundaries between academic disciplines tend to become less defined as cooperative teams pool their knowledge in the pursuit of integrated projects. As teachers learn about what other teachers are doing, they begin to see ways of integrating their efforts. In such classrooms, the language arts and social studies may begin to merge, and the arts may be put to use in the service of scientific and geographical knowledge.

A good example of this "blurring" of disciplinary boundaries is given by Charles Fowler. He writes:

> If, for example, students are studying the Grand Canyon, and we want to give them a general idea of it without actually going there, we often resort to a verbal description: "The Grand Canyon, the world's largest gorge, is a spectacle of multicolored layers of rock carved out over the millennia by the Colorado River." If we want to convey its vastness, we use measurements: "The Grand Canyon is over 1 mile deep, 4 to 18 miles wide, and more than 200 miles long." Each of these symbolic systems—words and numbers—permits us to reveal important aspects, but a picture or a painting can be equally telling.
>
> The arts—creative writing, dance, music, theater/film, and visual arts—serve as ways that we react to, record, and share our impressions of the world. Students can be asked to set forth their own interpretation of the Grand Canyon, using, say, poetry as the communicative vehicle. While mathematics gives us precise quantitative measures of magnitude, poetry explores our disparate personal reactions. Both views are valid. Both contribute to understanding. Together, they prescribe a larger overall conception of, in this case, one of nature's masterpieces.[15]

In a collaborative classroom, not only does content knowledge become something to be "learned," but also, more important, learning becomes more meaningful as students make connections between areas of knowledge that, after all, blend together in the world outside of school.

Assessment: Old and New

In all classrooms, methods of evaluating student performance should be compatible with the types of learning activities that characterize those classrooms. For example, traditional forms of evaluation, such as standardized paper-and-pencil tests, answers to questions posed by the teacher in a large-group format, and student reports, all seek to determine what and how much students "know" about a particular subject, such as math or English. Each assumes that subject matter knowledge can be "given" to students, who are then able to "give" such knowledge back as a sign that it has been learned. Perhaps the most efficient form of instruction for transmitting subject matter knowledge is that in which teachers talk and students listen, read, and are evaluated on the degree to which they have retained what they have heard and read.

In collaborative classrooms, however, learning is less dependent on teacher talk and more dependent on group activities (projects, problem-solving situations, study groups) that take place over time. In such classrooms, compatible evaluation techniques are those that measure performance over time, such as the creation of artifacts and portfolios and the demonstration of individual and group problem-solving ability. Although all of these will be discussed in more detail in Chapter 11, the point to make here is that these forms of assessment are a good match with instructional methods that emphasize collaborative teaching and learning.

In all teaching situations, however, it is good to remember that teachers are not required to choose only one kind of instruction, one kind of role, or one kind of evaluation. Indeed, the more variety one has in one's repertoire, the more effective one is likely to be and the more exciting the classroom will be for everyone.

PERSPECTIVES ON GENDER AND SEXUAL ORIENTATION

One of the earliest and most important learning experiences in any society is the development of a sense of self-identity—the knowledge that one is separate from mother, father, and family. This perception begins when an infant is about 7 or 8 months old and continues throughout his or her life. It is not unusual for one's sense of identity to undergo significant changes as one encounters new experiences.

An extremely important part of identity, and one that begins at least at birth, is gender. It is thought that identification in terms of sex begins at about 18 months of age, and, by the age of 3, is clearly internalized.[16] But sexual identity is more complex than simply "knowing" that you are male or female. More important to your sense of self is your identification as a member of a *gender* group—"I am a girl"; "I am a boy." While sex is a biological characteristic, gender is a social one. In all cultural groups, gender identity includes the knowledge of a large set of rules and expectations for what boys and girls should wear, how they should speak and act, and their "place" in the overall structure of society. Knowledge of these rules is knowledge of one's role as a member of a particular gender group, and it provides us with the ability to deal with many social situations without having to stop each time to figure out what to do. Sex role identity, however, also limits us in terms of our range of choices and, sometimes, the very quality of our lives.

Sex Role Socialization

The rules associated with one's sex role vary by race, by ethnicity, by social class, by religion, and even by geographical region. Such socialization takes place in a variety of ways, many of them small and incremental—simple routines of daily life and language. The process of such learning has been described in three parts:

1. The child learns to *distinguish* between men and women, and between boys and girls, and to know what kinds of behavior are characteristic of each.
2. The child learns to express appropriate sex role *preferences* for himself or herself.
3. The child learns to *behave* in accordance with sex role standards.[17]

While this process of internalizing one's knowledge of and identification with sex role is a part of all children's lives, it has been most studied in the lives of middle-class white children, especially girls. This is significant for at least two reasons. First, it reflects the predominant characteristics of the researchers themselves, many of whom have been both white and middle-class university scholars and feminists interested in rediscovering the reality of women's lives. Because the focus has been on girls, the consequences of sex role socialization on boys, which are great, have often been minimized.

Second, studies primarily located in the white middle class have reflected the dominant social group in the United States. Because dominance is often equated with universality, norms related to the sex role socialization of middle-class whites are often thought to apply to *all* American girls and boys—indeed, to *all* girls and boys everywhere. New research, which attempts to look at sex role socialization in terms of racial, ethnic, religious, and national groups is beginning to discover significant differences in value and orientation between white middle-class socialization practices and those of other groups. This is important, because the role of the school in teaching sex role attitudes and behavior is second only to the role of the family. As we have said before, schools normally represent the dominant culture, and gender role is no exception. Thus, schools often unconsciously attempt to "mold" boys and girls into dominant gender roles, while ignoring the different orientations and behaviors regarding gender that students bring with them to school.

227

CHAPTER *8*
Developing a
Collaborative
Classroom: Gender
and Sexual
Orientation

Sex Role Socialization in the Middle Class

For the white middle class, differences in socialization practices for boys and girls are many and obvious. Florence Howe describes some of them this way:

> We throw boy babies up in the air and roughhouse with them. We coo over girl babies and handle them delicately. We choose sex related colors and toys for our children from their earliest days. We encourage the energy and physical activity of our sons, just as we expect girls to be quieter and more docile. We love both our sons and daughters with equal fervor, we protest, and yet we are disappointed when there is no male child to carry on the family name.[18]

Sylvia Kramer has suggested a number of socialization agents in early childhood that reflect middle-class values.[19] The first, of course, is parents. Studies have demonstrated not only that infant boys are handled more roughly than their sisters and that infant girls receive more verbal attention but also that young boys are given more freedom to explore than young girls, who are often kept closer to the supervising parent. In addition, girls receive more help on tasks than boys, who are encouraged to "figure it out for themselves." Research also shows that parental reaction to the behavior of their children tends to be more favorable when girls and boys are behaving in ways traditionally associated with their sex.[20] Thus, parents shape the expectations and abilities of their children not only by overt behavior but also by rewards of approval when they behave "appropriately."

In contrast to the usually more traditional socializing influence of the family is another powerful socializing agent—television. While there is much that is still stereotypical about the images of boys and girls and women and men on television—particularly the sexual images on such networks as MTV—there has been a significant change in the nature of gender role images to be found in commercials. Indeed, males and females of all ages are shown in roles unheard of even fifteen years ago. Thus, young women are competing in sports and young men are taking care of their infants in a variety of commercial messages. Similarly, this kind of change can also be seen in the roles played by older people on television commercials, who today are climbing mountains and fording wild streams, rather than sitting on front porches with their grandchildren.

A third influence on young children's development of sex role identity is children's books. Although increasing numbers of nonsexist books are being published today, the "classics" are still being read with enthusiasm. Traditional fairly tales, such as Cinderella, Little Red Riding Hood, Snow White and Rose Red, and Sleeping Beauty present "heroines" who are browbeaten, tricked, chased, put to sleep by wicked witches (another ever popular female character), and/or eaten. Release from such vicissitudes, when it occurs, is always at the hands of a (handsome) young man, who finally shows up at the end of the story to whisk the young girl away on *his* horse, to live out her days in *his* castle.[21]

A fourth important gender socializer of children is toys. If the inclination of parents and relatives to buy "sex-appropriate" toys is not sufficient to the task, manufacturers provide useful clues to the gender of the child expected to use the toy on its package. Kramer notes that "with few exceptions, blocks, cars, trains, manipulative games, chemistry sets, doctor's kits, work tools, building games, and of course balls of all kinds show boys on the package. Dolls, kitchen or cleaning toys, needlework or sewing equipment, and nurse's kits show girls on the package."[22] Although many Barbie dolls come with brief cases, astronaut helmets, and computers, Barbie is still a *very* well-endowed young lady, and Ken is still lurking in the background.

Boys' toys are relatively more complex, more varied, and more expensive than girls' toys[23] and frequently have no counterpart for girls. Consider, for example, the range of remote-control cars, boats, and airplanes for sale, as well as electronic sports and adventure games that are marketed for boys. While there is no *law* preventing parents and others from buying "cross-sex" toys, most people still feel a bit uncomfortable doing so. Even in the 1990s, we buy toy lawn mowers for little boys and toy shopping carts for little girls and seldom do the reverse.

Other socializing influences of young children may be found in a variety of everyday places and activities. From nursery rhymes, we learn that young girls are frightened of spiders, while young boys are nimble and quick. In Bible stories, we observe that young boys are brave and able to do away with giants, while women have a tendency toward evil actions, such as cutting off a man's hair and robbing him of his strength. From familiar proverbs and sayings, we become aware that sometimes objectionable behavior on the part of boys must be excused on the grounds that "boys will be boys" (did you ever hear "girls will be girls"?) and that "It's a man's world." And from children's songs we learn that John Henry built a railroad, while Suzannah waited for her young man to return from Louisiana.

Masculine and Feminine Behavior

If middle-class sex roles seem to limit girls more than boys, it may be only that our society favors the active, the adventurous, and the aggressive and that those traits are largely associated with boys. However, there is a high price to be paid by boys for all their "freedom." First of all, boys are socialized much earlier to what is perceived to be "manly." A girl who participates in boys' activities, plays with boys' toys, is impatient with dresses and ribbons, and in general eschews "girlish" things is called a tomboy and is regarded with some tolerance by most adults, at least until adolescence. At that point, according to conventional wisdom, chances are good that she will "grow out of it." At the same time, from the age of 3 onward, boys who want to play with dolls, spend time with their mothers in the kitchen, cry easily, like to stay clean, and avoid contact sports are called sissies—a much more negative label. Adults viewing such behavior even in very young boys often become enormously uncomfortable and worried that "he is moving in the wrong direction." Adult intervention in these "girlish" activities is usually swift, direct, and unmistakable.

Second, boys are punished much more harshly for deviation from the norms of "masculine" behavior. Moreover, such punishment occurs at an age when they are too young to really understand the source of their "problem" or the reasons for adult distress. Hartley argues that

> To make matters more difficult, the desired behavior is rarely defined positively as something the child *should* do, but rather, undesirable behavior is indicated negatively as something he should *not* do or be—anything, that is, that the parent or other people regard as "sissy." Thus, very early in life the boy must either stumble on the right path or bear repeated punishment without warning when he accidentally enters into the wrong ones.[24]

One result of this socialization is that boys very early come to regard anything having to do with girls' play and behavior as something to be avoided at all costs, and this attitude increases during the elementary years until most boys would rather "drop dead" than play with girls. This is commonly regarded as a natural stage of development, rather than the result of careful socialization.[25] Thus, little is done to alter practices that lead to the separation of the sexes and the masculine disdain for the "feminine," which often lasts a lifetime.

That such lessons are well learned is without doubt, and little has changed in the twenty-five years since Hartley asked a representative group of boys (8 and 10 years old) to describe what boys and girls have to be able to know and do. Boys, they said,

> have to be able to fight in case a bully comes along; they have to be athletic; they have to be able to run fast; they must be able to play rough games; they need to know how to play many games—curb-ball, baseball, basketball, football; they need to be smart; they need to be able to take care of themselves; they should know what girls don't know—how to climb, how to make a fire, how to carry things; they should have more ability than girls . . . they are expected to be noisy; to get dirty; to mess up the house; to be naughty; to be "outside" more than girls are; not to be cry-babies; not to be "softies;" not to be "behind" like girls are; and to get into trouble more than girls do.[26]

Thinking about the roles boys must assume, it is hard not to question, with Hartley, "not why boys have difficulty with this role, but why they try as hard as they do to fulfill it."[27]

PERSPECTIVES ON SCHOOLS AS SOCIALIZING AGENTS

One answer to "why they do it" is that sex roles are *normative*—that is, the ideas about what attitudes, values, and behavior are associated with one's sex or gender have been coded by the social group into norms or stereotypes. A *norm* is a rule of conduct based on attitudes and values that are usually internalized through socialization until they become "of course" statements.[28] Schools have an important function as socializers to societal norms, particularly those associated with the middle class.

Because these norms are so much a part of us, they seem normal and "right," and we take them very much for granted. That sense of normality is probably the most powerful force operating to encourage obedience to norms. However, there are other factors involved in encouraging normative thought and behavior. In all societies, there are *sanctions,* or punishments, for deviation from norms. In terms of sex role, an important sanction for "unwomanly" or "unmanly" behavior is the belief that such behavior means that one is simply not a man or a woman. One is, in short, robbed of a vital sense of sexual identity by the belief that one is "deviant."

Sex Role Stereotypes in School

In our society, sex role stereotypes include the belief that boys and men are aggressive, independent, strong, logical, direct, adventurous, self-confident, ambitious, and not particularly emotional. Girls and women are passive, weak, illogical, indirect, gentle, and very emotional. Boys, the stereotypes say, are good at math and science, and girls are good at language and writing. Boys are loud and girls are quiet. Girls play with dolls and boys play with balls. While it is true that not every boy or girl believes or adheres to these stereotypes, it is generally the case that *society,* partly through schooling, attempts to enforce them. Moreover, this continues to be the case even in the face of contrary evidence, such as the fact that girls and women are now participating in nearly every aspect of life once "owned" by boys and men.

Sex role stereotypes vary not only in their content but also in the value ascribed to the content. In other words, not only are boys and men perceived to be *different* from girls and women, but their learned behavior is generally more highly valued. Thus, sex stereotypes "genderize," or assign value to traits that either males or females are *able* to display, in favor of one gender or the other.

The power of sex role stereotypes is enormous and frequently costly to girls and women. A classic study of the perception of clinical psychologists about mental health done in the late 1960s assessed their beliefs about traits associated with the healthy male, the healthy female, and the healthy adult. A list of 122 bipolar items (e.g., aggressive-passive) associated with stereotypically masculine and stereotypically feminine characteristics was given to three groups of male and female psychologists.

> Each group was given a different set of instructions: One was told to choose those traits that characterize the healthy adult male; another to choose those of the healthy adult female; the third, to choose those of the healthy adult—a person. The result: The clinically healthy male and the clinically healthy adult were identical—and totally divergent from the clinically healthy female. The authors of the study concluded that "a double standard of health exists for men and women." That is, the general standard of health applies only to men. Women are perceived as "less healthy" by those standards called "adult." At the same time, however, if a woman deviates from the sexual stereotypes prescribed for her—if she grows more "active" or "aggressive" for example—she doesn't grow healthier; she may, in fact . . . be perceived as "sicker."[29]

In other words, if a woman behaves like a man, she is perceived to be "unwomanly," while, if she behaves like a woman, she is perceived to be "childish."

Sex role stereotypes are equally hard on boys and men, but in a somewhat different way. As the woman's movement has succeeded in opening up to women public roles that have been traditionally associated with men, women have learned to assume those roles more or less well, and the sex role socialization of young girls has changed somewhat to accommodate their broader life opportunities. The same is not true of boys and men. Cooper Thompson tells the following story, which illustrates the point:

> I was once asked by a teacher in a suburban high school to give a guest presentation on male roles. She hoped that I might help her deal with four boys who exercised extraordinary control over the other boys in the class. Using ridicule and their status as physically imposing athletes, the four wrestlers had succeeded in stifling the participation of the other boys, who were reluctant to comment in class discussions.
>
> As a class, we talked about how boys got status in that school and how they were put down by others. I was told that the most humiliating put-down was being called a "fag." The list of behaviors that could elicit ridicule filled two large chalkboards; the boys in the school were conforming to rigid, narrow standards of masculinity to avoid being called a fag. I, too, felt this pressure and became very conscious of my mannerisms in front of the group. Partly from exasperation, I decided to test the seriousness of these assertions. Since one of the four boys had some streaks of pink in his shirt, and since he had told me that wearing pink was grounds for being called a fag, I told him that I thought *he* was a fag. Instead of laughing, he said, "I'm going to kill you."
>
> He obviously didn't and, in retrospect, I think that what I said was inappropriate. But, in that moment, I understood how frightening it is for a boy to have his masculinity challenged, and I realized that the pressure to be masculine was higher than I ever would have expected. This was, after all, a boy who was a popular and successful athlete, whose masculinity was presumably established in the eyes of his peers; yet because of that single remark from me, he experienced a destruction of his self-image as a male.[30]

Thompson goes on to say that much of the definition of masculinity held by these boys was based not on what boys *should* do but, rather, on what they *should not* do and that what they should not do was to be anything like a girl. Two forces that, in our society, help enforce male and female stereotypes are misogyny and homophobia. Simply stated, *misogyny* is the hatred of women, and *homophobia* is the fear of homosexuality and homosexuals. Thompson argues that, while these forces seem to target different kinds of people, they are really different aspects of the same thing. "Homophobia is the hatred of feminine qualities in men, while misogyny is the hatred of feminine qualities in women."[31] In both cases, the assumption is that feminine qualities are less valued, even contemptible.

While this story may seem almost melodramatic, it reflects a fundamental set of values in our society, values that, often unconsciously, guide our thinking, our behavior, and our policymaking. Carelli has made an effective distinction between sex role stereotyping, sex bias, and sex discrimination:

> Whenever specific behaviors, abilities, interests, and values are attributed to one sex, then sex role stereotyping is taking place. . . . Behavior that results from the underlying belief in sex role stereotypes is referred to as "sex bias." . . . Any action that specifically denies opportunities, privileges, or rewards to a person or a group because of their sex is termed "sex discrimination" if the action is against the law.[32]

231

CHAPTER 8
Developing a
Collaborative
Classroom: Gender
and Sexual
Orientation

Calling a boy a fag because he is exhibiting "female" qualities is an example of sex bias—an action based on sex role stereotypes. If that boy were prevented from, say, taking art classes on the grounds that drawing is a "feminine" activity and that all artists are fags, that would be sex discrimination, since denying access to specific educational activities is against the law.

Clearly, the power of sex role stereotypes is great, and the cost is high for everyone: boys and girls, women and men. Sex role stereotypes prevent girls and boys from having valuable human experiences; they limit growth and development both by denying such experiences and by creating anxiety in children. They also create social and institutional barriers against the development of interests, goals, and talents that may be outside sex role "parameters." The human cost in terms of discouragement, sadness, fear, and alienation is incalculable. Sex role stereotypes also contribute to the organization of schooling and to the subtle and not so subtle messages that boys and girls absorb about their identities, their expectations, and their futures.

Recent Studies

In the 1990s, a great deal was learned about the relationship between gender and schooling. The first such study, commissioned by the American Association of University Women (AAUW), was a national poll in 1991 that assessed the self-esteem, educational experiences, and career aspirations of girls and boys ages 9–15. It found lower self-esteem among the girls, differentiated educational experiences between the boys and girls, and gendered career aspirations among both the boys and the girls.[33] Following this study, the AAUW funded Susan McGee Bailey at the Wellesley Center for Research on Women to do an in-depth review (more than 1,300 studies) of gender and schooling, including thirty-five major studies of schooling issued by special commissions between 1983 and 1991.[34] What Bailey and her colleagues found was, first, a noticeable lack of attention to gender in national commission reports and, second, a similar lack of interest in assessing the educational experiences of girls and boys across the categories of race and class. Thus, what information *was* available on gender was not differentiated by other status categories, thus eliminating the ability of researchers to obtain a full picture of the *diversity* of educational experiences within gender categories.[35]

Following this landmark study, the AAUW funded a series of additional studies on a variety of issues, such as the incidence and impact of sexual harassment in American schools, the impact of different educational approaches on girls' school achievement, the influence of school climate on adolescents, and single-sex education for girls.[36] These studies and others suggest that, in the areas of academic achievement, curriculum materials, learning environments, sexuality education, and college attendance, there remain a number of problematic issues and practices that tend to, if not completely favor boys, or at least often fail to take girls' needs into account.[37]

In general, conditions that support the effective education of girls are those which have and are being recommended in various school reform initiatives. Hansen, Walker, and Flom[38] have found that girls are more likely to thrive

> . . . in learning environments that provide mentors and role models; opportunities for leadership and exploration of new ideas, active intellectual engagement with concerned adults and other students; cooperative learning models; and consciousness-raising about gender, race, and class issues.[39]

PERSPECTIVES ON GENDER AND
SCHOOL CULTURE

233

CHAPTER 8
*Developing a
Collaborative
Classroom: Gender
and Sexual
Orientation*

As we have said before, the cultural values associated with the dominant social group in the United States are also the values that are generally taught in schools. Issues of gender emerge from the question, Is gender a difference that makes a difference? From that perspective, an examination of some of these values can illuminate how the culture of the school influences the socialization of girls and boys.

Productive and Reproductive Processes

Jane Roland Martin has observed that formal education, in content and practice, stresses attitudes and values that are associated primarily with the *productive processes* of society—political and economic activities as well as the creation of art, music, dance, and drama. The *reproductive processes* of society—activities that generally involve the caretaking of homes, children, the ill, and the elderly—are not important areas of learning in school, nor are they included in the ordinary criteria used in evaluating the ideal of the educated person.[40]

This emphasis on productive processes has its roots in the Greek tradition, which focused on the *polis,* or political community. Thus, schools were not originally established to meet the needs of the individual but, rather, to socialize young people into the adult roles of the larger society. The primary role of the teacher in this regard was to develop in children loyalties outside the family. This process of encouraging independence from the child's primary social group often begins with transferring loyalty to their teacher.

In accordance with this "productive" orientation, the typical classroom in our society has maintained a competitive atmosphere. A related value, individualism, characterizes the practice of teaching students as individual units, even though large numbers of students are present in any one classroom. Typical evaluation and assessment methods encourage individual competition. The standard bell curve demands that there be both successes and failures in any group. The success of one, then, lies in the failure of another. This pattern mirrors what we perceive to be the characteristics of the "real" world for which we are preparing students. That "real" world, moreover, has been until quite recently a world of mostly male competition to achieve individual success.

Gender and European American Values in Traditional School Culture

It has been suggested that European American middle-class culture rests on six major values.[41] We can explore these values by looking at proverbs and sayings that have become a part of our folk wisdom and also by asking if they relate differently to males and females.

1. *European Americans have a tendency to view themselves as separate from nature and able to master or control their environment.* As a result, a high value is placed on science and technology as the predominant means of interacting with the world. The study of science is presumed to result in objectivity, rationality, materialism, and a need for concrete evidence. Proverbs and sayings

such as "Necessity is the mother of invention" and "We'll cross that bridge when we come to it" reflect this belief. It is also the case, however, that boys are generally encouraged to take courses in math and science, while girls are not, usually because boys are thought to "need" these traits, while girls are not.

2. *European Americans are action-oriented.* The measurement of progress and change are important concepts here. Our schools expect such an orientation, as evidenced by an emphasis on testing and measurement, as well as a nearly religious belief in the efficacy of paperwork assignments. Proverbs such as "Seeing is believing" and "The proof is in the pudding" emphasize this cultural trait. But, while girls generally get better grades than boys, boys are more likely to be challenged to do their work until they get it right, while girls are often graded on such qualities as neatness.

3. *European Americans have an optimistic, progressive orientation.* Middle-class European Americans believe that change will be in the direction of bigger and better. They are seldom content with the present; they wish not to be considered old-fashioned, and they believe that effort applied in the present will affect their future. Progress is, in many ways, their most important product. Proverbs such as "I think I can, I think I can," and "From little acorns, mighty oaks grow," and even the more recent "No pain—no gain" reflect this tendency. However, the socialization patterns of schooling are more likely to emphasize this future orientation for boys than for girls. The assumption (often unrealized by teachers) is that girls' futures involve reproductive processes, such as caring for families in the private sphere, rather than productive processes involving the public sphere. Seldom are girls encouraged to be "mighty oaks."

4. *European Americans are self-motivated and are comfortable setting their own goals and directions.* From an early age, European Americans are encouraged to reach out on their own, to attempt for themselves, to satisfy their own needs. Such proverbs as "Nothing ventured—nothing gained," "If at first you don't succeed, try, try again," and "The early bird catches the worm" reflect this trait. Again, these values are differentially associated with boys and girls. Girls are not often pushed toward the adventurous, aggressiveness traits that are necessary to "get ahead." Indeed, aggressiveness is not seen as a "womanly" trait at all.

5. *European Americans have a strong sense of individuality.* They believe that the individual "self" is separate from the collective self. This results in a tendency to emphasize individual initiative, responsibility, independence, action, and an internal locus of control. One should not depend on others for identity but should maintain one's individuality, even within the larger group. The school expects children to work alone in their seats, rarely coming together with others to share in problem resolution and task assistance. How many of you have heard teachers say, "Keep your eyes on your own paper" or "Don't talk with your neighbors"? A cursory review of most grade school report cards gives evidence of this trait: consider such statements as "Johnny is able to work independently," "Mary works well on her own," or "Shaun is a responsible student." Proverbs such as "Too many cooks spoil the broth," "Don't judge a book by its cover," and "God helps those who help themselves" stress this value. At the same time, girls are encouraged to help others, and teachers often expect that girls will "know what is going on in the class" and otherwise show evidence of social and caring attitudes.

6. *European Americans believe in the mutability of human nature.* That is, they subscribe to the notion that one's nature is relatively easy to change and that people can be molded by their cultural environment. This belief underlies the assimilationist ideology that has pervaded American public education for so many years. "A stranger is only a friend you haven't met yet" and "Leaders are made, not born" may reflect this notion. Girls, however, are more likely to be protected from strangers and less likely to be encouraged to take leadership roles. One of the reasons given for single-sex education, for example, is that, in an all-girl class or school, girls have more opportunity to practice leadership roles.

235

CHAPTER 8
Developing a
Collaborative
Classroom: Gender
and Sexual
Orientation

One of the results of such socialization practices is that a middle-class European American boy often attributes success to effort and skill and attributes failure to external factors. A middle-class European American girl is more likely to attribute success to luck and failure to a lack of effort. Both boys and girls from lower socioeconomic groups, who may also be members of ethnic minority groups, more often attribute failure at a task to lack of ability.

Gender and School Rules

Interestingly, the *rules* within school cultures often stress values associated with "feminine" behavior, which are quite different from the values associated with the larger society for which children are theoretically being prepared. LeCompte[42] suggests that there are baseline conditions that reflect the social and structural demands of schools. Successful students, for example, are expected to

1. Learn the whole range of tasks presented to them, rather than selecting those that are of interest
2. Learn in particular ways—for example, through the written word rather than orally
3. Learn from and be evaluated by adults
4. Obey school personnel
5. Be task-oriented
6. Delay gratification of desires in order to win later rewards

In short, children are expected to be relatively passive, obedient, industrious, and malleable, all of which are traits positively associated with girls. In part because of the disjunction between school rules and the overarching societal values of independence and competition, the socialization patterns of schooling are more difficult for boys than for girls, because boys tend to receive conflicting messages. Girls (at least middle-class European American girls), on the other hand, tend to "fit into" school rules more easily, in part because these rules reflect basic family socialization patterns.

Homophobia and School Culture

As public awareness of homophobia increases, largely as a result of gay and lesbian activism engendered by the tragedy of AIDS, some professional educators are beginning to consider the need to address issues of homosexuality in schools. Some studies suggest that, the more one knows about homosexuality, the less one will be homophobic and the more accepting one's attitudes toward homosexual people will be.[43] However, cognitive knowledge about homosexuality sometimes fails to neutralize the deep-seated attitudes of anger and guilt that accompany the issue.[44] It is also complicated by the fact that there are gender-related issues involved. For example, anger, hostility, and often violence are more often directed toward gay men than toward lesbian women, although less physical forms of violence against lesbians, such as losing jobs or being evicted from housing, are common. Furthermore, within the homosexual community, differences in masculine and feminine traits among individuals are numerous. The belief that gay men are "feminine" and lesbian women are "masculine" is a stereotype that bears little resemblance to reality, as is reflected by the surprise often expressed by parents, friends, and acquaintances when a person "comes out." Indeed, one of the most difficult aspects of being homosexual in a homophobic society is the separation of sexuality and gender role.

A particularly poignant report was recently published in the newspaper of a small midwestern city. Written by a recent high school graduate who called himself Daniel, this autobiographical statement is telling, both in its genuine pathos and in its demonstration of the power of sex role norms, even in today's more "liberal" society:

> I was born in 1979 to a middle-class family that was elated to have a new baby boy brought into the world. My family was very loving and I had a very normal childhood.
>
> At the age of three or four, I began to get little crushes on other boys. I knew that I was different from what society considers to be normal. I never had sexual feelings for these boys because I never knew what sex was. I would instead imagine dancing with them. All around me I saw heterosexual couples kissing and hugging. I began to feel very strange and develop low self-esteem.
>
> As I went through grade school, many of the other kids began to pick on me because they realized that I was different. I would come home and cry because I just wanted to be normal. I tried to befriend everyone I came in contact with. However, because many of my social skills were not in use, others distanced themselves from me. I had a deep loathing for the people of this world. The hate was even greater for myself.
>
> I went into sixth grade and many of the other kids around me started their little boyfriend/girlfriend relationships. I wished I was dead. In art class one day, after being told that I did something wrong, I told the art teacher that I wanted to kill myself. She made me speak with the guidance counselor at the junior high. Through these sessions, we never got anywhere. I wasn't about to tell anyone why I was really hurting.
>
> My summer between sixth and seventh grade was the most traumatic summer up until that point. I would get rushed to the hospital frequently because I was having severe stomach and chest pains. I thought I had AIDS because I knew I was gay.
>
> On to junior high, a child slowly changing into an adult. My body was changing, my voice was getting deeper and I was developing acne. Could life get any worse? I saw all of these kids who thought that they were in love around me holding hands, kissing and sharing what they did over the weekend. I started making up stories about my invisible girlfriends from other schools. I still got teased though. Sometimes people would be very blatant and ask me if I was gay. Of course, I said, "No."
>
> The first time that I actually heard the scientific word "homosexual" was in eighth-grade science. At the time, I made fun of the teacher for teaching it because I didn't want everyone to know that I was one. It was also in eighth grade that a

237

CHAPTER 8
Developing a
Collaborative
Classroom: Gender
and Sexual
Orientation

neighbor noticed that I was very depressed. She decided to take me to her church. At the church, I was very happy.

My entire life began to revolve around this church. Although everyone thought that I was a very "good little boy," I had my deep, dark, horrible secret. I thought that if I prayed hard enough, I would be "healed" of this awful affliction. I grew very sad. I didn't get "healed." Each week when it came time to share a prayer request, I mentioned an unspoken request. No one ever knew what it was.

It came time for me to go to high school. I met the first gay person I had ever come into contact with. He was an old, gray-haired, overweight man with a very annoying lisp. I really began to hate myself. I thought that all gay men became like this when they got older. I did not want to be like this. I wanted to lead a normal life.

To gain attention, I began to make up this big whopper of a story about how the doctors found a large tumor on my brain. I finally was found out by my pastor and church. All of the people who knew me were very disappointed in me. No one knew why I lied. I greatly regret it. This was to be the end of lying to myself and to others. I now felt as if I should tell the truth.

I began by telling one of my best friends that I was bisexual. I felt like a weight had been lifted off of my shoulder. She was very accepting. I finally could be understood.

I did not plan on telling anyone else. However, I was "outed" when my friend's boyfriend found a letter and showed it to some of his friends. Now everyone knew my deep, dark secret. People whispered about me and as I walked down the halls, I received horrible remarks and got some very bad looks. At this point, I wanted to kill myself.

As the week progressed, many people approached me and told me that they admired me for the courage to "come out." I felt awful because I never had this "courage" that they spoke of. If it had been my choice, no one would have known.

My pastor's wife approached me one Sunday after I had finally decided to return to church and asked if what she had heard was true. I couldn't bring myself to say "yes," so I lied. She said that she was glad that I wasn't *that* way. She went on to say that the church would not want someone living in such a sin to be there. I was devastated, and since that very moment, I have not and will not ever return to that church again.

I still feel the pain that was inflicted upon my heart, but I am slowly healing. In coming out, I gained many new friends. I also lost many friends. Some people have chosen to hate me even though they have no reason. I sometimes get called names and often have people telling me that my "choice" to be homosexual is wrong. I would never understand why someone would choose this kind of lifestyle. I could not wish this on my worst enemy. The desire to be "normal" will always exist in the back of my mind.

My family is slowly dealing with the whole issue. It must be very hard for them as it was very hard for me to accept myself. I feel much better that I am no longer living a lie.[45]

It is very clear that the culture of the school is overwhelmingly heterosexist. Butler and Byrne[46] suggest decreasing levels of homophobia by using gender-free terminology, such as *partners* and *persons* instead of *husband, wife, boyfriend,* and *girlfriend;* by systematically interrupting homophobic comments, as Tom Littleton did in the case study that opened this chapter; by overtly using homophobic misinformation to encourage students to use critical thinking; and by using educational materials that do not assume that all students are heterosexual. Remember that homophobia is learned behavior; it can be unlearned as well.

Ethical Issues

Clearly, there are many ethical issues involved in the consideration of gender and sexual orientation in the classroom. One important issue has to do with the degree to which all students, regardless of their beliefs and attitudes, are encouraged to be open, reflective, and critical thinkers. Children and adolescents are all in various stages of physical, intellectual, and moral development. It is unwise and unfair for teachers to either impose their own judgments on students or to differentially favor the students whose beliefs and attitudes are most nearly like their own. Rather, students should be enabled and encouraged to discuss all aspects of these issues in a context of thoughtful inquiry.

A second and related issue is the degree which such inquiry may place students in direct conflict with the values of their families and/or the communities in which they live. A great deal of judgment should be exercised by teachers in this regard, particularly when the family and community context is fairly rigid. It is possible for teachers to insist on an equitable set of language and behaviors while still recognizing and affirming contrary beliefs. To do otherwise is to set up a climate of "political correctness" that usually does more harm than good and does not do anything at all to promote self-reflection or inquiry.

While equity as a value is consistent with democracy, so is pluralism. In a society as diverse as the United States, it is not possible—or useful—to insist on a single set of attitudes, beliefs, and values. Rather, the role of the school should be to help students negotiate differences, to understand their origins, and to appreciate what is valuable about them. One of the goals of a collaborative classroom is to nurture *both* similarities and differences among people by enabling them to work together in ways that benefit everyone.

SOME REFLECTIVE QUESTIONS

If we were to read Tom Littleton's journal, we might find that he has asked himself some of the following questions:

1. Both competition and individualism are deeply held values in American society. Have I stressed collaboration in a way that omits these values from the students' lives or in a way that weaves them together?
2. All people need to feel that they belong, that they have a reliable sense of alliance with others. Has this class fostered such feelings?
3. The culture of some students centers on individualism, while the culture of others centers on a collective spirit. Is there a balance here? For example, are students given enough opportunity to be assessed individually as well as in groups?
4. Have I gone too far with Rebecca in stressing equity for girls? Have I put her in a position where she feels she has to choose between her community's emphasis on the male and my encouragement of her individual talents? How can I help her bridge these two sets of values and still maintain her family's trust in me?
5. To what extent has the collaborative structure of this class resulted in individual learning for all students? How can I measure that? How can I be sure that real learning is going on for everyone?
6. I can't keep all of these students together with me all day or for the rest of their schooling. How are they doing, and how will they do in more traditional classrooms that stress competition and individual performance? Is this class just a unique experience that will fade from memory as they get older?

It is obvious that Tom can have few definitive answers for these questions, but the fact that he asks them is important. He clearly believes that a collaborative classroom is both necessary and valuable, yet he knows that this approach to schooling is not shared by everyone, either in the school or outside of it. The decisions he makes as he thinks about these issues are always tempered by what he knows about his school and community. Still, he will probably continue to modify and improve his approach, knowing also that change is incremental and does not come all at once. It is a great challenge.

239

CHAPTER 8
Developing a
Collaborative
Classroom: Gender
and Sexual
Orientation

Active Exercises

The following exercises from *Human Diversity in Action: Developing Multicultural Competencies for the Classroom*[47] complement this chapter well:

Activity 19: Gender Role Socialization, p. 141

Activity 20: Observing Gender Differences, p. 143

Activity 21: The Plight of Women on a Global Scale, p. 147

Activity 22: Sexual Orientation: A Matter of Experience? p. 151

Accessing the World Wide Web: Resources for Diversity

For more information on cooperative learning, see the following:

http://miavxl.muohio.edu/~iascecwis/resources.htmlx   Resources for Cooperative Learning.

http://www.ncrel.org/sdrs/areas/rpl_esys/collab.htm   Article: "What is the Collaborative Classroom?" by M.B. Tinzman, B.F. Jones, T.F. Fennimore, J. Bakker, C. Fine, and J. Pierce.

http://ericir.syr.edu/Eric/   Use the AskERIC database to query for the term *cooperative learning*.

For more information on perspectives on sex role socialization, see the following:

http://www.askeric.org/Eric/index.html   Use the AskERIC database to search for materials on sex role socialization.

For more information on gender equity in schools, see the following:

http://www.albany.edu/twoyear/gender_equity/gui_1c.html   A little history of early efforts at gender equity and some ideas for teachers on what boys and girls need to know.

http://mdac.educ.ksu.edu/MDAC/resource/publications/teachgender/index.html Resources and activities for teaching students about gender equity.

http://www.aauw.org/2000/research.html   This is the home page of the American Association of University Women; it has multiple links to research and findings on gender equity sponsored by the AAUW, as well as information on the reasons for and history of the AAUW effort on gender equity.

References

1. Several elements of this case study—in particular, the land discovery project—are adapted from the experience of Bill Elasky and his students at Amesville Elementary School in Amesville, Ohio, and Dan Bisaccio and his students at Thayer Junior/Senior High School in Winchester, New Hampshire. Both are described in George Woods, *Schools That Work* (New York: Penguin Books, 1992). Elements of Gypsy education are taken from *The First S.T.E.P. (Systematic Training and Early Prevention) Program,* prepared by Sam Chandler and Rebecca Boglione, Tacoma Public Schools, 1992.

2. Milton Olson, "Lessons from Geese."

3. See, for example, Carol Gilligan, *In a Different Voice* (Cambridge, MA: Harvard University Press, 1982); and Nel Noddings, *Caring* (Berkeley: University of California Press, 1984).

4. See M. F. Belenky, B. Clinchy, N. Goldberger, and J. Tarule, *Women's Ways of Knowing: The Development of Self, Voice and Mind* (New York: Basic Books, 1986); and B. M. Clinchy, M. F. Belenky, N. Goldberger, and J. Tarule, "Connected Education for Women," *Journal of Educational Thought* 167, 3 (1985).

5. John I. Goodlad, *A Place Called School: Prospects for the Future* (New York: McGraw-Hill, 1984), p. 45.

6. Spencer Kagan, "The Structural Approach to Cooperative Learning," *Educational Leadership* 47, 4 (1989/1990): 12–15.

7. Ibid.

8. R. E. Slavin, *Cooperative Learning: Theory, Research, and Practice* (Englewood Cliffs, NJ: Prentice Hall, 1990).

9. David W. Johnson and Robert T. Johnson, *Learning Together and Alone* (Englewood Cliffs, NJ: Prentice Hall, 1987).

10. Slavin, op. cit., p. 12.

11. Ibid., p. 39.

12. Sudia Paloma McCaleb, *Building Communities of Learners* (New York: St. Martin's Press, 1994).

13. R. Greenspan, J. H. Niemeyer, and D. Seeley, *Principals Speak: Report #2: Parent Involvement* (New York: Research Foundation of City University of New York, 1991).

14. J. Cummins, *Empowering Minority Students* (Sacramento: California Association for Bilingual Education, 1989).

15. Charles Fowler, "Strong Arts, Strong Schools," *Educational Leadership* 52, 3 (November 1994): 4–5.

16. L. C. Pogrebin, *Growing Up Free* (New York: Bantam Books, 1980).

17. Lenore J. Weitzman, "Sex-Role Socialization," in *Women: A Feminist Perspective,* ed. Jo Freeman (Palo Alto, CA: Mayfield, 1975), p. 109.

18. Florence Howe, "Sexual Stereotypes Start Early," in *Nonsexist Curriculum Materials for Elementary Schools,* ed. Laurie Olsen Johnson (Old Westbury, NY: Feminist Press, 1974), pp. 25–32.

19. Sylvia Kramer, "Sex Role Stereotyping: How It Happens and How to Avoid It," in *Sex Equity in Education,* ed. Anne O'Brien Carelli (Springfield, IL: Charles C Thomas, 1988), pp. 5–23.

20. See, for example, B. Fagot, "The Influence of Sex of Child on Parental Reactions to Toddler Children," *Child Development* 49, 2 (1978): 459–565; and S. Dronsberg, B. Fagot, R. Hagan, and M. D. Lleinback, "Differential Reactions to Assertive and Communicative Acts of Toddler Boys and Girls," *Child Development* 56, 6 (1985): 1499–1505.

21. For an insightful analysis of the impact of several fairy tale "heroines" on the socialization of children, see Madonna Kolbenschlag, *Kiss Sleeping Beauty Goodbye: Breaking the Spell of Feminine Myths and Models* (New York: Bantam Books, 1981), p. 7.

22. Kramer, op. cit., p. 11.

23. "A Report on Children's Toys," in *And Jill Came Tumbling After: Sexism in American Education,* ed. Judith Stacey, Susan Bereaud, and Joan Daniels (New York: Dell, 1974),

241

CHAPTER 8
Developing a
Collaborative
Classroom: Gender
and Sexual
Orientation

pp. 123–125. (If one believes that the age of this citation belies contemporary reality, a short trip down the aisles of Toys R Us will quickly rid one of the notion that toys—and their packaging—have changed a great deal.)

24. Ruth E. Hartley, "Sex Role Pressures and the Socialization of the Male Child," in *And Jill Came Tumbling After: Sexism in American Education,* ed. J. Stacey, S. Bereaud, and J. Daniels (New York: Dell, 1974), pp. 186–187.

25. Kathleen Barry, "View from the Doll Corner," in *Women and Education,* ed. Elizabeth S. Maccia (Springfield, IL: Charles C Thomas, 1975), p. 121.

26. Hartley, op. cit., p. 90.

27. Ibid., p. 91.

28. Robert S. Lynd and Helen Merrell Lynd, *Middletown in Transition* (New York: Harcourt, Brace, 1937), p. 402.

29. Howe, op. cit., p. 28.

30. Cooper Thompson, "Education and Masculinity," in *Sex Equity in Education: Readings and Strategies,* ed. Anne O'Brien Carelli (Springfield, IL: Charles C Thomas, 1988), p. 47.

31. Ibid., p. 48.

32. Anne O'Brien Carelli, "Introduction," in *Sex Equity in Education,* ed. Anne O'Brien Carelli (Springfield, IL: Charles CThomas, 1988), pp. xiii–xv.

33. *Shortchanging Girls, Shortchanging America* (Washington, DC: The American Association of University Women Educational Foundation, 1991).

34. *The AAUW Report: How Schools Shortchange Girls* (Washington, DC: The American Association of University Women Educational Foundation, 1992).

35. Lynn Phillips, *The Girls Report: What We Know and Need to Know About Growing Up Female* (New York: The National Council for Research on Women, 1998), pp. 55–56.

36. *Hostile Hallways: The ASUW Survey on Sexual Harassment in America's Schools* (Washington, DC: American Association of University Women Educational Foundation, 1993); *Growing Smart: What's Working for Girls in Schools* (Washington, DC: American Association of University Women Educational Foundation, 1995); *Girls in the Middle: Working to Succeed in School* (Washington, DC: American Association of University Women Educational Foundation, 1996); *The Influence of School Climate on Gender Differences in the Achievement and Engagement of Young Adolescents* (Washington, DC: American Association of University Women Educational Foundation, 1996); and *Separated by Sex: A Critical Look at Single-Sex Education for Girls* (Washington, DC: American Association of University Women Educational Foundation, 1998).

37. Phillips, op. cit.

38. *Growing Smart.*

39. Phillips, op. cit., p. 70.

40. Jane Roland Martin, *Reclaiming a Conversation: The Ideal of the Educated Woman* (New Haven: Yale University Press, 1985), p. 6.

41. Larry Samover, Richard Porter, and Nemi Jain, *Understanding Intercultural Communication* (Belmont, CA: Wadsworth, 1981).

42. M. Lecompte, "The Civilizing of Children: How Young Children Learn to Become Students," *Journal of Thought* 15, 3 (1980): 105–128.

43. Joel W. Wells and Mary L. Franken, "University Students' Knowledge About and Attitudes Toward Homosexuality," *Journal of Humanistic Education and Development* 26, 2 (December 1987).

44. Kurt E. Ernulf and Sune M. Innala, "The Relationship Between Affective and Cognitive Components of Homophobic Reaction," *Archives of Sexual Behavior* 16, 6 (1987).

45. *The Akron Beacon Journal,* 5 January 1998, p. A6.

46. Karen L. Butler and T. Jean Byrne, "Homophobia Among Preservice Elementary Teachers," *Journal of Health Education* 23, 6 (September-October 1992): 357–358.

47. Kenneth Cushner, *Human Diversity in Action: Developing Multicultural Competencies in the Classroom* (New York: McGraw-Hill, 1999).

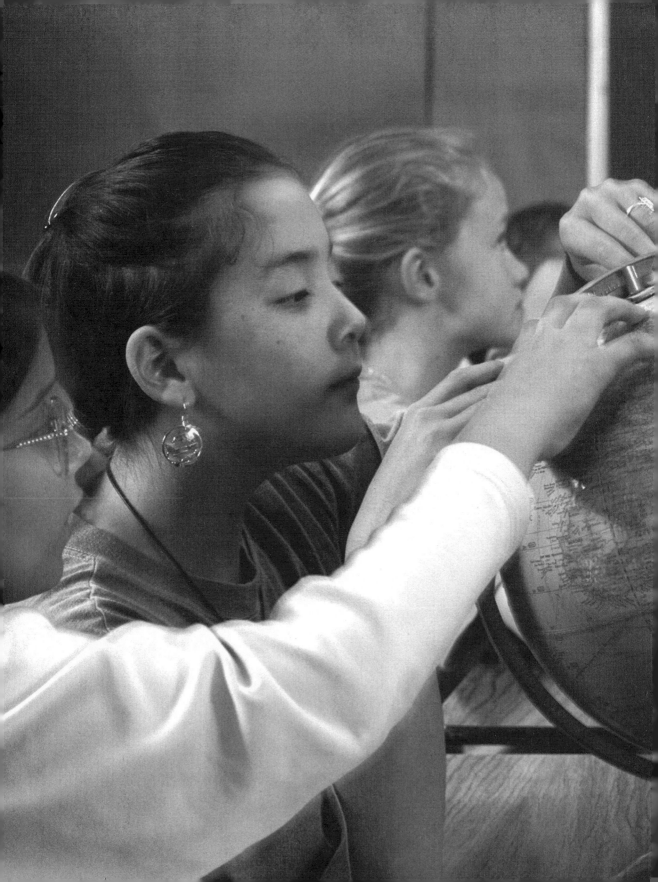

CHAPTER 9

The Classroom as a Global Community: Race, Ethnicity/Nationality, and Region

CHAPTER OUTLINE

RATIONALE FOR THE CLASSROOM AS A
   GLOBAL COMMUNITY
   Education for a Global Perspective
   Hoopes's Model of
      Intercultural Education
CHARACTERISTICS OF A
   GLOBAL CLASSROOM
   Pedagogies: Old and New
   Roles: Old and New
   Place of Content Knowledge: Old
      and New
   Assessment: Old and New
   Case Analysis

PERSPECTIVES ON A GLOBALLY
   ORIENTED CURRICULUM
   Curriculum Transformation:
      The Case of Prejudice
   Curriculum Transformation:
      The International Perspective
   Ethical Issues
SOME REFLECTIVE QUESTIONS
ACTIVE EXERCISES
SOME CRITICAL INCIDENTS
ACCESSING THE WORLD WIDE WEB:
   RESOURCES FOR DIVERSITY
REFERENCES

A multicultural education is an education for life in a free and democratic society. It helps students transcend their cultural boundaries and acquire the knowledge, attitudes, and skills needed to engage in public discourse with people who differ from themselves.

James A Banks

A Global Classroom: A Case Study

It is 8:00 A.M. on a Tuesday morning in early February as Jerome Becker rushes into the front office with good news. Yesterday's mail had brought the package his class had been anxiously awaiting—a completed story from a school in southern India. Now he would be able to share its contents with the class. Jerome is eager to tell his principal, Mrs. Lewis, because she had seemed so certain that this project would fail and that the children would be let down. Well, this time it hadn't, and Jerome is delighted.

243

The school year had started with great difficulties. Throughout the previous summer, children in the district had been in an increasing number of confrontations with one another in the malls, on playgrounds, and even on recreation department ball fields. Vandalism and fighting was new to this community of 60,000 in the suburbs of Grand Rapids. All the troubles people had read about in other major cities seemed to pass by this relatively peaceful area of Michigan. But here, too, things were beginning to change. And the problems didn't end with the summer. They came right into the classroom in full force with the new sixth grade class—name-calling, fighting, and threats of gangs. Tension seemed especially strong between the African American and European American students but was also present between the majority students and the three international students, of whom two had immigrated from Japan and one from Kenya. There was even talk of some Ku Klux Klan and militia activity in the community, and this worried Jerome a great deal.

After the first few weeks, Jerome decided that it was time to do something to alter the course of events. He had taken some workshops in multicultural education, global education, and cooperative learning over the past few summers and was eager to try some of the strategies he had studied. He was also beginning to integrate various parts of his curriculum; he saw several opportunities to link language arts, social studies, and the arts. He was even willing to try to integrate other areas of the curriculum while exploring how he might add a global perspective. After all, he had nothing to lose and everything to gain in his attempts to bring some peace to the class and to help his students live more peacefully with one another.

Since several of his students were first-generation children (their parents had recently immigrated to the United States), Jerome decided that an international perspective might provide them with concepts and activities that would cut across the various ethnicities and nationalities in his class. This might also help reduce some of the prejudice he was witnessing on a daily basis. With this in mind, Jerome began with a unit on immigration that he hoped would develop empathy in his students for newcomers to this country. He also hoped this sense of empathy would be applied to the relatives and ancestors of students with deep roots in America. Such an activity might also bring the group together as they explored both the similarities and the differences in their backgrounds. He asked his students to go home and interview family members about their own or their ancestors' experiences in coming to this country, asking them to inquire specifically about the following topics:

1. From what country did our ancestors come?
2. When did they leave their country of birth?
3. Why did they leave that place?
4. What was their experience when they first came to this country? Do people remember any hardships? Were any stereotypes and prejudice directed at them?
5. Where did they first arrive in this country?
6. How did they come to live in Michigan? When did they come here, and why?

7. Are there any traditions from the home country that are still practiced?
8. What makes our people unique in this country today?

245

CHAPTER 9
*The Classroom as a
Global Community:
Race, Ethnicity/
Nationality, and
Region*

A week later, Jerome had students come to the front of the room, share their stories, and locate their family's place of origin on the world map. He gave them each a piece of yarn, and, as they located their country of origin, he asked them to attach it to the map at that country and extend the yarn to Grand Rapids. He was surprised by the results of this exercise. Table 9.1 shows the origins of his students.

The discussion that ensued was enlightening for both Jerome and his students. Like Martina Chandler in Chapter 5, he was not surprised to see many of the students stand up and talk about their family history with a sense of pride. For many of them, this was the first time anyone had asked them about their ancestry. It seemed to Jerome that this was also the first

TABLE 9-1 Jerome Becker's Sixth Grade Class

Boys	Ethnicity	Origin	Generation
Tony	Italian American	Italy	Third
Peter	Danish American	Denmark	Third
Guy	Scandinavian American	Sweden/Finland	Hundreds of years
Bart	Irish American	Ireland	Third
Mark	African American	West Africa	Seventh
Steve	Exact ethnicity unknown	Adopted at birth; adopted family is third-generation German	
Peter	Hungarian American	Hungary	Third
David	Native American/Polish	USA/Poland	Mixed
Allen	European American	France/England/Germany	Sixth
Kamal	African American	West Africa	Seventh/eighth
Tsuyoshi	Japanese	Hiroshima	Short-term/new immigrant
Lenny	African American	West Africa	Ninth
Paul	Polish American	Poland	Fourth
Charles	Kenyan	Kenya	Short-term/new immigrant

Girls	Ethnicity	Origin	Generation
Jenny	Irish American	Ireland	Fourth
Mary	Irish American	Ireland	Second
Hannah	Polish American	Poland	Third
Gwendolyn	African American	West Africa	Seventh
Evgenia	Russian American	Russia	First
Yoshiko	Japanese	Japan	Short-term/new immigrant
Ronelle	Afrikaner English	South Africa	Short-term/new immigrant
Mariam	Lebanese American	Lebanon	First
Susan	German American	Germany	Third
Rebecca	European American	Germany/Poland	Third/fourth
Maria	Italian American	Italy	Fourth
Kathy	Danish American	Denmark	Third
Monisha	Indian American	India	First

time that the students had listened intently to one another's stories. There seemed to be a real sense of contribution for most of the students. They were especially interested in Guy's and Hannah's stories. Some of Guy's ancestors came to this country in the 1600s. He shared stories of people jumping ship off the New England coast and ending up in Vermont. Hannah shared stories of her grandparent's escape from Hitler's armies and how lucky most of her family had been to get out of the Holocaust alive. She did know, however, that two of her relatives had perished in the Holocaust.

What surprised Jerome, however, was the difficulty that some students had with the exercise, especially Steve and Kamal. At first, Steve avoided participating in the exercise by offering the excuse that he had left his notes at home. The next day, when urged again to participate, Steve stood in front of the class and mumbled something like, "I'm adopted and I don't know anything about my parents." There was complete silence. An awkward moment or two followed, until Jerome quietly said, "My Grandfather was adopted, too, and he didn't know much about his background, either. His adopted family helped him learn about their Polish background, and he grew up in that tradition. Perhaps there are some traditions that your adopted family follow that you can take for your own. What background is your adopted family?"

Jerome remembers Steve beginning to relax and feel as if he belonged in the group when he replied, "Well, I guess they're all German. I mean, my grandparents speak a little German when they visit, and my parents make it a point to go the Oktoberfest every year. My father really likes it when he has his German beer. They're even talking about visiting Germany in the next couple of years and plan on taking me and my sister. I guess I'm really German, but I'm not sure what it really means to be German. I feel very much American, if you know what I mean."

Jerome asked how many others felt more "American" than affiliated with their ethnic ancestry. Almost all of the students raised their hands. "Well," said Jerome, "it is good that we all feel American, because we are; but I want you to think about what being 'American' means." He let the matter drop there for a time.

Kamal's response to the exercise, however, was not as easy for Jerome to handle. Jerome knew that Kamal's family was, perhaps more than many African American families in the school, emphasizing their African heritage with their children. Kamal stood up and, with a certain anger in his words, stated, "I'm African, and I don't know my exact heritage. You see, you white folks took my people from their lands, mixed us up with all the other Africans you stole, and now lump us all together. My father tells me that African American people come from more than fifteen different groups in West Africa, and we don't even know which ones we belong to. That's why there's so much confusion in the world today. We've been stripped of our heritage."

Jerome, taken aback by Kamal's apparent anger, wasn't quite sure what to say. Jerome remembers feeling threatened and a bit angry at first that Kamal would make him and the class feel uncomfortable. But, after taking a deep breath and pondering the situation for a moment, Jerome

247

CHAPTER 9
*The Classroom as a
Global Community:
Race, Ethnicity/
Nationality, and
Region*

*began to hear and feel the anger that must be felt by people everywhere
who have been subjugated and forced to adapt to a more powerful group.
He began to ask Kamal a few questions, such as, "Can you tell us about
some of the things you and your parents are learning? Perhaps we can all
learn something new. I wonder if your parents would be willing to come
into class and teach us about your background? In fact, I'd like all of us to
consider bringing our families to class to teach us about your heritage.
Think this over, Kamal, and perhaps we can make some concrete plans."*

*With that, Jerome returned to his desk, feeling that he was at least tak-
ing the first steps toward opening up some lines of communication between
himself, his students, and their families. But neither the issue of adoption
nor the issue of slave families' historical records had crossed his mind
before. He was reasonably satisfied with his response to Steve but less than
happy with his response to Kamal. He knew he would have to think about
these issues more.*

*In a larger group discussion, students were asked to identify general-
izations in people's presentations and to pose hypotheses to explain what
they observed. Peter noticed that most people seemed to come to the United
States for better job opportunities or for more money, as he put it, both in
the past and today. A few people came for religious reasons. Kathy noticed
that everyone, except for one of David's relatives, came from somewhere
else. When encouraged, she went on to suggest that everyone was an immigrant at least once in his or her past. Kamal reminded everyone that his
ancestors didn't come here by choice, and perhaps that explained many of
the differences that exist between African Americans and other groups.
Jerome took this opportunity to discuss with the class the differences
between voluntary and involuntary immigration.*

*Jerome then began to probe into students' feelings about the immi-
grants they read about today. Most were familiar enough with the Haitian
refugees, the situation in Cuba, and the constant debate about Mexicans
crossing the border into the United States. A few were aware of immigrant
and refugee groups from Southeast Asia, the former Yugoslavia, and the
fact that many whites had left Zimbabwe and were now leaving South
Africa. Jerome was hoping that a discussion about the plight of today's
refugees and immigrant groups would enable students to identify with their
situation and to compare it with that of their own ancestors. A few were
able to make this leap, but most only nodded in half-hearted agreement.
Jerome was content that perhaps he had planted a few seeds for future discussion and activity, which he promised himself he would develop. He
ended the discussion by asking the students to read the following parable:*

Once there were three men who had never seen oranges. They had heard many
wonderful things about the fruit and wanted very much to have some. The first
man set out with excitement. He traveled for many days and began to worry that
he would get lost. The farther he went, the more he worried. Finally, he sat
under a tree, deep in thought. "No silly fruit is this important," he decided. He
got up and turned toward home.

The second man was a very bold fellow. He rushed off, dreaming about
oranges as he traveled, and ended up at the same tree. Round orange fruits were

all over the ground and in the branches. Thrilled with his success, he grabbed one of the fruits off the ground and bit into it. It was rotten and bitter. "Ugh! What a stupid fruit," he said and returned home empty-handed.

The third man did research before he left home. He also asked questions of people he met as he traveled. Lo and behold, he found the same tree full of oranges. He examined many oranges and chose one that was not too hard or too soft. It was juicy and delicious. He took some seeds home, planted them, and eventually became a famous grower of fruit.

Jerome asked his students to think about the possible meanings of the story overnight. Tomorrow they would begin a writing assignment using this parable to link some of the issues that had been raised in their discussion.

Two months into the semester, the classroom was alive with activity. Three parents had already been in to share part of their family traditions. The fact that the sixth grade social studies curriculum looked at world cultures made this comparatively easy. It was also rather easy to integrate a number of books on other cultures into the language arts program. Jerome's focus was always on prejudice, discrimination, and how people might overcome the differences that exist between one another. The students had already read such books as The Diary of Anne Frank *and had viewed and discussed a number of films. They were still to read a few more books by the winter holiday. Jerome had also started a Friday afternoon intercultural forum, in which students participated in a variety of activities designed to enhance their regular courses while expanding their horizons.*

One particular activity excited the students so much that it expanded into the whole language arts program and involved all the students in the grade. It was the end result of this activity that Jerome was so excited to share with Mrs. Lewis, the principal. Jerome had read about a project, a partnership story project, that was designed to integrate language arts, social studies, and cooperative learning.[1] Through small-group activity, students in one country begin writing a story. They decide on a topic or problem, identify main characters as well as a setting, and then begin writing the first half of the story. The first half is then mailed to children in another country, who complete the story and translate it into their own language. When completed, the classrooms have an internationally developed product translated into two languages. The book can also be co-illustrated. In addition to collaborating on the story, classrooms can exchange a variety of artifacts, photos, letters, and so forth.

Jerome had written to a relative of Monisha's who worked in a school in Madurai, India. She was interested in the idea of the story-writing project and was willing to collaborate if Jerome's class would agree to begin the project. The class broke up into three groups, each writing the beginning of a story. Since they had been studying a bit about the environmental crisis in social studies, Jerome asked them to build their storyline around this topic. Each group had started a story. One was an adventure story involving a school of fish in a polluted lake. Another was a mystery involving a missing mineral. A third focused on abuses of the world's wildlife. Then they mailed all three unfinished stories to the Indian sixth grade class.

The students were very excited that morning when Jerome told them that the completed stories had been returned. It had been six weeks since the class had mailed its story beginnings to India. Rather than just share the endings that had come back, Jerome decided to turn the activity into a real culture-learning experience by rereading their unfinished stories and then asking his students to imagine how they thought the Indian students would complete the story. After reading his students their part of the stories, Jerome showed them the beautifully written Tamil script and the pictures that the Indian class had used to complete the stories. Following is the third story sent by Jerome's class and co-written by children in Madurai, India.

Part One [United States]

Once in a circus there was a tiger that would not perform because he was lonely. The circus owner sent his daughter, Maryetta, to the jungle to find a friend to perform with the lonely tiger. Maryetta's father gave her one thousand dollars to purchase a tiger. Her father told her to spend the money wisely.

The next day on a boat trip to the jungle, Maryetta met a trapper named Toby. Although not the trapper Maryetta was to meet, Toby asked Maryetta why she was going to the jungle. Maryetta told him that she needed to purchase a tiger for her father's circus.

"What a coincidence," Toby remarked, all the while trying to figure out a way he might obtain Maryetta's money before the real trapper could reach her. "I am meeting a girl from a circus tomorrow."

"You are?" Maryetta asked, looking puzzled. "Do you know what circus she is from?"

"No," replied Toby, "but it must be yours. How many girls could there be going to the jungle tomorrow to buy a tiger?"

"I guess you're right. I'll meet you by the river at 10:00 tomorrow morning."

Toby wanted to get there before the real trapper did, so he said, "Why don't we meet at 9:00 and get an early start?"

They agreed to this and then went their own ways. The next day was a beautiful summer day, perfect for trapping tigers. Toby rented a boat and met Maryetta precisely at 9:00.

"I'll need to collect my fee of one hundred dollars each morning before we begin," Toby told Maryetta.

"I thought you told my father your fee was one hundred and fifty dollars per day," Maryetta said, wondering why he had lowered his fee.

"Oh, well, I guess I forgot what I said before. One hundred and fifty dollars it is then," said Toby.

"All right, but I don't have a lot of money. Do you think we'll be trapping for a long time?"

"Probably only two or three days," Toby reassured. "Well, then, let's get going!" exclaimed Maryetta.

At first, the boat trip down the river was pleasant. About noon, however, the boat struck a huge rock, which punctured its side. The rest of the day Maryetta and Toby spent repairing the boat. As a result, they had to spend the night on the river bank.

During the night, Maryetta thought she heard voices. When she peeked out of her tent, she saw Toby talking to a wolf. She couldn't believe her eyes or ears! Although she had been raised around the circus and always knew that animals were special, she had never talked to one! She listened intently.

"Go make friends with the tiger and bring him back here," Toby told the wolf.

"When do you want me to bring back that stupid tiger?" asked the wolf.

"Five days from now will be good. Then I will have enough money to buy the secrets I want from the old wizard."

"Okay, I'll see you then," said the wolf, and he crept away.

Maryetta silently closed the flap of her tent and slumped to the ground. Something was very, very wrong. How was she going to get back to the circus safely with the tiger and not let Toby know that she knew he was a fake?

The next morning, Toby told Maryetta the boat was fixed.

Toby then said, "I don't want to be rude, but where is my money?"

Maryetta answered, "I'll pay you later." She thought to herself, I have no intention of paying Toby. Toby said, "I want my money now!"

Maryetta said that because the boat accident was not her fault she should not have to pay for the first day. Toby replied, "Well, it's not my fault either, and, besides, we had an agreement."

They argued for a while and Toby finally agreed that Maryetta could pay him later. He told her he would begin to look for the tiger today.

They boarded the boat together to begin the search for the tiger. Along the way, they spotted a beautiful tiger being chased by a wolf.

Maryetta said, "Toby, I know you sent the wolf after the tiger and you better make sure the wolf doesn't harm him or you won't be paid!" They anchored the boat and went ashore.

Toby and Maryetta began to chase after the tiger and the wolf. Suddenly, Maryetta tripped over a vine and broke her leg. Toby came along, grabbed Maryetta's money, and ran off with it!

At this point, Jerome stopped reading. He asked how many students remembered this half of the story. All hands were raised. He then asked them to write down a few sentences about how they thought the story would end.

Of the twenty-six students in Jerome's class, eleven completed the story in a way that Maryetta's task was fulfilled. In these cases, Maryetta caught the tiger, she took it home, and it performed as desired in the circus. Three students resolved the story by creating a new character who saves Maryetta from her injury and from Toby. In six cases, the tiger frees Maryetta from her crisis, and, in three of these cases, the tiger catches Toby. In two cases, Maryetta escapes, finds the wizard, and seeks revenge on Toby. In one case each, the wolf helps Maryetta catch first the tiger and then Toby; Toby steals the money from Maryetta and does not catch the tiger; Maryetta is cured in a hospital and becomes friends with Toby; and Toby spontaneously recognizes and reconciles his evil ways.

Jerome could sense the excitement of the students as they waited to hear how their Indian colleagues had completed the story. He sat on the edge of his desk and continued with the second half.

Part Two [India]

The wolf that was chasing the tiger stopped after hearing Maryetta's cries and ran toward her. He finally reached her. He felt sad when he saw the flow of blood from her leg.

"Don't be afraid. I shall help you," said the wolf.

The wolf then ran into the forest and brought back rare herbs and placed them on her leg. At once, Maryetta felt relief from the pain and felt pleasant again. Maryetta looked at the wolf with love and gratitude.

The wolf asked Maryetta, "How did you fall?"

She explained everything to him. The wolf felt bad when he heard of Toby's treacherous deeds. The wolf told Maryetta that he would get the money from Toby.

Maryetta saw the birds, trees, and other creatures around her. She did not feel lonely. She felt happy she was a part of an endless creation of nature. She felt the encouragement and nourishment given by the surrounding birds and trees.

Toby went straight to the old wizard with the money he robbed from Maryetta. After getting the money from Toby, the wizard taught him the mantras (magic phrases) to conquer the animals and humans. He then proceeded quickly, greedy to make money.

Then Toby saw a tiger running toward him in a frenzy. He tried to conquer the tiger with the mantras he had learned from the wizard. But the tiger pushed him down and tried to attack him. At that time, the tiger heard the voice of a wolf and ran away.

The wolf and Maryetta saw Toby struggling for his life. The wolf did not like to help the treacherous Toby. He thought that this was the right punishment for his terrible deeds. But Maryetta was deeply moved by Toby's suffering. She felt sad that she did not have the money to admit him to a hospital.

Maryetta pleaded with the wolf to help Toby. The wolf halfheartedly ran and brought back rare herbs. Maryetta made a bandage with the herbs for Toby's wounds. She also gave him some juice from the herbs. He then recovered and could breathe easy again.

Toby slowly came to consciousness and appreciated the gentle qualities of Maryetta and apologized to her. He revealed that he had given the money to the old wizard. He felt sorry that he was spoiled by his own greed.

In the meantime, the wolf went to the tiger. He asked the tiger, "Why did you try to kill Toby?"

The tiger angrily replied, "It is but natural that we are angry toward men who prevent us from living independently in the forest and who try to hunt us. Toby is trying to destroy us totally by violence, tricks, and mantras. For him, money is bad."

The wolf said, "Toby cheats not only the animals but also the humans. For this greedy fellow, money is everything."

Toby was truly sad. He felt ashamed of himself and asked to be pardoned. Then the wolf, the tiger, Toby, and Maryetta danced together in joy in a circle.

Then Maryetta told the tiger, "In my father's circus, there is a male tiger suffering without a companion. If you can come with me, he would be very happy."

Maryetta looked at the female tiger with love and affection. The female was moved to tears. She began to wonder if that male tiger was the one that had been taken away from her long ago. She agreed to go with Maryetta.

All four returned to the circus. The male tiger was happy to see the female tiger that he had been separated from so very long ago. Soon they were able to identify one another. What a pleasure it is when separated ones come together again!

Maryetta was very happy. She had learned to talk with the animals. Her love toward them grew many times over. She looked after the tigers with special care.

One day, Maryetta fell asleep while playing with the tigers. She listened to the conversations of the tigers as she woke up. She pretended as if she was sleeping and continued to listen to them.

The female tiger said, "Maryetta is a wonderful girl. But she does not realize the fact that the forest is our heaven. Even this golden cage is still a cage."

Maryetta was deeply moved. The next day, Maryetta's father called her and said, "Maryetta, I have grown old. I am retiring from the circus as of today. Hereafter, you should run the circus."

Maryetta said, "I shall free those wonderful animals from this sorrowful, torturous caged life and I will go and live in the forest.

And that she did.

Jerome followed this reading with a discussion. To begin the discussion, he asked each student to respond, in writing, to the following questions:

Maryetta saw the birds, trees and other creatures around her. She did not feel lonely. She felt happy she was part of an endless creation of nature. She felt the encouragement and nourishment given by the surrounding birds and trees.

Toby went straight to the old wizard with the money he robbed from Maryetta. After getting the money from Toby, the wizard taught him the mantras (magic phrases) to conquer the animals and humans. He then proceeded quickly, greedy to make money.

தன்னைச் சுற்றிலும் பறவைகள், மரங்கள், மற்றும் பிற உயிரினங்களை மரியட்டா பார்த்தாள். அவள் தனி-மையை எண்ணவில்லை. இயற்கையின் எல்லையற்ற படைப்பில் தான் ஒரு பகுதி என்பதை அவள் உணர்ந்து இன்புற்றாள். சுற்றியிருந்த பறவைகளும் மரங்களும் தந்த ஊக்கக்கையும் ஊட்டத்தையும் அவள் உணர்ந்தாள்.

டொபி நேரே, மரியட்டாவிடமிருந்து கொள்ளை-யடித்த பணத்துடன், சூனியக்கார கிழவியிடம் சென்றான். டொபியிடமிருந்து பணத்தை பெற்றுக் கொண்ட பிறகு, சூனியக்காரி மிருகங்களையும் மானிடர்களையும் வெல்லு-வதற்குரிய மந்திரங்களை அவனுக்கு உபதேசித்தாள். பிறகு பணம் சேர்க்கும் பேராசையுடன், அவன் வேகமாக வெளியேறினான்.

253

CHAPTER *9*
The Classroom as a
Global Community:
Race, Ethnicity/
Nationality, and
Region

1. In what ways is the ending different from what you expected?
2. What surprised you as you heard the end of the story?
3. What do you think you learned about Indian culture?
4. What might reading this story tell you about American culture?

The discussion that followed was lively. Most of the children thought that good would prevail over evil. What seemed to surprise them, however, was that the bad characters changed for the good. On probing further, some of the children questioned if human nature could be modified so quickly, as if through sudden insight or experience. Many were also struck by the use of herbs and mantras in the story, as well as the apparent reverence for nature and living things.

When discussing what they thought they had learned about Indian culture, Peter began by suggesting that Indians seem to care about nature in general and animals in particular. He also asked about the possibility of humans really talking to animals. He remembered watching a television show about how researchers were trying to communicate with dolphins, whales, and gorillas. Kathy seemed particularly moved by Maryetta's change of heart toward Toby and thought that Indians might care that other people are safe and peaceful. Kamal said that he was learning about some of the ways African healers treated their patients and that the Indians use of herbs and mantras reminded him of this.

It was a bit more difficult, however, for the students to discuss what they might have learned about their own culture. With some probing, however, Jerome was able to get a discussion going. Some thought that both countries were alike in many ways. Others were surprised that, while most of them would let the characters in the story die, the Indian children seemed to have compassion for them.

The discussion of violence in American society, toward both people and animals, was the most lively. Finally, Maria pointed out that the way the story was completed showed that the Indian students believed that people's labels can change, whereas in the United States she thought a label might remain with a person for quite a long time. She was even bold enough to ask why so many in the class seemed to have difficulty getting along with one another. Jerome thought that was a good question and allowed it to develop into a whole class discussion about prejudice and racism in their classroom and community. At the end of the discussion, all of Jerome's students agreed with the Indian class that the two classrooms should continue a long-term friendship and exchange of ideas, resources, and letters.

RATIONALE FOR THE CLASSROOM AS A GLOBAL COMMUNITY

It is the business of schools to prepare students for life in the larger societies that surround a school. In a democratic society, this means preparing students not only to know about democracy but also to be able to put it into practice. In a globally interdependent world, this means preparing students for a future in which four-fifths of new jobs created are the result of foreign trade, more than six thousand American firms having offices in overseas locations and more than six thousand international firms having offices within the United States. Political boundaries are rapidly changing, thus creating opportunities and challenges not imagined in recent decades. More and more, daily activities bring people into closer contact with others who are different from themselves. Moreover, it is not necessary to leave one's own community in order to come into regular contact with people from other nations. As a result, educators are beginning to seek out concepts, skills, and strategies that will help students function effectively in a globally interdependent world. A central focus of this effort is to develop an education that is international and intercultural in scope.

Education for a Global Perspective

The National Council for the Social Studies defines a global perspective as the development of "the knowledge, skills, and attitudes needed to live effectively in a world possessing limited natural resources and characterized by ethnic diversity, cultural pluralism, and increasing interdependence."[2] Teaching toward a global perspective emphasizes that

1. The human experience is an increasingly global phenomenon in which people are constantly being influenced by transnational, cross-cultural, and multicultural interaction.
2. There is a wide variety of actors on the world stage, including states, multinational corporations, and numerous voluntary nongovernmental organizations, as well as individuals.
3. The fate of humankind cannot be separated from the state of the global environment.
4. There are linkages between present social, political, and ecological realities and alternative futures.
5. Citizen participation is critical at both local and international levels.[3]

Education for a global perspective helps individuals better comprehend their own condition in the community and world and make more accurate and effective judgments about other people and about common issues. It emphasizes the study of nations, cultures, and civilizations, including our own pluralistic society, and focuses on understanding how these are interconnected, how they change, and what individuals' roles and responsibilities are in such a world. An education with a global perspective provides a realistic, balanced perspective on world issues, as well as an awareness of how enlightened self-interest includes concerns about people elsewhere in the world. The catchphrase "Think globally, act locally" has served the field of social studies education well. Making global concerns concrete, immediate, and meaningful to students is difficult yet critical.

Hoopes's Model of Intercultural Education

One approach to an international perspective is to consider how the cognitive demands placed on individuals change as societies change. Hoopes used such an approach when presenting his model of intercultural education.[4]

Hoopes distinguished three levels of society and identified some basic cognitive requirements for operating at each level. At the first level, called the *local-traditional level*, people are able to attain their daily needs from within their rather small, closed society. Little interaction with outsiders is necessary for obtaining these needs. When interaction with outsiders does occur, it is usually fraught with conflict, disagreement, apprehension, and fear. There is little need, or desire, to understand the perspective of others. Historically, these characteristics were associated with hunting and gathering groups, with large extended families or clans living in close proximity, and perhaps with very small rural towns and villages.

At the second level, the *national-modern level*, individual and group needs have broadened to the point that they cannot be obtained within their immediate surroundings. The services, goods, and knowledge of outside groups may be desired and needed, thus leading to barter, trade, and other means of negotiation. The need to communicate between groups increases, and money as a medium of exchange becomes very important. These characteristics can be associated with most Western societies from at least the latter half of the seventeenth century onward. The degree to which people and societies are interdependent at this level, however, is small. For the most part, nation-states remain relatively autonomous, while towns and cities maintain a local focus. Individuals may not have to go very far beyond their neighborhoods to trade, buy, or sell the things they need or desire.

The third level, which Hoopes called the *global-postmodern level*, is one that many societies and nations of the world are entering today. At this level, people and nations are so inextricably bound together that they cannot satisfy their needs and wants without significant interaction and nearly instantaneous communication with outside groups. These characteristics are also associated with the daily lives of most individuals who live in societies at this level. People obtain their food, not from their own or neighboring farms but from a supermarket that carries foodstuffs from around the world. Their clothing comes, not from their own or their neighbors' fields, spinning wheels, looms, and needles but from stores that manufacture, buy, and sell on an international scale. People do not build their own or their neighbors' houses without materials from around the planet, nor do most build their own machinery at all. If there is an oil spill in the Bering Sea, it is likely to affect the lives of people in the Gulf of Mexico. If there is famine in India, it is likely to affect the lives of people in the United States. If a large international company in the United States is bought out by a large international company in Germany, it is likely to affect the jobs of people in Taiwan, Singapore, and China. When something happens in Tanzania, Venezuela, or Saudi Arabia, people in Alaska, Sweden, Australia, and South Africa know about it within minutes or hours. When there is war, it affects everyone.

Indeed, it appears that mere survival of the planet today may be dependent on the smooth, interdependent functioning of many governments, economies, technologies, and communications systems, as well as the people who make those institutions come alive. It is such a level that we refer to when we speak of a global society or a global economy. To the extent that these characteristics apply, people live in what has been referred to as a global village.

Most people would agree that, in order to develop satisfactory relationships, to understand others' motivations and needs, and to interact effectively with those who are different, a certain degree of empathy (the ability to understand the world from another's perspective) must be achieved. Hoopes suggests that the development of empathy is critical for the move from the local-traditional level to the national-modern level.[5] If empathy becomes more necessary for some (but not all) at the national-modern level, it is indispensable for everyone at the postmodern-global level.

Such a world has numerous players, each of whom has distinct wants and needs, different perspectives, and different ways of thinking, interacting, and communicating. A healthy, well-functioning global society demands that individuals have the ability to think, perceive, communicate, and behave in new and different ways. The preparation of individuals for these kinds of interactions is the goal of global education.

CHARACTERISTICS OF A GLOBAL CLASSROOM

Most national systems of schooling typically address the needs of the nation they serve, paying particular attention to transmitting the "proper" attitudes and beliefs thought to be necessary to maintain the society. By its very nature, most schooling is an ethnocentric activity. However, long-term goals in most schools reflect some of the ideals of a global perspective. If you were to examine closely the philosophical goal statements of most schools, you would probably find such goals as to appreciate people from other cultures, to develop sensitivity to the needs of people different from themselves, and to increase knowledge about people around the world.

While the philosophical stage has been partially set, the methods for implementing such goal statements have created a problem. Schools in the United States, as well as most parts of the world, typically present curricular experiences from a strictly cognitive Eurocentric point of view. In addition, until rather recently curriculum development efforts have had little input from or interaction with people of different backgrounds. Such assumptions and practices are presently being called into question.

In a classroom with a global perspective, global education is not merely an add-on to an already overcrowded curriculum. Relevant concepts and activities that develop a global perspective are woven throughout the curriculum. Most important, global classrooms seek to help students develop such critical cognitive skills and attitudes as empathy, interconnectedness, perspective-taking, cross-cultural understanding, action-orientation, and prejudice reduction. In such classrooms, students are active in building connections with others. They may have pen pals with children in other parts of the world. In addition to writing letters and thus developing their language skills, students may be sharing audiotapes, videotapes, photographs, classroom materials, and other artifacts that reflect their own and each other's cultures. Children may read books about lives in other communities, which helps develop a global perspective while achieving the goals and objectives of a language arts curriculum. Students may even be working on collaborative writing projects with peers in other countries, as Jerome's class was doing with students in India. In short, students develop their language arts and other skills with other people in mind.

Pedagogies: Old and New

All of the pedagogical techniques discussed in previous chapters also apply to the global classroom. Indeed, the use of developmentally appropriate practice, collaborative and cooperative groups, and student involvement in planning takes on a new and richer dimension when placed in the context of an international perspective.

However, a global perspective can also be introduced in more traditionally oriented classrooms. What is important is the notion of a broader perspective.

257

CHAPTER 9
The Classroom as a
Global Community:
Race, Ethnicity/
Nationality, and
Region

In addition, students in global classrooms may use technology in creative ways. Classroom computers can be connected to networks that enable children to communicate on a regular basis with others from around the world. Joint activities may develop whereby classes in two or more countries collaborate via computer to discuss a global issue. Classrooms or schools may also use fax technology or computer scanners to link classes, enabling them to transfer artwork, poetry, essays, and the like to other schools. Similarly, an increasing number of schools are using video teleconferencing technology to motivate young people in social studies and foreign language education. Students can conduct conference calls with peers around the world while transmitting pictures of themselves, thus adding a highly personal dimension to the interaction. Rather than simulate a French café in a typical French language class, some schools have had video teleconferences in French cafés, thus allowing students from overseas to see and interact directly with those in the real-life setting.

While it is helpful to have such technology in global classrooms, much can be done without it. One can, for example, make excellent use of maps, local and national newspapers, encyclopedias and other books, taped television programs, and United Nations materials. One does not need more advanced technology than the mail service to introduce students to pen pals around the world. Or, when crises occur around the world, children's messages to others can have quite an impact. Rennebohm-Franz (1996) reports that the impact of a group of first grade children sending letters of emotional support to children in Kobe, Japan, following the earthquake in 1995 helped both her students and those in Japan feel connected to one another. One child's drawing showed her family standing outside their house at night with the following message of hope and connectedness: "I hope you get your houses built. This is a picture of me and my family looking out at the night. Maybe you see the same stars and moon we do"[6] The class received a message back from the teacher, stating:

> We began receiving your heartwarming messages from around the world. . . . We have posted the pictures, letters and messages in the classrooms and hallway bulletin boards of city schools that are serving as refugee centers. For those of us living among the aftermath of Kobe's quake, these messages have had an immeasurable heartwarming effect. They have given us an opportunity to realize that emotional support is just as important as material support and that we are all inhabitants of the same small planet.[7]

Roles: Old and New

In global classrooms, the local international community is considered to be an integral part of the school. As events unfold around the world, representatives from the various communities are invited into classrooms to share their experience and perspectives. This may occur at regular specific times in certain classes (e.g., social studies, language arts) or during regular school assemblies devoted to world events. Such involvement breaks down some of the personal barriers that tend to develop between people. Not only are students introduced to different perspectives, but they are also introduced to various cultures and languages firsthand. Such activities add a personal element to the content under study that a textbook cannot. Thus, when a natural disaster occurs somewhere in the world, or when a conflict breaks out, children can associate it with real people; it is no longer an abstract event unfolding in a far-off, abstract corner of the world. Finally, having adults from other parts of the world serve as teachers helps students understand that teaching and learning can occur in a variety of ways.

Place of Content Knowledge: Old and New

Globally oriented classrooms, like collaborative classrooms, integrate subject matter from various academic disciplines. Often these integrated curricula are jointly developed by educators from many countries. This, of course, helps assure the accuracy of the content being studied. For example, the Pacific Circle Consortium, for well over a decade, has been developing educational materials that integrate the perspectives and contributions of educators from the United States, Canada, Australia, New Zealand, Japan, and some Pacific Island nations. One of its products, The Ocean Project (TOP), uses the Pacific Ocean as a curriculum vehicle for students located in countries on the Pacific Rim. Two such projects have been developed. One provides fifth and sixth grade students in two countries with an integrated look at the culture, environment, economics, and cultural interaction of the other group's region. At the beginning of the unit, each group of students studies local conditions (environment, culture, economics, etc.). Next, a simulated transoceanic voyage brings the students to the other country, where they study similar concepts in that location. Thus, students in Honolulu, Hawaii, and Hiroshima, Japan, for instance, learn about one another's way of life and local environment. A similarly developed unit for upper secondary school students looks at the use of the world's oceans, treaties, international law, and so forth. A project on Antarctica has also been developed.

Assessment: Old and New

Assessment itself in global classrooms may generally be described as global. That is, because of the wide variety of activities and the emphasis on cross-disciplinary or interdisciplinary studies, global classrooms can easily use both traditional and alternative forms of assessment. One example is provided by Alan Singer, who taught a class on the impact of industrialization on American society to students at Edward R. Murrow High School in Brooklyn, New York.[8] As part of their evaluation package, students were assigned to create a political cartoon, poem, song, rap, poster, button, or flyer that illustrated the experience of one group with industrialization. The assignment counted as an "essay" on their final exam. Singer notes that "on the statewide regents exam that all students in New York must take, these Murrow students had at least as high a passing percentage as students in more traditional classes."

If technology is used in global classrooms to stimulate curricular activities, it can also be used in evaluation. Everything from computer-generated tests in which students receive immediate feedback to the production of videos and computer games can be assessed for what they demonstrate that students know and can do. The central point to remember in the assessment of global classrooms, as well as in other kinds of classrooms described in this book, is that, when a wide variety of activities enhances the curriculum, they can be evaluated in a wide variety of ways.

How might all this look in action? Let's go back to Jerome Becker's sixth grade classroom and reflect on what he was doing.

259

CHAPTER 9
The Classroom as a
Global Community:
Race, Ethnicity/
Nationality, and
Region

Case Analysis

Jerome's classroom activities reflect a number of strategies related to global or intercultural education:

1. He has demonstrated that it is possible to combine global education and prejudice reduction with the development of traditional curriculum skills in such areas as language arts, social studies, and art.
2. He has not shied away from real but sensitive issues, such as prejudice and interpersonal conflict, that greatly affect the lives of his students. Rather, he has acknowledged them as problems worth confronting and analyzing, and he has done this in a subtle, creative manner that will set the stage for subsequent activity once everyone has a common foundation.
3. By integrating traditional content areas, the day is not broken into short time slots in which content and curricular experiences are segregated from one another. Rather, classroom activities are designed to be meaningful and relate to the lives and experiences of the students. Through the partnership story, for example, students have an opportunity to develop their language arts skills while learning valuable social studies concepts about culture, specific countries, and interpersonal interaction. At the same time, students work in cooperative groups and develop linkages with others around the world.
4. He has actively sought to reduce prejudice, not by simply telling students that it is wrong but by enabling them to learn, firsthand, about similarities and differences among at least two groups of people.

This represents just the beginning of what is possible in a globally oriented classroom.

PERSPECTIVES ON A GLOBALLY ORIENTED CURRICULUM

What Jerome has attempted to do in the first part of the school year is to integrate into his curriculum three types of knowledge that will help his students evaluate their interpersonal experiences, both inside and outside of school. First, he is integrating knowledge and understanding of prejudice formation and prejudice reduction. Second, he is tapping into the growing body of knowledge related to the development of an international perspective. Both of these will be developed in the following sections. Third, he is applying cooperative learning strategies (see Chapter 8), thus providing students with necessary practice in developing the skills needed for collaborative living and working.

Curriculum Transformation: The Case of Prejudice

Critical to establishing a globally oriented classroom is the teacher's understanding of intercultural sensitivity and prejudice reduction activities in the curriculum. Intercultural education and training are delicate and difficult endeavors that must be approached with the greatest of sensitivity. Bennett pointed out that intercultural interaction among human populations has typically been accompanied by violence and aggression, when he said,

> Intercultural sensitivity is not natural. It is not part of our primate past, nor has it characterized most of human history. Cross-cultural contact usually has been accompanied by bloodshed, oppression, or genocide. Education and training in intercultural communication is an approach to changing our natural behavior. With the concepts and skills developed in this field, we ask learners to transcend traditional ethnocentrism and to explore new relationships across cultural boundaries. This attempt at change must be approached with the greatest possible care.[9]

Understanding prejudice, its purposes as well as its forms, is also fundamental to achieving an education that is international in scope. It is our hope that the following discussion will stimulate personal reflections on your part and a commitment to expanding on the curriculum and instruction suggestions provided here.

Our earlier discussions of categorization and stereotyping (see Chapters 3 and 4) inevitably lead into a discussion of issues surrounding prejudice and discrimination. It seems to be human nature to surround oneself with others who provide social acceptance and help in times of need. As a result, people spend a considerable amount of time and energy learning the norms of the groups they wish to belong to. One consequence of this is that individuals begin to think that the familiar behaviors of their group are good and natural and those of others are less good and less natural. Recall that ethnocentrism is the tendency of people to make judgments based on their own standards and to apply those standards to others.[10] When people make nonreflective judgments about others that are harsh, are discriminatory, or involve rejection, then the judgments are called prejudicial. The word *prejudice* implies a lack of much thought or care in making a judgment; people's responses are quick, narrow in scope, and based on negative emotions rather than accurate information. Prejudice appears to be a cultural universal; that is, people around the world behave in similar ways toward certain other rejected groups.

Prejudice seems to be an entirely negative phenomenon. It is easy to judge others' prejudices (and even our own) rather harshly. But we need to understand that, if prejudice did not have a psychological function, it would quickly disappear. Just as fear encourages people to prepare for danger and pain makes people aware of a problem, prejudice also serves an adaptive purpose. Obviously it has not disappeared, and this has encouraged researchers to seek out the reasons for its existence.

The Functions of Prejudice

Katz[11] suggests that prejudice serves at least four functions:

1. *Adjustment function.* People need to adjust to the complex world in which they live, and, if holding certain prejudicial attitudes aids that adjustment, they will be maintained. For instance, a teacher who believes that members of certain minority groups or people with disabilities are incapable of achieving at a high level is provided with an excuse for not finding alternative methods of reaching them. This obviously reduces the work-related responsibilities of the teacher, thus making life a bit easier. However, it also prevents minority and disabled students from achieving their full potential.

261

CHAPTER 9
The Classroom as a
Global Community:
Race, Ethnicity/
Nationality, and
Region

2. *Ego-defensive function.* Katz suggests that people hold certain prejudicial attitudes because they protect self-concepts. If less successful students want to think of themselves as on equal terms with higher-achieving students, they may be inclined to view the comparison group as cheaters. Holding this attitude protects the self-image of these individuals without any painful self-examination of the reasons for their own lack of success. The ego-defensive function also protects a positive view of one's ingroup. Rejection of others, then, becomes a way of legitimizing one's own viewpoint, as well as a way of avoiding the possibility that others may have an equally legitimate point of view.

3. *Value-expressive function.* This refers to attitudes people use to demonstrate their own self-image to others. If people believe they are custodians of the truth about the role of education, for instance, or that the god of their religion is the one true god, then other groups must be incorrect in their thinking. If one's group has attained success through the use of highly valued technology, then those who do not have this technology must be backward. The value-expressive function presents a certain image to the world, while the ego-defensive function protects that image by blaming others when things go wrong.

4. *Knowledge function.* This has to do with the way information is organized. Some prejudicial attitudes make the stereotypical knowledge of one's ingroup (its ideology) the basis of one's personal judgments and actions. Some groups, for instance, might consider certain outgroup members undesirable peers or romantic partners. Holding these attitudes allows individuals to make quick, usually negative, decisions when faced with choices involving individuals from the outgroup.

There is often a close relationship between the knowledge and adjustment functions. The former has to do with the information that one's ingroup believes is important, the latter with how people use that information in making decisions. Consider the issue of friendships and romantic relationships. There can be severe consequences if there are violations of the ingroup ideology. People can be expelled from their ingroup, shunned by their families, and excommunicated from their church for entering into relationships with the "wrong" partners.

Extreme Cases of Prejudice: Hate Groups

The *Dictionary of Multicultural Education* defines a *hate group* as any organized body that denigrates select groups of people based on their ethnicity, race, or sexual orientation or that advocates the use of violence against such groups or their members for purposes of scapegoating.[12] The term, as used in the United States, is generally applied to white supremacist groups, such as the Ku Klux Klan, the White Aryan Resistance (WAR), and the Church of Jesus Christ Christians/Aryan Nations. While local chapters of hate groups tend to target racial or ethnic minorities in their immediate area, all of them are anti-black and anti-Semitic.

It is difficult to obtain accurate figures on the number of hate groups or individual membership, but estimates range from between 250 to 400 groups, representing 20,000 to 200,000 members. Some of these groups limit their activities to producing and distributing literature, as would be most typically observed in schools, while others are known to commit acts of violence, including vandalism, intimidation, assault, and murder.

Of course, not all hate groups are white. The Nation of Islam, a black Muslim separatist group, is regarded by some as a hate group, with its main targets being whites and Jews. Their activities, however, have been restricted to verbal assaults and printed material.

The Components of Prejudice

Psychologists generally consider there to be three components of prejudice: cognitive, affective, and behavioral. The *cognitive component* refers to the process of categorization discussed in Chapter 3. We have seen how narrowly constructed categories result in stereotypes. The *affective component* refers to the feelings that accompany one's thoughts about members of a particular group. The affect attached to any statement can, of course, be positive or negative. It is the affective component that is most often thought of when we think of prejudice. The *behavioral component* is the discriminatory behavior that those who harbor prejudices are capable of directing toward others, especially when prejudice and power go together in the same person.

Educators can work with each of these dimensions in different ways. In Chapter 3, we saw that the categorization process is a cultural universal that helps people simplify the multitude of stimuli they confront each day. As educators, we must recognize this fact, make a point of informing others about it, and work to broaden our students' (and our own) categories. One long-term goal of both multicultural and international education is for individuals to become broader, more complex thinkers. That is, people should be able to perceive and evaluate situations from a number of perspectives, not just from one's native perspective. The affective and behavioral components are also under the control of educators. Strategies and programs that have successfully reduced negative affect and behavior toward others will be discussed in the prejudice reduction section.

White Privilege

People can, in many ways, unknowingly contribute to the existence of prejudice. A particular situation, referred to as *white privilege,* exists when white people, who may have been taught that racism is something that puts others at a disadvantage, are not taught to see the corresponding advantage that their color brings to them. Peggy McIntosh refers to white privilege as "an invisible package of unearned assets that I can count on cashing in each day, but about which I was meant to remain oblivious. White privilege is like an invisible weightless knapsack of special provisions, maps, passports, codebooks, visas, clothes, tools, and blank checks."[13] White privilege, like its counterpart, male privilege, remains largely unconscious for most perpetrators, with people, generally, not seeing their own oppressive behavior. Rather, individuals typically attribute success and status to personal traits rather than situational factors (recall the fundamental attribution error discussed in Chapter 4).

McIntosh identifies numerous instances in which she (and whites in general) are at an advantage over people of color. Such examples include the fact that she can arrange to be in the company of people of her own race most of the time; that, should she have to move, she can be pretty confident that she can find a home in an area she can afford and in which she would want to live; she can go shopping alone most of the time without being followed or harassed; her children will find examples of their race as the foundation of the curriculum; she will not be asked to represent her entire race; and she can speak in public to a powerful male group without putting her entire race on trial.[14] In what ways can you see that you or others around you may have been privileged?

263

CHAPTER 9
The Classroom as a
Global Community:
Race, Ethnicity/
Nationality, and
Region

Prejudice Formation

Children are aware of differences in others from a very early age. It is in the early childhood and elementary school years that children's attitudes toward members of particular groups are being formed. It has been suggested that it is a critical role of the elementary school to provide positive experiences that cause children to rethink their beliefs about group differences.[15] In general, children are unlikely to do this on their own.

Byrnes summarizes the literature on prejudice formation in children and identifies four basic ways in which children learn to be prejudiced:[16] observation, group membership, the media, and religious fundamentalism:

1. *Observation.* Children learn prejudice by observing the behavior of others, particularly respected elders. If those who surround a child hold biased beliefs about a particular group (the disabled, members of a certain religion, the physically unattractive, etc.), children may be inclined to follow suit. While children learn much from the subtle messages given by others, some learn prejudice from more blatant efforts by parents and community.[17]
2. *Group membership.* Like other individuals, children want to feel that they belong to a group. If excluding or devaluing certain "others" is considered the proper thing to do by a group one identifies with, it is likely that one will adopt that behavior and those attitudes. Thus, children may learn prejudice simply as a survival technique, as a way to "fit into a group." Some children, for instance, are, from a very early age actively prepared for adult roles in various religious cults or in secular organizations, such as the Ku Klux Klan.
3. *The media.* The media present another way in which children learn prejudice. While the media may not actively teach prejudice, they sometimes reinforce stereotypes or introduce stereotypes where they may not already exist. Cowboy and Indian films, for instance, have been shown to have a significant impact on children's views of Native Americans.[18] Both electronic and print media, through children's stories, often equate beauty with goodness and ugliness with evil. The symbolic association with evil of physical disabilities, such as hunchbacks, peg legs, eye patches, and hooked arms, may encourage a negative attitude toward disabilities.[19]
4. *Religious fundamentalism.* The more orthodox or fundamental one's religious beliefs are, the greater the prejudice toward other religious and cultural groups is likely to be.[20] Strict adherence to certain religious practices may actively encourage one to believe that all other doctrines are at best "wrong" and at worst dangerous, as are the individuals who believe in them.

What can be done in schools to help reduce the occurrence of prejudice?

Prejudice Reduction

We are fortunate that the educational research literature supports efforts to reduce prejudice. Indeed, there is some indication that we may even be able to decrease the likelihood that prejudiced attitudes will develop.[21] In reviewing the literature,

Byrnes found that educational strategies that have demonstrated the ability to reduce prejudice generally fall into four basic categories: (1) improving social contact and intergroup relations, (2) increasing cognitive sophistication (3) improving self-esteem, and (4) increasing empathy for and understanding of other groups.[22] All of these have curricular implications which we will look at one at a time.

Improving Intergroup Interaction. From a programmatic standpoint, the most promising of all change efforts stems from the work of those interested in intergroup interaction. Gordon Allport, in proposing the contact hypothesis, suggested that one way to reduce negative prejudice is to bring representatives of different groups into close contact with one another.[23] While sometimes this proves helpful, it is not always the case; occasionally, negative prejudice is reinforced or, in fact, formed where it did not previously exist. A different hypothesis suggests that it is the conditions under which groups come together that is critical. Certain characteristics of the contact situation are required to assure positive outcomes. Considerable efforts under many different circumstances (bilingual classrooms, integrated housing and schools, summer camp programs) have led to recommendations concerning the best conditions under which social contact can be improved. These include the following:

1. *Equal status contact.* Amir, working in integrated school settings in Israel, found that, if individuals coming together perceive that they have equal status or equal access to any rewards available, conditions are set for improved relations.[24] In Switzerland, for instance, French, German, and Italian are all recognized as official languages of the country. Official documents are made available in all three languages. Speakers of diverse languages, therefore, are all appreciated, well informed, and encouraged to participate in the society at large.[25] (Note the current movement underway in many states in the United States to make English the official language, even though the United States boasts the fourth largest Spanish-speaking population in the world.) In the school context, equal access to rewards can be translated to mean such things as equal access to knowledge, grades, and extracurricular offerings. In order for all students to have equal access to knowledge and grades, culturally appropriate curricula and instructional strategies need to be used. Equally at issue is the necessity to encourage all students to participate in extracurricular offerings. In the "natural" course of events, this may not always occur. Social class status has significant impact on the kinds of school experiences a child has. Children from lower socioeconomic groups tend to participate in fewer after-school activities than do their middle-class counterparts, thus not reaping the potential benefits of such participation. For example, the development of skills related to group and team thinking and acting that have been shown to be associated with managerial or other higher-level employment are often learned through extracurricular activities, rather than in formal classrooms. Recent legislation regarding equal rights for disabled persons (of whom there are over 43 million in the United States) is also intended to bring equal access to children with disabilities.

2. *Superordinate goals.* Having equal status alone is not sufficient. Individuals who come together and work toward achieving a superordinate goal or common task that could not be satisfied without the participation of all involved are more likely to learn to get along. This concept stems from the work of Sherif,

who, successfully able to create hostility and aggression between two groups of boys at summer camp, found it quite difficult to bring them back together again as one larger, cooperative group.[26] Finally, after much trial and error, he was able to bring both groups together after staging an incident in which a bus got stuck in the mud while on the way to a camp outing. In order for the bus to continue on its way, all of the campers had to work together to push the bus back onto the road. This superordinate goal, which could not have been achieved without everyone's participation, enabled all to work together toward a common goal. In the school context, superordinate goals are readily available in the form of team sports, drama productions, and music performances, as well as through cooperative learning activities that can be easily integrated in the classroom setting (e.g., the land lab and the partnership stories). When students with disabilities participate in the mainstream of school life (extracurricular as well as academic activities), such coparticipation with nondisabled peers in pursuit of common goals is possible. Similarly, students who have opportunities to work with others across racial and ethnic boundaries in such activities tend to develop more positive attitudes toward one another. In schools that are more homogeneous, it is usually necessary to plan activities that involve different groups. Such attempts may involve learning to "see" invisible differences, such as differences in learning style, in religious attitudes, or in knowledge and perceptions related to sex role. They might also involve cooperative efforts with other communities and schools; an effort to encourage the implementation of international exchange students on a regular basis; or the encouragement of integrated activities between handicapped and nonhandicapped individuals, across traditional age barriers, between high school and elementary school students, or between older people in the community and students of all ages.

3. *School norms that encourage intergroup interaction and the reduction of prejudice.* In order to be effective, efforts to reduce prejudice must be seen as important at all levels of the school. Such efforts cannot be seen entirely as the whim or "cause" of a particular teacher or group. Teachers, school administrators, and as many other adults as possible must actively encourage and show support for such efforts. Do not mistake this caveat, however, as indicating that the efforts of an individual teacher cannot initiate such changes. As innumerable teachers acting independently or with a small group of colleagues have demonstrated, the initial efforts of a single individual can have broad effects, especially in curricular decisions. Although it is often the case that the school system controls much of one's ability to make significant and permanent change, partly in the way it controls available resources, it by no means controls everything. Indeed, many school systems today are eager and willing to support a teacher who is trying something new in the way of curricular revision. Careful documentation of the revision process and its results is needed in order to institutionalize the changes that are effective and to refine the teacher's initial work.

4. *Personal familiarity.* A high acquaintance potential must exist, encouraging rather intimate contact between individuals in a given situation. In other words, people must have the opportunity to get to know the other person in ways that render the stereotypic image clearly inappropriate. It is very difficult, for instance, to believe that all people on welfare are lazy when one knows firsthand that Susan and her mother are both working as much as they are allowed

to within the welfare rules and that, if Susan's mother were to take an available job that did not include health benefits, she would lose the health card she is using to treat Susan's chronic asthma.

In addition to the preceeding suggestions, students can be placed in different heterogeneous groups for a variety of purposes and can be encouraged or required to participate in mixed team sports—any scheme that will enable students to get to know others personally. Time for informal activity, perhaps even structured into the day or on weekends, must be found.

Increasing Cognitive Sophistication. A second area that has been shown to have a positive impact on prejudice reduction includes strategies designed to increase cognitive sophistication. A considerable amount of research points to the fact that individuals who think in rather narrow terms are more likely to have a high degree of prejudice. Strategies designed to help individuals avoid stereotypes and overgeneralizations, as well as to become aware of the biases in their thinking and behavior, help people become less prejudiced. This means focusing teaching efforts on improving students' critical thinking skills. Thinking in a critical manner, as Walsh says, is antithetical to prejudicial thinking.[27] Rather than acting quickly out of an emotional response, people must search for and examine the reasons or motivations behind their thoughts and actions. When one thinks critically, one questions, analyzes, and suspends judgment until all available information has been collected and examined.

Ten essential criteria in the development of critical thought have been identified by D'Angelo:

1. Intellectual curiosity
2. Objectivity—relying on evidence in making one's argument, not on one's subjective emotions
3. Open-mindedness—willingness to consider a wide range of possibilities
4. Flexibility in one's thinking—the ability to change one's method of inquiry
5. Intellectual skepticism—evaluating considerable evidence before accepting a hypothesis
6. Intellectual honesty—a willingness to accept evidence even if it conflicts with a previously held belief
7. Attempts to be systematic or consistent in one's line of reasoning
8. Persistence
9. Decisiveness, but making conclusions only when enough supporting evidence is available
10. Attentiveness, by having respect for other points of view and responding appropriately, to what others are saying[28]

Teachers should work hard to create the kind of classroom environment that encourages critical thought. Walsh suggests that such a classroom is characterized by the following factors.[29]

First, the classroom and school climate must be one in which students feel respected and have a certain degree of trust. Students cannot function at higher levels of cognitive activity when their anxiety level is high. Feelings of safety and trust are thus a corollary of student risk taking. Recall the culture-general themes of anxiety, belonging, and status.

267

CHAPTER 9
The Classroom as a
Global Community:
Race, Ethnicity/
Nationality, and
Region

Second, the classroom must reflect, as Lipman states, a "community of inquiry"[30] or, as we have stated, "a learning community." Such an environment is characterized by questions of all kinds, those for which there are "right" answers and those that have more than one right answer. Indeed, some feel that, in order to prepare students for the real world outside of school, teachers' questions should force students to consider all sides of a problem, some of which may be conflicting.

Third, a balance should be maintained between teacher talk and student talk. Students must believe that their ideas are important and that what they have to say is critical. It is through discussion with others, and the sharing of ideas and problems, that critical thinking develops. It is important that, within the context of a safe, open classroom discussion, all students are allowed to participate and to feel that their participation is successful. More will be said about this later in the chapter.

Finally, students should be taught to think about their thinking and should be able to justify their reasoning with evidence. An emphasis should be on *metacognition*, or the awareness of how one has come to a decision. Being aware of how one arrives at defensible positions is key to becoming an independent, self-regulated learner.

To think critically means to think broadly, to take all sides of a problem into account and to weigh the resulting evidence. In short, to think critically is to avoid simplistic approaches. Too often, students are encouraged to "learn what is in the book," which frequently means to avoid thinking altogether. Teachers who create an environment that encourages risk taking, where cooperation in problem solving is stressed and where mistakes are not perceived as sins or personal faults, are more likely to engender achievement in students.[31] In such classrooms, an emphasis on thinking skills is not seen as an "addition" to an already overcrowded school day. It does not require a special course or time of day. Rather, it is a goal that permeates every lesson and all teacher-student contact.

Improving Self-Confidence and Self-Acceptance. Pettigrew established a clear inverse relationship between the degree of prejudice a person harbors and the person's sense of self-worth.[32] That is, the more confident one is in one's own sense of identity and competence, the lower one's degree of prejudice, and vice versa. While the relationship is not necessarily cause and effect, there are strong indications that self-acceptance is critical to mental, physical, and emotional health. Classroom activities designed to increase self-confidence also tend to bring about a decrease in levels of prejudice. Children can develop confidence in themselves when they are in educational environments where they feel secure and accepted, where their participation is valued, and where they know the boundaries and limits.[33] Creating such environments should be of prime concern to educators.

Increasing Empathy for and Understanding of Others. Although prejudice reduction is enhanced through social contact, cognitive sophistication, and increased self-esteem, long-term gains require educational activity that actively engages the emotions. Activities designed to help students see the world from another's perspective are useful in achieving this purpose. Classroom simulations are an excellent tool for helping children become sensitive to others who appear to be different from themselves. Shaver and Curtis, for example, offer a simulation to help children understand what it is like for those with speech difficulties.[34] They suggest that students put something in their mouths (such as a small, clean rubber ball or dental cotton—something large enough that it won't be swallowed) and then make a telephone call to a store and ask for information. Students can then discuss how it feels to be unable to communicate effectively.

The classic cross-cultural simulation BAFA BAFA—or the children's version, RAFA RAFA—provides an excellent way for students to gain an understanding of what it is like to move into another cultural group.[35] In this experience, individuals learn the "proper" behavior associated with the creation of two cultural groups. After some time, the members of each group have the opportunity to interact with one another. They very quickly experience feelings of anxiety, rejection, apprehension, and confusion—the feelings often referred to collectively as *culture shock*. Such feelings are encountered by most individuals who have made a significant move from one country or culture to another. This simulation allows students (and teachers or parents) to explore the feelings and experiences of immigrant, migrant, and refugee students; international exchange students; students in newly desegregated schools; newly mainstreamed children with disabilities; or just about anybody cast in the role of "new kid on the block."

Students may also write stories or act out plays and dramatizations of situations that characterize acts of prejudice and discrimination. In this manner, students step into the shoes of another, thereby gaining an "insider's" perspective of what it is like to be discriminated against.

Curriculum Transformation: The International Perspective

Most discussion of what is called global or international education refers to Robert Hanvey's paper, "An Attainable Global Perspective."[36] In this work, Hanvey identified five elements of a global perspective that educators can transform into teachable skills and perspectives that cut across academic disciplines and grade levels. Each of these elements is examined in the discussion that follows.

Perspective Consciousness

Perspective consciousness is one's awareness that one has a view of the world that is not universally shared, that this view is shaped by unconscious as well as conscious influences, and that others may have profoundly different views. This element differentiates opinion from perspective. *Opinion* refers to the surface layer of one's innermost thoughts. It is the tip of the iceberg, so to speak, showing only a small portion of its totality. Underneath the surface lie the generally hidden, unexamined assumptions and judgments people make about life, about others, and about right and wrong. The assumption that human dominance over nature is both attainable and desirable is an example of a perspective that lies deep in many Western minds. It was not until this traditionally unexamined assumption surfaced that many philosophical choices that previously had escaped our attention were raised. As a result, debate involving our relationship with the environment arose, stimulating considerable thought, activity, and discussion. Similarly, the feminist movement raised the consciousness of women and men regarding the role of women in society. In the process, deep layers of chauvinism inherent in much of our thinking about male and female roles was revealed. Likewise, concerned parents, addressing the unmet needs of their exceptional children, pointed out how the educational system (and society in general) discriminated against a large segment of society.

Children can develop perspective consciousness in a number of ways. Social studies curricula, for example, can help students examine their own culture's behavior from another point of view. Ethnocentrism suggests that most individuals have a tendency to overemphasize their own culture's accomplishments and point of view. Children can be encouraged to question their own cultural perspectives and to consider how others might view them. When studying people in other parts of the world, for instance, they can be asked to explore why most people prefer to live in their native habitats, despite sometimes difficult conditions. Children in your classrooms might ask why anyone would want to live in the arctic, where people have to contend with extremes in temperature and have to hunt for their food. Or, for example, when studying people of the Amazon River in South America, children might want to know how anyone would want to live where the temperature was extremely hot year round; where there are poisonous animals and annoying insects to contend with; and where the food staple, the poisonous manioc, has to be boiled and pounded over hot fires in the sweltering heat just to make it edible. Likewise, children growing up in those regions of the world might ask the same of our young students: how can anyone live in an environment where the air is polluted; where the water is trapped in pipes and treated with chemicals; and where food is not freshly hunted and prepared but packaged and loaded with preservatives so its shelf life can be extended? It is probably safe to say that our own behavior looks as strange to others as theirs might appear to us.

Children can also develop perspective consciousness by reading some of the numerous books that have been written either from another's perspective or from an insider's point of view. Reading the children's book *The True Story of The Three Little Pigs as Told by A. Wolf,*[37] for instance, is a good way to help children see that other points of view exist around most topics.

State of the Planet Awareness

An awareness of prevailing world conditions and trends includes such things as population growth and migration; economic conditions; resources and the physical environment; political developments; advancements in science and technology, law, and health; and various forms of conflicts. Most people, even from highly mobile societies such as the United States, spend most of their time in their local area. However, developments in communications technology have brought the world within most people's reach, if not into most people's homes. Extensive global media coverage via television news is making its impact felt at the diplomatic table as well. The liberal weekly *Die Zeit* of Hamburg, Germany, related two incidents that capture the extent of the impact made by the aggressive CNN news broadcasting team:

> In the summer of 1989, when the U.S. government was searching for a response to threats that hostages in Lebanon would be killed, a White House advisor was asked where President George Bush was spending the day. "He is in his office, watching CNN," the advisor said. "CNN is interviewing Middle East experts; maybe one of them will have an idea that the president can use." And when the Americans marched into Panama in December, 1989, Soviet leader Mikhail Gorbachev made use of the medium. CNN's Moscow correspondent was called to the Kremlin in the middle of the night. There, a press aide read a condemnation of the invasion for the

269

CHAPTER 9
*The Classroom as a
Global Community:
Race, Ethnicity/
Nationality, and
Region*

camera. The official note to the U.S. ambassador was not delivered until hours later. The Kremlin's excuse was that it was counting on Washington's getting the Kremlin's reaction immediately via CNN.[38]

Another illustration of the media's educational role can be seen in its coverage of the Gulf War in the winter of 1991. The United States military, knowing that Iraq was watching CNN's coverage of the war, actually planned its movements differently from those they were reporting to the American public so as to confuse the enemy. Thus, while the media make state of the planet awareness a possibility as never before, they also make the spread of misinformation easier and faster than ever before. Also, if we are not careful, it is very easy to believe that the real world consists only of televised images of the world according to CNN. Recall the storyline in the successful film *Wag the Dog*, which portrays a media-produced war to divert public attention from unethical presidential behavior.

Another problem is that television and print news are selective. For example, an outbreak of the measles (as has happened in recent years in various parts of the United States) or a famine in Ethiopia is deemed newsworthy, while chronic hunger and disease, which affects millions of Americans and others around the world, is not. Also, not all parts of the world receive the same news. For example, a drastic rise in the rate of skin cancer in Australia during the late 1980s and early 1990s was thought to be tied to an increase in the size of the hole in the ozone layer. In recent years, the hole spread from Antarctica to the southern parts of Australia. Consequently, major efforts were underway throughout the country to warn people against unprotected exposure to the sun. Parents went to all extremes to make certain their children's skin was covered while they played outside. Everyone wore hats. Even adolescents, who typically might go to any length to show off a suntan, made efforts to protect themselves. Attempts were also made to make high-SPF sunscreens prescriptive medications so people could deduct their cost from their income tax, thereby encouraging their use. For some reason, however, the American public was prevented from knowing about the extent of the hole and the severe impact it had on life in Australia. This is an example of selective news coverage.

General public awareness of the state of the planet must become a priority. Children must be encouraged to reflect on national and world conditions and to ask questions that go beyond the obvious. For example, they should be aware that, despite all of the United Nation's accomplishments, conditions for most of the world's people show serious deterioration:

1. The world's population has more than doubled in the past fifty years and is increasing by 250,000 per day, over 90 million every year. By the year 2050 there will be an extra 4 billion mouths to feed. This number alone is equal to what the total world population was in 1975.

2. Four hundred million people are unemployed in the "South" (the preferred term for those once referred to as undeveloped, or third world). Forty million new jobs are needed each year just to maintain the present world condition. Under present North-South imbalances, there is not the remotest chance of this happening.

3. More than 1 billion people live in poverty, 40 percent more people than in 1980. In 1960, the wealthiest one-fifth of the world's population was thirty times richer than the poorest one-fifth. By 1989, the wealthiest one-fifth of the world's population was sixty times richer than the poorest one-fifth. Viewed

from the perspective of a single country, such conditions represent the classic condition for a massive and violent revolution.

271

CHAPTER 9
*The Classroom as a
Global Community:
Race, Ethnicity/
Nationality, and
Region*

4. Television, radio, and video spread to the poor knowledge of the affluent lifestyles of the minority in the North and some southern elites, permitting angry comparisons with the desperate poverty of the vast majority in the South.

5. The exhaustion of natural resources and lack of work opportunities are prompting massive migrations across frontiers in Africa and Asia. In the early 1970s, there were 16,000 applicants for asylum within western European countries. By 1991, there were 545,000 asylum seekers. By 1993, country after country was beginning to close its gates.

6. In 1951, when the United Nations High Commission on Refugees (UNHCR) was founded, there were 1.5 million legally classified refugees worldwide. In the mid 1990s, there were roughly 20 million refugees worldwide. A further 24 million people are displaced within their own countries due to ecological, economic, and political causes.

7. World grain production per capita has shrunk by half since 1950. In Africa, grain production has dropped by 28 percent since 1967 due to the effects of drought, desertification, erosion, and population growth.

8. The rate of environmental deterioration continues unabated despite the best intentions of the *Earth Summit and Agenda 21*. The problems posed by global warming, ecosystem destruction, and ozone depletion demand urgent attention.

9. Between 1990 and 1994, the United Nations mounted as many peacekeeping missions as it had done in its entire history. On a global basis, only $1.90 is spent, per person, per year on the United Nations. This compares with $150 spent per person worldwide on weapons.[39]

Within the United States, most people do not know that 43 million Americans are considered disabled or handicapped. Nor do people know that 35,000 children around the world die each day due to hunger-related causes. How many people go hungry or are homeless in our own nation? How many children are born addicted to cocaine or suffering from AIDS-related complications? Students must be actively encouraged to expand their knowledge base, to review international news sources, and to inquire into the knowledge and perspective of international visitors. This, incidentally, would help develop the first dimension of global education, perspective consciousness.

Cross-Cultural Awareness

The dimension of cross-cultural awareness includes an awareness of social and cultural diversity around the world and at least a beginning awareness of how one's own culture and society might be viewed from other vantage points. Hanvey suggests that this dimension may be the most difficult to attain, since people typically do not have the time or expertise needed to truly understand those who are different from themselves. We now know that understanding about others does not necessarily follow from simple contact. Rather, lengthy, intimate contact under certain conditions is needed in order to "get into the heads" of those in another culture.

How can schooling best develop cross-cultural awareness in young people? To define what school might reasonably hope to accomplish in this direction, it may be helpful to consider four levels of cross-cultural awareness posited by Hanvey.

Level one involves an *awareness of superficial or extremely visible cultural traits,* the kind that often become the basis for stereotypes: skin color, dress, language patterns, ceremonies, and so on. Much of this information is obtained through textbooks, television, and tourism. At this level, the individual outside a given culture typically interprets the observed actions of others as exotic or, worse, bizarre.

Level two involves an *awareness of significant but more subtle cultural traits that contrast markedly with one's own.* Such information is gained as a result of culture conflict situations and is often interpreted as unbelievable. The reaction, however, is more on an emotional level. Interactions are considered frustrating, irrational, and against common sense.

Level three also includes an *awareness of significant and subtle cultural traits that contrast markedly with one's own.* However, this level is characterized by more intellectual emphasis and analysis. Others' behavior is then interpreted as believable because it can be understood.

Level four involves an *awareness of how members of another culture feel from the perspective of an insider.* People attain this perspective through cultural immersion—that is, from living the culture. Information is perceived as believable not simply because it is understood at the cognitive level but because of its familiarity at the subjective or affective level. This might be likened to reaching the state called "home" on the U-curve that was introduced earlier in the book.

Effective culture learning is more of an affective and behavioral process than a cognitive process. One truly learns about another culture by living it, not by being told about it. The development of intercultural competence may be, as Hanvey and others have noted, the most difficult, yet the most critical, of the five dimensions to achieve.[40]

However, strategies do exist that can assist one on the way to becoming interculturally competent. The culture-general framework used throughout this text has demonstrated the ability to have a significant impact on cognition, affect, and behavior in cross-cultural settings. It is a cognitive tool that engages the emotions, and it may be just the tool for the school context.

Knowledge of Global Dynamics or World Systems

Attaining the fourth dimension of a global perspective requires a modest understanding of how world ecosystems operate. The interconnectedness of things is stressed as students are asked to consider the impact of one particular decision or action on another. Examples such as the following can be used to illustrate the interconnectedness.

In southeastern Australia, the fluctuation of various fish populations in area river basins was found to be caused by an increase in estrogen in the water. Following an extensive investigation, it was determined that this hormone found its way into area waterways by being flushed out in toilet wastewater. Women using birth control pills eliminated higher than usual levels of estrogen in their urine. This directly affected the development of fish downstream. This is a good example of an unanticipated, unintended outcome.

Now consider an example of the vulnerability of ecological systems to changes in distant parts of the world. The recent increase in mosquito populations across the United States can be directly tied to our tremendous appetite for inexpensive fast-food hamburgers. An increasing proportion of the meat in our diet comes from cattle raised on land that was once rain forest in Central and South America. These rain forests provide the winter nesting sites for many of the northern hemisphere's migrating bird populations. As an increasing percentage of the rain forest is destroyed, so, too, are the winter nesting sites for these birds, which are dying. The decline in bird population has resulted in fewer songbirds returning north and, consequently, an increase in the mosquito population, which forms a major part of their diet. This is a vivid example of the impact that individual choice—in this case, eating habits—can have. "Think globally, act locally" again becomes paramount.

When a new element is introduced into any system, it has unanticipated effects. Hanvey suggests that there are no "side effects," only surprise effects. Thus, when we intervene in any system, we should be prepared for some surprising consequences. We confront numerous other examples of this principle in action almost every day. The depletion of the ozone layer, the greenhouse effect, the poisoning of groundwater, and the weakening of the eagle's egg as a result of DDT moving up the food chain are all examples of these surprise consequences, which we are now trying to correct. We must learn, as Hanvey suggests, to look for the "concealed wiring," the hidden functions of elements in a system.

Awareness of Human Choice

Hanvey's fifth dimension, awareness of human choice, represents the final critical step in developing a global perspective. The problems of choice that confront individuals, nations, and the human species as they increase their knowledge of the global system are addressed here. Until rather recently, people were generally unaware of the unanticipated outcomes and long-term consequences of their actions. This is no longer the case. A global consciousness, or cognition, is emerging. We now need to consider the implications of our expanded knowledge and communication base. Negligence, or even making an unwise choice out of ignorance, may set the stage for countless problems in the future.

Fortunately, we know a great deal more than we used to, and choices do exist. Consider the use of chlorofluorocarbons (CFCs) and the growing problem of ozone depletion. We have two choices: we can continue to use CFCs because at the present time they make refrigeration and propellants possible, or we can stop using them because of their effect on the environment, while actively seeking a replacement product. The simple substitution of pump spray mechanisms for propellant sprays on a variety of products is a good example of a successful alternative. It is awareness of the problem, however, that often makes the difference in the success of alternatives.

Children can make remarkable strides toward realizing their power and ability to bring about change. In the 1970s, Israeli elementary schoolchildren went on a campaign to protect some of their nation's threatened wildflower population. They raised the awareness of adults to such an extent that the adults stopped indiscriminately picking the flowers. Many of the threatened flowers have since been removed from the endangered species lists.

During the early 1980s, one of the authors of this text initiated a school exchange program between fifth and sixth grade children in northeast Ohio and schoolchildren in the Yucatan in Mexico and in Belize. Seventeen children went on the first trip from Ohio to Belize. One gesture of appreciation the Ohio children made to their host community was to present the village school with a world atlas signed by everyone at the visitors' school. This gift seemed to be the first book the

Belize school actually owned. This made such an impression on the students from Ohio that, on their return home, they decided to do something about the situation. All the fifth and sixth grade students in the school became involved in operating an after-school snack bar, collecting usable books from the community, and packaging them for shipment overseas. With the proceeds from their snack bar and their collection efforts, students were able to send more than 500 books to their peers in the small village in Belize. Needless to say, they felt tremendous pride, realizing that they, personally, could have such an impact on individuals so far away. This is a lesson no textbook could teach them and one they will never forget.

Teaching the Global Perspective

The development of a global perspective should be integrated throughout the school curriculum, not restricted to the social studies. Although large-scale infusion is desirable,[41] an international perspective can be integrated into the curriculum by individual teachers through any of the following means: by offering international focus courses, by internationalizing instructional methods and materials, and by internationalizing the disciplines.[42]

International focus courses exist in such areas as anthropology, regional history, geography, global or world studies, foreign languages, art and music, world religions, ethnic group studies, and international business. Such courses seem most appropriate at the secondary level and quite readily emerge from the disciplines themselves.

Internationalizing instructional methods and materials might emphasize intercultural interaction in the classroom using the special experiences of immigrant and international students as resources. Teachers should use culturally appropriate instructional and assessment strategies. Textbooks should be reviewed for balance. Partnership programs with other schools and countries, such as those with the schools in India and Belize, can also be developed.

Internationalizing the disciplines involves infusing key elements of a global perspective across the entire curriculum. There are numerous ways this can be accomplished at all levels and in all content areas. For instance, in reading and language arts, students might study how non-American and non-British writers use the English language. World literature courses should strive to include numerous examples from a non-Western origin. And literature should be integrated with the social sciences as a way to introduce multiple perspectives on abstract concepts. Children's literature can be used to present concepts of interest in international education. Classic Dr. Seuss books, such as *The Lorax* and *The Butter Battle Book*, can be used in a study of the environment and the nuclear arms race, respectively. Students might also analyze the portrayal of minorities and internationals in basal textbooks.

In science education, teachers might help students observe and understand the natural world and study the problems created as a result of increased technology and innovation. Students should be encouraged to ask questions, such as why there is drought in some parts of the world, why there is pollution, and why there is a growing hole in the ozone layer. Then, students should be encouraged to propose solutions to many of these problems, solutions that require knowledge and input from diverse peoples and cultures, all of whom "own" the problem. While technology may be universal, its application is quite specific. The study of what constitutes appropriate technology in a given situation demands sensitivity to such things as local environment, culture, history, and language. The topic of unplanned change can be introduced through the study of biology and evolution. Inequities of energy consumption across the planet can be explored. Finally, the global nature of such systems as the water cycle, the mineral cycle, and the energy cycle can be studied.

In foreign language education, cultural studies can be expanded beyond the mother country to include colonized people, as well as immigrant and refugee populations. The role of translators in world diplomacy can be studied. Foreign languages can be taught through folk songs, and English as a second language can be introduced to foreign language teachers and students.

Mathematics education should stress the metric system. The United States is the only nation in the world not actively using metrics. Math concepts can be illustrated by using problems that simultaneously teach about world trends and global issues. Traditional numeration systems from other cultures can be studied. The mathematics and possible computer application of Islamic art can be analyzed. Likewise, the impact of women on the development of mathematics can be introduced.

Finally, history and the social studies should look at various perspectives on similar issues. The American Revolution, for instance, certainly looked different through British eyes. Studying other nation's textbooks and discussing various events with international students can go far in developing perspective consciousness. Issues of population growth, personal family migration, history, and cultural diffusion can become the focus of historical inquiry, as can the interaction between geography, culture, and the environment. Students should be encouraged to ask difficult questions and to explore possible reasons and solutions. For instance, why does one-fifth of the world's population (in the developed countries) use two-thirds of the world's natural resources, and what might be done to counterbalance this? What does it really mean to be an overpopulated nation when one individual in the developed world has the same impact on the earth in terms of pollution and resource use as do about twenty-five individuals in the developing world? And why should soybeans, for instance, be exported from Brazil to feed cattle in the Western nations, to the detriment of the small farmers in the South and the benefit of wealthy corporations in the North? These are difficult questions to explore but, ultimately, ones that have to be addressed if the people of the world are ever to live in true balance.

Ethical Issues

Clearly, there are a variety of ethical issues involved in developing a global classroom. Among them are the fair allocation of available resources (including computers and other technology), the need to consider families and communities when discussing global concerns, and, perhaps most important, the need to balance advocacy with inquiry. While it is tempting to become an advocate when discussing the world's problems, the role of schooling remains one of inquiry. Assessing students on the degree to which they are able to use the tools of inquiry, such as breadth and depth of research, analytical skills, and creativity in proposing solutions, is more appropriate for schools than assessing them on the degree to which they subscribe to a particular point of view.

Similarly, there are ethical considerations involved in the length of time given to new ideas, such as global education. Its emphasis on attitude and behavior change may make it necessary to allocate large amounts of time in order to achieve even modest gains. Social psychologists have had a difficult time demonstrating that significant, long-lasting behavioral change follows from short-term attitude change. While it may be possible to demonstrate a change in attitude as a result of a short-term intervention (efforts at a summer camp program, for instance), there has been little evidence to demonstrate either that the attitude change persists or that it leads to a subsequent long-term change in behavior.

The converse may, in fact, be true, as seen in research concerning attitudes toward people with disabilities. An individual who has had little contact with disabled persons may initially react with discomfort and/or pity, being acutely aware of the disability. For example, in one study, teachers participating in an intensive five-week summer training institute on teaching young children with disabilities initially demonstrated a negative change in attitude, as measured by the Attitudes Toward Disabled Persons scale.[43] Positive attitudes, as defined by this scale, are those that regard a disabled person as essentially like everyone else, not someone "special." For many of the teachers in this study, this was the first exposure to children with disabilities; as a result, they had difficulty not being overly solicitous and eager to help. Follow-up experiences with disabled students gradually led to more "normalized" attitudes.

Studies of the classroom integration of children with disabilities generally have shown that mere exposure does not necessarily result in the formation of friendships. Teachers need to actively promote social interaction, model an accepting attitude toward all children, and design activities that enable handicapped and non-handicapped children to work together.[44] Too often, insufficient time is provided for these activities; consequently, initial assessments are disappointing. For example, in one study involving preschool children, initial observation revealed that typical children seldom selected children with disabilities in play situations, but repeated observations several weeks later showed significantly more acceptance.[45]

To summarize, when people encounter situations that induce or require them to behave in new and different ways for an extended period of time, there is a real possibility for long-term changes in attitude and behavior. If, for instance, school organizational structures can be modified to encourage or require intergroup interaction over an extended period of time, the likelihood that all students learn to regard themselves as tolerant, understanding, and able to get along with people increases. Government legislation that provides mandates for altering organizational structure on a national level is based on this idea. Official support and status for bilingualism in Canada and multilingualism in Switzerland are promising examples of this policy in action. Never believe, however, that mandates alone will do the job. What is required is persistent face-to-face activity and a good deal of trial and error.

SOME REFLECTIVE QUESTIONS

Our case study teacher, Jerome Becker, has developed a number of activities and curricular redesigns that infused global awareness into his sixth grade curriculum. Still, he is bothered by several aspects of his work.

1. How can he continue to educate himself about new methods of global education while keeping up with student needs and school requirements? Time is definitely a problem.

277

CHAPTER 9
The Classroom as a
Global Community:
Race, Ethnicity/
Nationality, and
Region

2. He knows that the United States is a widely diverse country with many unsolved problems regarding race and ethnicity. How can he justify moving to a global perspective when the problems at home remain so critical?

3. Kamal's "bottom-line" comments on the loss of cultural heritage experienced by those brought to the United States as slaves surprised him. How can Jerome be more sensitive to these issues while still encouraging a wider perspective?

4. Although he has been relatively successful in incorporating a global perspective into social studies, language arts, and some of the arts, how can he do the same with such seemingly "culture-neutral" subjects as mathematics and science?

5. He has found that many students do not relate at all to the idea of ethnicity. Rather, they think of themselves as Americans and have neither a knowledge of nor emotional ties to their own ethnic roots. How can he encourage these students to appreciate and value ethnic and racial diversity without seeming to denigrate the American way of life?

6. Michigan (as well as other states) appears to be home to a variety of groups that are extremely suspicious and fearful of what they believe is an effort to constitute a "world order." How can he approach the parents of the children in his class who have such fears?

7. Not every teacher and administrator in his school appreciates the direction Jerome is taking toward a global perspective. How can he continue to broaden his students' perspectives in the face of criticism from his colleagues?

Active Exercises

The following exercises from Human Diversity in Action: Developing Multicultural Competencies for the Classroom[46] complement this chapter well:

Activity 7: Family Tree Exercise, p. 38

Activity 30: Modifying Existing Instructional Material to Reflect the Goals of Diversity, p. 192

Some Critical Incidents

A Delayed Response

A couple of days after Jerome's class received the completion of their partnership story, he overheard Lenny and Paul giggling and talking about how silly it seemed that those in India would use rare herbs as medicines. They thought it more unusual that they would consider using mantras to control people and animals and began referring to the people in derogatory ways. Why do you think Lenny and Paul would, after two days, begin to ridicule those whom they had spent time studying about? What might you as a teacher do to prevent this from happening? What would you do at the moment?

Nurturing a Gang?

Steve, Bart, and Allen had been spending quite a bit of time together, and Jerome, as well as many of the other teachers, had noticed that they seemed to be excessively close to one another while excluding most others. This was especially apparent before and after school hours, when the boys could be seen hanging around corners close to the school. Other students had begun complaining that the boys were verbally abusive, calling some by derogatory names, and occasionally even being physical toward them. There was even talk that the boys might be involved in some gang activity, which might explain their increase in fighting and verbal assaults on some of the ethnic minorities in the school. Jerome, with the assistance of the principal, called in their parents for a conference.

Consider this first meeting between Jerome and the parents. How would you go about planning for this meeting? What aspects of the boys' behavior would you focus on first? Next? Why? What strategies might you use to make the meeting as positive as possible? How would you use your knowledge of prejudice, the functions of prejudice, and prejudice reduction as a central part of your discussion? In your discussions with the principal and other teachers, what efforts at the school level might you integrate? Why did you choose these activities?

Accessing the World Wide Web: Resources for Diversity

For more information and ideas on various types of prejudice and strategies for reducing them, the following web sites will be useful.

http://www.adl.org   Anti-Defamation League: this group monitors anti-Semitic activity and offers prejudice reduction programs.

http://www.newswest.com/crossingline/skagit2.html   Information on how to fight hate groups in your community.

http://www.vrx.net/aar/home.html   Artists Against Racism; musicians, composers, writers, actors, and other performing artists have joined to create this antiracist resource page.

http://www.euroamerican.org/   Center for the Study of White American Culture; a multicultural center that examines European American culture, with a special focus on how the prejudice of white Americans toward other ethnic and cultural groups can be confronted through antiracist dialogue and action.

http://www.splcenter.org/   The Southern Poverty Law Center, founded in 1971, is a nonprofit organization that combats hate, intolerance, and discrimination through education and litigation.

http://www.splcenter.org/klanwatch.html   Klanwatch and its Militia Task Force monitor extremist and militant activity throughout America and provide comprehensive updates to law enforcement agencies, the media, and the general public.

http://www.magenta.nl/crosspoint/   European Crosspoint Anti-Racism Webpage, maintained by the Netherlands International Centre for Human Rights; this web site provides links organized by continent and country to antiracist organizations around the world.

http://www.globaled.org/index.htm   American Forum for Global Education.

http://www.unicef.org/voy/   Unicef Voices of Youth. Live from the World Youth Forum THE MEETING PLACE where you can share ideas about important world issues and where you'll find activities to do and problems to solve; Where teachers (and others) can discuss global education and online learning.

279

CHAPTER 9
*The Classroom as a
Global Community:
Race, Ethnicity/
Nationality, and
Region*

http://www.halcyon.com/FWDP/fwdp.html   The Center for World Indigenous Studies Fourth World Documentation Project; provides access to documentation on the social, political, strategic, economic and human rights situations being faced by fourth world nations (indigenous peoples).

http://www.aaaid.org/   American Association of the Advancement for Individuals with Disabilities.

References

1. K. Cushner, "Creating Cross-Cultural Understanding Through Internationally Cooperative Story Writing," *Social Education* 56, 1 (January 1992): 43–46.
2. National Council for the Social Studies, *Position Statement on Global Education* (Washington, DC: Author, 1982).
3. Ibid.
4. David Hoopes, *Intercultural Education. Phi Delta Kappa Fastback*, no. 144 (Bloomington, IN: Phi Delta Kappa Educational Foundation, 1980).
5. Ibid.
6. K. Rennebohm-Franz, "Toward a Critical Social Consciousness in Children: Multicultural Peace Education in a First Grade Classroom," *Theory into Practice* 35, 4 (autumn 1996): 265.
7. Ibid., p. 266.
8. Alan Singer, "The Impact of Industrialization on American Society: Alternative Assessments," *Social Education* 58, 3 (March 1994): 171–172.
9. Milton Bennett, "Toward Ethnorelativism: A Developmental Model of Intercultural Sensitivity." In *Education for the Intercultural Experience,* ed. R. M. Paige (Yarmouth, ME: Intercultural Press, 1993), pp. 21–71.
10. Gordon Allport, *The Nature of Prejudice* (New York: Doubleday, 1958).
11. D. Katz, "The Functional Approach to the Study of Attitudes," *Public Opinion Quarterly* 24, (1960): 164–204.
12. C. Grant and G. Ladson-Billings, *Dictionary of Multicultural Education* (Phoenix: Oryx Press, 1997), p. 129.
13. P. McIntosh, "White Privilege: Unpacking the Invisible Knapsack," *Creation Spirituality* (January/February 1992): 33–35, 53.
14. Ibid.
15. P. A. Katz, "Developmental Foundations of Gender and Racial Attitudes," in *The Child's Construction of Social Inequality,* ed. R. H. Leahy (New York: Academic Press, 1983), pp. 41–78.
16. Deborah A. Byrnes, "Children and Prejudice," *Social Education* 52, 4 (April-May 1988): 267–271.
17. R. M. Dennis, "Socialization and Racism: The White Experience," in *Impacts of Racism on White Americans,* ed. B. P. Bowser and R. G. Hunt (Beverly Hills: Sage, 1981).
18. Deborah A. Byrnes, *Teacher, They Called me a . . . !: Prejudice and Discrimination in the Classroom* (New York: Anti-Defamation League of B'Nai B'rith, 1987).
19. D. Bicklin and L. Bailey, eds., *Rudely Stamp'd: Imaginal Disability and Prejudice* (Washington, DC: University Press of America, 1981).
20. D. A. Byrnes and G. Kiger, "Religious Prejudice and Democracy: Conflict in the Classroom," *Issues in Education* 4, 2 (1986): 167–176.
21. G. Pate, "What Does Research Tell Us About the Reduction of Prejudice?" Presented at the 1987 Anti-Defamation League Conference, American Citizenship in the Twenty-First Century: Education for a Pluralistic, Democratic America, Washington, D.C.

22. Byrnes, "Children and Prejudice."

23. Allport, op. cit.

24. Yehuda Amir, "Contact Hypothesis in Ethnic Relations," *Psychological Bulletin* 71, 5 (May 1969): 319–343.

25. Ibid.

26. M. Sherif, "Superordinate Goals in the Reduction of Intergroup Tension," *American Journal of Sociology* 63, 4 (1958): 349–356.

27. Debbie Walsh, "Critical Thinking to Reduce Prejudice," *Social Education* 52, 4 (April-May 1988): 280–282.

28. Edward D'Angelo, *The Teaching of Critical Thinking* (Amsterdam: B. R. Gruner, 1971).

29. Walsh, op. cit.

30. Matthew Lipman, *Philosophy in the Classroom* (Phildelphia: Temple University Press, 1980).

31. Walsh, op. cit.

32. T. F. Pettigrew, "The Mental Health Impact," in *Impacts of Racism on White Americans,* ed. B. P. Bowser and R. G. Hunt (Beverly Hills: Sage, 1981), pp. 97–118.

33. S. C. Samuels, *Enhancing Self-Concept in Early Childhood* (New York: Human Sciences Press, 1977).

34. J. P. Shaver and C. K. Curtis, *Handicapism and Equal Opportunity: Teaching About the Disabled in Social Studies* (Reston, VA: Council for Exceptional Children, 1981).

35. R. Gary Shirts, *BAFA BAFA, a Cross Cultural Simulation* (Del Mar, CA: SIMILE II, 1977).

36. Robert Hanvey, *An Attainable Global Perspective* (New York: Center for Global Perspectives, 1978).

37. Jon Scieszka, *The True Story of the Three Little Pigs as Told by A. Wolf.* (New York: Viking, 1989).

38. In "CNN: Television for the Global Village," *World Press Review* 37, 12 (December 1990): 34.

39. E. Childers and B. Urquhart, *Renewing the United Nations System* (Geneva: United Nations, 1994).

40. Kenneth Cushner and Gregory Trifonovitch, "Understanding Misunderstanding: Barriers to Dealing with Diversity," *Social Education* 53, 5 (1989): 318–322.

41. Ibid.; see also A. DeKock and C. Paul, "One District's Commitment to Global Education," *Educational Leadership* 47, 1 (September 1989): 46–49; and A. Crabbe, "The Future Problem-Solving Program," *Educational Leadership* 47, 1 (September 1989): 27–29.

42. K. Cushner, "Adding an International Dimension to the Curriculum," *The Social Studies* 81, 4 (July-August 1990): 166–170; and Gail Hughes-Wiener, "An Overview of International Education in the Schools," *Education and Urban Society* 20, 2 (February 1988): 139–158.

43. J. Stahlman, P. Safford, S. Pisarchick, C. Miller, and D. Dyer, "Crossing the Boundaries of Early Childhood Special Education Personnel Preparation: Creating a Path for Retraining," *Teacher Education and Special Education* 12, 1 (January 1989): 5–12.

44. P. Safford, *Integrated Teaching in Early Childhood* (White Plains, NY: Longman, 1989).

45. K. Dunlop, Z. Stoneman, and M. Cantrell, "Social Interaction of Exceptional and Other Children in a Mainstreamed Preschool Classroom," *Exceptional Children* 47, 2 (October 1980): 132–141.

46. Kenneth Cushner, *Human Diversity in Action: Developing Multicultural Competencies for the Classroom* (New York: McGraw-Hill, 1999).

Religious Pluralism in Secular Classrooms

CHAPTER OUTLINE

RATIONALE FOR ATTENDING TO RELIGION
  IN PUBLIC SCHOOLS
  Definitions of Religion
  Religious Pluralism in the
    United States
CHARACTERISTICS OF A CLASSROOM THAT
  ATTENDS TO RELIGIOUS PLURALISM
  Pedagogies: Old and New
  Roles: Old and New
  Place of Content Knowledge: Old
    and New
  Assessment: Old and New
  Analysis of the Case Study
PERSPECTIVES ON RELIGION AND
  SCHOOLING IN THE UNITED STATES
  Private Freedoms: Religion and
    Compulsory Attendance

Private Freedoms: The Practice of
  Religious Beliefs in Classrooms
Public Freedoms: Public Funding
  for Religious Schools
Public Freedoms: The Provision of
  Religious Instruction
PERSPECTIVES ON RELIGIOUS IDENTITY
  Religion as a Form of
    Personal Identity
  The Influence of the "Religious
    Right"
  Ethical Issues
SOME REFLECTIVE QUESTIONS
ACTIVE EXERCISES
ACCESSING THE WORLD WIDE WEB:
  RESOURCES FOR DIVERSITY
REFERENCES

> **W**ithout knowledge, the people perish.
>
> **Book of Proverbs**

Religion in a Secular Classroom: A Case Study

Melissa Morgan had been teaching fifth grade in a small town in her home state of Georgia for four years and she loved it. She had been married for two years, lived only five blocks from the school, and walked to work most mornings, passing on her way the principal's house, the local Baptist church, and the drug store on the town square. Two evenings a week, she attended classes at the local university, where she was almost finished with her master's degree in reading. On Sundays, she and her husband sang in the Methodist church choir, where many of her students' families also attended. It was a peaceful life in a town known primarily for the neatness of its surrounding farms, the beauty of its old magnolia trees, and the computer technology developed at the university where her husband taught English. At least it had been a peaceful life until last year.

It all started during the spring semester a year ago, when she took a children's literature course taught by a colleague of her husband's, a woman who, prior to becoming a professor, had been a youth minister in Chicago. One of her assignments had been to select several books written at the upper elementary level that could be used to introduce common themes from several of the world's major religions. From subsequent class discussions on ways in which children's literature could be used for a variety of purposes, Melissa had begun to develop an idea that seemed to solve one of her recurring problems. Because her school was in a university town, her students often represented a greater variety of cultural backgrounds than one would normally expect to find in a small southern town. In the past four years, she had had students from Japan, South Africa, and Ireland, as well as a number of students from various parts of the country who were the children of university faculty. As a result, her own classroom sometimes reflected the same split between local people and newcomers that now and then caused misunderstanding and strife in the community. For the most part, she had been able to help students who were new to the town (and the country) adjust to life in Georgia. But there was one element of the cultural differences in her classroom that had stumped her; that was the difference in religion that had created a number of overt conflicts in the past.

Armed with some new insights about using literature for purposes in addition to reading instruction, Melissa spent the summer developing a series of lessons designed to take advantage of the religious diversity in her class not only by using books and other materials about different religious faiths but also by planning activities that would lead children to discover more about their own religious backgrounds.

When school began in the fall, she was ready—convinced that it would be a wonderful year. She was doubly excited because students in her class represented a wider variety of religious backgrounds than had been the case the year before. Along with the usual Southern Baptists, Methodists, and Presbyterians were a Catholic student who had come to the United States from Brazil three years ago, three local Jewish students, five African American students who attended the African Methodist Episcopal church in town, two Muslim children from Pakistan whose parents worked in the Computer Science Department at the university, and two children who had been schooled at home until this year by parents who belonged to a conservative evangelical church. She also had students whose families were part of a small Unitarian congregation made up almost entirely of university faculty and their families.

The year began calmly enough, and her initial efforts to weave information about various religions seemed to go well. During September, she had made home visits to her students' families, some of whom she already knew. In the course of these visits, she was able to talk informally with parents and other family members, interact with her students in their home settings, and learn something about the cultural and religious backgrounds of those she did not know well. The father of one of her Pakistani students turned out to be a professor of architecture and promised to come in to her class one day to talk about both the mathematics and the art in Islamic mosque architecture. She was thrilled!

Near the end of October, Melissa's school held its annual open house for parents and community members. Her class was eager for everyone to see the exhibit they had been working on since the beginning of school— models of houses of worship from around the world that included a mosque, a Jewish synagogue, a Gothic cathedral, a Greek Revival Congregational church, and a Quaker meeting house. Each model stood against a map of the part of the world where such a building might be found, and each display was surrounded by pictures and books related to that particular place of worship.

About a week after the open house, Melissa's principal asked her to stop in his office after school. After a little small talk, he got to the point: "We've had some complaints," he said, "about the fact that you're dealing with religion in your class."

Melissa was astonished. "Who's complained?" she asked. "And what about?"

"It seems," continued Mr. Johnson, "that there are two kinds of complaints. Some parents object to their children talking about religion in school at all, and others believe their children are being exposed to ideas that they believe are not Christian. One family wants to come in and look at the books we have in the library to see if there are any offensive materials there."

"Well," said Melissa, "you know what the children and I have been doing; you've seen the models and maps. Did you explain our project to the parents who called? I really didn't intend to upset anyone, you know."

"Yes, I do know," said Mr. Johnson, "but I'm afraid we've got something of a problem here. At least one of these families has a history of suggesting that the school might not be 'purely' Christian. They're part of the small group of parents in this school who objected so strenuously to celebrating Halloween because they felt it encouraged pagan beliefs and devil worship. As you know, several years ago we did away with the Halloween party in favor of a 'Dress Up As Your Favorite Book Character' day every fall."

"What do you think I should do?" Melissa asked.

"I'm not sure," replied Mr. Johnson. "Perhaps you should put your models away and let it just die down."

A little shaken, Melissa went home that evening, wondering if all her ideas about building on religious diversity would be stalled. She certainly hadn't intended to find herself in the middle of a battle over religion! She also didn't want to stop the discussions and activities in class that had led to such a good project as the models, because her students were learning a great deal and seemed to be loving it. On an impulse, she called her own minister and told her about the problem. Melissa asked if Reverend Southworth could suggest anything.

"Indeed I can," said Maggie Southworth. "The clergy in the area all belong to a regional clergy council that meets next week. Let me bring this

up and see what they say. Perhaps you'd like to attend and tell us about what you're doing in class so everyone can hear it at the same time."

Melissa agreed and met the next week with the clergy council, where she carefully explained that, although she wasn't teaching any particular religious beliefs, she did think that learning about other religions was a good thing for students. She told them that the idea for building the models had come from the students and that she had been able to bring mathematics and geography as well as both reading and writing into the project, and she told them how proud the students were of their work. At the end of the meeting, each member of the council agreed that what she was doing was a good thing, even if it had never been done before. Several expressed a desire to see the models for themselves, and Melissa promptly issued an open invitation to all. She was pleased that one of those who wanted to see the exhibit was the pastor of the church attended by several of the families who had complained.

"Perhaps," she thought as she drove home, "there is an ecumenical spirit in this town after all." Then she found herself thinking about the coming holidays. "I wonder if we should talk about the way we emphasize Christmas at school?"

RATIONALE FOR ATTENDING TO RELIGION IN PUBLIC SCHOOLS

Since our national beginnings, the citizens of the United States have been deeply concerned with the role of religion in matters of state. Some of our earliest settlers came to this continent to escape religious prejudice, and all who have come in the years since have brought with them their religious ideas, beliefs, rituals, and habits of mind. Even those who profess to be agnostic or atheist have formed their spiritual values in express rebellion *against* varieties of formalized religion that exist or existed in their particular cultural worlds.

In addition, much of the cultural capital of human societies emerges from philosophical, literary, musical, and artistic attempts to answer fundamentally religious questions: Who are we? Where did we come from? What is our purpose on earth? What happens when we die? Thus, whether individuals see themselves as "religious" or not, religious references and allusions permeate their lives. In most, if not all societies, religious references are used in everyday language; families, schools, and other institutions organize time around religious observances; and places of worship exert influence in community affairs. Even many forms of money have religious symbols and language.

In part, this connection to religious ideas and symbolism emerges from a seemingly universal human need to be associated with a spiritual dimension. In some societies, that connection permeates not only the ways in which the society is organized but also nearly every minute of daily life. When that is the case, as it was in our own history in the Massachusetts Bay Colony and is currently in such places as Iran, the society is called a theocracy. In other societies, the connection is looser, with some degree of separation between secular and religious life. That was the intention of the founders of the United States, who wrote such a separation into the Constitution in the First Amendment, which reads:

Congress shall make no law respecting an establishment of religion, [*establishment clause*] or prohibiting the free exercise thereof [*prohibition clause*]; or abridging the freedom of speech, of the press; or the right of the people peaceably to assemble, and to petition the Government for a redress of grievances [italics added].[1]

Notice that, while the writers of the Constitution did not *establish* a religion as a dimension of the state, they also were careful to ensure that religion could be freely practiced by individuals, that religious speech (as well as other forms) was protected by the Constitution, and that peaceable assembly to practice religious beliefs (as well as for other purposes) was guaranteed. It was the passage of the Fourteenth Amendment in 1868, however, that granted to citizens of the states all the rights they had as citizens of the nation, which made the issue of separation of church and state a direct influence on schooling.[2]

Definitions of Religion

Uphoff notes that religion is a concept that seems easily definable until one actually tries to define it.[3] Both universal definitions (those that apply to all religions) and sectarian definitions (those that apply only to a specific denomination or sect) of religion are available to us. Yinger, for example, defines religion broadly as "a system of beliefs and practices by means of which a group of people struggle with . . . the ultimate problems of human life."[4] Sociologist Emile Durkheim defines it a bit more concretely but still in a universal manner when he says, "A religion is a unified system of beliefs and practices relative to sacred things, that is to say, things set apart and forbidden—beliefs and practices which unite into one single moral community called a church, all those who adhere to them."[5] Similarly, Berger and Berger view religion as an overarching view of reality concerned with ultimate meanings that provides a cohesive view of the world, explains evil and prosperity, and offers guidelines for social action in the secular realm."[6] Most broad definitions of religion encompass concepts of a deity, of shared values and an orientation toward the sacred, and of a sense of community.

On the other hand, narrower, sectarian definitions of religion (e.g., Presbyterian, Catholic, Jewish, Buddhist, Seventh Day Adventist) have relatively different answers to the following questions:

1. What theological outlook does this religion acknowledge?
2. What kinds of religious practice do the people who belong to this religious denomination accept as expressive of proper worship and devotion?
3. What kinds of religious experience—feelings, perceptions, and sensations—ensure that some contact will be made with ultimate reality—that is, a supernatural agency?
4. What knowledge about the basic tenets of faith, scriptures, and traditions are necessary to the practice of this religion?
5. What are the consequences of this religious belief, practice, experience, and knowledge on an individual's daily life?
6. What are the consequences of falling away from the practice, experience, and knowledge of this religion?[7]

In large measure, answers to these questions determine the differences between one religious group and another. Furthermore, it would be a mistake to regard these differences as simply "interesting" variations on a theme. Rather, beliefs about one's very identity and relationship with God and other human beings are vested in these beliefs, which are generally regarded by members of a particular faith as true in some ultimate sense. Thus, for example, religious beliefs about the proper kinds of food to eat, the proper way to prepare and eat it, the relative places of males and females in society, and the kinds of rituals required to receive the deity's blessing, as well as the number and relative importance of deities themselves, all have a bearing on how an individual conducts his or her daily life. These ideas are so strongly held and so central to a religious person's sense of individual and collective identity that conflicts of belief among various religious groups can—and often have—led to war.

Still, religious pluralism in the United States has been a part of American life since the beginning. What has changed over time is the degree to which religious belief has been deemed a necessary part of *public* life and, more important, the number, strength, and variety of religious denominations present in the society in any given period.

Religious Pluralism in the United States

While religious pluralism in the United States is so great that a complete accounting is not possible in a short chapter, it is possible to describe major religious groups that flourish here and to give a brief history. Prior to colonization by Europeans in the sixteenth century, the Americas were home to a wide variety of religious practices by native peoples. Although Native American societies differed widely in various aspects of culture, in language, and in appearance, all shared a fundamentally religious outlook that emphasized the centrality of a creator, a reverence for the natural world, and a belief that human beings were a part of nature and were obligated to preserve and protect it.

Europeans brought with them another set of religious variations, this time Christianity and Judaism, as well as a belief that human beings were apart from nature and were intended to conquer and control it. This difference in worldview with respect to the place of human beings in the natural world is perhaps the most significant and profound difference between so-called Western religions and all others.

In New England, puritan Protestantism took hold as a dominant theme; in the middle colonies, a greater diversity of religious belief, including Catholic, Quaker, Anabaptist, and others, meant that no particular denomination prevailed; in the South, the dominant religion stemmed from the Anglican church of England. Jews also were among the earliest immigrants, first Sephardic Jews from Spain and Portugal and then German Jewish immigrants, until, by the American Revolution, there were about three thousand Jews in the colonies.[8] Religious diversity continued to expand in the late eighteenth century. In the nineteenth century, large numbers of Catholics from Ireland and Italy and Jews from Russia and eastern Europe immigrated to the United States, each group containing within it great diversity of belief and practice. In the twentieth century, particularly since the 1960s, the United States saw increasing Catholic immigration from Cuba, the Caribbean, and Central America.

In the seventeenth, eighteenth, and nineteenth centuries, large numbers of Africans were brought to the United States as slaves, bringing with them another large set of their own nativist religions, which combined with and enriched the primarily Protestant Christian traditions they found here. Indeed, the creativity with which Africans interpreted and used Protestant scriptures and music to make their daily lives more bearable and to further the cause of freedom produced a unique contribution to American religious and political life. Negro spirituals, for example, were very often used as a form of clandestine communication to spread news of slave activities. After slavery was finally abolished in the middle of the nineteenth century, African American churches continued to have an immense influence on the cultural and educational lives of their members and are still central to African American culture and social and political struggles.

The late nineteenth and twentieth centuries saw a growth in the Muslim faith in the United States, partly through conversion and partly through immigration. In fact, Islam is one of the fastest-growing religions in the United States. The converted Muslim population is primarily African American and often identifies itself as the Nation of Islam, a group that has a history in the United States that goes back to the 1930s, when it grew out of the works of W. D. Fard and Elijah Muhammad. The Nation of Islam was—and, in some respects, still is—a separatist group that empha-sizes freedom, justice, and equality for African Americans, actively discouraging intermarriage with whites. Perhaps its most well-known leader was Malcolm X, the converted son of a Baptist minister, who, as a result of his experience during a pil-grimage to Mecca (a Hajj) and shortly before his assassination in 1965, began to shift his beliefs away from separatism and toward brotherhood among all human beings.[9]

Muslim immigrants are from Middle Eastern countries, such as Jordan, Lebanon, and Syria, from both North Africa and sub-Saharan Africa, and from such Southeast Asian countries as Malaysia.[10] Like their European counterparts, many Muslims have come to the United States as a result of social and political unrest in their native countries. Al-Ani notes that Muslims have come in three waves. The first, largely poor and uneducated, came from what is known as Bilad ash-Sham, or Greater Syria—an area that after World War I was Jordan, Lebanon, Palestine, and Syria—and from Turkey, Albania, India, and elsewhere.[11] The sec-ond wave immigrated after World War II, particularly from the Middle East and North Africa and were primarily educated professionals uprooted by political changes, including the creation of the states of Israel and Pakistan.[12] The third wave, which continues today, began in the 1960s with the liberalization of Ameri-can immigration laws. These individuals came not only from the same areas as their earlier counterparts but also from the former Yugoslavia.[13] In addition, begin-ning in the 1970s, the oil-producing countries of the Middle East have sent many Muslim students to study in the United States, and these students have played an active role in Muslim communities.[14]

While the United States has always been a religiously pluralistic country, today that pluralism is greater than it has ever been. Along with ethnic and racial plural-ism, to which it is closely related in a variety of ways, religious pluralism has become a daily experience in classrooms all over the country—a fact that has edu-cational implications in terms of curriculum materials, subject matter, school rules and customs, student services, school calendar decisions, the scheduling of student activities, cafeteria offerings, holiday celebrations, teaching methods, and school financing.[15] Rather than considering these "problems," however, some teachers and schools are finding that such diversity of religion offers unique opportunities for teaching and learning.

CHARACTERISTICS OF A CLASSROOM THAT ATTENDS TO RELIGIOUS PLURALISM

How would one design a classroom not only to affirm religious pluralism but also to build on it?

Pedagogies: Old and New

As is the case with other forms of difference, teaching in a classroom that is sensitive to religious diversity is in large measure a matter of getting to know the children with whom you are working, their families, and the communities in which they live. Most teachers quickly learn the individual idiosyncrasies of their students with respect to psychological issues and traits: attention span, motivation, perceived intelligence, and so on. What is often less well known is the sociocultural background of students, yet the best context for learning is one in which students are able to build on what they already know. Thus, knowing as much as possible about your students' backgrounds is also central to everything else that happens, because you will be designing your classroom around *your* students and the experiences they bring with them to school.

Because formal religious teachings and values may *or may not* be a part of your students' lives, it is important to know something about the religious composition of your class. Chances are good that you will not have an overwhelming number of different religions represented in one room, so you need to know something about only those that are represented at any given time. However, you do need to know something about the worldview of those religions, as well the worldview of those who do not subscribe to any religious tenets, particularly with respect to issues of gender and to the relationship between young people and elders. It is also wise to know whether or not a particular religious group values such skills as critical thinking and questioning for their children, because some do not. In some contexts, one simply does *not* question authority, age, or religious doctrine.

Knowledge about religious groups does not, of course, mean that you must design a classroom to match each child's unique experience. Indeed, one of the purposes of schooling is to help students expand their experience beyond the relatively small world in which they live. However, it is important to know something about the religious values of your students, so that you can make decisions about how to approach new learning, where conflicts may develop, and when you can intercede to help students (and, often, parents) bridge the gap between their own experience and what they are learning in school. At the same time, it is important for a teacher to understand and respect the community's primary values, so that he or she does not get too far beyond the readiness level of community members. As Gollnick and Chinn note, schools

> are influenced greatly by the predominant values of the community. Whether evolution, sex education, and values clarification are part of instruction in a school is determined in great part by the religious beliefs of a community. Educators must be cognizant of this influence before introducing certain readings and ideas that stray far from what the community is willing to accept within their belief and value structure.[16]

Within a framework of the desire to built on religious diversity, it is perhaps even more important that a teacher vary the instructional methods used in the classroom.

As we have discussed before, the culture of the traditional American public school stresses certain teaching methods, patterns of instructional interaction, and assessment strategies. Some examples of these patterns include teachers talking while students listen; individual students answering teacher-directed questions; individual students giving oral reports to their class; students following detailed, teacher-given instructions in how to carry out a task; and students taking paper-and-pencil tests. In the United States, these patterns emerge from a Western cultural worldview that emphasizes individualism, middle-class values, and generally a Protestant Christian belief system that stresses the importance of the minister as teacher and the individual's direct relationship with God. Such a pattern may be relatively or totally unfamiliar to some students. Native American students, for example, whose religious worldview emphasizes communal patterns of interaction and individual choice, may be more interested in the activities of their peers than of the teacher and may feel that the teacher must earn their respect, rather than simply getting it by virtue of his or her position. That is, students may believe that one should follow a teacher's directions because one has chosen to, rather than because one is compelled to do so.[17] Another example is African American students, whose churches use an emotive "call and response," or choral pattern of interaction; they may respond to teachers' questions with emotion, hand gestures, changes in vocal tonality, and in chorus, because that is a pattern they have learned.[18] In general, what may be *new* about pedagogy for a classroom that pays attention to religious diversity is the subtle but important ability of the teacher to vary and alter instructional patterns, so that all students find both familiar and new ways of learning.

Roles: Old and New

Sensitivity to potential and real areas of conflict among students of different religious backgrounds requires that teachers adopt the role of interpreter and, sometimes, mediator. Once again, teachers must learn as much as they can about the religions represented in the classroom, not only so that they can help students find the commonalities among different religious beliefs but also so that they can help students interpret differences. Parents and community members are often helpful in this regard, as long as they understand that their role is to explain rather than to convert. Indeed, perhaps more dissension regarding religious tenets has been caused by teachers' failure to communicate closely with parents about what they are trying to accomplish in class than by any other single factor. Generally speaking, if parents understand that their children will not be deprived of either respect or affirmation because of their religious beliefs, most will be happy to help teachers in any way they can. Students, too, if they are old enough, can serve as teachers to their peers, as can other school staff and members of the community.

Another set of issues to consider in a religiously sensitive classroom is the role of school rules and customs, from attendance policies to dress codes. Attendance, for example, should be flexible for students involved in religious celebrations and/or duties, and such policies as dress codes should take into account religiously based regulations and customs. One example is the dress code that stipulates that students should not wear hats in school. Such a code must exempt an Orthodox Jewish boy who wears the yarmulke as a token of respect to God and an Amish girl who wears a dimity bonnet and long dress as a gesture of modesty.

Similarly, the fact that the school calendar conveys the importance of religious diversity is significant. For example, vacation times scheduled on traditional school calendars, as well as celebrations usually held in schools, tend to be based on the Christian holidays of Christmas and Easter. Moreover, such common practices as scheduling games on Friday nights (when many Jewish families begin the celebration of the Sabbath) or homecoming activities early in the autumn (which may fall on the Jewish High Holidays) should also be considered seriously. Later in the school year, teachers need to be sensitive to the demands placed on older Muslim students who observe Ramadan and refrain from eating and drinking during the daylight hours. It is important that the customs involved in these special cases be discussed openly in terms of their religious significance, so that other students both learn about different traditions and respect the reasons for them. Much of this kind of discussion can take place in the context of learning about religious beliefs and customs as a part of more general curricular study.

Place of Content Knowledge: Old and New

When religion is the cultural focus of your thinking, remember that religion, unlike some other kinds of difference, has a powerful element of "truth" built into it. That is, it may be more difficult for a student to "stand apart" from his or her religious worldview in order to look at others, because religious "truth" is often linked to fundamental ideas of the relationship between individuals and a supernatural power. Nevertheless, religious history and traditions, architecture, art, music, and ideas can become the basis for an enriched and affirming classroom.

Although in recent years educators have been reluctant to consider teaching about religion in public schools, the *study* of the contributions of various religions to world civilization is worthwhile. In 1964 the American Association of School Administrators published a book called *Religion in the Public Schools,* in which the authors assert:

> A curriculum which ignored religion would itself have serious implications. It would seem to proclaim that religion has not been as real in men's lives as health, or politics, or economics. By omission it would appear to deny that religion has been and is important in man's history—a denial of the obvious. In day by day practice, the topic cannot be avoided. As an integral part of man's culture, it must be included.[19]

The study of religion generally can be incorporated into a variety of places in the curriculum; often, the best place is the most obvious. Religious dietary regulations might be included in a home economics class, for example, or the intricate, geometrical designs of an Islamic Mosque might be part of a math or an art class. Because religion has been so fundamental to human life and history, locating its study in the context of a variety of subject matters is not difficult. At the same time, separate courses in the study of comparative religion or interdisciplinary courses that study the impact of religion on history, law, and art can be instituted, particularly at the secondary level.

Regular curriculum materials and resources in a religiously sensitive classroom should be carefully screened for bias of various kinds, including omission, not so much in order to exclude those materials as to point out the bias to students and to let the bias, itself, become the subject of inquiry, discussion, and debate (see Chapter 12 for an excellent list of forms of bias in curricular materials that can also be applied to religious bias). At the same time, curricular resources—including books, articles, paintings, music, sculpture, maps, and such artifacts as wearing apparel and icons—that represent various religions can be made available for examination by students. Similarly, students who belong to particular religious groups may educate their classmates about their own religious beliefs and values. In all cases, the basis of study and discussion should be inquiry, not evangelism.

Assessment: Old and New

When one is teaching or learning about a belief system, such as religion, it is important that assessment focus not only on the knowledge that has been acquired but also on the form that assessment takes. Uphoff offers a good example of religious sensitivity when he writes about creating exam questions having to do with the concept of evolution. As you may be aware, the teaching of evolution is the subject of much controversy in some communities, with many people calling for balancing the curriculum by including the study of "creation science" in biology and other classes. The difference between showing respect for families who accept the story of creation in Genesis as a fact and giving the impression that those families are wrong can be seen in the following test questions:

> *Poor.* It took millions of years for the earth to evolve to its present state. (True/False)

> *Better.* Evolutionists believe that it took millions of years for the earth to evolve to its present state. (True/False)[20]

In the first question, the student must agree with a factual statement, while, in the second, the student can agree that one group (not necessarily one to which he or she belongs) asserts that something is the case. As Uphoff notes, it is a subtle but powerful difference.[21]

Another issue concerns such assessments as psychological testing and health screening and care. Some families—generally, those who profess a fundamentalist Christian faith—believe that psychological assessment by school personnel is an invasion of family rights, a corruption of values based on strict adherence to biblical teaching, and an attempt on the part of school officials to alter or interfere with students' religious beliefs. These families tend to think that psychological interventions to raise self-esteem or encourage self-expression, such as classroom games or the use of puppets as a way to enable children to speak freely, are suspect, sometimes in the extreme.

Similarly, health screening and assessment, especially when it involves somewhat invasive procedures, such as tine or PPD (purified protein derivative or Mantoux) tests for tuberculosis, are often the focus of parental objections on a variety of religious grounds. Some parents also may have religious reasons for objecting to their children having their blood typed in biology classes or to giving blood in high school blood drives. As schools increasingly become the place where a variety of health and social services for children are located, it is likely that an increasing number of objections will be raised by families from a variety of religious backgrounds.

Pang and Barba note that culturally affirming instruction should include culturally familiar interaction patterns, culturally familiar strategies, a culturally familiar environment, culturally familiar content, culturally familiar materials, and culturally familiar analogies, themes, and concepts.[22] Let's explore now some of the reasons that Melissa Morgan's classroom is one in which these guidelines were followed with respect to religious sensitivity and appreciation.

Analysis of the Case Study

Those who have been involved in school disputes about religion might think that this case study has an improbably positive resolution. Certainly, many schools have become the center of highly emotional and long-lasting acrimony about such issues as using counseling techniques to build self-esteem in children and have experienced major attempts at censorship of library and other materials.

However, Melissa demonstrated several attributes of a good teacher in a religiously sensitive classroom. First, she took advantage of her students' idea to build models as a way to get them to cooperate in a hands-on activity and to encourage students from different religious backgrounds to bring their own specialized knowledge to their classmates. Second, she skillfully integrated several aspects of the curriculum into the project, so that students could see that knowledge is interrelated. Rather than dry lecturing about various religions, she involved the students in finding out about various religious beliefs in terms of the meaning underlying the parts of the house of worship itself.

When objections came, Melissa did not try to withdraw, nor did she get angry or dismiss the objections as unreasonable. Rather, she went to her own minister as a possible way to create linkages with the religious leaders of the community. That there happened to be a clergy council meeting the next week and that she happened to be a persuasive speaker might be viewed as fortuitous; however, many communities have organizations to which various clergy belong, and the notion of enlisting help from community members is always a good one.

As diversity of all kinds is increasingly prevalent in schools, and as teachers such as Melissa learn to appreciate and build on those differences, experiences like Melissa's will also increase. Thus, it is a good idea for those who will be teachers to consider both the opportunities and possible implications of being an educational leader in the classroom and in the community.

PERSPECTIVES ON RELIGION AND SCHOOLING IN THE UNITED STATES

Because a religious or spiritual dimension is so close to both the cognitive and emotional lives of human beings, and because the founders of the United States believed that religion was so important that it should be addressed in the Constitution, the few words in the First and Fourteenth Amendments have been both the source of religious freedom and the source of educational battles around religion in the schools ever since. In schooling, the fundamental problem has been how to resolve the tensions created by seemingly opposing principles: (1) the need for schools, as an arm of the state, to support a basic freedom guaranteed by the Constitution and

(2) the need for schools, also as an arm of the state, to uphold the separation of church and state. Throughout our history, these tensions have resulted in continually shifting opinions about a number of issues.

R. Freeman Butts has cast these issues into two broad categories. The first is education's role in protecting *private freedoms,* or "those that inhere in the individual, and therefore may not be invaded or denied by the state."[23] He writes:

> In the most general terms, freedom was sought for parents and their children on the grounds that every human being has the right, and should have the opportunity and the ability, to live one's own life in dignity and security. Further he or she is entitled to a chosen cultural or religious group without arbitrary constraint on action or coercion of belief by the state or by other community pressures.[24]

"Most often," he notes, "appeal was made to the free exercise of religion guaranteed by the First Amendment of the Constitution (and as applied by the Fourteenth Amendment to the states) as a protection against coercion of belief or action by school or government authorities."[25]

The second category is education's role in guaranteeing *public freedoms,* "that is, those that inhere in the welfare of the democratic political community and which the . . . state is obligated actively to safeguard, protect, and promote whether threatened by a majority or minority in the community."[26]

> He describes the ground for public freedoms for teachers and students as the belief that every person in his or her capacity as a teacher, learner, and citizen had the right and should have the opportunity to speak, to read, to teach, to learn, to discuss, and to publish without arbitrary constraint on action or coercion of belief by the state or by other pressures.[27]

The approach to protection of public freedoms has run into opposition from those who see it as a threat to the established order—that is, as a threat to the dominance of Protestantism as the foundation of public schooling. It has also been opposed by those for whom the protection of private freedoms is paramount—that is, by those who see in the protection of *public* welfare a threat to *private* freedoms of parents to control the education of their children.

Several of the more important concrete issues over which these debates have raged are compulsory attendance; the freedom to practice religious beliefs with respect to the Pledge of Allegiance, salutes to the flag, and prayer and Bible reading in schools; the use of public funds for religious schools; and release time for religious instruction. Each of these issues has reflected the tension between private and public freedoms.

Private Freedoms: Religion and Compulsory Attendance

As we have said before, the history of schooling in the United States is characterized by a continually expanding effort to include all children. One way in which this has been done is by requiring all children to go to school until a certain age. This requirement was little regarded in the early years of the country; indeed, for much of our history, schooling was not only not required but also not really necessary to earn a living and develop a good life.

Beginning in the nineteenth century, with the advent of industrialization and the major waves of immigration, compulsory schooling gained acceptance largely as a way of protecting young children from exploitation in factories and keeping children off the urban streets. In general, however, the move toward compulsory schooling can be seen as part of a larger movement toward the establishment of a social institution (the common school) that would ensure a common citizenship and loyalty to the state among diverse individuals. Thus, early on, the issue of compulsory schooling was seen by some as an issue of the rights of parents versus the rights of the state.

In 1922, the state of Oregon narrowly passed an initiative requiring that "all normal children between 6 and 18 must attend a *public* school, or that any who attend a private school must obtain the permission of, and be examined by, the county superintendent of schools."[28] Fearing that such a law would destroy parochial schools, a Roman Catholic teaching order filed suit to have the law declared unconstitutional. In 1925, the Supreme Court did just that in *Pierce v. Society of Sisters,* saying,

> The fundamental theory of liberty upon which all governments in this Union repose excluded any general power of the State to standardize its children by forcing them to accept instruction from public teachers only. The child is not the mere creature of the State; those who nurture him and direct his destiny have the right, coupled with the high duty, to recognize and prepare him for additional obligations.[29]

Although affirming the right of parents to send their children to private religious schools, the Court also stipulated that the state had a right to require children to go to *a* school, and that the state could also regulate all schools. Thus, the precedent was set for the development of a protected parochial school system alongside the public schools.

As is often the case, however, support for compulsory schooling ebbs and flows. By the 1960s and 1970s, many educators had doubts about requiring attendance of all children to the age of 16 or 18. Again, religious beliefs provided the means for the Supreme Court to further the cause of private freedoms and parental rights. In *Wisconsin v. Yoder* (May 1972), the Court upheld the decision of the Wisconsin Supreme Court that stipulated that Old Order Amish parents could disobey Wisconsin's compulsory schooling law and remove their children from school at the end of the eighth grade. The Court held that

> a state's interest in universal education, however highly we rank it, is not totally free from a balancing process when it impinges on other fundamental rights and interests, such as those specifically protected by the Free Exercise Clause of the First Amendment and the traditional interest of parents with respect to the religious upbringing of their children so long as they, in the words of *Pierce,* "prepare [them] for additional obligations."[30]

Today the move toward compulsory schooling is once again on the rise, largely because of the state's perceived interest in a technologically oriented workforce that can compete economically with other nations. Indeed, the second goal of the national Education 2000 plan for schooling requires that "by the year 2000, the high school graduation rate will increase to at least 90 percent."[31] Interestingly, at least since the Supreme Court's decisions in 1963 declaring that the *requirement* to begin the school day with prayer and Bible reading was unconstitutional, schools have often dealt with religious issues by ignoring them.

Private Freedoms: The Practice of Religious Beliefs
in Classrooms

297

CHAPTER 10
*Religious Pluralism in
Secular Classrooms*

Public sentiment regarding the role of religion in public schools, like public opinion on other issues, must always be seen in a historical context. In the decisions cited in the previous section, for example, parents' right to foster religious beliefs in their children versus the state's right to compel school attendance was part of the larger question of child labor and the development of schools as the primary socialization agents of citizenship in a democracy.

Similarly, the debates over the practice of religious beliefs in classrooms have often been part of the larger question of loyalty to the United States and the debate about the state's role to protect a citizen's rights to equality. In the beginning of the common school movement, there was little question that religious practice—and religious sources of instruction—was a fundamental part of public schooling. Such practices as school prayer and the reading of the Bible on a daily basis were common, if not universal, and such curricular materials as the widely used McGuffy Readers taught moral values derived from Christian Protestantism along with vocabulary and grammar. Although the influence of particular religious ideas and values on schooling has always been partly a matter of the religious composition of the community in which a school is located, the basic structure of public schooling in the United States emerged from an allegiance to a Judeo-Christian heritage as much as it did from the development of an economically capitalist state. Indeed, the Judeo-Christian God has been a more or less involuntary party to a wide variety of legislative and judicial meetings, deliberations, and decisions at the federal, state, and local levels. Note that, although we say we separate church and state, the president of the United States still places one hand on the New Testament when taking the oath of office.

The question of loyalty to the government usually arises in times of major political disagreement or war. In 1919, for example, in the wake of World War I and fears of involvement with world affairs, Nebraska passed a law requiring that all instruction in the public schools be given in English and prohibiting the teaching of any foreign language to children younger than the ninth grade. In *Meyer v. Nebraska*,[32] however, the Supreme Court ruled that such a law was unconstitutional, stating that the right of parents to guide their children's education is a constitutional right.

Similarly, during World War II, the Minersville, Pennsylvania, board of education set a policy that required all teachers and students in the public schools to incorporate the Pledge of Allegiance and a salute to the flag on a daily basis. One set of parents named Gobitis, who were Jehovah's Witnesses and prohibited by their religion from worshiping "images," objected that the requirement set aside their First Amendment rights to free exercise of religion. In *Minersville v. Gobitis*,[33] the Supreme Court ruled in favor of the state's right to impose the flag salute rule. The dissent to this ruling was written by Justice Stone, who, on becoming the Chief Justice three years later, reversed the Gobitis decision in *West Virginia State Board of Education v. Barnett*,[34] saying, in effect, that, while the state could require the study and teaching of civic matters, it did not have the right to impose an ideological discipline that "invades the sphere of intellect and spirit."[35]

The debate about the role of the state in providing equality of opportunity, on the other hand, has influenced other decisions regarding religion in the public schools. Today, for example, a more widely known controversy revolves around the issue of prayer and Bible reading in public schools. In a widely referenced case in 1963—*Abington v. Schempp*[36]—the Supreme Court ruled that *requiring* student participation in sectarian prayers and reading from the Bible, particularly the New Testament, violated the First Amendment separation of church and state. The argument was that school prayers were fundamentally Christian (and usually Protestant), that all students were not Christian, that so-called nonsectarian prayers satisfied no one, and that therefore the removal of all religious practice from public school classrooms was necessary.

Unfortunately, many people, including the national and local media, confused the argument with the actual decision, which did not "ban" prayer in schools but only said that *requiring* students to participate in sectarian prayers and Bible reading was unconstitutional. Indeed, in the majority opinion written by Justice Clark, the Court strongly supported the study of religion in public schools:

> It might well be said that one's education is not complete without a study of comparative religion or the history of religion and its relationship to the advancement of civilization. It certainly may be said that the Bible is worthy of study for its literary and historic qualities. Nothing we have said here indicates that such study of the Bible or of religion, when presented objectively as part of a secular program of education, may not be effected consistent with the First Amendment.[37]

Uphoff suggests that it was the self-censorship of educators and publishers based on both an inadequate reading of the Court decisions and a desire for equal representation for non-Christian religions that was responsible for the relative removal of religion from public schools. The vacuum created by this removal has enabled a strong challenge from the so-called Religious Right to reinstate religious practices into classrooms. Although this challenge will be discussed in greater detail in a following section, for now it is sufficient to say that the pendulum of social opinion on the role of religion in public schools seems to be swinging in the direction of more rather than less influence.

Public Freedoms: Public Funding for Religious Schools

Arguments for public funding for religious schools stem from the doctrine contained in the *Pierce v. Society of Sisters* decision previously discussed. As Butts notes,

> if parents have a private *right* to send their children to religious and private schools to meet the compulsory attendance requirements of the state, then distributive justice requires that the state provide parents with public funds to enable them to do what they have the private right to do.[38]

Arguments against public funding for religious schools stem, on the other hand, from the establishment clause of the First Amendment on the grounds that the taxpayer has a right to be free of taxation that promotes a religious doctrine.

Until about the middle of the twentieth century, the American public in general was inclined to believe that both national and religious interests were better served if public funds were not used for religious schools.[39] The debate arose again, however, at mid-century, with positions being taken about both *direct* and *indirect* aid. Proponents of direct aid argued that, since compulsory attendance laws served the state, and parochial schools contributed to the ability of those laws to be enforced, parochial schools should also benefit from public financial support. Further, they argued that, since all citizens were required to pay taxes to support public education, those parents who wished—*and had a right*—to send their children to religious schools would have a double financial burden. In addition, they argued that the provision of separation of church and state in the Constitution said nothing about the ability of public and parochial schools to *cooperate* with one another.

A more moderate view favored *indirect aid* to religious schools. As early as 1930, precedent was set for such aid when, in *Cochran v. Louisiana Board of Education,*[40] the Supreme Court upheld a Louisiana law that affirmed the purchase of texts for use in private sectarian schools on the grounds that the books benefited the children and, thus, the state. After World War II, however, a variety of religious groups began to push the limits of *Cochran* by asking for public support for health and medical services, school lunches, and books. The greatest demand was for help with the transportation of parochial students to their schools.

Perhaps the most cited and argued over case regarding religion and public education,[41] *Everson v. Board of Education*[42] was the landmark case with respect to bussing parochial school children, largely supported by American Catholic Bishops. Emerging from a New Jersey case in which the state allowed public funds to be used to transport Catholic children to parochial schools, the Court ruled that payment for such transportation essentially benefited the children (and thus the state, as it had said in *Cochran*), rather than the school. The vote was 5–4, however, with the minority arguing that such support did, indeed, help children and parents maintain religious instruction at public expense.

A third position, generally taken by Protestant, Jewish, and civil libertarian supporters of the public school, as well as by many professional educators, argued that both direct and indirect aid to parochial schools were unconstitutional. Those who took this position based their argument on a strict separation of church and state. In 1950, 1951, and 1952, both the National Education Association and the American Association of School Administrators adopted the following language as policy:

> We believe the American tradition of separation of church and state should be vigorously and zealously safeguarded. We respect the right of groups, including religious denominations, to maintain their own schools so long as such schools meet the educational, health, and safety standards defined by the states in which they are located. We believe that these schools should be financed entirely by their supporters. We therefore oppose all efforts to devote public funds to either the direct or indirect support of these schools.[43]

Over the next three decades, the action regarding federal aid to private schools moved from the courts to the legislature. At the federal level, the School Lunch Act of 1948, the National Defense Education Act of 1958, the Higher Educational Facilities Act of 1963, the Higher Education Act of 1965, and the Elementary and Secondary Education Act of 1965 provided financial support for school lunches in parochial schools; massive funding in a variety of areas for private, often sectarian, colleges; and funds for school libraries, textbooks, and secular instructional materials for private as well as public schools. The courts, however, continued to cut down state statutes supporting direct and indirect services to parochial schools, although they did create some conditions in which such aid was permissible. Thus, in 1977, the Supreme Court ruled that states could use public funds to pay for therapeutic, remedial, and guidance counseling services for parochial school children, provided that those services were offered in a "neutral site." That ruling resulted in a great many trailers parked on the tree lawns of parochial schools, in which some types of special education, health, and guidance counseling were offered.

Today the debate about tax support for parochial education continues, made perhaps even more strident because of current efforts to greatly reduce governmental support of social programs more generally. This effort is also helping create conditions in which supporters of a greater role for religion in public schools can argue that such a role will either eliminate the need for, or take the place of, governmental support.

Public Freedoms: The Provision of Religious Instruction

Current charges that public schools are too secular and lack the moral tone that will help children grow up to be better citizens are not new. If, at the end of the nineteenth century, a consensus had developed that religious instruction should not be a responsibility of public schools, after World Wars I and II many thought that the schools were "godless" and that some sort of religious instruction should be returned to public classrooms. Throughout the 1940s and 1950s, efforts were made to get around Court decisions regarding the separation of church and state but were largely unsuccessful. Two arguments were generally offered.

Some people—mostly Protestants and Catholics—sought a revival of sectarian instruction, usually through the demand for released time in the school day, so that students could receive religious instruction from teachers of their own religious faith. Most often, this instruction was to be offered apart from the school building, usually in a nearby church. Others—primarily Protestants—urged that more attention be paid to nonsectarian religious instruction through daily reading of the Bible and recitation of nonsectarian prayers in school. Both propositions were denounced by many as an infringement of the separation of church and state.

While a number of states and the U.S. Supreme Court ruled in various ways on the issue of released time for religious instruction, the Supreme Court finally decided in 1952, in a New York case, a situation in which students left the school building for religious teaching was permissible under the First Amendment, because the schools did not actively promote a sectarian form of instruction and because no public funds were expended for the effort.[44]

The issue of Bible reading has also been decided variously. By the 1970s, a number of states had decided Bible reading was *not* religious instruction. At least six state courts, however, ruled that the Bible *was* a sectarian document, at least to Catholics, Jews, and nonbelievers. For Catholics, the King James version of the Bible was thought to be Protestant sectarianism; for Jews, reading the Bible does not hold the same significance that it does for Christians; families of unbelievers objected to any religious practices at all.

Nonsectarian prayers were usually objected to by everyone, on the grounds that they "watered down" any "real" religious belief in an effort at compromise among belief systems and on the grounds that they, nevertheless, promoted religion against the establishment clause of the First Amendment. In 1963, the Supreme Court did away with all these arguments in the previously mentioned cases that declared *required* prayer and Bible reading to be unconstitutional even while they affirmed the value of teaching *about* religion in public schools.

In the past thirty years, new issues have arisen that bring religious pluralism in the classroom once again into sharper focus. First, immigration from various parts of the world by people whose religious structures and beliefs are very different from the so-called big three—Protestantism, Catholicism, and Judaism—has populated public school classrooms with students from a wide variety of religious backgrounds. Second, changes in the institutions of the family and the economy have weakened the social cohesion that normally helps bind communities together and provide the common socialization processes necessary to raise the next generation. In such circumstances, young people often feel rootless, answerable to no one, and alienated from a system that no longer really exists, except in the minds of their elders. One result of these societal conditions is the increase in violence we are now witnessing in all segments of society, but particularly among our youth. Finally, the growth of and importance attached to science and technology in our society tend to mask the smaller, more human dramas that contain the very essence of religious questions and meaning. It is little wonder that, in response, the call for religious instruction and moral values in public schools has become a widespread demand.

PERSPECTIVES ON RELIGIOUS IDENTITY

Religion as a Form of Personal Identity

Of all the groups to which a person can claim loyalty, a religion is perhaps the most common. Some researchers suggest that Americans are more likely to identify themselves as members of a religious group than anything else.[45] It is also the case, however, that to identify oneself as a member of a religious group often means a close association with an ethnic group as well. Thus, an Irish Catholic may consider herself or himself substantively different from an Italian Catholic, and a Russian Jew may feel quite different from a German Jew. Consider a professor who was teaching about diversity at an urban university in a highly ethnic city. After several class sessions on the subject, a student came up after class to tell her that she (the student) could relate to the lesson. "You know," the student said, "I went all through Catholic school in my own Irish neighborhood, and it wasn't until I got to college that I met some Italian Catholics. You're right; they sure are different."

In part, this differentiation results from differences in ethnic histories and in part from differences in the development of religious practices among members of the same general faith. One has only to attend services at churches of three or four different Protestant denominations (e.g., Presbyterian, Southern Baptist, high Episcopalian) to know that there is great diversity *within* the same religious tradition. Moreover, to identify oneself with a particular religious group also usually means that one has placed oneself in a particular social as well as geographical location. The term *Southern Baptist,* for example, says a great deal about the geographical roots of one's religious identity, and the term *high Episcopalian* may indicate something about the social class to which one belongs.

Religious identity has its strongest roots in the family, and many families not only encourage but demand that their children follow in their religious traditions. In fact, some families go so far as to deny the existence of a child who breaks with the faith, and some religious groups, such as the Old Order Amish, occasionally invoke the practice of "shunning" (never speaking to or acknowledging the presence of the person being shunned) when a community member strays from the fold. The belief that one's religious identity is an integral part of one's essential self can be seen in the reaction of parents whose children join a cult. Such parents believe that their children have been brainwashed and many hire an "expert" to "deprogram" them.[46]

Religious identification also places a person in a particular relationship with a deity (e.g., Catholics as part of a community of believers, Protestants in a one-to-one relationship with God). On that relationship may depend one's view of the possibility of a life after death, a set of moral codes for living, and the nature of rewards or punishments for the life one has led. Given the profound nature of these issues, it is not surprising that individuals, families, and communities react strongly to perceived threats to their religious beliefs.

At the same time (and perhaps paradoxically), in a religiously heterogeneous society, such as the United States, a great deal of switching occurs from one religion to another. The move from one religious affiliation to another may involve a formal conversion process, or it may be a move from a conservative to a more liberal branch of the same church (or vice versa). It may occur as the result of marriage between people of two faiths, or it may occur in an individual as an outgrowth of intellectual analysis. Gollnick and Chinn note that switching from a conservative to a more liberal church may be the result of upward mobility. They write, "Those shifting to the liberal churches have tended to be older, more educated, holding higher-status occupations, and, as might be expected, more liberal on moral issues. As a group, they tend to be less active in their new churches than the members of the conservative churches they have left."[47]

The switch from conservative to liberal is not, however, the current trend in the United States. The fastest-growing churches in the United States tend to be conservative, sometimes evangelical or pentecostal, Protestant denominations, with an accompanying decline in membership of so-called mainline churches. There are probably a variety of reasons for this trend, not least among them the desire of many people for a solid, unquestioning, and dependable religious orientation at a time when change in all institutions means a dissolution of traditional rules for living. One might also argue that the trend toward conservatism reflects, in part, the shrinking of the middle class and the increasing economic gap between those who are wealthy and those who are not. If switching to liberal religious affiliations is a function of upward mobility, then the opposite is perhaps also the case. For the first time in American history, there is a general perception that children may not "do better" than their parents, and the real or perceived fact of downward mobility can be related to an increasing desire and need to be a part of a community in which one can identify with virtue and righteousness.

The Influence of the "Religious Right"

While the so-called religious right in this country is composed of a politically oriented and loosely connected set of relatively fundamentalist Christians, it would be a mistake to think that conservatism is the property of the Christian faith. Indeed, fundamentalism is gaining strength in all the religions of the world as people begin to feel the effects of globalization and institutional change. In the United States, however, the determinedly *political* nature of a coalition of conservative Protestants is having a profound effect on the direction of American government and its legislative and judicial processes. Such national issues as the size of the federal government and the need to reduce the incidence of crime, abortion, and violence in and out of schools are the issues of choice of the religious right, and information and exhortations about these issues are carried to millions of people through televangelists, and radio networks sponsored by such organizations as Dr. James Dobson's Focus on the Family, as well as by such national figures as Pat Robertson and Pat Buchanan. The influence of the religious right is also observable in the rhetoric of otherwise more moderate politicians, and political campaigns at all levels will undoubtedly be driven in large measure by conservative and even fundamental beliefs.

Nowhere is the influence of the religious right felt more strongly, however, than at the local and grassroots levels, and no institution is of more concern than the school. As we noted in the preceding sections, the tension produced by the constitutional separation of church and state has meant a continual debate over the part played by schooling in both protecting religious liberty and enabling religious practice.

As it has been in the past, the issue of school prayer is once again at the forefront of public debate, fueled in part by the vocal participation of those who believe that the *absence* of regular prayer in schools is one of the elements of what they see as a lack of morality in American society. While the current status of prayer in schools, as determined in part by Supreme Court decisions, is that prayer is individual and voluntary (one wit remarked that, as long as there is academic testing, there will be prayer in schools), conservative groups continue to press for a return of mandated school prayer with the stipulation that individuals can choose not to participate.

Similarly, the issue of funding for private and parochial schools is also the subject of much debate, this time using the language of tuition tax credits. Some proponents argue (again) that, because student enrollment in private schools reduces the pressure on public schools and contributes to the overall education of America's children, financial support for private tuition is justified. They argue further that parents should not have to pay twice for the education of their children and that support for private schools encourages pluralism. Interestingly, unlike the Great School Wars in the nineteenth century, in which Protestants opposed parochial schools in general, the proponents of public funding for private schools who are members of the religious right would now like public support for private Christian schools. Opponents, on the other hand, argue that allowing such a use of public funds would weaken the public school system, facilitate the ability of parents to avoid integrated schools, and create a dual system of education that is antithetical to the ideal of a democratically educated citizenry. In a time of social change such as we are experiencing, this debate is likely to continue for some time and promises to be another large part of the conservative political agenda.

Perhaps the most serious challenge to public education by the religious right, however, lies in the area of censorship. Conservative and fundamentalist religious groups are not the only groups to advocate censoring the materials to which schoolchildren have access, but they are among the most vocal. Gollnick and Chinn describe the seriousness of this challenge in the following way:

> Censorship, or attempts at censorship, have resulted in violence, where involved parties have been beaten and even shot. It has resulted in the dismissal or resignation of administrators and teachers. It has split communities and in the past thirty years has created nearly as much controversy as the desegregation of schools.[48]

While most people would not doubt that those who urge the censorship of school materials are sincere and fully convinced that they are espousing a cause that is morally right, the question arises as to whose morality is to be the basis for whatever guidelines are selected. In a religiously pluralistic society, the public schools have an obligation to educate as broadly as possible. Moreover, the issue of academic freedom for teachers to select the materials they deem most suitable is an important one. Of particular concern to many conservative religious groups are the books and materials that deal with alternative family lifestyles and sex and/or sex education, that contain realistic language, and that are written about ethnic minority groups. Indeed, some object to any materials that do not portray the ethnocentrically patriotic, small-town, middle-class, family-oriented values of Norman Rockwell.

Among the targets of self-styled censors have been such books as Mark Twain's *Huckleberry Finn* and John Steinbeck's *Of Mice and Men,* such curricula as Man—a Course of Study (a social studies curriculum developed by the National Science Foundation), biology texts that do not give equal space to "creation science," dictionaries containing words deemed offensive, and the holding of school Halloween parties, which are believed by some to encourage the worship of devils and witches. Further, many conservative groups object to any materials and practices that seem to them to represent "secular humanism," which they define as thought and action not based on a God-centered universe. Often referred to as a religion by conservative religious groups, secular humanism does not have a church, a set of rituals and practices, or a set of doctrines and dogma. Rather, humanism is a movement begun in the Renaissance that centers its intellectual attention on human beings and their affairs, including the many ways in which they engage in religious endeavors. Nevertheless, some determined religious groups believe that a "religion" called secular humanism exists and are committed to defeat it.

Clearly, those who claim to be part of a religious revival in the United States are currently in a strong position. It is difficult to argue that we, as a society, should not be concerned about crime, about the high rate of unwed parents, and about raising the next generation to be respectful of the traditions of this country. Indeed, many who do not profess affiliation with conservative religious groups are deeply concerned about those issues and many others. Furthermore, if the United States is to be a truly religiously pluralistic society, those who profess fundamentalist beliefs have every right to hold them and every right not to be discriminated against because of them. What seems to separate the religious right from more moderate citizens, however, is the belief—based on a strict interpretation of one book, the Bible—that they have the one and only, true, and virtuous answer and that it should be applied to everyone. It was this very problem, of course, that led the writers of the Constitution to stipulate that, while citizens of a free country should be allowed to practice whatever religious beliefs they espouse, the *government* (and, thus, the public schools) should not establish one particular religion as the religion of the state.

Ethical Issues

As mentioned earlier, it is important when considering religious issues related to classrooms that teachers understand their communities and not go too far beyond the values the community holds. While this may appear to be common sense, as well as carrying with it a certain degree of self-preservation, it also suggests the belief that *all* deeply held religious beliefs are worthy of respect.

Within the classroom, it is also important to be on the lookout for and to intercede in religious prejudice, particularly as it might be expressed in the kind of casual name-calling children do so easily. Like all other forms of prejudice, religious prejudice is learned and can be unlearned (though not easily). Respectful behavior toward others, however, can and should be insisted on.

Another ethical issue concerns teachers' responsibility to be familiar with federal and state laws with respect to religion and schooling. The classroom teacher often must serve in the role of instructor to parents and community members, as well as to students, and should be knowledgeable about the development of and debates about religious differences that are a part of the fabric of law and judicial decision in the United States.

With respect to relations with parents and the community, teachers should also be knowledgeable about the bases of various religious beliefs and should be as ready and willing as possible to answer questions and discuss objections calmly. There are times when consensus is not possible, and finding effective ways of agreeing to disagree is both useful and wise.

SOME REFLECTIVE QUESTIONS

In the opening case study, with the very best of intentions, Melissa Morgan found herself in the center of a controversy that could have turned into a major issue, both in her classroom and in her community. On reflection, it is likely that Melissa might have asked herself the following questions:

1. Having grown up in a town very much like the one in which she taught, and having taught in her school for five years, how is it that Melissa didn't think about what she knew to be a streak of deep-seated conservatism present in the community?
2. Once her students' project was underway, were there strategies she could have used that might have forestalled the objections voiced by some parents after they saw the exhibit at the open house?
3. As we saw in the case of the new kindergarten teacher in Chapter 6, acting as an agent of change can be a tricky business, particularly when the school in which one teaches is a very traditional one. Certainly, it is often easier to "go with the flow" of traditional school culture than to try to change it. It does not appear, however, that Melissa thought of herself as a change agent; rather, she was attempting only to use existing human and intellectual resources in a better way for the sake of her students. What are some of the factors that turn a seemingly innocent curricular activity into a potential source of protest?
4. Melissa attempted to resolve the issue by going to a number of community leaders. Are there dangers in this strategy? What might some of them be?
5. Melissa could have simply dismissed the objections raised to her use of religious information in the classroom as ignorant, unenlightened, or prejudiced behavior. How would that view have undermined her strong belief in religious pluralism?
6. When the episode was over, Melissa began to think about some of the long-standing practices of American schooling, such as the way most schools use Christian holidays—particularly Christmas and Easter—as sources for both curricular and extracurricular activities. Are such traditional practices fitting subjects for review and rethinking?

7. In her meeting with the clergy council, Melissa did not mention that, according to the most recent Supreme Court decisions, she was well within her rights to teach *about* religion in her classroom. Should she have raised that issue? Might there have been some negative results if she had?

Active Exercises

The following exercises from *Human Diversity in Action: Developing Multicultural Competencies for the Classroom*[49] may be adapted to explore the cultural elements of religion in one's life experience:

Activity 9: The Culture Learning Process, p. 45

Activity 10: How Culture Is Learned: The Socializing Agents, p. 58

Accessing the World Wide Web: Resources for Diversity

For more information on many of the world's organized religions, as well as on broad religious/spiritual ideas, see:

http://home.miningco.com/cultures   Click on name of religion or idea.

For more information on the common school-Catholic school controversy, see the History of American Education web site at:

http://sun1.iusb.edu/eduweb01/   Click on "Common School".

For information on, as well as the language of, the Court decision for any of the church-state decisions to which this chapter refers, try:

http://oyez.nwu.edu/cases   Type in the name of the decision.

For more information about the values and activities of conservative activists, try:

http://www.cc.org   The web site of the Christian Coalition.

To simply search the web for sites with information about or from religious groups, use a search engine by typing the term *religion* and seeing what you find.

References

1. First Amendment to the Constitution of the United States, 1791.
2. James K. Uphoff, "Religious Diversity and Education," in *Multicultural Education: Issues and Perspectives,* 2nd ed., ed. James A. Banks and Cherry A. McGee Banks (Boston: Allyn & Bacon, 1993), p. 95.
3. Ibid., p. 91.
4. J. M. Yinger, *The Scientific Study of Religion* (New York: Macmillan, 1970), p. 7.
5. Emile Durkheim, "The Social Foundations of Religion," in *Sociology of Religion,* ed. R. Robertson (Baltimore: Penguin Books, 1969), p. 46.
6. Peter L. Berger and Brigitte Berger, *Sociology: A Biographical Approach* (New York: Basic Books, 1972), pp. 348–352.
7. Adapted and extended from R. Stark and C. Y. Glock, "Dimensions of Religious Commitment," in *Sociology of Religion,* ed. R. Robertson (Baltimore: Penguin Books, 1969), p. 46; cited in Donna M. Gollnick and Philip C. Chinn, *Multicultural Education in a Pluralistic Society,* 3rd ed. (New York: Macmillan, 1990), p. 175.
8. Thomas Sowell, *Ethnic America: A History* (New York: Basic Books, 1980), p. 77.

9. Salman H. Al-Ani, "Muslims in America and Arab Americans," in Christine L. Bennett, *Comprehensive Multicultural Education: Theory and Practice,* 3rd ed. (Boston: Allyn & Bacon, 1995), p. 139.

10. Ibid., pp. 134–135.

11. Ibid., p. 135.

12. Ibid.

13. Ibid., p. 136.

14. Ibid.

15. Uphoff, op. cit., pp. 102–103.

16. Gollnick and Chinn, op. cit., p. 196.

17. Ibid., p. 346.

18. Ibid., p. 347.

19. Cited in Uphoff, op. cit., p. 95.

20. Uphoff, op. cit., p. 104.

21. Ibid.

22. Valerie Ooka Pang and Roberta H. Barba, "The Power of Culture: Building Culturally Affirming Instruction," in *Educating for Diversity: An Anthology of Multicultural Voices,* ed. Carl A. Grant (Boston: Allyn & Bacon, 1995), pp. 345–356.

23. R. Freeman Butts, *Public Education in the United States: From Revolution to Reform* (New York: Holt, Rinehart & Winston, 1978), p. 272.

24. Ibid.

25. Ibid.

26. Ibid.

27. Ibid.

28. Ibid., p. 275.

29. *Pierce v. Society of Sisters,* 268 U.S. 510 (1925), pp. 534–535. Cited in Butts, op. cit., p. 276.

30. *Wisconsin v. Yoder,* 406 U.S. 213 (1972).

31. See *Phi Delta Kappan* 72, 4 (December): 1990, with articles by L. Cuban, S. L. Kagan, N. L. Gage, L. Darling-Hammond, I. C. Rothberg, L. Mikulecky, and R. A. Hawley, all addressing national goals.

32. *Meyer v. Nebraska,* 262 U.W. 390 (1923).

33. *Minersville v. Gobitis,* 310 U.S. 586 (1940).

34. *West Virginia v. Barnett,* 319 U.S. 624 (1943).

35. Butts, op. cit., p. 279.

36. *Abington Township District School v. Schempp,* 374 U.S. 203 (1963).

37. Quoted in Uphoff, op. cit., p. 95.

38. Butts, op. cit., p. 286.

39. Ibid., p. 287.

40. *Cochran v. Louisiana State Board of Education,* 281 U.S. 370 (1930).

41. Butts, op. cit., p. 289.

42. *Everson v. Board of Education,* 330 U.S. 1 (1947).

43. "School Administrator," *Journal of the American Association of School Administrators* (April 1950): p. 2; cited in Butts, op. cit., p. 291.

44. *Zorach and Gluck v. Board of Education,* 343 U.S. 306 (1952).

45. W. Herberg, *Protestant-Catholic-Jew: An Essay in American Religious Sociology* (New York: Anchor Press, 1960), p. 56.

46. Gollnick and Chinn, op. cit., p. 193.

47. W. C. Roof and W. McKinney, "Denominational America and the New Religious Pluralism," *Annals of the American Academy of Political and Social Science* 480 (July 1985): 24–38; cited in Gollnick and Chinn, op. cit., p. 194.

48. Gollnick and Chinn, op. cit., p. 199.

49. Kenneth Cushner, *Human Diversity in Action: Developing Multicultural Competencies for the Classroom* (New York: McGraw-Hill, 1999).

ARTS

Enjoys and participates in art activities

Recognizes eight basic colors

Cuts on line

Uses glue sparingly

PHYSICAL SKILLS

Hops on one foot

Walks a balance beam

Catches and throws a ball

Kicks a rolling ball

Skips

Jumps rope

Climbs stairs using alternating feet

First Report Period

TEACHER'S COMMENTS

Teacher's Comments:

Your student is progressing nicely. He has a positive attitude and is a pleasure to have in my class.

CHAPTER 11

Assessing Progress:
The Importance of Social Class
and Social Status

CHAPTER OUTLINE

RATIONALE FOR A BROADENED DEFINITION
  OF ASSESSMENT
    The Case Against
      Standardized Testing
    The Case for Alternative Forms
      of Assessment
CHARACTERISTICS OF A CLASSROOM
  USING BOTH TRADITIONAL AND
  ALTERNATIVE ASSESSMENTS
    Pedagogies: Old and New
    Roles: Old and New
    Place of Content Knowledge: Old
      and New
    Assessment: Old and New
    The Importance of Criteria
    The Issue of Grading
    Case Analysis
PERSPECTIVES ON SOCIAL CLASS AND
  SOCIAL STATUS

Definitions of *Social Class*
Social Class and Minority
  Group Membership
The Working Poor
Social Class and
  Childrearing Practices
Social Status
The Importance of
  Teacher Expectations
PERSPECTIVES ON
  ALTERNATIVE ASSESSMENT
  Demand Versus Support
  Ethical Issues
SOME REFLECTIVE QUESTIONS
ACCESSING THE WORLD WIDE WEB:
  RESOURCES FOR DIVERSITY
REFERENCES

> **A**lice: *"Would you tell me, please, which way I ought to go from here?"*
> *The Cat: "That depends a good deal on where you want to get to."*
>
> **Lewis Carroll**

Redesigning the Jefferson Schools' Math Assessment
Program: A Case Study[1]

*It had been a busy semester, and Beth Bradley, chair of the Jefferson City
School District Mathematics Committee in Jefferson, Texas, was relaxing
and reflecting with some of her fellow teachers in the conference room at
the district office one particularly hectic Tuesday afternoon in late January.*

The day was gray and chilly outside, but students and staff from through-out the district were busy preparing for the first mid-year evaluation. This was to be like no other mid-year evaluation they had ever experienced in the school system. No longer were grades at the middle and high school so heavily dependent on final examinations, as had so often been the case at this time of the year. This was the first year the new evaluation plan was to be put into effect. Parents, teachers, and students would come together over three afternoons and evenings to review student work that was now in the process of being displayed throughout the three elementary schools and the newly combined middle and high school. It had not been an easy tran-sition, and there were still quite a few uncertainties as the evaluation days approached. And, while most were enthusiastic and optimistic that the transition would be made smoothly, this wasn't the case for everyone. Even after the two years of discussion and planning that had preceded this year, there were still some teachers who resisted the changes that had been decided on. Beth hoped they would come around after they saw the success of this year's activity.

Beth, a veteran junior high and then middle school math teacher who had been with the school district for fifteen years before taking over responsibility as chair of the Math Committee, was talking with John Pinto, a new student teacher in math, who was just beginning his student teaching experience at the high school. John was finishing a program at a nearby state university, where he would graduate with a master of arts in teaching. Prior to this, John had spent five years as a computer consultant with area businesses. He felt fortunate to have been so warmly welcomed at the high school and was especially excited about being with the math faculty as they were in the process of redesigning the whole math curricu-lum—including their practices in evaluation.

With them in the district office were two other math teachers, Mr. Goodwell, who was responsible for the math program at the elementary level, and Miss van Ryan, the math teacher at the high school who was to be John's cooperating teacher. Since all the mathematics teachers in the district were to have started using alternative means of assessment this year, Beth was relating to John how some of the changes had taken place, at least for her.

"Our decision to redesign the way we did math assessments was based on the National Council of Teachers of Mathematics Curriculum and Eval-uation Standards," began Beth. "When I first read them, I was impressed and excited about the depth and breadth of the changes they recommended. Before I started to think about making any changes in my classes, I took the time to do a thorough self-evaluation of my assessment practices. And was I surprised at what I discovered! First, I realized that one of the main rea-sons I gave most tests was to produce a score that could be entered into my grade book. But, while I may have had a score in my book, I really didn't know much about my students' learning or their abilities with respect to the content of the exams. Another thing that really stood out for me was that, as I thought about the way I constructed exams, I knew that I could accu-rately predict which of the students could answer which questions. And I

had to admit that my predictions were often based on—or at least consistent with—my knowledge of the students' socioeconomic status. Finally, it occurred to me that, unless I designed tests that provided opportunities for students who worked at different paces to demonstrate their abilities, I was not really testing learning, but speed instead."

311

CHAPTER 11
Assessing Progress:
The Importance of
Social Class and
Social Status

Beth recalled her first attempts to introduce alternative forms of assessment in her eighth grade general math class. "My goal was not to give separate, stand-alone tests but to assess student growth and understanding through the use of performance assessments, observations of students, interviews with students, and oral as well as written student reports. Nevertheless, old habits die hard. After administering and grading one early test, I realized that I really had received no new information from the results. You see, we should use tests primarily as diagnostic tools, and I had no "diagnosis" to offer. I somewhat hesitantly abandoned the testing approach in favor of having students assigned to groups or pairs, each having certain tasks to perform. Then, through coaching, observing, and interviewing students as they worked on these tasks, I began to be more aware of each student's work and more able to assess their knowledge and growth. This information was much more comprehensive and complete, and I was able to give students grades that more accurately reflected their progress. The students, too, seemed much more relaxed with this approach. Now that I have more experience with these methods, tests do not have to be the primary, or sometimes even necessary, means of assessment. Furthermore, I suspect that tests may even be an impediment to effective instruction, because they tend to reinforce what I already 'know' about my students—that is, who is likely to do well and who is not."

"How did you get started?" asked John. "I mean, textbooks don't seem to offer much more than they did years ago. Just what does it mean to provide students with performance-based assessment?"

"That's a good question, and it did take quite a bit of rethinking and reformulating at first," replied Beth. "I found that the first step in using performance tasks was to find or create some intrinsically useful and interesting activities and problems. A good initial source of these is, in fact, the textbook itself. Using these activities, you then have to consider how students might demonstrate their understanding of a given concept. They might use manipulatives, for instance. Having class presentations, constructing mathematical models, keeping journals, and producing bulletin boards are other ways students can demonstrate their understanding. You can also change the wording of textbook word problems so that they elicit further explanation. For example, instead of asking, How many are left? you can change the directions to read 'Explain how you would find out how many are left.' What's important is that students learn how to organize data, set up their own problem-solving strategies, identify their own mistakes, and demonstrate their own thinking as much as possible. This will require students to do things that many of them have not been asked to do before. It may be difficult at first, but you will be amazed at how fast they come around."

"There are many ways students can be asked to demonstrate their understanding of mathematical concepts," added Mr. Goodwell, entering *the conversation. "For instance, by using manipulatives, young children who are studying fractions can show how they would divide different items, such as five candy bars, ten pencils, or eleven comic books among 4 students. Instead of a traditional division test with twenty items, groups of students can be given different problems to solve. Groups can then be responsible for making posters that explain to others the methods they tried in solving their problem. Older students can be asked to find and demonstrate the value of pi by measuring diameters and circumferences, expressing the ratio, and finding decimal equivalents on the calculator. Students can be free to choose the way they explain and display their findings. When studying sampling techniques, students might be asked to estimate how many bicycles, or any other items, are within two miles of the school. A group can be asked to make a plan for investigating the question and to prepare an oral report, complete with graphs or other displays. They might also keep a log of their activities. Our major goal, you must remember, is to design ways that make it possible for students to demonstrate what they know, and the way in which they went about solving their problem. Students should be the active workers and decision makers. It is ultimately what we do in the real world on a daily basis, anyway. We balance our checkbooks; we decide which price is a better buy. We must learn to estimate expenses and live within a budget. Life doesn't test us with rows or columns of problems to solve. And, more often than not, the problems in real life are open-ended, with more than one correct answer. We should strive to integrate this in our work with young people as well—the understanding that there might be more than one solution to many problems. This not only provides the teacher with insight into the student's thinking, but it encourages the student to verbalize and share his or her strategies."*

"That's right," said Beth as she eagerly rejoined the conversation. "Teachers really must decide what is important for students to know and what skills are really essential. There are some surprises here as well. Many of our students do not go on to college, but the jobs they will find are increasingly skilled and technical and require rather sophisticated leadership and problem-solving capacities. We also have to get away from thinking that every bit of student work or activity must be evaluated or observed. You might start by assessing a single simple but important idea. For instance, over a period of several days, we might want to find out if students can paraphrase the problem they are working on, while teaching in our usual way the rest of the time. We might then observe whether students can formulate a plan. All the time, we keep notes or other records of our observations."

Miss van Ryan chimed in. "I had an interesting experience with my secondary classes. At the start of last year, I persuaded Mr. James, the principal, to replace my standard desks with tables that could seat four students. I was then forced to change my entire approach to teaching mathematics. Since last year, I've taught my students in a cooperative manner. I'm really thrilled with the results. I have never known students to be so involved with mathematics. I am convinced that their learning was more effective when they were allowed to work in groups, to discuss concepts, and to solve problems with their peers. Even the noise is productive—students actually talk about mathematics!"

"Of course," Miss van Ryan continued, "my assessment strategies had to change as well. I couldn't justify assessing group work only with written quizzes and unit tests, as I had always done. I added three techniques of assessment: by pairs, by observation, and by individual presentation to the whole group. Assessment by pairs of students is very effective. Students are randomly paired. I give each pair two copies of the quiz—one for a rough draft and one to turn in to me. Both students are awarded the same mark. They particularly like this approach, because it allows for collaboration and adds another dimension to the thought process—students feel responsible for each other's success."

"Assessing students by observation is also quite natural when teaching in a small group format. I assess students on their contribution to the group, their observed understanding of the concepts, and their ability to clarify and explain questions as they arise. I move freely among the groups and can easily identify students who are in need of extra help. And, because students are accustomed to talking with one another about math problems, they are not as shy about asking for help from me."

"Assessment by presentation allows students to demonstrate the solution to a problem I present on the overhead projector or chalkboard that comes from the work they are currently studying. Each group is responsible for making certain that all members understand and can explain the solution. I then randomly choose individual students to present their solution to the entire class in a clear and concise manner. The same mark, based on quality of presentation, clarity, creativity, and correctness of solution, is then awarded to each member of the presenter's group."

John was pretty surprised at what he was hearing and glad he had the opportunity to listen to others from the department. "What about the use of portfolios in math?" he asked. "I've heard quite a bit about them, but I've not had the opportunity to see them in use. Has anyone here been using portfolios?"

"We all have," replied Mr. Goodwell. "I began with my fifth grade math class's unit on ratio, proportion, and percents just this year. I told my students that the basic reason for the change was to encourage high-quality work. I was really challenged each day to think of different ways to present topics so that the portfolio would show variety. The textbook by itself certainly wouldn't, nor would any of my supplemental worksheets. Most of the activities and applications had to come from me. Quality was the criterion. Growth in thinking and understanding needed to be seen in assignments that involved applications in activity-based projects. Such assignments were not readily available and required considerable time and thought at first. It's gotten quite a bit easier as time has gone by and I have become more experienced. Needless to say, I found my teaching style had to change and found new excitement within my classroom. I looked forward to seeing how the various assignments would be received and to discovering what value they would have in promoting understanding. We became more like partners in learning—my students and I."

313

CHAPTER 11
Assessing Progress:
The Importance of
Social Class and
Social Status

"I did not abandon testing altogether, but I felt better about having something to back up my test scores," said Miss van Ryan. "The criteria for evaluating the portfolios were listed. A cover sheet was required that had a list of all the assignments given. Students had to indicate how many activities they had done out of the total assigned. They were to select four samples of their best work and to include them with two assignments I required. The work had to show variety and evidence of thought. They had to explain why they chose what they did. Students quickly went to work. They were allowed to make revisions and attach them to the original work. At first, students balked at having to tell why they chose a particular piece of work, but, in time, this seemed to smooth out. We took two days with this final activity, but the end result was quite rewarding and definitely worth the time. Parents will see the results of this when they come in for conferences."

"When it comes to grading, I use a holistic method. I sort portfolios into three main piles and then subdivide within those piles. I find myself basing my decisions on the kinds of assignments selected, and I tend to value those with writing rather than those with strict calculations. I also look at the quality of the assignments and value those that show more mathematical understanding over others. I feel very good about the whole process. And the students seem to like the portfolio process as well. They feel it allows them to 'mess up' a bit and not be penalized. They like being able to choose the quality of the work. A test is only one grade, and it may not always be the student's best effort. They feel that a combination of the two, tests and portfolio, is a good measure of what they have learned. The portfolio really is a culmination of everything I've been trying to do. It reflects a wide variety of assessments and assignments. It also forces me to use and acknowledge some of the principles of learning that are currently being uncovered by researchers. Students like being a part of something new and exciting as well."

"You know, we've studied quite a lot about diversity and education across cultures and socioeconomic groups in college," said John, "and there seems to be considerable diversity here in the Jefferson schools. Has this approach been beneficial to all the individuals from various backgrounds who are in this school?"

"It sure has, at least from my perspective," replied Beth. "We are a school with tremendous diversity, and we haven't always been good about addressing the particular needs or reaching some of our students, particularly those whose families are poor. Exciting and involving some of these students about school seemed to be difficult if not impossible at times. Now that we've begun to alter our assessment strategies, as well as our instructional approaches, a much greater percentage of students seem to be more actively involved in their learning more of the time. The more verbal student, for instance, is now encouraged to discuss and reflect more with open-ended questioning, and he or she has more opportunity to dialogue with others. Because we use more interviews and individual conferences, there is a greater opportunity for both teacher and student to get to know one another better, to develop trust, and to increase that essential sense of belonging among students. This, incidentally, also helps build confidence and self-esteem in students."

315

CHAPTER *11*
Assessing Progress:
The Importance of
Social Class and
Social Status

"With portfolios, students become an integral part of the system," Mr. Goodwell added. "Students are co-creators of what they are to be responsible for. No longer is it only the teacher who tells students what it is they are to know. Students help determine the direction of their learning, the means by which it is assessed, and the level of acceptability. It is also easier for students to see how their progress has evolved. They are no longer merely collecting a series of marks on papers and exams. They become part of the process of documenting growth over time."

"We also find that there is greater opportunity to communicate with parents," interjected Miss van Ryan. "First, our method of reporting student progress has had to change. We are now piloting a variety of checklists and descriptive reports to determine the most beneficial way to communicate student progress. It is also much easier to sit down at conferences and be specific with parents about their children's strengths and weaknesses when you have a collection of their actual work in front of you. It becomes much more meaningful than merely looking at numbers in a gradebook, which I'm now embarrassed to say that I've done in the past. It is easier to take a more individualized approach to my teaching and working with students now that we all are much more focused on their actual products. This also helps build the necessary bridges within the community between parents and the schools. We have started asking students to assess themselves and to become critical of their own progress, as well as of our work. This is somewhat difficult for many of the students to do well, but I'm pretty sure they will become better self-evaluators as time goes on."

"Are other teachers using alternative forms of assessment?" asked John. "Can they be used outside the traditional classroom?"

"Of course," replied Beth, "this is a districtwide effort. The same principles which we have applied in math are used across the curriculum. We are constantly seeking out ways that our students can demonstrate the skills they are learning. Why don't you spend some time during the evaluation period observing what others are doing. I think you'll find it quite interesting."

"And," Mr. Goodwell added, "our emphasis on performance assessment has forced us to ask the bigger questions; those dealing with our narrow approach and perspective that we have always found so comfortable and easy to adopt. We're all learning a tremendous amount about how our own culture, for instance, has conditioned us to see the world from one perspective and, thus, to judge others according to our own culture's standards. This means that we have had to develop more elaborative, comprehensive, and inclusive means to evaluate students across the board. We're beginning to rethink our whole policy on participation in many of the so-called extracurricular activities. Our goal really is full inclusion. We do want as many to participate in as much as possible. We think we can create a structure that will allow as many students who wish to participate in an activity to do so while striving toward quality and excellence. Maybe we won't build school spirit by having the region's best sports teams, but we'll build it by having more students who are active and involved in their school community. By looking at alternative forms of assessment, we have been *forced to concentrate on actual student behavior—and, in the process, encourage greater participation."*

At that moment, Dr. Gerard, the district superintendent passed by the office. "Hope you're looking forward to our upcoming evaluation activities," she said, as she put her head in the office. "I've never seen faculty so busy and excited. I think we're on the long overdue road to uniting the schools. Hope it all goes well."

RATIONALE FOR A BROADENED DEFINITION OF ASSESSMENT

While the task of assessing student progress has always been of central importance to educators, in the past decade or so there have been an increasing number of teachers, parents, administrators, and policymakers who have questioned the nature and outcomes of traditional evaluation practices, as well as the uses to which these are put. Particularly called into question is the primary use of standardized "objective" tests as an accurate and useful measure of student achievement.

Much of the current discussion about educational evaluation and testing is a contemporary version of an old debate, brought about most recently by the perceived failure of American students to compete academically with students in other industrialized nations. The debate, itself, however, has to do with arguments about the very purpose of schooling in a democratic society.

Theobald and Mills[2] frame the argument in terms of the ideas of psychologist Edward Thorndike and philosopher John Dewey at the turn of the twentieth century. Although thinking and writing at a time when science seemed to offer the clearest and most reliable way of understanding the world, the two men nevertheless applied it to schooling for democracy in very different ways.

Thorndike emphasized the precise methods of science, particularly the habits of the natural sciences that included breaking down problems into small pieces and applying careful measurement. For him, a democratic society was one in which excellence could rise to the top from whatever place in the society it emerged, and schooling was a way of finding the young people whose intelligence and ability merited their rise. At the same time, he conceived of the concept of intelligence as an individual and relatively unchanging characteristic of human beings that could be measured and that largely determined how far and in what directions an individual could go. Thus, the purpose of schooling was to take advantage of such "intelligence" as resided in students in ways that would promote individual achievement and allow the most meritorious to rise to the surface of leadership. Schooling, therefore, should be highly individualized, "breaking curriculum down to its lowest skills or conceptual elements, and then, through behavioral objectives, putting it back together."[3] Such an approach required the mass use of individual testing in order to see just how far students had come and to give criteria for the apportionment of rewards (usually advanced education, which led to the most prestigious and rewarding occupations).

Dewey, on the other hand, emphasized the experimental and social nature of science. He believed that a democratic society was one in which all people cooperated willingly in their own governance and that the purpose of schooling was to develop and encourage in all young people the kind of creative intelligence that would lead them as citizens to apply a wide variety of knowledge and skills to public and private problems. For this reason, his ideas about what counts as good education involved "cooperation, wholistic curriculum and instruction, and minimal individual assessment."[4]

317

CHAPTER 11
Assessing Progress:
The Importance of
Social Class and
Social Status

Into the contemporary context of public concern for educational accountability has once again come the debate over what counts as good education, how such education is demonstrated, and what consequences flow from demonstrated results—in short, a debate not only about curriculum but also about evaluation and the ways in which we assess student progress in schools.

Throughout the 1970s and early 1980s, the use of standardized tests increased across the United States in response to the minimum competency testing movement that swept the nation. Proponents of this movement argued that U.S. students, in comparison with students in other industrialized nations, were lacking basic skills, particularly in literacy and mathematics. Such insufficiency, they argued, was due to two factors. On the one hand, proponents argued that American education suffered from too much "child-centered" educational practice and the wide latitude of curriculum in U.S. schools that was commonplace. In addition, children from racial minority groups, poor children, and those for whom English was a second language routinely scored lower than white upper- and middle-class children on tests of basic skills. These combined factors only proved that U.S. schools were not doing their job with respect to basic knowledge.

Today the loudest calls for educational reform from business and government include an insistence on standardized testing as a way of measuring how well American schools are doing. Thus, in many states, standardized achievement tests at various grade levels are mandated, and there is continued discussion about the creation of national standardized achievement tests for schoolchildren. So popular is the appeal of an "objective" and standardized test as a way of measuring student achievement, and so strong is the belief that such tests actually do measure the knowledge that students have acquired, that standardized testing has come to be accepted as *the* measure by which many educators assess students' academic achievement.[5]

The Case Against Standardized Testing

Over the years, many concerned educators, as well as some well-informed politicians, have been raising questions and concerns over such issues as poor validity between the stated purpose of a given test and what it actually measures; the reliability and comparability of test scores; cultural bias in the design and use of tests; the often unethical or questionable use of test results; and the narrow approach and application of tests that, while providing relatively easy quantitative analysis, tend to measure out-of-context learning while downplaying actual student performance. Most standardized tests, for instance, don't truly tell us if a student can write a coherent sentence but, rather, indicate only if he or she can identify one. Further, there is little correlation between a student's ability to identify which word in a series of words is misspelled (which is easy to measure on a standardized test) and the individual's subsequent ability to spell correctly (which is really the preferred goal).[6] Performance-based assessment, on the other hand, requires that students demonstrate their ability to actually perform the skill.

While the goal of most responsible policymakers is to improve the outcomes of schooling by assuring that most students master some basic skills, the effect is often quite different. For example, in order to use multiple-choice standardized tests, complex academic and intellectual skills often must be broken down into discrete elements, which, although easy to measure, often tend to neglect both the context in which knowledge and skills can be used and the ability to connect one idea or skill with another. Teachers, on the other hand, often teach within a context that is familiar to their students but unknown to test makers. Thus, two results are common: (1) students don't recognize out-of-context questions and (2) students' thinking skills and ability to synthesize information or to solve problems is not ordinarily tested very well. In addition, because such areas of knowledge as art, drama, and music are difficult to assess in this manner, many schools have deemphasized these aspects of the curriculum. Educators, feeling pressure to "teach to the test," have often overemphasized the discrete, low-level elements while ignoring the more complex cognitive, affective, and behavioral skills and processes needed by individuals in a highly interrelated and rapidly changing society.

The Case for Alternative Forms of Assessment

The federal government has described performance standards as "concrete examples and explicit definitions of what students must know and be able to demonstrate, such that students are proficient in specific skills and knowledge."[7] Performance-based assessment, contrary to traditional standardized testing, tends to examine student performance on specified tasks that are deemed important in life.[8]

Three ideas are central to the argument underlying alternative assessment. First, students must leave school with more than low-level basic skills. They should be able to solve complex problems and integrate knowledge across disciplines, as well as have an appreciation for and knowledge of the arts. Alternative forms of assessment enable teachers to determine more accurately if, in fact, a student can actually perform the skills or behaviors that are expected of them.

Second, because the world in which students will live is becoming increasingly interdependent, young people must learn cooperation and collaboration. Thus, instruction and evaluation must become somewhat less individualistic, and students should be able to work with others in groups, both as leaders and as followers.

Third, greater accuracy in assessment across cultural groups must be achieved in order to understand more clearly just what students do know and can do, and to assist all students in developing their own potential to the highest level possible. Since the use of standardized tests (including IQ tests) has become so widespread, educational researchers have been investigating the reasons that some groups tend to perform less well than others. Theories to explain discrepancies between groups have tended to look for deficiencies in the people and not in the tests themselves. Thus, explanations for poor performance have included sociocultural and genetic deficiencies among particular groups of people. Critics of these theories point out that differences in test results do not represent deficiencies in the upbringing or in the genetic differences of certain groups of children. Rather, research suggests that many tests—IQ tests, for example—are inherently unreliable due to such factors as cultural bias or the fact that tests may not measure features of intelligence that are deemed essential among particular groups. Children, therefore may lack exposure to certain knowledge and experiences, which are the basis of the tests or the test administration. Tests, thus, are inconclusive with regard to the basic assumptions about intelligence and its inheritability.[9]

319

CHAPTER 11
Assessing Progress:
The Importance of
Social Class and
Social Status

Performance assessment is congruent with the practice of many groups. Prior to European contact in the Americas, for instance, nearly all native people used performance-based assessment to determine how each individual could best contribute to the survival of the group. As children grew up, adults observed their level of knowledge and skill in such tasks as hunting, running, consensus building, healing, and spiritual leadership. Children who demonstrated superior skills were the ones who later led hunting parties, provided spiritual guidance, and performed other necessary tasks. In what ways have you been evaluated by performace-based assessment as you were developing?

Today performance-based assessment is gaining wide acceptance as a legitimate way to evaluate learner success, as schools begin to question the use of standardized, norm-referenced tests, including achievement, ability, aptitude, and intelligence tests.

At the same time, proponents of alternative forms of assessment argue that teachers are most often the best judges of student performance, because they are aware of both the context in which students have learned and the individual variations in students' learning styles. Furthermore, they assert that, since standardized means of assessment, particularly simple multiple-choice tests, do not lend themselves well to analysis of these more complex behaviors and skills, teachers should develop the skills necessary to make informed and accurate judgments in a variety of contexts and across a variety of groups. These goals have prompted educators to look more closely at alternative forms of assessment and to develop more comprehensive approaches in the area of performance assessment.

CHARACTERISTICS OF A CLASSROOM USING BOTH TRADITIONAL AND ALTERNATIVE ASSESSMENTS

It is important that we distinguish between the processes of assessment and testing. When one is engaged in assessment, one is looking carefully at the whole individual within the educational process and context. *Assessment* implies a comprehensive, individualized evaluation of a person's strengths, as well as areas which are in need. It is formative; that is, it is an in-process act, in which the information derived is used as feedback to both teacher and students as to how and where one might begin to look if change is desired.

Testing, on the other hand, implies standardization, in which the individual is compared against a norm-referenced set of scores or a known group of individuals. Testing tends to be a summative activity. That is, the resultant scores represent a final statement of how an individual compares with others who have taken the same test. Too often, teachers neglect the ongoing nature of assessment and rely on a summative test to obtain a picture of how well a student has performed. Once this result is obtained, it is usually too late, at least in the standard classroom, to take corrective action.

Pedagogies: Old and New

Classrooms that actively use performance and alternative forms of assessment are typically classrooms where students are engaged in meaningful projects, multiple activities, and discussion with teachers about self- as well as teacher-evaluation. Rather than completing workbook page after workbook page, or endlessly doing repetitive exercises from a textbook, students may be seen working on open-ended projects that begin with focused problems and move into larger, more complex problems that demand a variety of skills. Such classrooms are characterized by a lack of standardized, objective-type tests. Rather than accumulating a series of test papers, a certain number of projects may be required each grading period—a certain percentage of which must be passed better than satisfactory. And there is a certain understanding that the entire community may also wish to have knowledge and access to student work. As a result, performance tasks and portfolios of student work often become the means by which students demonstrate mastery of content.

Roles: Old and New

In such classrooms, the use of portfolios allow students to become active contributors and responsible partners in documenting their learning. With a portfolio, each student puts together a folder, which may contain classwork, journals, and projects. At the end of a grading period, teachers and students work together to select the pieces that provide an honest picture of the work the student can accomplish and has accomplished. Portfolios developed early in the year enable students and teacher to see growth and changes that occur over time. Together they choose what is worth documenting—because the ideas are important, because the work is something the student is especially proud of, or because progress is easily visible. Based on the contents of the portfolio, students are given narrative reports, which detail the students' strengths, areas for improvement, development, special interests, and so forth. Parents may also become active in such an evaluation process by being encouraged to review the contents with their children and to call or write a response to the teacher. All the while, students reflect on what they have learned and what they desire to know in the future.

Place of Content Knowledge: Old and New

As in many, if not all, of the classroom case studies presented in previous chapters, content knowledge has a somewhat different place in classrooms using a variety of traditional and alternative assessments. First, much of the time in such classrooms, content is presented and acquired in the service of other activities. Thus, language arts content is necessary for the production of a newspaper, a report, or a story. Similarly, math content is necessary for building models, measuring water samples, and making maps. This attitude toward content information closely mirrors the way we acquire knowledge and skills outside of school; in general, we learn something because we need to know it in order to do something else.

It may be argued that, if the only information and skills we acquire are directly linked to what we need to know, we miss much that is both useful and beautiful. Schooling is, in part, an invitation to escape the boundaries of our current lives by discovering that which lies outside our experience. Such was the case, for example, in Chapter 10, when students were encouraged to build models of various types of places of worship and, in the process, discovered much about comparative religion that was "unnecessary" in their daily lives. It is up to teachers to provide the context and the environment in which students do learn to go beyond their present experience. Indeed, it is the very nature of a liberal education to provide students with new experiences of all kinds (including exposure to literature, music, and art) that will enrich their lives. The major difference here is that such knowledge is not taught only as an end in itself but also as a means toward other ends.

321

CHAPTER 11
Assessing Progress:
The Importance of
Social Class and
Social Status

Assessment: Old and New

As teachers have become more sophisticated in their understanding of the manner in which students learn and have paid particular attention to the variety of learning styles, they have recognized the relative inadequacy of a single approach to assessment. Some children who perform tasks quite well in real life demonstrate poor performance on paper-and-pencil tests, the result not of an inability to demonstrate the requisite skill but of an incongruency between their knowledge and the manner in which it is assessed.

Often, in classrooms that use alternative means of assessment, students and teachers together arrive at acceptable standards for good work. Assessment of such projects is not based on such terms as *neat* or *correct*. Rather, students are evaluated on their ability to solve problems, to demonstrate clearly how their thinking was done, or to collaborate well with others.

The time limits and criteria of acceptability are also generally broader. It is understood that some students may take more time than others to complete various projects; the standards, however, remain the same for all students. It is more important that students ultimately achieve the objectives—not that they achieve them by a certain deadline. In such classrooms, students might also keep working and submitting their work for suggestions and critiques, not only from the teacher, but from other students as well. Rather than considering a project or particular learning task completed at a particular date, as with a final test, students are encouraged to return to earlier work time and time again as they gain new knowledge.

Student work may also be used to teach others. Classroom folders may contain student work from previous years. Students can see others' thinking and realize that projects may have multiple solutions. Students may also be encouraged to, and evaluated on their ability to, find good help—in the form of primary source material or outside people. Parents and other community volunteers may take an active role in student work and in such things as after-school "homework halls," where cross-age tutoring is encouraged.

At the end of each semester, there may be a portfolio week, much like the old finals week, during which student work is displayed, as the faculty in the Jefferson schools were preparing for in the case study presented at the beginning of the chapter. The portfolio, in such circumstances, is the basis for a conference with the teacher or advisor. The subject of the conference focuses not only on the content of the portfolio but also on the student's future plans, any major learning tasks still to be addressed, and any changes in direction that might have occurred since the previous conference. Students ultimately take their work home and share it with another adult.

The Importance of Criteria

Determining the specific criteria for satisfactory performance may be the most difficult aspect of assessment.[10] One must step back and ask what it means to master a specific ability or skill. Just what would a student be able to do who has mastered certain skills?

For instance, a long-term goal of an American history class might be for students to demonstrate empathy for people in different periods in history. To demonstrate this, using the Civil War as a context, students might be asked to do such things as the following:

1. Write a diary as though they were the mother of two sons during the Civil War, one fighting for the South and one fighting for the North. Attach a statement about what you think was hardest for the mother.
2. Create a play about a family in the Civil War, where the action revolves around the decision to join the army. Attach a commentary about how the members of this family are like or unlike families you know.
3. Create a chart of the aspects of the Civil War that affected families. Compare them with the experiences of families during the Persian Gulf War.

Making judgments about the appropriateness of student responses is another issue. Some criteria that might be used in the analysis of student responses to the tasks about the Civil War include (1) the student accurately uses information from the historical period, (2) the student uses sufficient detail to create a sense of what it was like for people who lived at the time under study, (3) the student draws out relationships between that period of history and the present, and (4) the student uses affective language in dealing with the experiences of people—in history as well as today.

Finally, communicating achievement to students and parents is a critical issue. Teachers have always been faced with the difficulty of integrating a number of sources of student information into a single grade. However, today especially, with the emphasis on broadening the range and types of assessments, boiling down all the information into a single grade can be overwhelming, if not impossible, to do. Seeking alternative methods of reporting grades has also been an important task in recent years.

The Issue of Grading

While issues of assessment (how well students are doing) have long been a part of the educational landscape, grading (how well students are doing in relation to others) seems to be a relatively recent phenomenon. As far back as ancient Greece, assessment was used in a formative manner. Teachers questioned students orally so they could demonstrate what they knew, thus giving insight into the areas or topics that required more work or instruction. Grading and reporting were virtually unknown until the mid 1800s. Prior to that time, few students went beyond an elementary education. It wasn't until later, as school populations grew and the new ideas of scientific measurement gained popularity that the perceived need to grade children emerged. A brief history of grading can be seen in Table 11.1.

In any discussion of grading, especially if traditional grading methods are being called into question, it is good to consider the basis on which grades are

TABLE 11-1. History of American Grading

Mid to late 1800s

Progress evaluations begin to be issued by schools. Teachers simply record the skills students have mastered. Once students have completed the requirements of one level, they move on to the next.

Early 1900s

As the number of high school students increases, teachers begin introducing percentages as a way to certify students' accomplishments in specific subject areas. While written descriptions continue to be used in elementary schools, few question the gradual shift in emphasis at the high school.

1912

Starch and Elliott[11] publish a study that questions the use of percentages as a reliable measure of student achievement. Their study asks 142 teachers to grade two papers written for a first-year high school English class. Grading on a scale from 0 to 100, 15 percent give one paper a failing mark while 12 percent give the same paper a score of 90 or more. The other paper receives scores ranging from 50 to 97. While neatness, spelling, and punctuation influence the scoring of some of the teachers, others simply consider how well the paper communicates its message.

1913

In light of criticism that good writing is, by its very nature, subjective, Starch and Elliott[12] repeat their investigation, this time using geometry papers. Greater variation occurs with this assessment, with scores on one paper ranging from 28 to 95. Some teachers deducted points only for wrong answers, while others took neatness, form, and spelling into account.

1918

Teachers begin using grading scales with fewer and larger categories. One 3-point scale uses the categories of Excellent, Average, and Poor. Another scale has five categories: Excellent, Good, Average, Poor, and Failing, with corresponding letters of *A, B, C, D,* and *F.*

1930s

Grading on a curve increases as an attempt to minimize the subjectivity of grading. This method begins to group students according to an arbitrary scale, with top percentages receiving As, the next percentage receiving Bs, and so forth. Some even go as far as suggesting the proportion of grades be assigned as 6-22-44-22-6. Grading on a curve seems fair and equitable, especially in light of research at the time that innate intelligence approximates a normal probability curve. The debate over grading and reporting intensifies. Many schools abolish formal grades altogether and return to using verbal descriptions of student achievement. Some schools introduce pass-fail systems, distinguishing only between acceptable and failing work. Still other schools emphasize a mastery approach; once students demonstrate mastery of a skill or content, they are allowed to move on to other areas of study.

1958

Ellis Page[13] investigates how student learning is affected by grades and teachers' comments. In his classic study, seventy-four secondary teachers administer a test and assign a letter grade of *A, B, C, D,* or *F* to each paper. Scored papers are then randomly assigned to one of three groups. Papers in one group receive only the numerical score and a letter grade. The second group, in addition to the score and letter grade, receive the following comments: *A*—Excellent! *B*—Good Work. Keep at it. *C*—Perhaps try to still do better. *D*—Let's bring this up. *F*—Let's raise this grade! For the third group, in addition to the score and letter grade, teachers write individualized comments. Page looks closely at students' scores on the next test as a measure of the effect of the comments and grades. Results demonstrate that students in the second group achieve significantly higher scores than those who receive only a score and grade. The students who receive individualized comments do even better. Page concludes that grades can have a beneficial effect on student learning, but only when accompanied by specific or individualized comments from the teacher.

Source: H. Kirschenbaum, S. B. Simon, and R. W. Napier, *Wha-ja-get? The Grading Game in American Education* (New York: Hart, 1971); and T. R. Guskey, "Making the Grade: What Benefits Students?" *Educational Leadership* 52, 2 (October 1994): 14–20.

assigned in the first place. Kohn[14] suggests three levels of inquiry into questions regarding the assignment of grades that distinguish their depth of analysis and their willingness to question the basic assumptions about why grading is undertaken.

Level One considers the most superficial elements—primarily, how to grade students' work. The assumption at this level is that everything that students do must receive a grade and that, as a result, students should be concerned about the ones they ultimately will receive.

Level Two begins to question whether, in fact, traditional grading is really necessary or even useful for assessing student performance. Alternative or authentic means of assessment, when used for more than merely determining a letter grade, fall into this category. The basic idea is to provide a deeper description of students' achievement.

Level Three begins to move beyond the discussion of how to grade and begins to question why students are to be evaluated. Regardless of how we go about evaluating students, if our reasons for doing so are not valid, our results will not be constructive.

Sorting

One reason we evaluate students is to sort them into groups based, generally, on their performance. Level One questions ask if we are placing individuals in the "correct" group. A major problem here is that, at the secondary and university levels, too many are placed in the "excellent" category. Most studies, interestingly enough, suggest that there is no subsequent increase in student performance when teachers grade more stringently. Conversely, students do not do inferior work when it is relatively easy to get a good grade.

At Level Two, discussion centers around whether grades are reliable indicators with which to sort students. The subjectivity as well as the variability of grading suggest the rather questionable nature of much of our "objective" assessment.

Level Three concerns ask not if we may be sorting students poorly but why we are sorting them at all. What are our reasons in school for sorting students? Is it to segregate students and to teach them separately? Are we acting as inexpensive personnel screening services for business? Are we attempting to maintain a power structure built on an outdated foundation? Whatever the ultimate reasons, it is suggested that sorting is often incompatible with the goal of helping all students learn.[15]

Motivation

A second often-stated reason behind the giving of grades is to motivate students to work harder so they will, in turn, receive favorable evaluations. This use rests on the assumption that there exists a single entity, called motivation, that students have to a lesser or greater degree. What is often overlooked or not well understood, however, is the distinction between extrinsic and intrinsic motivation. That is, some motivation comes from outside the student (extrinsic), as in an attempt to avoid punishment or receive greater rewards; other motivation comes from within the student (intrinsic), as when learning occurs for its own sake. These two sources of motivation, unfortunately, often conflict with one another. That is, when people work for external rewards, they tend to lose interest in whatever they have to do to earn those rewards. Either obtaining the reward or avoiding a punishment becomes the principle motivator. Many studies, across age as well as culture, have found that, the more students are induced to think about their evaluation on an assignment, the less their desire to learn and the less they will do, especially in areas where creativity is the focus.[16] As Butler and Nissan[17] suggest, grades may actually encourage an emphasis on the quantitative aspects of learning, depress creativity, foster fear of failure, and result in a loss of interest on the part of the student.

325

CHAPTER *11*
Assessing Progress:
The Importance of
Social Class and
Social Status

Feedback

Some educators state that their purpose in evaluating students is to provide feedback, so that students can learn more effectively. From a Level Two perspective, this is a legitimate goal. Unfortunately, grades are not a good means to provide feedback. In most instances, students experience grades as rewards and punishment—not as information. For instance, reducing a paper to a *B+* or *D-* provides the student with little information about how the paper might be improved. A good Level Three question asks, Why do we want the student to improve?

Increasingly across the United States, such questions are being asked—and answered in surprising and interesting ways. When teachers and administrators begin to question seriously the form and function of traditional grades, the answers they come up with frequently alter traditional views.

Case Analysis

Now let's reflect on the case study presented at the beginning of the chapter. Performance assessment and authentic evaluation have been the buzzwords of the past few years when it comes to looking closely at the manner in which teachers gain knowledge about student achievement. Such efforts force educators, such as those in the Jefferson School District, to look well beyond simply testing students. When teachers look at the broader issue of assessment, they are encouraged to examine the purposes of education, clearly stating the specific skills they wish students to master while empowering themselves to take greater charge of their curriculum.[18] This process also brings into question the manner in which teachers tend to make judgments about students, as well as attempts to broaden that approach. Indeed, the testing of individuals in and of itself seems to be solely a Western concept associated with Western models of schooling.[19]

In addition, the desire to compete with others may also be a foreign concept for some cultures or groups. In other words, the whole concept of testing, in the formal sense that we use the word, may be relatively uncommon to some groups of people. Educators are also forced to look closely at the manner in which schools communicate achievement to both students and parents.

In the traditional sense, testing as we have known it draws our attention to whether or not students get the right answers. The ways in which students arrive at their answers, while perhaps important in the development of such tests, are typically not evident or even asked about at this stage. When students take a multiple-choice test—in math, for instance—there is no way a teacher can differentiate students who select the correct answer because they truly understand the problem from those who do not know where to begin but simply guess correctly. A key feature of performance assessment is that students demonstrate their knowledge or skill. The process by which they go about solving problems, therefore, becomes as critical as the final solution. Whereas a traditional test might ask students the steps involved in preparing a biological specimen to be viewed under a microscope, a more authentic assessment might ask students to demonstrate how to prepare a slide for use on a microscope. Instead of testing students' knowledge about the rules of grammar, students might be asked to edit a poorly written passage. Whereas a traditional technology test might ask students to identify the steps involved in programming a computer, a performance assessment would have students produce a program that runs well.

Another key element of all performance assessments is that students become active participants. Instead of choosing from preselected options, as is typical of multiple-choice or most other simple objective measures (e.g. true/false, matching), students become active learners, responsible for creating or constructing their responses. A wide range of assessment techniques are possible, some of which are summarized in Table 11.2.

Another issue that is central to alternative forms of assessment is the assumption that some students will take longer than others to arrive at mastery. The concern, however, is not that some students will take longer or need extra help to achieve the goals and objectives that have been set. The standards will remain the same for all students. What differs is how they are achieved. We must ask if it is more important for a student to "get the concept" by a certain date or that they "get it" at all. Underlying alternative forms of assessment is the notion that learning is developmental—that assessment is not final or summative but, rather, provides insight into where on the path one is at a particular time. Assessment, thus, plays a more important role as a formative tool, enabling all parties—teacher, student, and parents—to derive a sense of where a student is at a particular time, so that subsequent learning experiences can be developed that aid in student growth.

There are some important questions that must be asked before we even begin to determine the most appropriate form of test questions to use. In most cases in the past, teachers and schools have focused solely on the content they were teaching. The goals of a biology course, for instance, were often stated in terms of phyla of the plants and animals the students were expected to study. Emphasizing what it is we want students to know and be able to do forces us to look at the curriculum in much broader terms. We begin to ask what personal abilities and sensitivities we want students to develop. What behaviors and orientations should students exhibit toward the environment around them? What will they be able to do to demonstrate these abilities?

A related issue concerns our definition of *intelligence.* Standard classic definitions, from which the most commonly used intelligence tests are developed, tend to be narrow in scope, assuming that because something has a name it can easily be measured. The traditional use of the term *intelligence* tends to overemphasize convergent thinking in the areas of verbal and spatial reasoning. While IQ tests may be able to predict school success, it has not been easy to correlate school performance with most other abilities—except, perhaps, doing well on tests.[20] In other words, the generalizability of the concept of intelligence as commonly used in educational contexts has been brought into question. Little evidence exists, for instance, that the school aptitude results of college students correlate with their accomplishments later in life. This may be disheartening news for some educators but refreshing news for those looking to bring about change to a system in need of redesign to match changing world conditions.

TABLE 11-2. Some Examples of Performance Assessment Techniques

Projects

Projects are comprehensive demonstrations of skills or knowledge. They are often interdisciplinary in focus, require a broad range of competencies, and require student initiative and creativity. Teachers or trained judges score each project against standards that are known to all participants ahead of time. Projects can take the form of competitions between individual students or groups, or they may be collaborative projects that students work on over time. Students may be required to conduct a demonstration or give a live performance before a class. Science fair projects are a form of this type of assessment. Group projects enable a number of students to work together on a complex problem that requires planning, research, discussion, and group presentation. Such an approach helps develop and integrate students' skills of cooperative learning.

Interviews and Oral Presentations

Such approaches allow individuals to verbalize their knowledge. This is especially useful with young children, with students with learning disabilities, or with those relatively new to a second language. In such an approach, the interview is likely to elicit more information than open-ended written questions. Examples occur rather frequently in foreign language education, where fluency can only be determined by hearing an individual speak. The use of audio and video technology allows such an approach to be used more frequently.

Constructed-Response Questions

Such questions require students to produce their own responses rather than select from an array of predetermined responses (such as multiple-choice). Constructed-response items may have just one correct response or may be more open-ended, allowing for a range of possible answers. Examples include answering fill-in-the-blank items, writing a short answer, producing a graph or diagram, or writing out a proof for geometry.

Essays

This approach has long been used to assess a student's understanding of a subject through written description, analysis, explanation, or summary. Essays can demonstrate how well a student uses facts in context. Answering well-constructed essay questions may also allow a teacher to assess a student's ability to use higher-level cognitive processes, such as critical thinking, analysis, and synthesis. Essays may also be used to assess students' composition skills, such as spelling, grammar, and sentence structure.

Experiments

Experiments allow teachers to assess how well students understand various scientific concepts and can carry out scientific processes. Students are encouraged to "do" science by posing hypotheses, designing experiments to test their hypotheses, writing up their findings, and applying various scientific skills, facts, and concepts.

Demonstrations

Demonstrations allow students the opportunity to show their mastery of subject-area content and procedures. Students in biology class might demonstrate the production of a microscope slide. Students in a first-aid class might demonstrate skill in bandaging by working with a partner.

Portfolios

Portfolios are usually files or folders that contain collections of a student's work. They provide a broad portrait of an individual's performance over time. Students, if allowed to put together their own portfolio, gain skill in evaluating their own work. Portfolios are increasingly common in English and language arts, where drafts, revisions, works in progress, and final papers demonstrate student development.

Source: Lawrence M. Rudner, "Assessing Civics Education," *ERIC Digest Series* (1991), and *Testing in American Schools: Asking the Right Questions* (Office of Technology Assessment, Congress of the United States), cited in Lawrence M. Rudner and Carol Boston, "Performance Assessment," *The ERIC Review* 3, 1 (winter 1994): 3.

In many ways, one's cultural experiences (defined rather broadly) determine the kinds of abilities that are important and therefore learned, as well as the context and strategies in which they are expressed. Howard Gardner's theory of multiple intelligences[21] is useful to consider here in that it challenges our more traditional concepts of intelligence and suggests that there are multiple contexts in which individuals develop and demonstrate their skills. Gardner hypothesized there to be at least eight areas in which people can express competence—musical, linguistic, logical-mathematical, spatial, body-kinesthetic, interpersonal (social or "street-smarts"), naturalistic, and intrapersonal (showing great insight into self). Note that only three of these, linguistic, logical-mathematical, and spatial, are presently assessed by standard intelligence tests. All eight of these dimensions, it is proposed, are of importance in today's world. When applied to school, the main emphasis of Gardner's theory suggests that children may demonstrate the different kinds of intelligence in ways not necessarily associated with traditional subjects in school, and certainly not associated with traditional methods of assessment.

PERSPECTIVES ON SOCIAL CLASS AND SOCIAL STATUS

In previous chapters, we have suggested that differences in school achievement may be attributed to a variety of cultural influences. Two of those that have not yet been addressed are the cultural aspects of social class and social status.

Most Americans believe they live in a classless, egalitarian society. At the least, American ideology promotes the idea that, through proper attention, diligent effort (and some luck, which Americans also believe in), an individual may "rise above" his or her social class. Part of what has been called an "American religion,"[22] this faith in the reality of upward mobility may account for the relative lack of attention given to the concept of social class in much of the educational and psychological literature in the United States.[23] Certainly, it accounts for the difficulty encountered by sociology professors in helping young people understand the bases of class differences in this society. Nevertheless, as we all know, there are significant variations in economic standard of living, status of occupation, and extent of expectations for upward mobility among American citizens.

Definitions of Social Class

Social class has been defined in a number of ways, all of which refer to a hierarchical stratification, or "layering," of people in social groups, communities, and societies. Assignment to social class categories is one of a number of stratification systems that can be used to distinguish one individual or group from another in such a way as to assign worth. The urge to organize people in layers appears to be a human characteristic; it has been said that, whenever there are more than three people in a group, there will be stratification. Someone will be more respected, more powerful, or more "worthy" than the rest. While many Americans would identify class membership in terms of income,[24] it is important to understand that money alone does not determine one's social class. Rather, one's social class standing depends on a combination of prestige, power, influence, and income.[25]

Traditional class markers in the United States, thus, include family income, the prestige of one's father's occupation, prestige of one's neighborhood, the power one has to achieve one's ends in times of conflict, and the level of schooling achieved by the family head. Among other nations and cultures, markers of one's social class may include such determiners as bloodline and status of the family name, the caste into which one was born, the degree to which one engages in physical labor, and the amount of time one devotes to scholarly or leisurely activities of one's choosing.[26]

329

CHAPTER *11*
Assessing Progress:
The Importance of
Social Class and
Social Status

One reason that social class is so difficult to talk about and truly understand is that, while class distinctions are real and observable in concrete daily experience, they are also highly abstract. It is no accident that social class categories are often assigned by others (often sociologists), for social class in the real world is often in the eyes of the beholder. Nevertheless, for purposes of analysis, American society can be divided into five social classes.[27] At the top there is a very small upper class, or social elite, consisting of those who have generally inherited social privilege from others. Second is a larger upper middle class, whose members often are professionals, corporate managers, and leading scientists. This group usually has benefited from extensive higher education, and, while family history is not so important, manners, tastes, and patterns of behavior are.

The third (or middle) social class has been called the lower middle class.[28] Most members of this group are people employed in white-collar occupations earning middle incomes—small business owners, teachers, social workers, nurses, sales and clerical workers, bank tellers, and so forth. This is the largest of the social classes in the United States and encompasses a wide range of occupations and incomes. Central to the values of the lower middle class are a "desire to belong and be respectable. . . . Friendliness and openness are valued and attention is paid to 'keeping up appearances.' "[29]

Fourth in the hierarchy of social class is the working class, whose members are largely blue-collar (industrial wage earners) workers and employees in low-paid service occupations. Working-class families often have to struggle with poor job security, limited fringe benefits, longer hours of work, and more dangerous or "dirtier" work than those in the classes above them. It is not surprising, then, that members of the working class often feel more alienation from the social mainstream.

Finally, fifth in the hierarchy is the lower class—the so-called working poor and those who belong to what has been termed the "underclass," a designation that refers to people who have been in poverty for so long that they seem to be unable to take any advantage of mobility options and thus lie nearly outside the class system. Clearly, poverty is both the chief characteristic and the chief problem of this group. Webb and Sherman point out that this simple fact needs to be underscored:

> Being poor means, above all else, lacking money. This statement would be too obvious to mention were it not for the fact that most Americans see poverty in other terms. Middle-class conversations about the poor often depict them as lazy, promiscuous, and criminal. Misconceptions about the poor are so widespread that it is difficult to appreciate fully what life is like at the lowest stratum of society.[30]

Social Class and Minority Group Membership

Complicating the issues of social class is the fact that in the United States there is a large overlap between lower-middle-class, working-class, and lower-class membership and membership in minority groups. African Americans, Hispanics, and Native

Americans (including American Indians, Eskimos, and Hawaiians) are the most economically oppressed and depressed of all groups in the United States. The highest school dropout rates also occur among these groups. To the extent that social class status depends on income and occupation (and, therefore, usually prestige and power), women and children across racial, ethnic, and religious groups constitute a large proportion of the lower classes. This is, in part, a consequence of the descent into poverty that characterizes the lives of divorced women and their children. At the present time, nearly 25 percent of all American children under 6 are members of households trying to exist below the poverty line.[31]

The Working Poor

Members of the working poor—those who do work but in jobs that pay minimum wage or slightly above, with no benefits, and hardly any job security—must also struggle to make it in today's society. To reach a middle-class lifestyle, a family of four has to have an annual income of about $35,000. In many cases, in order to reach this level, both husband and wife must work. Only 25 percent of families reach this level if only one partner in the marriage earns an income. Thurow states that,

> although the dominant pattern today is a full-time male worker and a part-time female worker, the pattern is rapidly shifting toward a way of life in which both husband and wife work full time. . . . As an increasing number of families have two full-time workers, the households that do not will fall farther and farther behind economically.[32]

In commenting on the effect this reality has on women and children, Brislin adds,

> The people left behind in the movement through social class levels include households headed by women. . . . Dependence on one income, combined with the well-known fact of lower salaries earned by women, can result in poverty. Women and children constitute 77 percent of people living in poverty, and 50 percent of these poor people live in female-headed households with no husband present.[33]

Social Class and Childrearing Practices

Those who share similar socioeconomic status, whatever the level, also share similar cultural knowledge, attitudes, and values. These can be seen in various patterns of childrearing; various attitudes toward and expectations about dress, food, and shelter; and various beliefs about the necessity and value of schooling. Gordon suggests that the socioeconomic level to which a family belongs may be the strongest factor in determining differences among groups.[34] Of prime interest to us is the influence social class has on educational opportunity, behavior, and achievement in schools.

Brislin has reviewed a number of sources in this area that are useful.[35] Kohn, for example, argues that parents from different class backgrounds emphasize different values when raising their children.[36] Parents in the middle classes tend to emphasize intellectual curiosity, self-control, and consideration of others. This leads to adult characteristics of empathetic understanding and self-direction. Working-class parents, on the other hand, stress neatness, good manners (often involving quietness and invisibility when adults are present), and obedience.[37] These emphases lead to a concern with external standards, such as obedience to authority, acceptance of what other people think of as good manners, and difficulty in articulating one's wishes to

331

CHAPTER *11*
Assessing Progress:
The Importance of
Social Class and
Social Status

authority figures. The middle-class emphasis leads to adolescents and adults who are relatively comfortable with self-initiated behaviors and at ease when interacting with others outside their immediate family or friendship networks. Kohn suggests that the skills children of the middle classes learn prepare them to assume professional and managerial positions that demand intellectual curiosity and good social skills.[38] In addition, Argyle suggests that social skills, such as those learned by children of the middle classes, may be central to success in the professions, as they may take precedence over purely intellectual skills in many promotion and hiring decisions.[39]

In contrast, the skills working-class children learn lead them to take wage labor jobs that are closely supervised and demand physical effort. The implication is that these jobs are taken partly as a result of less emphasis on intellectual curiosity and partly as a result of parental concern for external standards and obedience to the standards and demands of a visible supervisor. However, jobs involving strictly physical labor have all but disappeared, a fact that only makes life for lower-class individuals that much more frustrating.

Lindgren and Suter suggest many reasons that students from middle-class backgrounds may do better in school than their working-class peers.[40] One difference can be attributed to perceived parental expectation. Students from working-class backgrounds think their parents expect less of them with regard to future school achievement, even when this is not the case. Parents who have attended college or have participated in other forms of postsecondary education are more likely to encourage their children to attend college than are parents who have not.

While family income may be a factor that discourages college attendance among the lower classes, the cultural context of schooling may also discourage many lower-income and inner-city children.[41] Success in school, for example, demands linguistic competence. Children from working-class backgrounds tend to have less exposure, less expertise, and less confidence with language skills. Working-class children may not understand the teacher's questions as well as middle-class children. Gullo found that 3- to 5-year-old working-class children have more difficulty answering various "wh" questions (who, when, where, and why, but not what) than do middle-class children.[42] Since a considerable amount of teacher-student interaction consists of questioning, it is conceivable that lower-class children may benefit less from lessons that use questioning.

Another view, however, is taken by Knapp and Shields,[43] who seriously question the efficacy of emphasizing the so-called deficits of "disadvantaged children." To do so, they assert, is to

> risk making inaccurate assessments of children's strengths and weaknesses . . . [to] have low expectations...and set standards that are not high enough to form the foundation for future academic success . . . [and, in] focusing on the deficits of students from disadvantaged backgrounds, . . . [to risk] overlooking their true capabilities. Finally, a focus on the poor preparation of disadvantaged children often distracts attention from how poorly prepared the school may be to serve these youngsters.[44]

While statistically there are significant differences in school performance of students from different class backgrounds, there are some students from working- and lower-class backgrounds who do quite well in school. Social class, by itself, may not be the best predictor of school success. Rather, the relation of school success to social class appears to be mediated by a number of other factors, not the least of which is the teacher's perception of what social class means.

Social Status

As we discussed in Chapter 3, the term *social status* refers to a hierarchical position determined not so much by one's wealth (or lack of it) but by the prestige, social esteem, and/or honor accorded one within one's own social milieu. It is quite possible, in fact, to have high social status without having commensurate money. Members of the clergy are good examples of this condition, as are, quite often, teachers. Conversely, it is also possible to have a great deal of money but occupy a low-status position, at least in terms of general community norms. One thinks, for example, of drug lords and of gang leaders.

In the social hierarchy of schools, individual students usually achieve high status because of roles they assume, such as star athlete, academic achiever, and cheerleading captain. Interestingly, the social status of a particular student often differs from the point of view of students and teachers. Thus, students may often accord athletes with high status, while teachers generally accord high status to students who achieve well academically. In neither case are economic considerations necessarily predominant.

All of which, of course, is not to say that social class and social status don't sometimes go hand in hand. To the extent, for example, that teachers believe that middle- and upper-middle-class students will achieve more than working- and lower-class students, such expectations are often reflected in reality.

The Importance of Teacher Expectations

Teacher expectations regarding the possibilities and potential of academic success for individual students are a critical factor in student achievement. *Teacher expectation* refers to the attributions that teachers make about the future behavior or academic achievement of their students, based on what they presently know about them. Teacher expectation effects are student outcomes that occur because of the actions taken by teachers in response to their own expectations.[45]

An important type of teacher expectation is the self-fulfilling prophesy. In this effect, a false belief leads to behavior that causes an expectation to become true. For instance, if false rumors begin to spread that the stock market is going to crash and millions of people rush to sell off their stock holdings, the market may, in fact, crash. The outcome, however, is not due to any event that was predicted accurately but because people responded to the false information that was rumored.

In the classroom setting, teachers may tell themselves about the potential for success or failure of the students in their charge. For instance, let's assume that a teacher looks at her roster for the upcoming year and sees that she will have in her classroom a particular student—Sandra, whose sister, Sally, was in the same classroom two years earlier. Let's assume that Sally had a difficult year. Not only did she struggle academically, but (perhaps as a result of academic failure) she also had behavioral problems. The teacher, vividly remembering her problems with Sally, may expect that Sandra will repeat the pattern. When Sandra walks into the classroom at the start of the year, the teacher may greet her in a cool manner, may be hesitant to approach her, and may even avoid personal contact with her as much as possible. Such behavior on the part of the teacher may alienate Sandra, may make her feel as if she doesn't belong, and may generate many feelings of anxiety and uncertainty. These feelings may, in turn, result in certain acting-out behaviors on Sandra's part. The teacher may have set the stage for a self-fulfilling prophesy.

333

CHAPTER 11
Assessing Progress:
The Importance of
Social Class and
Social Status

Just the opposite can also be true. For whatever reason, a teacher may believe a certain child will be a good student, when, in fact, he or she may be just about average. This belief may translate into certain actions by the teacher that demonstrate care and concern and an expectation of success to the student. The teacher may call on this student to read more than other students, may trust this student with certain responsibilities, and may afford greater attention and privilege to him or her, which may, in turn, result in increased gains in achievement. This outcome may not have happened if the teacher did not have high expectations for this student.

A tremendous amount of research has been undertaken over the past twenty-five years that looks at the effect of teacher expectations on student achievement.[46] Many teachers expect students of color as well as those from lower socioeconomic groups to perform less well on school-related tasks than their middle-class peers. When these expectations are upheld, the teacher's beliefs are reinforced, thus perpetuating an erroneous cycle.

It is a part of our folk wisdom that children tend to live up (or down) to the expectations that significant adults have for them. For some children, their teachers will be the only adults who may ever have high expectations for them. Clearly, to automatically disregard the possibility of achievement because of the color of a child's skin or the evidence of a child's economic situation is discrimination of the most insidious kind, because it is unspoken and largely invisible. It is perhaps not too much to say that the greatest gift a teacher can offer a child is not knowledge, skill development, or evaluation but, rather, a fundamental faith that the child can acquire knowledge, develop skills, and demonstrate ability.

PERSPECTIVES ON ALTERNATIVE ASSESSMENT

The belief that all children can and should learn is, in essence, at the heart of alternative assessment as an educational movement, and a number of scholars have looked at ways in which this philosophical position can be translated into classroom practice.

Demand Versus Support

Kohn[47] suggests there are classroom orientations that distinguish between what students "ought" to be able to do versus how we as educators can support students' development, thereby helping them learn. He calls these opposing approaches demand versus support.

In the demand model, students are perceived as workers who are obligated to "do a better job." Students who do not succeed are said to have "chosen" not to study or not to have "earned" a given grade. Under such an approach, responsibility is removed from the teacher, with attention being deflected away from the curriculum and the context under which learning is meant to occur. In reporting to parents, teachers state whether students did what they were supposed to do. Even programs that reportedly emphasize performance objectives often adopt such an approach under the guise of the common buzzword—*outcomes*. Unfortunately, in the context of the demand model, many working- and lower-class students appear to "choose" not to study and thus "earn" lower grades.

The support model, on the other hand, assumes that students are active contributors to the learning process, or, as Kohn puts it, the "adventure of ideas."[48] Under such an approach, the teacher has the major responsibility of guiding and stimulating all students' natural curiosity and desire to learn and explore the unfamiliar, to construct meaning in their world, and to develop the competence for using words, numbers, and ideas. Teaching and learning are child- or student-centered, in which the goal is helping students build on their desire to make sense of, and to become competent in, their world. Student evaluation is, in part, a way to determine how effective we have been as educators. We seek to measure improvement in students because it indicates, in part, that we have been successful in engaging students and in creating a context in which they become motivated. Assessment, then, is supportive.

Kohn[49] offers five principles of assessment that follow a supportive model.

1. **Assessment should not be overdone.** The United States seems to be a test-happy nation, and American young people are the most tested in the world. When students become preoccupied with how they are doing, they begin to lose interest in what they are doing. An excessive concern with performance can erode curiosity and, thus, reduce the quality of performance. Students excessively concerned with their performance may tend to avoid difficult tasks so they can avoid any negative evaluation.

2. **The best evidence we have of whether we are succeeding as educators is to observe the behavior of children.** Test scores tell us if students perform well only on that specific test. Most tests are not true indicators of one's subsequent ability to perform a specific task. When we observe children talking about a topic, seeking answers to their own questions, or reading on their own, we know that we have sparked their interest and that they will probably acquire related skills.

3. **Schools must be transformed into caring, safe communities.** Such characteristics are critical for helping students become good learners willing to take risks and to seek guidance and support. Only when there is no fear of humiliation or punitive judgment are children free to acknowledge their mistakes and take the guidance of others. When the environment stresses grades and standardized testing, or when teachers feel there is a certain amount of the curriculum that must be covered, pressures increase and learning diminishes.

4. **Any responsible discussion about assessment must attend to the quality of the curriculum.** The easy question to answer is whether the student has learned anything. The more difficult question is whether the student has been given something worth learning. Research has supported what good teachers already know. That is, when students have interesting things to do, artificial inducements to boost their achievement are not necessary. If the need to evaluate students has directed the design of the curriculum, you can be certain that students will not be actively engaged in their learning.

5. **Students must become part of the discussion in determining the criteria by which their work will be judged and then play a role in that judgment.** Such participation gives students greater control over their own education, makes evaluation feel less punitive, and provides an important learning experience in and of itself. If letter grades must be given, consideration should be given to the following. Refrain from giving a letter or number grade for individual assignments, even if you must give one at the end of the term. Numerous research studies support the use of comments instead of grades as more effective assess-

ment devices. Also, never grade students while they are in the process of learning something. Never grade on a curve, thus limiting the number of good grades available. If students master the work, let them know this by giving them the appropriate grade. Do not artificially limit the number of students who are said to do well.

335

CHAPTER 11
Assessing Progress:
The Importance of
Social Class and
Social Status

Ethical Issues

Regardless of the means of communicating performance to others, it is inherently a subjective process. Ornstein[50] has suggested that the more detailed the reporting method and the more analytic the process, the more likely that subjectivity will influence the results. Subjectivity, however, is not always a negative factor. After all, teachers who truly know their students understand their progress in far greater detail than any test might uncover.

It is when subjectivity turns into bias that we get into trouble. Teacher's perceptions, and subsequent expectations, can significantly influence their judgments of scholastic performance. Students with behavioral problems, for instance, often face the obstacle of their infractions overshadowing their performance. These effects are especially evident with boys. A student's handwriting, dress, family background, and so forth can influence a teacher's judgment.

The official labeling of children and the identification of cognitive difficulties happen chiefly in the elementary years. Public schools typically label children as mentally retarded when their measured IQ is below 79. Children with African American and Spanish surnames are more likely to score below 79 than are European Americans and, subsequently, are more likely to be placed in special education classes. Of the students placed in special education classes, only 19 percent ever get out—23 percent drop out of school, 46 percent are ultimately placed in other institutions or other programs, and 11 percent age-out of the system. African American and Spanish surnamed children are overlabeled as mentally retarded by public agencies; European Americans are underlabeled when compared with the general population. Such a situation suggests that we are using tools of analysis that favor some over others and actively discriminate against some groups. The special education literature is replete with evidence of individuals wrongfully identified as in need of special education services when all that was really at issue was their inability to communicate as expected in the English language at the time the exam was administered. How many have been cheated or wrongfully labeled as failures due to an inadequate means of assessment?

Standardized testing in its many forms often results in the use of labels that may not be accurate and comprehensive. Such labels may be limiting on the individual and difficult to shed. The unofficial labeling of students, usually in the form of teacher expectations with respect to social class attributes, can occur at any age. All that is required is a teacher who does not really know the child. Do we really want to use our power as teachers to prematurely limit one's growth and development or to make judgments that will be perceived by others as final statements of one's skills and abilities? What about the late bloomer? What about the individual who is penalized because her first language is not English? What about the child who has not had all the early advantages others may have had? Are we willing to say that these children cannot and will not succeed as well? As a teacher, you should provide the structure and opportunity for all to develop to their full potential—whenever they are ready.

Imagine, for a moment, that you are viewing the files of the following two students.[51] What kinds of judgments would you make about these children? What kind of academic program would you recommend? Would you expect them to fit into your regular class program? Would you suggest any special intervention, such as special classes for gifted or handicapped students? Would you recommend any extracurricular activities that would help develop special skills in these children?

Sam Edder did not begin speaking until he was 3 years old. He has always had trouble with school, often remaining withdrawn and unsociable. He was even removed from school at one time because of his emotional instability. Sam's test scores are well below average, except for his performance on creativity measures. In this area, he shows some potential. Other than reading intently and playing a musical instrument, Sam seems to have few interests and expresses little in the way of personal or vocational goals. Sam's parents are of European descent, with high school educations.

Bill Ridell has never spent much time in school. He started late because of an illness and was withdrawn several times due to continued sickness. Bill has been labeled "backward" by school officials. He has suffered from a variety of ailments and is going deaf. Although his creative performance shows some promise, Bill's IQ score is low (81), as are his scores on other achievement indices. However, Bill enjoys building things and mechanical pursuits, has good manual dexterity, and would like to be a scientist or railroad mechanic someday. Although Bill's mother is well educated, his father has no formal schooling and is unemployed.

What do you think? What judgments are you able to make about these two children, given the preceding descriptive information? As a teacher, what other information would you like to have? How might you go about working with these children?

This exercise can be used to check the accuracy of your attributions, as well as the assumptions you were making. The descriptions of Sam Edder and Bill Ridell are actually case studies of real people. Sam Edder's file is that of Albert Einstein, and Bill Ridell's is that of Thomas Edison. How quick were you to make faulty attributions about the potential for success of these students? How many other potential geniuses have been overlooked or have slipped through the cracks because of our narrow approaches to assessing and judging students?

Increasingly, teachers are searching for more effective ways to communicate performance to both students and parents. Many issues converge as we consider exactly what it is we wish to communicate to others. For one, as already discussed in Chapter 6, children develop at different rates. Determining specific outcomes that all students could be expected to learn by the end of a given school year is a difficult task. In addition, identifying which of these outcomes are the most critical to assess must also be decided on.

SOME REFLECTIVE QUESTIONS

1. Beth Bradley and her colleagues in the Jefferson Schools undertook a major change in the way they assessed students in mathematics, based on guidelines set by the National Council of Teachers of Mathematics. These guidelines, like those set by other subject area teacher associations, are often adopted by individual states as requirements for all teaching of that subject in the state. As a teacher, how might you become involved in the organizations that set these standards?

337

CHAPTER 11
Assessing Progress:
The Importance of
Social Class and
Social Status

2. Two years of planning went into the new assessment program discussed in the case study. Why do you think it took so long? What happens to teachers who continue to disagree with a proposed change?

3. One of the first things that Beth and her colleagues discovered was that using alternative forms of assessment required them to alter their instruction in significant ways. What does that finding imply about the relation between instruction and evaluation?

4. Beth recalls in the case study that even though she believed in the assessment changes that were to be adopted, she continued to test in the old way because "old habits die hard." What do you think might help teachers develop new habits? What characteristics of the school environment would facilitate change in teachers' behavior?

5. How might tests be an impediment to effective instruction (that is, instruction that results in student learning)?

6. A common criticism of alternative forms of assessment is that two teachers, using the same assessment procedures, might arrive at different evaluations of students' achievement. Assuming that this criticism has some validity, how might conditions be set so that variation in teachers' evaluation is minimized?

7. Alternative forms of assessment raise critical issues about the relation between project-based collaborative work in classrooms and standardized testing. Given the political climate of the United States at the present time, it is unlikely that standardized testing, at least on the state level, is going to be abandoned any time soon. Many teachers believe that the knowledge and skills acquired through new types of instruction and assessment will transfer easily to demonstration through standardized tests. Others are not so sure. What are the arguments on each side?

Accessing the World Wide Web: Resources for Diversity

For information on standardized testing, see the following:

http://www.ericae.net/   ERIC Clearinghouse on Assessment and Evaluation—search capacity, articles, fairness in testing, and a large number of other resources on assessment.

http://www.edweek.org/ew/vol-17/28chic.h17   Article by Lynn Olson from *Education Week* regarding overdependence on standardized test scores.

http://www.azstarnet.com/public/packages/iowatest/118-4380.htm   Article by Roderick Gary of the *Arizona Daily Star,* discussing the Iowa Test of Basic Skills and its use and misuse in the schools.

http://www.nsf.gov/sbe/srs/seind93/chap1/doc/1f193.htm   National Science Foundation article on assessment, the pros and cons of standardized testing, and new approaches to assessment, with many links to other sources.

For more information on alternative assessments, the following web sites may be useful:

http://www.ncrel.org/sdrs/areas/issues/methods/assment/as8lk30.htm   Links to articles on alternative assessment.

http://www.col-ed.org/smcnws/assessment.html   Links to articles and professional associations' activities related to alternative assessment.

http://kennedy.soc.surrey.ac.uk/qb/topics/soclass_level_1.htm A resource from the Centre for Applied Social Surveys by the UK Economic and Social Research Council.

http://www.eval.org/ American Evaluation Association; documents, other links.

References

1. This case study has been adapted from material found in J. K. Stenmark, *Mathematics Assessment: Myths, Models, Good Questions, and Practical Solutions* (Reston, VA: The National Council of Teachers of Mathematics, 1991).
2. Paul Theobald and Ed Mills, "Accountability and the Struggle over What Counts," *Phi Delta Kappan* 76, 6 (February 1995): 462–466.
3. Ibid.
4. Ibid., p. 462.
5. Ron Brandt, "A Fresh Focus for Curriculum," *Educational Leadership* 49, 8 (May 1992): 7.
6. Ibid.
7. PL 103-227 - Goals 2000: Educate America Act (Washington, DC: U.S. Government Printing Office, 1994), p. 129.
8. B. R. Worthen. "Critical Issues That Will Determine the Future of Alternative Assessment," *Phi Delta Kappan* 74 (1993): pp. 444–448.
9. A. M. Villegas, *Culturally Responsive Pedagogy for the 1990's and Beyond* (Trends and Issues Paper, No. 6) (Washington, DC: ERIC Clearinghouse on Teacher Education, 1996, ED 339 698).
10. M. E. Diez and C. J. Moon, "What Do We Want Students to Know?. . .and Other Important Questions," *Educational Leadership* 49, 8 (May 1992): pp. 38–41.
11. D. Starch and E. C. Elliott, "Reliability of the Grading of High School Work in English," *School Review* 20 (1912): pp. 442–457.
12. D. Starch and E. C. Elliott, "Reliability of the Grading of High School Work in Mathematics," *School Review* 21 (1913): 254–259.
13. E. B. Page, "Teacher Comments and Student Performance: A Seventy-Four Classroom Experiment in School Motivation," *Journal of Educational Psychology* 49 (1958): pp. 173–181.
14. Alfie Kohn, "Grading: The Issue Is Not How but Why," *Educational Leadership* 52, 2 (October 1994): p. 38.
15. Ibid.
16. Ibid.; see also R. Butler, "Task-Involving and Ego-Involving Properties of Evaluation," *Journal of Educational Psychology* 79 (1987): pp. 474–482; W. S. Grolnick and R. M. Ryan, "Autonomy in Children's Learning: An Experimental and Individual Difference Investigation," *Journal of Personality and Social Psychology* 52 (1987): pp. 890–898; and M. Kage, "The Effects of Evaluation on Intrinsic Motivation," paper presented at the meeting of the Association of Educational Psychology, Joetsu, Japan (1991).
17. R. Butler and M. Nissan, "Effects of No Feedback, Task-Related Comments, and Grades on Intrinsic Motivation and Performance," *Journal of Educational Psychology* 78 (1986): pp. 210–216.
18. M. Smith and M. Cohen, "A National Curriculum in the United States?" *Educational Leadership* 49, 1 (September 1991): pp. 74–81.
19. B. Nurcombe, *Children of the Dispossessed* (Honolulu: University Press of Hawaii, 1976).
20. Ibid.
21. Howard Gardner, *Frames of Mind: The Theory of Multiple Intelligences* (New York: Basic Books, 1983).

339

CHAPTER 11
Assessing Progress:
The Importance of
Social Class and
Social Status

22. Robert N. Bellah, "Civil Religion in America," in *American Society: Problems and Dilemmas,* ed. Alan Wells (Pacific Palisades, CA: Goodyear, 1976), pp. 351–368.

23. R. Brislin, "Increasing Awareness of Class, Ethnicity, Culture and Race," in *The G. Stanley Hall Lecture Series, Vol. 8,* ed. I. Cohen (Washington, DC: American Psychological Association, 1988), pp. 137–180.

24. Gilbert and Kahl, for example, suggest that in the United States individual or family income is the central variable from which other opportunities follow. For instance, income reflects the neighborhood in which one lives. This determines, to a great degree, the educational experience one has, in school and outside of it. The education one has then influences one's profession or occupation, which determines the prestige one obtains, and so forth. D. Gilbert and J. Kahl, *The American Class Structure: A New Synthesis* (Homewood, IL: Dorsey, 1982).

25. Rodman B. Webb and Robert R. Sherman, *Schooling and Society*, 2nd ed. (New York: Macmillan, 1989), pp. 397–398.

26. Brislin, op. cit., p. 144.

27. Webb and Sherman, op. cit., pp. 399–417.

28. Ibid., p. 405.

29. Ibid., p. 407.

30. Ibid., p. 412.

31. Nancy Gibbs, "Shameful Bequests to the Next Generation," *Time,* 8 October 1990, p. 43.

32. L. M. Thurow, "A Surge of Inequality," *Scientific American* 256, 3 (May 1987): pp. 30–37.

33. Brislin, op. cit., p. 146.

34. J. Gordon, *Assimilation in American Life* (New York: Oxford University Press, 1964).

35. Brislin, op. cit.

36. M. L. Kohn, *Class and Conformity*, 2nd ed. (Chicago: University of Chicago Press, 1977).

37. Gilbert and Kahl, op. cit.

38. M. L. Kohn, op. cit.

39. M. Argyle, "Interaction Skills and Social Competence," in *Psychological Problems: The Social Context,* ed. M. P. Feldman and J. Orford (New York: John Wiley & Sons, 1980).

40 H. C. Lindgren and W. N. Suter, *Educational Psychology in the Classroom*, 7th ed. (Monterey, CA: Brooks/Cole, 1985).

41. A. W. Boykin, "The Triple Quandary and the Schooling of African-American Children," in *The School Achievement of Minority Children: New Perspectives,* ed. V. Neisser (Hillsdale, NJ: Lawrence Erlbaum, 1986).

42 D. Gullo, "Social Class Differences in Preschool Children's Comprehension of Wh—Questions," *Child Development* 52, 2 (June 1981): 736–740.

43. Michael S. Knapp and Patrick M. Shields, "Reconceiving Academic Instruction for the Children of Poverty," *Phi Delta Kappan* 71, 10 (June 1990): pp. 753–758.

44. Ibid., p. 754.

45. Thomas Good and Jere Brophy, *Looking in Classrooms*, 4th ed. (New York: Harper & Row, 1987).

46. Ibid.

47. A. Kohn, op. cit., pp. 39–40.

48. Ibid., p. 40, citing J. G. Nichols and S. P. Hazzard, *Education as Adventure: Lessons from the Second Grade* (New York: Teachers College Press, 1993).

49. Ibid.

50. A. C. Ornstein, "Grading Practices and Policies: An Overview and Some Suggestion," *NASSP Bulletin* 78 (1994): pp. 55–64.

51. From a simulation developed by John Rader.

CHAPTER 12

Classrooms of Today and Tomorrow

CHAPTER OUTLINE

CREATION OF AN INCLUSIVE ENVIRONMENT
    Sociocultural Inclusion
    Curriculum Inclusion
      and Expansion
    Modification of Pedagogy
    Modification of
      Assessment Strategies

COMMUNITY AND THE SCHOOL
THE PROCESS OF CHANGE: FROM SELF
    TO OTHER
IN CONCLUSION
REFERENCES

Sometimes you change your world; sometimes you change your mind about your world.

Kenneth Cushner

In many ways, this book is about boundaries—boundaries that we impose on ourselves, that we impose on others, and that are imposed on all of us by factors often beyond our conscious or direct control. It is a book about physical boundaries of geography; about social boundaries of language, gender, race, ethnicity, and religion; and about political and economic boundaries of many kinds. However, and more important, it is also a book about breaking boundaries, building bridges, and finding commonality across differences.

In today's world, many old boundaries are fading away and new ones are emerging. In Germany, the Berlin Wall has disappeared. In the former Yugoslavia, in Eastern Europe, and in Russia, newly revived ethnic boundaries are reappearing. In the Middle East, political and religious boundaries shift and harden as all people struggle to ensure an identity for their grandchildren and great-grandchildren. Around the globe, the old antagonisms of political ideology that pitted East against West have given way to new antagonisms based on economics in which the countries in the South struggle to survive in the face of an inequitable distribution of resources weighted toward those in the North. And at home, even within our schools, boundaries seem to be hardening between ingroups and outgroups to such an extent that atrocities such as school shootings in Littleton, Colorado result.

As we have already suggested, social categories of various kinds do not arise arbitrarily. They help us understand the world we live in; they offer the comfort of familiarity; they allow us to proceed through our days without having to identify and

341

re-identify everything and everybody. Social categories help give meaning to our lives. They are also often responsible for sustaining hatreds among people, for enabling human beings to turn away from human suffering, and for encouraging war.

In the age we live in, old boundaries created by traditional definitions are becoming increasingly dysfunctional. We are well on the way to shedding many of our Second Wave characteristics as we evolve into a Third Wave society. In the face of new circumstances, it is necessary to rethink some of our old ideas and to find ways to cross the boundaries that separate people. Many people may not like this expectation. Indeed, many today are reacting to change by pulling back, by hardening their resolve to "keep things as they were." Note the resistance to talk of a "New World Order," the rise in membership of various hate groups, and the recent terrorist attacks within our own borders. It is quite likely that we will see much more of this kind of response in the years ahead; however, in the end, change will have its effect. Whether that effect is positive or negative is up to us. In large measure, teachers play a very important part in the process, because it is teachers who can exercise the power to engender new ideas and new ways of doing things in the children with whom they come into contact.

In this book, we have attempted to present a number of ideas that are helpful in leading us to remove, redefine, or bridge old definitions or theories that may stand in our way as we attempt to create educational environments that are more inclusive in terms of culture, gender, race, exceptionality, and the many other aspects of culture from which we derive our own sense of cultural identity and loyalty. Our goals, you will recall, were (1) to recognize social and cultural change, (2) to understand culture and the culture-learning process, (3) to improve intergroup and intragroup interactions, and (4) to transmit cross-cultural understandings and skills to students.

CREATION OF AN INCLUSIVE ENVIRONMENT

While we used the term *inclusive* in reference to its use in the field of special education, we use it here in a more global sense to refer to the process of creating a classroom and school environment that welcome the contributions of *all* its members. The raw material to achieve full inclusion, at least in terms of ideology, has existed in our nation since its inception. The United States is a democracy, truly one of the first experiments in such a process of government. The Declaration of Independence, signed on July 4, 1776, begins with these words:

> We hold these truths to be self-evident, that all men are created equal, that they are endowed by their Creator with certain unalienable Rights, that among these are Life, Liberty, and the pursuit of Happiness.—That to secure these rights, Governments are instituted among Men, deriving their just powers from the consent of the governed.

On September 17, 1787, eleven years after the Declaration of Independence laid the foundation for our nation, the Constitution was signed. This document outlines the structure of the American government and captures the basic principles on which the nation is to operate. The first ten amendments of the Constitution, known as the Bill of Rights, establish the basic rights to life, liberty, and property, which are to be available to all the citizens of the republic. Included are freedom of speech, of the press, and of religious practice; freedom to assemble and petition the government; freedom from unwarranted search and seizure; and the right to have a speedy and public trial by jury.

Our nation embodies these principles today as much as ever, and it is constantly faced with the awesome task of preparing a populace that is not only knowledgeable about these principles, but also able to put them into everyday practice. The American common school originated as a way of enabling young people to learn to participate in a democratic polity. Today, in addition to that polity having global implications, it seems that we must work to establish a new form of common school that works for all its members. In a sense, we must learn to establish an effective, dynamic, multicultural community.

We have repeatedly stressed that knowledge alone is rarely sufficient to bring about significant change in behavior. Educational philosopher John Dewey reflected this idea when he insisted that children learn through experience as well as through instruction. Jean Piaget has been known to utter the simple phrase "Teaching is not telling." The transmission of the democratic ideals of our nation, then, cannot be relegated to the mere giving of information. Students *must* have concrete experiences that enable them to develop the necessary skills and outlooks needed to fulfill the goals of our nation's charter.

The school and classroom provide a perfect environment in which to put into practice the very ideals and behavior we hope our students will one day express and exhibit as adults—those of participatory, reflective, and informed decision makers who act within their multicultural community, nation, and world. Educators must create an environment that enables individuals to act in such a manner that the ideals sought by our founders become second nature. The school, then, can be envisioned as a mini-society where appropriate classroom structure can emerge to ultimately create a climate conducive to democratic and inclusive practice. Establishing a democratic, learning community classroom and school community assures that all students participate, are recognized, and have a say in helping establish a structure that considers the needs of all its members.

Building an inclusive Third Wave environment, whether it be the learning community within the classroom or a sense of community from within and outside the school, requires a comprehensive approach. Basically, we are attempting to remove the barriers of access to knowledge, to the mainstream society and culture, and to one's own identity. In general, the schools that are successfully addressing this challenge are concerned with at least four areas: sociocultural inclusion, curriculum inclusion and expansion, modification of pedagogy, and modification of assessment strategies. We have addressed these areas in some detail in earlier chapters of the book. Here we provide a summary of key points.

Sociocultural Inclusion

The classroom that accepts and integrates various cultures, languages, abilities, and experiences helps its students begin to learn to negotiate life in a society characterized by multiple layers of identity and affiliation. This can be realized in many different ways and at numerous levels. In successful schools, the physical surroundings might be transformed in an attempt to make the school look less "institutional" and to reflect the various groups that are present. Hallway walls may include photographs of children, of families, and of the local community. The school, as in the wheat-growing society referred to at the beginning of the book, integrates the ideas, perspectives, and contributions of all and begins to look like a place where real people live and work together—people who can be identified, recognized, and admired as participants and role models. The family is woven into the fabric of the child's experience in school. Parents may become tutors, classroom aides, and decision makers in the school community. Such efforts go far in helping children see the ethnic (or other) makeup of adults as more congruent with those of their local community. Remember that, until a greater diversity of people enters the teaching force, most people who become teachers will be members of the dominant culture. Children may thus come into contact with few role models similar to themselves. We have a responsibility to establish greater opportunity for children to interact with people in a variety of roles and with a variety of backgrounds.

Equally important is a dialogue that can develop within a community and its schools, particularly with regard to negotiating between the purposes of the school and community expectations. Culturally appropriate means to introduce the community to the school are critical. The frequent complaints of Vietnamese immigrants, for instance, that the school does not value respect for age or authority and that children waste time in school without significant teacher-directed instruction suggest that distinctly different values exist. A variety of approaches are possible in this situation; however, one can be more "right" in a given context if care is taken in advance to think about the approach from the point of view of the listener. Prudence, as well as good sense and a simple interest in justice, for example, may suggest that specific learning styles inherent in the socialization of particular populations be accommodated at the outset. Later on, as has been demonstrated by various culture-specific programs in different parts of the country, individuals can be taught other styles, which then allows for successful entry into a greater society.

In addition, a sense of community can be developed within the ranks of teachers and administrators, as well as within the student population and between teachers and students. In successful schools, teachers share ideas, materials, and feedback. They perceive themselves as helpers to their colleagues. Parents are often included in school activities and learn ways of keeping their children's learning alive outside of the school day and during the summer months, when many gains made during the school year are lost. And teachers work to establish a sense of order in the school. For many children, life at home and in the neighborhood is chaotic and hazardous. In such circumstances, a relatively high degree of anxiety, ambiguity, and uncertainty may exist. In order for children to feel safe, secure, and loved, the school must strive to be an orderly, predictable environment.

Children, too, can work to create a sense of community within a school environment. Pairing younger and older children within a school, between schools, or even across district lines can go a long way toward helping individuals reach out and participate in the lives of those around them. Successful "reading buddy" programs that bring early readers and older students together over a continuous period of time help develop bonds such that children begin to look out for one another. All these efforts act to include individuals at various levels in the activities of the school, recognize and encourage various contributions, and enable diverse individuals to find their niche. Thus, a sense of belonging and personal identity develops, and a reduction in anxiety and ambiguity occurs.

Curriculum Inclusion and Expansion

Until recently, little attention was given to the more subtle messages conveyed by school curricula and classroom materials. Sensitivity to gender, ethnicity, and disability, among many other sources of diversity, were seldom thought to influence the learner. In reality, the exclusion of such factors harms all, the individual or group that has been excluded as well as the majority, which may develop an unrealistic perception of the world around them. We now know that, to build positive self-esteem for all children as well as a sense of inclusion or belonging, the educational materials presented to children must reflect the diversity of groups found in the society at large.

Materials also must be free of bias, or extreme ethnocentrism, where the tendency is to view or express an event from one firmly held point of view. Biases and stereotypes are especially powerful when people (1) deny that they exist; (2) ignore them or accept them when they occur; (3) deny that they affect their own as well as other's lives; and (4) support them, knowingly or not, through their own behaviors.[1] While subtle and often implicit, these behaviors may have significant impact upon the values and attitudes of teacher behavior and intentions. Various forms of bias may affect issues of gender[2] and culture alike, including: (1) exclusion or tokenism; (2) inequality or imbalance; and (3) isolation or segregation.

Exclusion suggests the elimination from or invisibility in curriculum materials. Many groups in society, including women and people of color, have historically been absent from most educational material; if they have been present, it has been in such a token manner as to be trivialized or perceived as having second-class status. The discoveries, inventions, and contributions of people of color or of women are often absent from the history books (some would suggest that is why the very word is *his*tory). Exclusion and tokenism are also apparent when persons with disabilities rarely appear in curriculum materials, or when the origins of ideas, concepts, or technology are not credited with its founders but merely assumed to be associated with the mainstream—such as the fact that the concept of zero was discovered by the Mayans. Consider the fact that the proportion of children's books portraying people of color even in the mid 1980s was only 1 percent.[3] This figure is now beginning to change.

Inequality, or *imbalance,* refers to the practice of representing only one side of an issue or event. When we learn of Martin Luther King, Jr., and not Rosa Parks in a study of the Civil Rights Movement, or when children learn about the colonization of the Americas without learning that the people who were already present had well-developed cultures and societies, we are not providing a balanced perspective on the issue. Too, when the origins of our democratic principles do not credit the Iroquois nation, we are not providing adequate balance and perspective.

Often, events are glamorized or sanitized and, as a result, present an unrealistic image. When children study the atrocities of the Holocaust but do not learn of the internment of Japanese Americans during World War II or when students do not learn that Thomas Jefferson, one of the authors of the Declaration of Independence, was himself a slave owner and fathered at least one child with a slave, they are not being presented with the reality of the times but, rather, with an image that can go far to create a false impression.

Isolation, or *segregation,* occurs when the history or concerns of a particular group are relegated to special sections in the textbook or special times of the year.

When February becomes the only time of the year when African American contributions are discussed, or when women's contributions to the development of the nation are presented only as a special chapter at the end of the book, their content is often overlooked, viewed as "extra credit," or simply passed over due to lack of time.

Attention to issues of diversity through curriculum transformation requires the teacher and/or school to look at issues of process as well as content. One must determine what knowledge, skills, and attitudes already exist, as well as those that must be developed. Teachers should strive to achieve multiple perspectives by emphasizing many different groups in many different ways, not just the experiences of one group. Certainly, in a pluralistic nation such as the United States, more than one kind of cultural content is valid and worth knowing. Beyond providing an expanded knowledge base, this also helps reduce people's tendency to form and use stereotypes in their thinking. As much as possible, a curriculum that addresses diversity should be interdisciplinary. That is, efforts to address issues of diversity should not be restricted to the social studies, language arts, or the performing arts. Attention to diversity in all areas, including mathematics, the sciences, and physical education, is necessary. Equally important is that, if the curriculum is to help students make broad connections, it must develop cognitive, affective, and behavioral skills. Especially in the areas of culture learning and in developing students' skills in making changes, significant active participation on the part of the student is necessary. As has been repeatedly stressed throughout this book, these areas are not achieved using only a cognitive approach. Finally, in efforts to bring people from different backgrounds into closer contact and, thus, to improve understanding while broadening one's experience base, local populations should be emphasized and used whenever possible. Individuals from the community who are able to share their lives, special knowledge, and talents, and thus help bring community members closer together, should be used.

Modification of Pedagogy

Successful teaching reflects both the living hand of cultural tradition, including culturally specific learning styles, and the particular social, linguistic, and cognitive requirements of the future in a rapidly changing post-industrial society. This suggests that it is necessary for teachers and other school personnel to meet the student wherever he or she is, to accommodate and adapt learning activities to the needs and abilities the student presents, and to work from that point toward assisting all to become better able to function effectively in diverse settings. Teaching from this perspective does not mean throwing out the knowledge and understanding necessary for success in the dominant society, however. Quite the reverse is true. As long as we live in a society in which individuals are punished economically, socially, and sometimes physically for their inability to participate in a dominant society, it is the teacher's responsibility to see that children acquire that knowledge and those skills. However—and this is a big "however"—it is not at all necessary to do so by negating, ignoring, and not taking advantage of the knowledge and skills children bring with them to school. Indeed, one could argue that the dominant society in the United States has not done well in terms of its relations with its fellow citizens and with its international co-citizenry. Clearly, members of the dominant society have a great deal to learn from those who live "other" lives. Viewed from this perspective, teaching and learning among diverse individuals are transactional experiences. As it is possible for people to function quite effectively in bilingual settings, so, too, can all individuals become increasingly bicultural, multicultural, or pluralistic. It is not in any sense a process of loss but, rather, a process of gain.

Modification of Assessment Strategies

Methods of student assessment that consider the complex interrelationships of race, class, ethnicity, religion, gender, and disability in students are also found to vary in effective schools. Assessment is used in determining student achievement vis-à-vis particular instructional objectives, in decisions on advancement from one grade level to another, in diagnosing individual student needs, and in gaining insight into the appropriateness of a given curriculum or instructional intervention. Test reliability studies have repeatedly indicated that considerable bias (cultural, gender, linguistic, experiential, etc.) may exist such that a given test administered to an individual may produce results that are significantly determined by factors other than actual achievement or ability. Based on such testing, students are often limited *a priori* from the variety of curricular and instructional choices available in a school. For example, students with inferior skills in the majority language who perform poorly on a given test early in their educational careers may have restricted subsequent educational experiences and, thus, may be prevented from access to knowledge that is potentially available.

Students and parents need accurate assessment of their work. Behavior described in terms of individual performance and development, often taking advantage of parent participation in the process, frequently provides a more accurate and sensitive measure of achievement than do paper-and-pencil tests. Assessment strategies that consider cultural and other differences provide students and parents with better indicators of actual student performance. Assessment strategies that measure individuals in terms of their achievement relative to a particular starting point provide a clearer picture of an individual's growth in a given area.

COMMUNITY AND THE SCHOOL

This book is also about building community, and perhaps a few words about this are necessary at this time. We use the term *community* in the context of the school to mean the "spirit" or "sense of community." In this sense, all individuals need to be 'in community' with one another. In such a context, diversity is central to our way of perceiving and acting—it is not seen as an obstacle that must be overcome. In a truly democratic community, all members' contributions are actively sought out and viewed as equally worthy of consideration. But creating a classroom community, as in creating any viable community, is not an easy task. Community growth and identification are evolutionary processes that, with concerted effort and constant guidance, emerge over time.

Peck described the qualities of a community, which are particularly relevant to multiculturalism, in the following manner:

> Community is integrative. It includes people of different sexes, ages, religions, cultures, viewpoints, life styles, and stages of development by integrating them into a

whole that is greater—better—than the sum of its parts. Integration is not a melting process; it does not result in a bland average. Rather, it has been compared to the creation of a salad in which the identity of the individual ingredients is preserved yet simultaneously transcended. Community does not solve the problem of pluralism by obliterating diversity. Instead it seeks out diversity, welcomes other points of view, embraces opposites, desires to see the other side of every issue. It is "wholistic." It integrates us human beings into a functioning mystical body.[4]

It was not too long ago that children, parents and teachers lived, worked, and interacted in relatively close proximity to one another. It was, thus, relatively easy and common to feel a true sense of community—parents could expect to run into teachers while doing their shopping, many parents and teachers shared common places of worship, and teachers had extended interaction and involvement with children as they grew and developed. Such a situation allowed for numerous models of good parent-teacher interaction and resulted in the community being a central, supportive component in a child's development. Today, in many instances, the situation is quite different. Many teachers, especially those who teach in urban areas, tend to live a good distance from the school in neighboring suburbs and, thus, leave the neighborhood soon after the school bell rings. The result is that the so-needed sense of community knowledge and experience is much more difficult to achieve. Teachers have a much more difficult time understanding the world in which their students live and are socialized, they struggle to build relationships with parents, and, thus, they cannot be as effective at reaching students as they might be.

Woodruff[5] suggests that the mostly untapped bridge between urban teachers and more desirable levels of student knowledge is the local community itself. And Banks[6] reminds us that the most effective schools are those in which the curriculum is rooted in the needs and experiences of the children served. The emphasis within the school, as such, should be as much about the child's life as it is about the curriculum and academics. As such, life in the school should reflect, to a large extent, life in the home and community, and classrooms should be organized in such a manner that children feel central and cared for. Teachers and staff should strive to reflect and value the child's community, belief systems, and culture, if school is to be seen as relevant in the eyes of the child.

Parents are often the key element in linking successful schools to students and community, yet one of the most difficult and unresolved issues for many urban schools has been the problem of how to involve minority and low-income parents in the education of their children. Irvine[7] found that parents who consistently participate in school activities and have frequent interactions with their child's teachers and principal are a key element in a school's success. Unfortunately, in many urban schools, these good parent-teacher interactions do not exist.[8]

As suggested in earlier chapters, a significant gap often exists between the culture of the school and that of the community and family. Many researchers have recognized that a key obstacle to establishing fruitful home-school relationships and academic focus among students is the misunderstanding that exists between these cultures.[9] In many situations, the interpersonal dimension in the urban community is at odds with that of the school, thus creating ongoing problems that are rooted in cultural dissonance. When there is agreement, this harmony, which extends between the school and the wider community, is critical for stimulating parental involvement and teacher effectiveness. James Comer, when discussing the evolution of a school-community development program, identified this dissonance when he said,

> We quickly discovered an extremely high degree of distrust, anger, and alienation between home and school—the two most important institutions in the developmental life of a child—that were only vaguely apparent and routinely misunderstood. School people viewed parents' poor participation . . . as indicative of a lack of concern. . . . Parents often viewed the staff as distant, rejecting, and sometimes even hostile toward them and their children.[10]

Maximizing parent and community involvement in the school has been the subject of much debate and considerable effort. Ladson-Billings[11] introduced the concept of culturally relevant pedagogy for teachers' use of students' lived experience and backgrounds as one way to link the students to the broader world of learning. In this view, academic development is seen as inextricably linked with psychosocial and emotional growth and development, and it is the teacher's responsibility to understand these dimensions and how they intersect. Culturally responsive pedagogy links the classroom curriculum to the learning styles and experiences of the students in a manner similar to Bell's[12] description of holistic learning. In Bell's description, sociopolitical, historic, and economic factors outside of the school are recognized as having impact in the classroom; the student's background, not that of the teacher, is the determinant of culturally responsive teaching; school language and communication patterns reflect the students' home and community language and communication structures; teacher effectiveness is dependent on both personal warmth and academic rigor; and the curriculum reflects students' lived experiences.

There are well-founded reasons related to academic success and cognitive development that support community or culturally relevant teaching, particularly in terms of language, communication, and the development of curriculum materials. A variety of cognitive processes that are important for school success, such as memory, comprehension, task focus, and attention to cues, have been enhanced in students of color by teachers who use culturally appropriate pedagogy.[13] Such research suggests that the cognitive demands required in problem-solving tasks are reduced when the tasks are introduced in ways that are familiar to the student's existing knowledge background. Linking instruction with contextual relevance enables teachers to add a personal dimension to their school and classroom and, thus, link more closely with students.

The sense of community is not static. That is, it is a process that must be constantly worked toward. Peck[14] contends that it is possible for community to happen on national and international levels. In fact, if we are ultimately to survive as a species, it must be toward this level that we all must strive. It is incumbent on us, then, to work at the classroom and school levels to establish such a state.

As we have mentioned before, schooling in the United States has two principle functions: to preserve the society and, at the same time, to change it. Historically, these two functions have been viewed as at odds with one another: either schooling preserves or alters the society, but it doesn't do both at the same time. In a society characterized by pluralism, it frequently appears that the primary role of schooling is to bind us together. Indeed, one of the fundamental notions at the heart of the common school movement was the provision of a common educational experience that would provide a kind of "glue" to hold the society together. This belief is a powerful factor in resisting attempts to alter schooling; there is a sense in which such alteration can be perceived to go against the preservation of our democratic experiment.

Apart from the degree to which transforming schooling is perceived to be a disservice to the nation, there are other difficulties inherent in the nature of the school as a social organization. Seymour Sarason is one of a few people who have attempted to look at the problems inherent in changing organizations, including the school.[15] In his work, Sarason has developed several propositions about changing organizations that are worth considering.

First, "real" or fundamental change, as opposed to cosmetic or surface change, requires a different way of thinking. This is extraordinarily difficult for people to do, particularly when they are caught up in day-to-day activities embedded in traditional ways of thinking and acting. Some evidence for this proposition can be found in the knowledge that schools seem always to be "changing": curriculum content changes; new activities take place; the things people talk about in terms of the school change. But life in schools goes on pretty much as it did before.

Second, altering thinking about schools requires the questioning of what Sarason calls "existing regularities," or structures that have become unquestioned "givens" in schools. And that requires that some alternative perspectives exist, for contrast, if for no other reason. In other words, people must be aware of other possibilities in order to seriously question what exists. The "regularities" of schooling are so much a part of our way of thinking about schools that it is hard to distance ourselves from them long enough to imagine them in different ways. Ask yourself, for example, the question that Sarason asked a number of school personnel: Why is it that math is taught every day? Sarason writes:

> The naive person might ask several questions: Would academic and intellectual development be adversely affected if the exposure was for four days a week instead of five? Or three instead of five? What would happen if the exposure began in the second or third grade? What if the exposure was in alternative years? Obviously, one can generate many more questions, each of which suggests an alternative to the existing programmatic regularity. From this universe of alternatives how does one justify the existing regularity?[16]

The responses—many of them emotional—that Sarason received to this question reveal a good deal about the difficulty inherent in thinking differently about that which already exists. The first response, he relates, was usually one of humor: the listener assumed he was making a joke and laughed. In order to keep the discussion going, he often set forth the view that no one, with the exception of those whose work entailed the use of mathematical concepts, used any but the simplest computation skills in life after school and, thus, the legitimacy of twelve years of mathematics every day was at least open to question. He then continues:

> And now the fur begins to fly. Among the more charitable accusations is the one that I am anti-intellectual. Among the least charitable reactions (for me) is simply an unwillingness to pursue the matter further. (On one occasion some individuals left the meeting in obvious disgust.) One can always count on some individuals asserting that mathematics "trains or disciplines the mind" and the more the better, much like Latin used to be justified as essential to the curriculum.[17]

Clearly, the consideration of alternatives to existing regularities is a profoundly difficult matter. Moreover, asking questions about existing structure often connotes to the listener a feeling of threat to the establishment and to the questioner a feeling of being alone and somehow weird. Neither of these feelings are conducive to an environment in which asking fundamental questions is encouraged.

A third problem, too often ignored by those who wish to see significant change, is that not all people in the school can be counted on to share that wish. As Sarason notes,

> there are those among the "change agents" whose ways of thinking are uncluttered by the possibility that others see the world differently than they do. In my experience, the number of these individuals is far exceeded by those, in and out of school systems, who know that their plans and intended changes will not be viewed with glee but who seem to assume that either by prayer, magic, sheer display of authority, or benevolence, the letter and the spirit of the changes will not be isolated from each other. Far more often than not, of course, letter and spirit are unrelated in practice if for no other reason than that in the thinking of planners the relation between means and ends was glossed over, if it was considered at all.[18]

All of this, of course, does not in any way mean that attempts to fundamentally alter schooling should not be made. It is to suggest that the processes of fundamental change are difficult, fraught with distractions and unconsidered problems, and probably will not occur in the lifetime of one set of transformers. What this means, in practical terms, is that one has to know that success will not be immediate, or even, perhaps, in the foreseeable future; nevertheless, one must act as if it were just around the corner.

A final difficulty that we wish to consider here (and there are, of course, more that we will not even discuss) is that those who wish to undertake new ways of thinking about and doing things in schools often are ignorant of the history of education and, thus, are simply unaware of possible alternatives that have already been conceived and attempted. This is one reason for the common belief that there is nothing new under the sun. This problem is not, of course, unique to educators who do a poor job of educating teachers in the history of their own profession. Most professions and skilled crafts today exist in a kind of modern time warp in which past and future are lost to one another. What this leads to, in part, is a kind of double bind: because we don't know much about our own history, we are inclined to think that what is has always been; at the same time, we are deprived of examples of potentially useful alternatives for thought and action. Thus, educators have been criticized for either moving too slowly or, worse, retaining models and strategies deemed effective in the past that fail to recognize the times in which we now live. The words of June Edwards echo the concerns of many before her:

> Today's secondary schools are designed as though students will face the same kind of life as their grandparents did. In previous generations, children were trained for industrial work. They learned to be punctual, obedient to authority, and tolerant of repetition, boredom, and discomfort, for such was the lot of factory workers. Judgment, decision-making ability, creativity, and independence were neither taught nor desired.
>
> Industries have changed in recent years, but schools have not. Students, herded by bells, are still for the most part expected to be obedient, dependent, and accepting of discomfort and boredom. Though some outstanding instructors encourage creativity and critical thinking, the majority of secondary classrooms are teacher-centered, focused on isolated facts, and constrained by standardized curricula and tests.[19]

Edwards follows this statement with a review of an educational model designed by Helen Parkhurst in 1921 known as the Dalton Plan, a model she suggests would serve our needs well today.[20] In examining this plan, think about the ways in which it required a way of thinking about schools that is significantly different from the way we currently approach schooling.

Under the Dalton Plan, the entire school day was restructured into subject labs whereby students determined their own schedules. Traditional classrooms were dismantled, bells were eliminated, schedules were dropped, and students were entrusted to have considerable say in the manner in which they carried out their day. Basically, the Dalton Plan was student-centered, self-paced, and individualized by means of monthly contracts. Teacher-designed contracts stressed academic learning as well as independent thinking and creativity. Homework was not assigned; however, students could complete work at home if desired. Movement from one grade to another was carried out when a student completed his or her contracts for a year's work, and, like college today, students graduated when they completed the requisite number of courses. Edwards suggests that this model is quite appropriate today, given the postindustrial, or Third Wave society in which we are living:

> As we move into the postindustrial age—with corporations splintering into mini-centers, with work being done on home computers at all hours of the day and night, and with diversity rather than standardization fast becoming the norm—the single-skilled employees who are punctual and can follow orders are no longer in great demand. Instead, the need is for employees who are self-disciplined, creative, capable of carrying out a variety of tasks, and able to work well alone or with others.[21]

The Dalton Plan could benefit students in many ways. Students might learn responsibility and self-discipline; might work slowly and learn thoroughly or quickly and advance rapidly if desired; might feel freer to take risks and fail without penalty; might actively be involved at all times; might work in a nonthreatening, noncompetitive environment; might be able to request individual help as needed; might develop and enjoy long-term relationships with peers and teachers; might be able to miss school for days if needed without falling behind; and might have the freedom to vary the hours they spend in school. Teachers might benefit by spending all their time on educational matters; having the opportunity to be friend and counselor, as well as teacher to students; working in a room free from disruptions; working with students who are interested, motivated, and self-reliant; and being able to specialize as well as working cooperatively with colleagues as needed. School districts, too, might benefit by reducing complex scheduling; being able to accommodate mid-year and other transient students more readily; enabling limited-English-proficient students to join English immersion groups as needed; more easily integrating students and first-year teachers to the professional ranks; and having the flexibility to reassess the organization of the school day to include early morning, evening, and holiday hours.

Notice that we have said that students, teachers, and school organizations *might* benefit from this kind of plan. The point is not that this is a model for imitation; the point is that it is an actual plan that was carried out at one time that seems to have some potential for today's school life. What is required, at this point, is questioning, discussion, and thought. Would such a plan really resolve some of the issues we face? How? What would be its constraints? What constraints would there be to adopting such a plan? Are there any portions of the plan that seem more applicable than others? Why?

Despite the obvious difficulties in instituting change in schools, numerous projects have been carried out around the United States, as well as in other countries of the world, to increase school effectiveness. Successful practices from the effective schools research are being applied in many inner-city school districts and are being explored by many state departments of education.

In some instances, significant school achievement gains have been recorded. In Milwaukee, Wisconsin, a school improvement effort known as Project RISE (Rising to Individual Scholastic Excellence) has demonstrated a continual improvement in test scores in reading and mathematics.[22] The School Development Program, a school empowerment model developed by James Comer designed to close the gap that often exists between students, parents, and schools, has demonstrated that positive school-community relationships can be established.[23] Similar results have been recorded in numerous schools that have applied various findings from the effective schools movement.

However, while successful projects can be identified, there exists a corresponding number of projects in which implementation has not resulted in improvement. Kritek suggests what we might expect, that perhaps a distinct culture is at work in schools that are moving toward effectiveness.[24] In more successful schools, for instance, staff appear to have accepted responsibility for school improvement and are active in the pursuit of excellence.[25]

While we have been suggesting all along that significant change must occur with the individual teacher in the classroom, we are not naive to the fact that a teacher's responsibilities, especially the new teacher's, are such that it will be extremely difficult to attend to behavioral and curriculum modification in the task of day-to-day teaching. Such change takes time. It also takes an awareness of the processes by which change occurs on an individual basis.

THE PROCESS OF CHANGE: FROM SELF TO OTHER

Combs identified the importance of recognizing and involving the individual's beliefs and patterns of behavior when considering the change process. He stated:

> [Changing] must concern itself with the inner life. Simple exposure to subject matter (or new information or ways of doing things) is not enough. The maturation of an effective professional worker requires changes . . . in perceptions—his feelings, attitudes, and beliefs and his understanding of himself and his world. This is no easy matter, for what lies inside the individual is not open to direct manipulation and control. It is unlikely to change except with the active involvement of the . . . [person] in the process.[26]

We have repeatedly identified the slow nature of change. Change cannot occur on a large scale until the individuals involved are able to alter their perceptions and see themselves as active participants in the process. Change is also facilitated when it is a welcome and sought-after process. We have looked closely at the adjustment process and have recognized that there will be predictable stages that individuals pass through as they internalize any new situation. People must also perceive themselves from a new perspective in order to fully internalize and actualize their new situation. Only then can one become a role model for change. Again, we stress that this change cannot come about simply as a result of new information. Active participation in efforts designed to bring about significant change are required for the individual.

Teachers, like all people, experience a myriad of obstacles and emotional reactions when they confront change. Seven levels of concern that teachers confront as they face any innovation have been identified in the literature:

- *Level 0—Awareness.* Although the teacher may be aware of the problem, the teacher has little concern about or involvement in the innovation.
- *Level 1—Informational.* The individual has some general awareness of the possible change and is beginning to show some interest in learning more.
- *Level 2—Personal.* The individual is beginning to question his or her own adequacy, as well as the demands that will be required to make the intended change.
- *Level 3—Management.* The individual is focusing on the details of seeing the change through and is beginning to identify the various tasks required to make the change happen.
- *Level 4—Consequence.* The teacher is focusing on the potential impact the innovation will have on the students in his or her immediate sphere of influence.
- *Level 5—Collaboration.* The teacher is beginning to think beyond him- or herself by cooperating with others in carrying out the innovation.
- *Level 6—Refocusing.* The individual is focusing on universal benefits of the innovation and what alternatives or modifications may be in order.[27]

Restructuring schools in such a manner that they become more inclusive and that individuals become empowered toward equity and excellence on all fronts does, however, require individual teachers to become mavericks, so to speak. This idea may go against the typical image people have of teachers. Teaching tends to be a rather conservative activity, with most teachers acting to maintain the status quo. In fact, some innovative teachers may rightly perceive themselves to be punished by the system in which they work when it comes to taking a stand and encouraging change. However, change must occur if schools and society are to become more equitable and inclusive.

Cherrie Banks identifies five responsibilities of the potential leader when it comes to implementing change toward diversity in an educational context.[28] These five tasks include challenging the process, inspiring a shared vision, enabling others to act, modeling the way, and encouraging the heart. *Challenging the process* is an active effort initiated by the individual who wants change. The individual at this time must be a risk taker and must be willing to confront the status quo. Such an individual must be willing to experiment, to make mistakes, and to remain aware of new ideas. *Inspiring a shared vision* refers to the individual recognition of the need, and the potential, for change. A major responsibility is to voice such issues and to enlist the assistance of others. Strong interpersonal and communication skills are required in order to reach out and affect others. Teachers, for instance, must strive to communicate that everyone can learn, improve, and meet with success. *Enabling others to act* recognizes the difficulty one will have encouraging and making change by oneself. Collaboration must be fostered and have the effect of enlisting other's assistance and efforts. In doing so, one must make every effort to strengthen others, so that they perceive themselves to benefit by the effort as well. A collective orientation, or identification as "we," should be a goal. *Modeling the way* requires that the teacher set an example. The individual should plan small, in order to demonstrate successes rather than failures. The teacher's actions alone will do much to demonstrate his or her commitment and concern, as well as show others what is possible. *Encouraging the heart* asks that the individual recognize the contributions of others and that he or she celebrate accomplishments. Teaching for diversity is an ongoing process that must be continuously addressed.

IN CONCLUSION

Throughout this book, we focused on ways to better prepare today's teachers to achieve their goals of delivering an effective education to diverse students who are living in a complex, interdependent world. The approach we chose began by recognizing the kinds of experiences many, but not all, individuals who become teachers bring with them. It is through the classroom teacher, in concert with their peers and community, that effective education can occur. For the most part, today's teacher education students are from the majority culture and have limited experience with people of different backgrounds. For that reason, they must attend to such issues as people's emotional responses and other kinds of experiences when they encounter diversity. Understanding the socialization process in terms of cultural development and the obstacles to culture learning helps teachers gain insight into the reasons for typical responses and facilitates the processes necessary to transcend one's conditioning. Understanding how such processes as communication and learning style impact on interaction and learning is also critical to effective teaching. We then looked at how society and education have responded to cultural diversity in a variety of contexts. Each of the diversities addressed in this book mediate one another and do not act in isolation, which further complicates our task but is nonetheless critical to the understanding of classroom interaction.

Our nation has been seriously addressing issues related to diversity only relatively recently. In only a few decades, development in related fields has tended to move from that of totally ignoring diversity in the hopes of complete assimilation to that of encouraging and recognizing the value of pluralism in a diverse democratic society. Schools, as well as individuals, who have been successful at addressing such issues *have been working on them for a long time.* Innovations in individual perspective and behavior, as well as in curriculum and instructional modification, do not come quickly and cannot show immediate results. Such efforts require a long-range commitment by many actors—teachers, administrators, students, parents, community, and material developers—before any of the hoped for changes can be realized. Removing the various barriers and modifying conditioned behavior takes time. We must be willing to act and work accordingly over the long haul; that is, we must take the time necessary to realize such changes and not be discouraged in the short run. Successes must be measured in inches, rather than miles, and must be perceived by all as being developmental, or evolutionary, not revolutionary. As such, efforts must begin in the early stages of education, both for children and adults, and must continue throughout. Such efforts are not ones that can be effectively addressed in one short course, class, or for a short period of time. Continuous efforts must be made at many different levels in the educational process. We hope for you that this is just one step on a personal and professional path of continual growth, development, and interaction.

References

1. E. W. King, M. Chipman, and M. Cruz-Janzen, *Educating Young Children in a Diverse Society* (Boston: Allyn & Bacon, 1994); and David Sadker and Myra Sadker, *Handbook on Sex Equity for Schools* (New York: Longman, 1982).

2. Sadker, op. cit.

3. K. M. Reimer, "Multiethnic Literature: Holding Fast to the Dream," *Language Arts* 69, (1992): 14–21.

4. M. S. Peck, *The Different Drum: Community Making and Peace* (New York: Simon & Schuster, 1987).

5. D. W. Woodruff, "Keeping It Real: The Importance of Community in Multicultural Education and School Success," *Theory into Practice* 35, 4 (1996): 234–235.

6. J. Banks, *An Introduction to Multicultural Education* (Needham Heights, MA: Allyn & Bacon, 1994).

7. J. J. Irvine, *Black Students and School Failure* (New York: Praeger, 1991).

8. Woodruff, op. cit.

9. B. A. Allen and A. W. Boykin, "African-American Children and the Educational Process: Alleviating Cultural Discontinuity Through Prescriptive Pedagogy," *School Psychology Review* 21, 4 (1992): 586–596; see also C. Ascher, "Improving the School-Home Connection for Poor and Minority Urban Students," *The Urban Review* 20, 2 (1988): 109–123; and S. Forham and J. Ogbu. "Black Students' School Success: Coping with the Burden of 'Acting White.'" *The Urban Review* 18 (1986): 176–206.

10. J. Comer, "Parent Participation: Fad or Function:" *Educational Horizons* 69, 4 (1991): 185.

11. G. Ladson-Billings, "Culturally-Relevant Teaching: Effective Instruction for Black Students," *The College Board Review* 155 (1990): 20–25.

12. Y. R. Bell, "A Culturally-Sensitive Analysis of Black Learning Style," *Journal of Black Psychology* 20, 1 (1994): 47–61.

13. C. L. Lopez and H. J. Sullivan, "Effect of Personalization of Instructional Context on the Achievement and Attitudes of Hispanic Teachers," *Education, Technology, and Research* 40, 4 (1992): 5–13.

14. Peck, op. cit.

15. Seymour B. Sarason, *The Culture of the School and the Problem of Change* (Boston: Allyn & Bacon, 1971).

16. Ibid., p. 69.

17. Ibid., p. 70.

18. Ibid., pp. 8–9.

19. J. Edwards, "To Teach Responsibility, Bring Back the Dalton Plan," *Phi Delta Kappan* 72, 5 (January 1991): 399.

20. Ibid.

21. Ibid., p. 400.

22. W. J. Kriteck, "School Culture and School Improvement," paper presented at the 67th annual meeting of the American Educational Research Association, San Francisco, CA, April 1986.

23. Woodruff, op. cit.

24. Kriteck, op. cit.

25. D. U. Levine, "Creating Effective Schools: Findings and Implications from Research and Practice," *Phi Delta Kappan* 72, 5 (January 1990): 389–393.

26. A. W. Combs, *The Professional Education of Teachers* (Boston: Allyn & Bacon, 1965), p. 14.
27. G. E. Hall, A. C. Wallace, and W. A. Dossett, *A Developmental Conceptualization of the Adoption Process Within Education Institutions* (Austin: Texas Research and Development Center for Teacher Education, University of Texas, 1973).
28. Cherrie Banks, remarks made in presentation at the National Council for the Social Studies Annual Convention, Anaheim, CA, November 1989.

Photo Credits

Chapter Opener 1 : PhotoDisc/Education   Vol. 24

Chapter Opener 2 : PhotoDisc/Far Eastern Business and Culture   Vol. 23

Chapter Opener 3 : PhotoDisc/Education 2   Vol. 41

Chapter Opener 4 : PhotoDisc/Education   Vol. 24

Chapter Opener 5 : PhotoDisc/Education   Vol. 24

Chapter Opener 6 : PhotoDisc/Education 2   Vol. 41

Chapter Opener 7 : PhotoDisc/Education 2   Vol. 41

Chapter Opener 8 : PhotoDisc/Education   Vol. 24

Chapter Opener 9 : PhotoDisc/Education   Vol. 24

Chapter Opener 10 : PhotoDisc/Far Eastern Business and Culture   Vol. 23

Chapter Opener 11 : PhotoDisc/Education   Vol. 24

Chapter Opener 12 : PhotoDisc/Earth in Focus, Background Series   Vol. 14

Author Index

Abelard, 132
Abercrombie, N., 91
Addams, J., 202
Al-Ani, S. H., 289, 307
Allen, B. A., 356
Allport, G., 264, 279
Amir, Y., 264, 280
Argyle, M., 331, 339
Ascher, C., 356

Bailey, L., 279
Bailey, S. M., 232
Baker, C., 157, 158
Baker, G., 51
Baker, K. A., 147, 149, 150, 158
Banks, C. M., 51, 306, 354, 357
Banks, J. A., 35, 48, 51, 52, 90,
    243, 306, 348, 356
Barba, R. H., 294, 307
Barnlund, D., 157
Barry, K., 241
Barsch, R. H., 141, 157
Beardsley, E., 70, 90
Beaudry, J., 157
Beers, M. K., 200, 211
Belenky, M. F., 240
Bell, Y. R., 349, 356
Bellah, R. N., 55, 90, 339
Bennett, C. L., 90, 143, 157,
    260, 307
Bennett, M., 260, 279
Bereaud, S., 240, 241
Berger, B., 77, 80, 91, 134, 135,
    156, 287, 306
Berger, P. L., 77, 80, 91, 134, 135,
    156, 287, 306
Bernier, N., 24
Bicklin, D., 279
Boglione, R., 240
Boston, C., 327

Botstein, L., 161, 168, 181, 182
Bowser, B. P., 279, 280
Boyer, J., 39, 51
Boykin, A. W., 339, 356
Braille, L., 202
Brandt, R., 338
Bredekamp, S., 173, 181, 182
Brislin, R. W., 91, 100, 117,
    330, 339
Bronte, C., 213
Brophy, J., 339
Broudy, H., 156
Brown, D. A., 50
Bruner, J. S., 171
Bullivant, B. M., 90
Butler, K. L., 237, 241
Butler, R., 237, 325, 338
Butts, R. F., 156, 295, 298, 307
Byrne, T. J., 237, 241
Byrnes, D., 263, 264, 279

Cantrell, M., 280
Carelli, A., 51, 231, 240, 241
Carnes, J., 155
Carroll, L., 309
Castenada, A., 156
Celeste, R. F., 121
Chandler, S., 240
Childers, E., 280
Chinn, P. C., 85, 90, 91, 138, 140,
    156, 157, 290, 302, 303,
    306, 307
Chipman, M., 356
Chomsky, N., 91, 178
Christensen, K. M., 91
Clerc, L., 202
Clinchy, B., 240
Cohen, I., 339
Cohen, M., 338
Combs, A. W., 353, 357

Comenius, John Amos, 133, 171
Comer, J., 349, 353, 356
Cooper, S. M., 109, 117
Copple, C., 181, 182
Cottrell, R. J., 91
Counts, G., 24
Crabbe, A., 280
Cruz-Jansen, M., 356
Cuban, L., 171, 181, 307
Cubberly, E., 34
Cummins, J., 148, 157, 224, 240
Curtis, C. K., 267, 280
Cushner, K., 25, 52, 91, 100, 117,
    152, 158, 180, 182, 209, 211,
    239, 241, 277, 279, 280,
    306, 307
Cutsworth, T., 202

D'Angelo, E., 266, 280
Daniels, J., 240, 241
Dao, M., 157
Darling-Hammond, L., 307
DeCroly, O., 194
de Kanter, A. A., 150, 158
DeKock, A., 280
Delgado, G., 91
Dennis, R. M., 279
Dewey, E., 131, 156
Dewey, J., 83, 91, 131, 156,
    316, 343
Diez, M. E., 338
Dinnerstein, L., 50
Diringer, E., 157
Dossett, W. A., 357
Down, J., 62
Dronsberg, S., 240
Dundes, A., 91
Dunlop, K., 280
Dunn, K., 156
Dunn, R., 156, 157

Durkheim, E., 287, 306
Dyer, D., 280

Edelman, M. W., 24
Edwards, C., 181, 356
Edwards, J., 351, 352, 356
Elijah Muhammad, 289
Elliott, E. C., 323, 338
Elliston, F. A., 90
English, J., 90
Erikson, E. H., 91, 177, 178, 182
Ernulf, K. E., 241

Fagot, B., 240
Fard, W. D., 289
Farris, P. J., 109, 117
Feagin, J. R., 90
Feldman, M. P., 339
Flom, 232
Foreman, G., 181
Fordham, S., 356
Fowler, C., 225, 240
Franken, M. L., 241
Freeman, J., 240
Frenkel-Brunswick, E., 52
Freud, A., 178
Freud, S., 178
Friedman, I., 91
Froebel, F., 173
Frost, R., 50

Gage, N. L., 156, 307
Gandini, L., 181
Gardner, H., 328, 339
Gartner, A., 24
Gary, R., 337
Gendell, M., 24
Gesell, A., 174, 177, 178, 181, 182
Gibbs, N., 338, 339
Gilbert, D., 90, 339
Gilligan, C., 240
Giroux, H., 55, 89
Glock, G., 306
Goldberger, N., 240
Gollnick, D. M., 85, 90, 91, 138,
    140, 156, 157, 290, 302, 303,
    306, 307
Gonzalez, G., 135–136, 156
Good, T., 339
Goodlad, J., 220, 240
Gordon, J., 330, 339
Gove, M., 182
Graham, S., 182
Grant, C., 42, 45, 46, 51, 279, 307
Gray, T., 156
Greenspan, R., 224, 240
Grolnick, W. S., 338
Gross, D. E., 51
Grossman, H., 144, 156, 157

Gullo, D., 331, 339
Guskey, T. R., 323

Hagan, R., 240
Hall, G. E., 357
Hall, G. S., 167, 174
Hamer, D. H., 90
Hansen, 232
Hanvey, R., 268, 271, 272,
    273, 280
Harris, 64
Harris, K. R., 64, 182
Hartley, R. E., 229, 241
Hauy, V., 202
Havighurst, R. J., 171, 181
Hawley, R. A., 307
Hazzard, S. P., 339
Heider, F., 117
Hellmuth, J., 157
Henry, W., 24
Herberg, W., 307
Herek, G. M., 90
Hernandez, H., 151, 157
Hill, S., 91
Hoffman, N., 51, 117
Hollingworth, L. S., 203, 211
Hoopes, D., 254–256, 279
Howard, G., 91
Howe, F., 227, 240, 241
Howe, S. G., 194, 201, 203, 211
Hughes-Weiner, G., 280
Humphries, T., 87, 91
Hunt, D. E., 156, 280
Hunt, R. G., 279, 280
Hunter, W., 51
Huxley, F., 90

Innala, S. M., 241
Irvine, J. J., 348, 356
Irwin, R., 202
Itard, J-M. G., 201

Jain, N., 157, 241
Janney, R. E., 200, 211
Jefferson, T., 63
Johnson, D., 52, 240
Johnson, L., 193, 210
Johnson, L. O., 240
Johnson, R. T., 240
Jung, R. K., 24

Kagan, S., 222, 240, 307
Kage, M., 338
Kahl, J., 90, 339
Kaplan, R., 143, 157
Katz, D., 260, 261, 279
Katz, P. A., 279
Keefe, J. W., 157
Keller, H., 202

Kennedy, J. F., 31
Kennedy, M. M., 24
Kiger, G., 279
King, E. W., 356
Kirgel, R. B., 210
Kirschenbaum, H., 323
Klavas, A., 157
Klein, J. W., 202
Kluckhohn, C., 89
Knapp, M. S., 331, 339
Koestler, F., 51
Kohlberg, L., 178
Kohn, A., 324, 330, 331, 333, 334,
    338, 339
Kohn, M. L., 338, 339
Kolbenschlag, M., 240
Kramer, S., 225, 227, 228, 240
Kritek, W. J., 353, 356
Kroeber, A. L., 89

Ladson-Billings, G., 51, 279,
    349, 356
Languis, M., 157
Leahy, R. H., 279
LeCompte, M., 235, 241
Leubitz, L., 139, 157
LeVay, S., 90
Levine, D. U., 356
Lightfoot, S. L., 95, 117
Lindgrun, H. C., 331, 339
Lipman, M., 267, 280
Litcher, J., 52
Lleinback, M. D., 240
Lopez, C.L., 356
Lynd, H. M., 241
Lynd, R., 241

Macchiarola, F. J., 24
Maccia, E. S., 241
Macdonald, C., 211
McDonald, F. J., 156
MacMillan, M., 174
Madsen, R., 90
Mallory, B. L., 169, 181, 182
Mann, Horrace, 171, 201
Martin, J. R., 233, 241
McCaleb, S. P., 156, 224, 240
McClelland, A., 24
McDonald, F. J., 156
McIntosh, P., 91, 262, 279
McKinney, W., 307
Meisels, S. J., 176, 182
Mikulecky, L., 307
Miller, C., 280
Mills, E., 316, 338
Mitchell, C., 46, 47, 51
Montessori, M., 194
Moon, C. J., 338
Moore, C., 156
Moyers, W., 117

Napier, R. W., 323
Neisser, V., 339
New, R., 169, 179, 181, 182
Nguyen, L. D., 145, 157
Nichols, J. G., 339
Niemeyer, J. H., 224, 240
Nirje, B., 210
Nissan, M., 325, 338
Noddings, N., 240
Nurcombe, B., 338

Ogbu, J., 45, 51, 356
Olson, L., 337
Olson, M., 240
Olszewski, L., 157
Orford, J., 339
Orland, M. E., 24
Ornstein, A. C., 335, 339
O'Shea, M. V., 211
Oxford-Carpenter, R., 24

Page, E. B., 323, 338
Paige, R. M., 279
Paley, V., 93
Pang, V. O., 294, 307
Parker, F. W., 171, 174
Parkhurst, H., 352
Pate, G., 279
Paul, C., 280
Peabody, E., 173
Pearce, R. H., 90
Peck, M. S., 347, 349, 356
Pedersen, P., 90
Pegrebin, L. C., 240
Peng, S., 24
Pestalozzi, J., 171
Pettigrew, T. F., 267, 280
Phillips, L., 241
Piaget, Jean, 135, 169, 175,
    178, 343
Pisarchick, S., 280
Pitt-Rivers, J., 90
Plato, 132
Pogrebin, L. C., 240
Pol, L., 24
Porter, R., 157, 241
Provenzo, E. F., 50
Pugach, M., 193, 210

Rader, J., 339
Rainforth, B., 211
Rash, J. E., 25,
Raynes, M., 200, 211
Reagan, R., 42
Reich, R., 8, 15, 24
Reimer, K. M., 356
Reiners, D. M., 50
Reinert, H., 156
Rennebohm-Franz, K., 257, 279
Richards, L. E., 211

Robertson, R., 306
Rockwell, N., 304
Roof, W. C., 307
Rothberg, I. C., 307
Rousseau, Jean Jacques, 171
Rudner, L., 327
Ryan, R. M., 338

Sadker, D., 356
Sadker, M., 356
Safford, E. J., 181, 210, 280
Safford, P. L., 181, 210, 280
Samover, L., 157, 241
Samuels, S. C., 280
Sapir, E., 90
Saracho, O., 181
Sarason, S. B., 350, 351, 356
Schmerl, R., 39, 51
Schurz, M. M., 173
Scieszka, J., 280
Seeley, D., 224, 240
Sequin, E. O., 195, 201, 211
Shade, Barbara J. Robinson, 157
Shaffer, D. R., 176, 182
Shakeshaft, C., 11, 24, 51
Shaver, J. P., 52, 267, 280
Shearer, A., 210
Sherif, M., 264, 280
Sherman, R., 51, 59, 90, 329, 339
Shields, P. M., 331, 339
Shirley, O., 52
Shirts, G., 280
Siccone, F., 155
Simon, R., 55, 89
Simon, S. B., 323
Singer, A., 258, 279
Slavin, R. E., 52, 222, 223, 240
Sleeter, C., 42, 45, 46, 51
Smith, M., 338
Snell, M., 200, 211
Sowell, T., 306
Spencer, H., 196, 211
Spodek, B., 175, 181
Stacey, J., 240, 241
Stahlman, J., 280
Starch, D., 323, 338
Stark, R., 306
Steinbeck, J., 304
Stenmark, J. K., 338
Stiles, L., 51
Stone, E., 129, 156
Stoneman, Z., 280
Strober, M. H., 117
Sullivan, H. J., 356
Sullivan, W. M., 90
Suter, W. N., 331, 339
Swindler, A., 90

Tarule, J., 240
Teidt, I., 51, 142, 155, 156, 157

Teidt, P., 51, 142, 155, 156, 157
Theobald, P., 316, 338
Thernstrom, S., 157
Thompson, C., 231, 241
Thorndike, E., 316
Thurow, L. M., 330, 339
Tipton, S. M., 90
Toffler, A., 7, 8, 13, 23, 24
Tozer, S., 24
Triandis, H., 90
Trifonovitch, G., 117, 280
Trujillo, R., 51
Turner, B. S., 91
Twain, J., 304
Tyack, D., 117

Uphoff, J. K., 287, 293, 298,
    306, 307
Urquhart, B., 280

Vacca, J., 182
Vacca, R., 182
Vetterling-Braggin, M., 90
Villegas, A. M., 338
Vygotsky, L., 91, 169, 170, 181

Wagley, 64
Wald, L., 202
Walker, 232
Wallace, A. C., 357
Wallin, J. E. W., 51
Walsh, D., 266, 280
Warren, D. M., 62, 63, 90
Webb, R., 51, 59, 90, 329, 339
Weber, L., 181
Weber, M., 90
Webster, N., 26
Weinberg, M., 51
Weitzman, L. J., 240
Wells, A., 339
Wells, J. W., 241
Whitmore, S., 23
Whorf, B., 90
Wilder, T., 56, 89
Williams, L. R., 169, 179, 181, 182
Witkin, H. A., 141, 156, 157
Wolfensberger, W., 210
Wood, G. H., 156, 181, 240
Woodruff, D. W., 348, 356
Worthen, B. R., 338

Yatvin, J., 207, 211
Yetman, N. R., 70, 90
Yinger, J. M., 287, 306
York, J., 211

Zangwill, I., 34, 51
Zelizer, V. A., 61, 90
Zimpher, N. L., 13, 24

Subject Index

Ability, 10–11, 13, 16, 71, 200–201. *See also*
    Disabilities
Abington School District v. Schempp, 40, 298, 307
Accents, 136–137
Active exercises, 23, 49, 88, 116, 152, 180, 209, 239,
    277, 306
Adjustment, 96–98
African Americans, 31–32, 46, 64, 89, 103, 105, 106,
    139, 140, 144, 145, 289, 291, 329
  experience in schools, 31–32, 38
Afrocentric curriculum, 81
Age, 73–74, 167, 176–180
AIDS, 200
Ambiguity, 101–102, 111
American Association of Colleges of Teacher
    Education, 36, 39
American Association of School Administrators, 299
American Association of the Advancement for
    Individuals with Disabilities, 279
American Association of University Women (AAUW),
    232, 239
American Federation of Teachers, 207
American Forum for Global Education, 278
American Sign Language (ASL), 61, 87, 88
Americans with Disabilities Act (ADA) (1992), 38, 41,
    191, 192, 210
Amish, 40
Anglo-conformity, 34
Anthropology, 59–63
Anti-Defamation League, 278
Anxiety, 96, 101, 111
Appalachia, 85
Arab culture, 114–115, 139
Architectural Barriers Act (1968), 37
Asian Americans, 89, 144
Asians, 34
Assessment, 13, 16, 21, 81, 233, 309–338, 347. *See*
    also Testing
  alternative, 318–322, 326, 327, 333–335, 337–338

Assessment—*Cont.*
  old and new, 134, 175–176, 196–198, 225–226,
    258–259, 293–294, 321, 347
  performance, 318–319, 326, 327
Assimilation, 28, 34–35, 36, 43, 46–47, 48, 235
Assimilationist ideology, 34–35, 42, 43, 49
Association for the Care of Children's Health, 210
Attitudes, 12, 17, 46, 47, 49, 61, 85, 97, 261, 276
  racial, 48
Attributions, 1–6, 21, 47, 107–108, 109, 336

Balance theory, 148–149
Belonging, 17, 102, 109, 112, 114
Bias
  in curriculum, 292–293, 345–346
  gender bias, 231–232
  test bias, 151, 318–319, 335, 347
Bicultural education, 37
Bidialectalism, 138
Bilingual education, 37, 38, 40, 48, 98, 145–151, 155
Bilingual Education Act (1968), 33, 37, 40, 148. *See*
    also Title VII, Elementary and Secondary
    Education Act (1968)
Bilingual Education Act (1984), 40, 146
Bilingual Education Act (1988), 40, 41
Bilingual Education Act (1990), 40
Board of Education of Westside Community Schools v.
    Mergens, 40
Brown v. Board of Education, 28, 36, 37, 40
Buddhism, 9

Case studies, 3–6, 22–23, 28–29, 56–59, 99–100,
    121–130, 161–167, 185–190, 213–218, 243–253,
    283–286, 309–316. *See also* Critical incidents
Categorization process, 81–82, 106–107, 108, 109, 111,
    112, 113, 260, 262
Catholics, 10, 30–31, 35, 110, 228, 299, 300, 301, 302
Catholic schools, 31, 50, 296, 306
Central High School, 28, 29, 49–50

362

Centralization, 14

Change, 6–10, 17–19, 22, 80, 353–355
  cultural, 20–21
  demographic, 6–8, 10, 48, 49
  difficulty of, 17–18
  economic, 8
  family, 8–9, 134–135
  institutional, 7–10
  mediators, 96
  political, 8
  resistance to, 18, 80
  schools, 19, 29
  social, 6–7, 10, 20–21

Children
  of color, 11
  with disabilities, 11, 32, 37, 276

Children's Defense Fund, 174

Chinese, 31, 38

Choice, 7, 15

Citizenship education, 30, 130, 131–132, 193, 253,
    316. See also Democracy

Civil rights, 32, 36

Civil Rights Act (1964), 33, 36, 37, 40

Civil Rights Movement, 5, 28, 32–33, 36, 45, 192, 345

Civil War, 31–32, 321

Cochran v. Louisiana Board of Education, 299, 307

Cognitive style, 48, 108. See also Learning style

Cognitive sophistication, 266–267

Collaboration, 15, 173, 193, 204–206, 219–226
  home-school, 224

Collective orientation. See Group orientation

Columbus, arrival, 30

Common school, 11, 30, 31, 50, 95, 173, 201, 202, 203,
    306, 343, 349–350

Communication, 43, 103–104, 109, 112, 115, 144–145.
    See also Language
  nonverbal, 139–140
  style, 144–145
  verbal, 136–139

Community, 12, 15, 16, 17, 19–20, 343–344, 347–353
  learning, 15, 16, 17, 19–20, 49, 94, 130–134

Competition, 14–16, 48

Compulsory attendance, 295–296

Conflict, 10, 31

Conflict management, 21

Constructivism, 60–61, 169–173, 179–180, 194

Contact hypothesis, 264

Cooperation, 16, 48

Cooperative learning, 48, 94, 108, 175, 221–223, 239

Council for Exceptional Children, 210

Critical incidents, 22, 110–116, 152–154, 277–278

Critical thinking, 266–267

Cross-cultural awareness, 271–272

Cross-cultural interaction, 21. See also Intercultural
    interaction

Cross-cultural misunderstanding, 102

Cross-cultural psychology, 65–68, 89, 93, 99

Cross-cultural simulations, 268

Cultural competence, 46–47

Cultural deficiency, 43

Cultural emancipation, 47

Cultural identity, 21, 47, 55–56, 68–75, 94, 96–98

Cultural knowledge, 60, 69–75, 79, 84–88, 98

Cultural mediators, 96

Cultural pluralism, 35, 39

Cultural relevant pedagogy, 349

Cultural understanding, 21, 46, 84–86

Culture, 21, 28, 43, 55, 59–68, 140–141, 142–144
  Amish, 296, 301
  of the deaf, 61, 89
  dominant American, 30, 34, 70, 86, 95, 106,
    227, 233
  objective, 61–62
  of the school, 47, 93, 233–238, 348
  subjective, 61–62

Culture clash, 11–12

Culture general framework, 21, 65–67, 93, 99,
    100–109, 110, 272

Culture general knowledge, 21, 65–67, 100, 116

Culture learning, 21, 23, 59, 68–88

Cultures
  American, 35
  school, 95
  student, 94, 233–237
  teacher, 94–95

Culture shock, 113, 268. See also Adjustment

Culture specific knowledge, 43–44, 66–67, 86, 110

Curriculum, 13, 14, 21, 36, 43. See also Knowledge,
    old and new
  Afrocentric, 81
  Eurocentric, 80, 256
  expansion and inclusion, 43, 44, 345–346
  global, 259
  intervention and impact, 48

Dalton Plan, 352

Deaf culture, 61, 71, 87–89

Decentralization, 17

Democracy, 12, 30, 32, 132, 238, 316–317, 342–343.
    See also Citizenship education
  cultural, 12, 36
  political, 12, 36

Demographics, 6, 7, 8–9, 10, 23, 253–254, 270–271
  of students, 7
  of teaching force, 11–12, 94–95
  in transition, 7

Desegregation, 36

Developmental domains, 177–178

Developmental knowledge, 178–180

Developmentally Appropriate Practice (DAP),
    167–176, 177–180, 194

Dialects, 137

Diana v. State Board of Education, 38, 40

Differentiation, 107, 108

Disabilities, 11, 32, 41, 62, 70–71, 222–223, 276. See
    also Ability

Disconfirmed expectations, 102, 111, 113

Discrimination, 33, 36, 45, 46, 47, 64, 260, 268
  in education, 33, 36, 45, 333
  in social life, 64

Diversity, cultural, 10, 30, 43, 47
  as a problem, 30–33

Diversity, cultural—*Cont.*
    in schools, 10, 11, 12, 16
    religious, 30–31
Down's syndrome, 198

Early childhood education, 169–175, 176–177
Ebonics, 137, 145–146, 154–155
Economy, global, 8
Education of All Handicapped Children's Act (1975),
        10, 33, 37, 41, 191, 196, 203. *See also* Public Law
        94–142
Education that is multicultural, 44–46
Elementary and Secondary Education Act, 33, 37,
        40, 299
Ellis Island, 34
Emotional response, 96, 101–103
Empathy, 255, 267–268
English Black. *See* Ebonics
    rural, 138
    standard, 138
Epperson v. State of Arkansas, 40
Equal Educational Opportunities Act, 41
Equal educational opportunity, 42, 49
Equal Pay Act (1963), 33
Equity in education, 33
Ethical issues, 150–151, 206–209, 275–276, 304–305,
        335–336
Ethics, 205–209, 238, 275–276, 304–305, 335–336
Ethnic group, 35, 36, 64
Ethnic identity, 35, 46. *See also* Identity, ethnic
Ethnicity, 43, 46, 72
Ethnocentrism, 44, 80–81, 260, 269
Eurocentric curriculum, 80–81
European-Americans, 94–95, 103, 105, 108, 145,
        233–235
Everson v. Board of Education, 299, 307
Exceptionality, 43, 201
Eye contact, 102, 103, 106

Family, 8–9
Feminist movement, 45, 268
Field dependent. *See* Field sensitive
Field independent, 141
Field sensitive, 141
First Amendment, 39, 294, 298, 306
First Wave civilization, 13
Fourteenth Amendment, 32, 39, 40, 294
Freedman's Bureau, 31, 50
Freedman's School, 31–32

Gangs, 94
Gallaudet University, 61
Gender, 11, 41, 43, 70, 83, 220, 226–228, 233–235
Gender-sensitive education, 32, 42, 226, 239
General Agreement on Tariffs and Trade (GATT), 8
Generalizations
    different from stereotypes, 86
    of groups of people, 87
Geographic location as cultural influence, 73
Global education, 42, 253–259, 275–276

Global perspective, 254–259, 268–275
Global society, 253–254
Grading, 322–325
Group orientation, 106, 108, 109, 115
*Guadalupe Organization, Inc., v. Tempe Elementary
        School District No. 3,* 41
Gullah, 137
Gypsy culture, 215–218

Hate groups, 261–262
Hawaii, 43, 108, 224
Health, 16, 70–71, 198–200
High culture, 89
Higher Education Act (1965), 299
Higher Education Facilities Act (1963), 299
Hispanic, 38, 64, 65, 89, 103, 144, 329
Homophobia, 231, 235–237
Homosexuality, 231, 235–237
Human relations, 43

Identity, 36, 83
    ethnic, 34, 38, 46, 47
    racial, 38, 47
    religious, 72–73, 301–304
Immigrants, 7, 27, 30, 31, 34, 36, 50
Immigration, 7, 33–35
Inclusion, 11, 21, 42, 43, 190–198, 200, 206–210,
        342–347
India, 248–253, 256
Indian Removal Act, 31
Individual Education Program (IEP), 192, 193, 196,
        197, 204
Individualism, 14, 15, 106, 109, 115, 220, 233, 234
Individuals with Disabilities Education Act (IDEA)
        (1990), 11, 41, 191, 193, 197, 201, 203, 207, 210
Industrial Age, 13
Industrial Revolution, 30
Information Age, 13, 17
Ingroups, 94, 108, 109, 112, 113–114, 142, 143,
        261, 342
Institutions, 6–12, 18
    in transition, 7–10
Instruction. S*ee* Pedagogies, old and new
Intelligence, 326–328, 335
    multiple, 328
Intercultural education, 96, 254–256
Intercultural interaction, 93, 99, 100–110. *See also*
        Cross-cultural interaction
Intergroup interactions, 21, 264–266
International education, 42
International perspective. *See* Global perspective
Intragroup interactions, 21
Islam, 9, 289

Japanese, 72, 78, 106, 142
Jewish people, 10, 31, 34

Kamehameha Early Education Program (KEEP), 43
Keyes v. School District #1, 41
Kindergarten, 173–174

Kinesics, 139–140
Knowledge, old and new, 133–143, 175, 196, 225, 258, 292–293, 320–321

Lakota Sioux, 74
Language, 10, 11, 12, 21, 28, 34, 38, 40–41, 74–75, 103–104, 109, 140–141
    acquisition, 134–136, 177
    fluency, 134–136, 177
    learning, 34, 38
    variation, 10, 11, 136–140
Lanham Act, 174
Large scale, 14
Larry P. v. Riles, 38, 40
Latin Americans, 34, 139
Lau v. Nichols, 38, 41, 147
Learning. *See also* Cognitive style
    community, 15–17, 129–134, 154, 267
    disabilities, 71
    in-context, 66–67
    out-of-context, 66–67
    style, 36, 61, 65, 66–67, 108, 109, 110, 140–144, 154
Least restrictive environment, 191, 206
Legislative and judicial mandates regarding equity in education, 39–41
Leman v. Kurtzman, 40
Liberty, 12
Little Rock, Arkansas, 28–29, 49–50

Macroculture, 94
Mainstreaming, 32, 192
Martin Luther King Junior Elementary School Children v. Ann Arbor School District Board of Education, 41
Melting pot, 34, 35, 36
Metropolitan Museum of Art, 89
Metropolitan Opera, 89
Mexican Americans, 64, 103, 106, 109, 110
Meyer v. Nebraska, 297, 307
Microculture, 64, 94
Middle school, 172–173
Minersville v. Gobitis, 297, 307
Minority group, 64, 329–330
Mitchell Typology, 46
Monocultural perspective, 34–35, 38
Monolinguistic perspective, 38
Motivation, 324
Multicultural education, 20, 21, 32, 33, 36, 38, 39, 42, 43, 44, 45, 46, 47, 48, 50, 79, 106, 116
    approaches, 42–47
    goals, 19–22, 79, 106
    group specific approaches to, 65–66, 86
    historical perspectives, 32–38
    outcomes, 47–49
    public response, 38–39, 42
    teaching, 22
Muslims, 9, 10, 82

National Association for the Advancement of Colored People (NAACP), 28, 29
National Association for the Education of Young Children (NAEYC), 169, 170, 173, 180

National Association of Elementary School Principals, 24
National Association of Secondary School Principals, 24
National Council for the Social Studies, 254, 279
National Defense Education Act (1958), 299
National Education Association, 36, 299
Nationality, 72. *See also* Ethnicity
Nation of Islam, 289
Native Americans, 30, 31, 60, 64, 65, 66, 89, 105, 108, 146, 179, 199, 288, 291, 329
"No One Model American," 36
Normalization, 191
Norms, 14, 47, 61, 70, 74, 97, 229–230
North American Free Trade Agreement (NAGTA), 8
North Central Regional Education Laboratory (NCREL), 24

Ocean Project, The, 258
Office of Civil Rights, 37
Outgroups, 94, 108, 109, 111, 112, 261, 342

Pacific Circle Consortium, 258
Palmer v. Board of Education, 40
Parable, 18, 22
Paralanguage, 140
Parent involvement, 348–349
Pedagogies, old and new, 132–133, 171–173, 194, 221–223, 256–257, 290–291, 320, 346–347
Pegagogy, 19, 346
    culturally relevant, 349
People of color, 64–65, 101
Perception, 81, 140
Perspective, 268–269, 275
Pierce v. Society of Sisters, 296, 298, 307
Plessy v. Ferguson, 32, 40, 50
Pluralism, 20, 30, 35–36, 238. *See also* Cultural pluralism
    in education, 32–33, 38, 39, 43
    historical perspectives, 30–33, 35
    religious, 30–31, 286, 288–294, 304
    in United States, 20, 28, 33, 43
Pluralist ideology, 35–36
Portfolio assessment, 16, 320, 321, 327
Poverty, 9, 329
Power, 95
Prayer in schools, 298, 303
Pregnancy Discrimination Act, 41
Prejudice, 18, 46, 47, 102–103, 259–268, 278, 305
    functions of, 260–261
    reduction of, 46, 256–268
Project Head Start, 175, 176
Proposition 227, 146, 147
Protestants, 10, 30–31, 33, 35, 288, 289, 297, 298, 300, 301, 302–303
Prototype image, 82
Proxemics, 139
Public Law 94–142, 10, 11, 37, 48, 191,196, 203, 223
Puerto Ricans, 64

Race, 31–32, 40, 46, 69–70
    in public education, 31–32
Racial identity. *See* Identity, racial

Reflective practice, 22
Reggio Emilia, 172, 179
Rehabilitation Act of 1973, 41, 191
Rejection, 102
Religion, 9–10, 12, 13, 30–31, 40, 46, 72–73, 283–306
   definitions of, 287
Religious fundamentalism, 10, 293, 302–304
Religious instructions, 300–301
Religious schools, 296, 298–300, 303
Rituals, 104–105, 109
Roles, 14, 20, 35, 61, 75, 105, 109, 198, 112, 134. *See*
   also Situational behavior
   old and new, 133, 173–175, 194–196, 223–224,
      257–258, 291–292, 320
   sex roles, 226–229
Rural English, 138. S*ee* English, rural

Schemata. S*ee* Categorization process
School Lunch Act, 299
School reform, 24, 44, 49
Schools
   civilization, 13–14, 19, 342
   institutions, 7
   in transition, 10, 13–15, 17, 23–24
   schools, 13–15, 17
   Second Wave, 7, 13–14, 17, 19
Segregation, 32
Sex, 70, 226–232. *See also* Gender
Sexuality, 74
Sexual orientation, 13, 74, 226, 235–237
Sign language, 138–139. *See also* American Sign
   Language
Single group studies, 43–44
Site-based management, 17
Situational behavior, 105
Slavery, 31
Slavic people, 34
Small scale, 7, 17
Social class, 11, 33, 43, 71–72, 79, 95, 109, 227–228,
   328–332
Socialization, 36, 65, 75–88, 142
   childhood, 77–79
   primary, 77–79
   secondary, 79–80
   into sex role, 226–232, 239
Socializing agents, 75–77, 86–88, 229–233
Social reconstructionist, 44–45, 47
Social status, 75, 95, 105, 109, 112, 332. *See also*
   Status
Sociology, 63–65
Southern Poverty Law Center, 278
Spatial orientation, 105. *See also* Proxemics
Special education, 14, 35, 38, 42
   historical perspective, 33, 35, 37, 62, 195, 201–204
   overrepresentation of minorities, 38–40
Specialization, 14
Spirituality, 72–73. *See also* Religion
Standardization, 13, 14, 16

Standardized tests, 317–318, 336, 337
Status, 109. *See also* Social status
Stereotypes, 46, 82–83, 86, 106–107, 108, 110,
   229–232, 260, 263, 266, 272
Stories, 22
Subculture, 63
Superstition, 104–105
Syncronization, 14

Taino, 30, 50
Teacher education, 12
Teacher expectations, 332–333
Teaching the culturally different, 43
Technology, 76
   in classroom, 257
Testing, 81, 316, 319. *See also* Assessment
   bias in, 38, 318–319
   IQ, 203, 318, 335, 326
   standardized, 317–318
Third Wave, 7, 13, 15, 19
   civilization, 13, 19, 23, 342, 352
   institutions, 7
   schools, 15–17, 343
Thresholds model, 149
Time orientation, 105
Title VI, Civil Rights Act (1964), 40
Title VII, Civil Rights Act (1964), 33, 37, 40, 41
Title VII, Elementary and Secondary Education Act
   (1968), 37. *See also* Bilingual Education Act
   (1968)
Title IX of the Education Amendments, 33, 37, 41
Trail of Tears, 31

U-Curve hypothesis, 96–98, 272
United National High Commission on Refugees, 271
U. S. Civil Service Commission, 37
U. S. Commission on Civil Rights, 36
Universal health precautions, 200

Values, 12, 17, 47, 48, 79, 85, 104, 109, 113,
   233–235, 344
Vietnam War, 32, 36
Vocational Education Act (1963), 41
Vocational Rehabilitation Act (1973), 37, 41, 191, 210
   Section 504, 37, 41, 191, 192
Voting Rights Act, 33, 40

West Virginia State Board of Education v. Barnett,
   297, 307
White Privilege, 262–263
Whites, 139, 140. *See also* European Americans
Wisconsin v. Yoder, 40, 296, 307
World Wide Web, recources, 23–24, 49–50, 88–89,
   116, 154–155, 180–181, 209–210, 239, 278–279,
   306, 337–338

Zorach v. Clausen, 40, 307